A
Straight-out
Man

A Straight-out Man

F. W. Albrecht and Central Australian Aborigines

Barbara Henson

MELBOURNE UNIVERSITY PRESS
1994

Reprinted in paperback 1994
First published 1992

Designed by Lynn Twelftree
Typeset by Bookset Pty Ltd, North Melbourne, Victoria
Printed in Hong Kong by
South China Printing Co. (1988) Ltd. for
Melbourne University Press, Carlton, Victoria 3053
U.S.A. and Canada: International Specialized Book Services, Inc.,
5602 N.E. Hassalo Street, Portland, Oregon 97213-3640
United Kingdom and Europe: University College London Press,
Gower Street, London WC1E 6BT, UK

National Library of Australia Cataloguing-in-Publication entry

Henson, Barbara, 1942– .
A straight-out man: F. W. Albrecht and Central Australian
Aborigines.
Bibliography.
Includes index.
ISBN 0 522 84569 X

1. Albrecht, F. W. (Friedrich Wilhelm), 1894–1984.
2. Lutheran Church—Missions—Northern Territory—
History. 3. Missionaries—Northern Territory—Biography.
[4]. Aborigines, Australian—Missions—Northern
Territory. I. Title.

266.41092

To my mother and father,
remembering especially my mother's interest and feeling for
a world and people beyond her immediate ken,
and my father's capacity for commitment to a chosen task.

CONTENTS

ILLUSTRATIONS

PREFACE

I am sometimes asked why I have written a biography about a Lutheran missionary in Central Australia. The answer goes a long way back, and lies in the kinds of questions which arose out of finding myself, partly European, living in Terra Australis, a vast southern continent which seemed to have little to do with Europe.

I felt the disparity even as a child. There seemed to me to be only two landscapes in Australia—the coast and the inland. Growing up at the base of Cape York Peninsula, west of the Great Dividing Range, the Pacific coast was a mere seventy miles away. Yet, in my childhood experience, it might have been another country. Cairns and its surrounds were lush, green, tropical—a place where life seemed easier and my aunt's hibiscus shrubs grew two or three feet a year. On the dry, sandy ridge west of Mareeba where my parents had established a tobacco farm, my mother's flowering trees and shrubs seemed, for all her diligent watering, to remain perpetual dwarfs—that is, if they were not eaten off by brumbies or burned in bushfires that came too close. As an adult, I was surprised to find they had eventually grown into sizeable trees. But within the strange stasis of childhood, where things are forever the same, life inland of the range seemed on the whole harsh and difficult.

Yet the bush also gave me other experiences—the beauty of its brief but brilliant greening in the wet season, a deep contentedness in roaming the hills and gullies, the crazy exhilaration of burning fire-breaks at night. And something that never ceased to amaze me—the recurring transformation of dry brown hills, with distance, into the most serene and transcendent of blues.

There was another puzzle connected with the landscape. To my childhood eyes, the hills and rough trees bore no imprint of the Christian teaching I was trying to absorb—ideas of God, events in Palestine so long ago. Nor did the small town we lived near, for all its Catholic church at one end of the main street. I could find no way to bring the Christian story into the place where I lived.

But life quickly drew me away from the bush—high school, university, work. It seemed inevitably urban, thoroughly centred in a European tradition. Asked about the Australian Aborigines while studying in the United States in 1968, I was astounded, embarrassed. Yes, I had seen them, knew their existence. But I had never really *thought* about them. Nor did I for many more years until I was back in Australia, and starting to write.

An inner question was becoming increasingly clear, even urgent: What was this strange enterprise called 'Australia', this large, dry continent peopled primarily by representatives of two such different cultures—Aborigines who had spread across much of its surface and lived in tangible relationship to it, and white Europeans who in the majority still lived on its edges, transposing a culture which often seemed inappropriate and misplaced. It was not a new theme, but it had become explicit and personal for me. And as a writing question, I knew I had no desire to write about an Australian who had lived purely out of the European, 'coastal' mode. I wanted to touch the Aboriginal part, and the continent itself. I thought and read about Albert Namatjira, an Aborigine who had become very visible within European Australia. But I came to feel that the cultural gap was too great to be bridged by someone who could not spend considerable time in Central Australia.

In that search, I had come across the name of Pastor F. W. Albrecht, superintendent of the Hermannsburg mission in Central Australia, and involved in Namatjira's beginnings as an artist. I learned that he and his wife had come from Europe to Central Australia in the 1920s and had lived there for almost forty years. I also discovered that he was still alive, aged eighty-nine, living in retirement in Adelaide.

Several aspects caught me. This man was a European, yet he had spent a large part of his life with Aborigines. This encounter, the point of contact between Aboriginal and European, interested me most. And that lifetime Christian commitment—that was still a point of search. Nor could I even begin to imagine what it would be like to come from northern Europe to the dry red heart of Australia. My childhood dilemmas of coast and inland paled into insignificance.

I wrote to Pastor Albrecht at the nursing home in Adelaide where he lived with his wife, and later telephoned him. Waiting for the voice on the other end was one of those moments in life: one feels blank, unknowing—yet one is hoping for something. What is there, or more accurately, what is there for me? It was an old man's voice that answered, rather slow, a little quavery, the voice of an old man in a nursing home. My heart almost sank. Perhaps it was not there. I listened, trying to catch this unknown thing through the thin thread of a voice at long distance.

'Pastor Albrecht', I said after some moments, 'You were involved for so long with the Aborigines, do you still think about those issues?'

'Oh, yes', the reply came stronger, 'Oh yes, in spirit, I'm still there. *They were my life, you see.*'

I must have breathed out. I had heard what I was searching for.

CONVERSIONS

1 inch	2.54 centimetres
1 foot	0.30 metre
1 mile	1.61 kilometres
1 ounce	28.35 grams
1 pound (lb)	0.45 kilogram
1 gallon	4.55 litres
1 acre	0.40 hectare

ACKNOWLEDGEMENTS

An Australian Literature Board Grant in 1984 and Northern Territory History Grants in 1985 and 1986 greatly assisted towards research expenses for this project and were also a much appreciated encouragement. My thanks go also to Perry Japanangka Langdon for permission to include extracts from his father's account of the Coniston massacre in Chapter 2, to Allen & Unwin for permission to use a quotation from Richard Broome's *Aboriginal Australians* in Chapter 16, and to Collins/Angus and Robertson for permission to use an extract from T. G. H. Strehlow's *Songs of Central Australia* in Chapter 13. My thanks go also to the Strehlow Research Centre in Alice Springs for the use of that extract and of a photograph, and to Philip Brackenreg of the Legend Press, Sydney, for kind permission to reproduce a painting of Albert Namatjira's on the dust jacket. I am also most grateful to staff and decision makers at Melbourne University Press for their commitment and effort in the shaping of this book, especially editors Sally Nicholls and Jean Dunn who have each made very special contributions to the final outcome.

A note on orthography and place names. Several Aranda orthographies have been developed in the span of European contact, but the one used in this book is consistent with that used in F. W. Albrecht's time, having been developed by the first missionaries and by the Reverend Carl Strehlow. A map has been included to show the whereabouts of most Northern Territory places mentioned in the text. A few are missing: places which Albrecht visited on his camel treks in the 1930s and early 1940s and mentioned in his diaries and reports, but which were not known to my informants.

I am very grateful for the immense help and support given me in this project by the family of the late Pastor and Mrs F. W. Albrecht, staff and friends of the Finke River Mission, and Aboriginal people at Hermannsburg and Alice Springs: Helene and Dudley Burns, Paul and Helen Albrecht, Min and Paul Sitzler, Garry and Liz Stoll, Sally and Ted Pohlner, Glen and Julie Auricht, Robert Arnold, the late Ossie Heinrich, David Shrowder, the Reverend Dr Les Grope, Christine Benz, Pastor Conrad Raberaba, Pastor Traugott and Lottie Malbanka, Joyce Malbanka, Pastor Eli Rubuntja, Joylene Abbott, the late Pastor Nahasson Ungkwanaka,

Mary Wolski, the late Helmut Pareroultja, Jimmy Jugadai, and many others. I had invaluable assistance from Finke River Mission staff in travel to distant Aboriginal communities, introductions to Aboriginal people, translation and interpreting, and in the preparation of a map to accompany the book, as well as much kindness and hospitality. I was given generous access to material in the Lutheran Church Archives in Adelaide by the Reverend Philipp Scherer, and special help in German translation by Herma Roehrs and the late Dorothea Raasch. My grateful thanks go also to the South Australian Museum for access to their photographic collections. Professor Henry Reynolds, the Reverend Philipp Scherer, Philip Jones and others read my manuscript and made helpful comments and suggestions. Personal friends and my family shared the long journey with much love and stalwartness, especially Rod, without whose encouragement and support the task could not have been undertaken. And I remember with special affection the late Stephen Murray-Smith who with characteristic generosity of spirit encouraged me a decade ago to write biography.

One other explanation. I have already spoken of the Aboriginal and part-Aboriginal people at Hermannsburg and elsewhere who shared their experience of the Albrechts and of mission life in their time. As I later struggled with the seeming impossibility of conveying Aboriginal thinking and feeling within a European-style biography, I decided to use direct quotations from these taped interviews within the larger narrative. It will be obvious to readers that they come from different individuals with a range of opinion. But I trust that they also constitute a collective Aboriginal presence within the book which I did not find another way to achieve.

If he had something to say, he would tell it straight out, you would not shift him, that would be finished then. He was a straight-out man.

BEGINNINGS

1894~1926

Pastor Albrecht, he come from somewhere else, he not an Aboriginal boss, but he bring this good news.

L ate in his life, his thoughts were returning more to beginnings. 'It's a strange pattern you see at the end of your journey.' He was thinking of his lameness—that had caused him such anguish as a child when he couldn't run with his friends. 'Yet, if it were not for that, I would have been under ice and snow in Siberia with my brothers and sisters.'

It was his handicap which had turned him to reading. And it was reading the Lutheran mission tracts and becoming aware of people and countries across the world that had kindled in him the idea of becoming a missionary. It was that dream that had taken him away from Poland to the missionary institute in Germany, and thrown his life in a completely different direction.

He had not forgotten those early years, and his children were accustomed to the moments of reminiscing. Snow fights in the village in winter, his grandfather who had helped to build the church at Kamien, the Christmas there had been so little food and he'd found a bag of potatoes left at the door. Connecting it in his own mind to his mother's faith. Sometimes, too, he talked about the war, almost dying of cholera, escaping from Poland in 1919. There, too, he was seeing a pattern, how he'd been preserved almost miraculously more than once. And the call to Australia.

As his children grew into adulthood and middle age themselves, they asked with real interest. How did his family get back from Siberia? Which sister was it that came to Germany as a refugee after World War II? He finally got out the old black box of family papers, unwrapping its carefully folded contents: names, dates, births, deaths, confirmations, baptisms. His own birth was recorded: Friedrich Wilhelm Albrecht, born Planawice, County of Chelm, Poland, 15 October 1894, to Ferdinand Albrecht, a farmer in Kroczyn and Helene Albrecht, née Reichwald. Another document, the *Sterbefaelle*, embellished with a drawing of the resurrected Jesus near the empty tomb, recorded family deaths. And there were details of his wife's family as well. He translated them from the old German script, typed out some additional explanation, and sent a copy to each of their five children.

If the living reality of his first thirty years was hardly encapsulated in the documents, neither could it really be communicated in his reminiscing. The gap was large—separate generations, another world. The stories were truthful, yet telescoped, condensed with the passing of years. But there was much that he remembered clearly, and he told stories well, so there were always people who liked to listen to him, enjoying his warmth, the animation in his face as he remembered.

Kroczyn, the village in eastern Poland in which he grew up, could have been almost any village in Europe—thirty or forty farms, and a road running through the middle. Fields stretched away from the houses, and crops, barns and animals were a part of the village itself. The only public building was a small congregational school. Kroczyn was one of thirty-seven predominantly German villages between Lublin and the Russian border. After a Polish nationalist uprising in the 1860s, the Russian administration had stripped Polish landowners of large estates, sub-divided them, and offered them to German settlers. This resulted in villages with large numbers of German Lutherans existing within a larger Catholic Poland.

The social and religious differences were visible at the local level but did not greatly impair the solidarity of village life. For all, daily life centred on the necessities of making a modest livelihood. Social occasions in the village were rare, but the geese-plucking evenings in winter were one of the times he remembered most in old age. Hundreds of geese were plucked of their feathers, with the soft under-feathers kept for pillows and bedding. Children played wildly in the snow when the work was done, coming in later for tea and hot cake.

For the German families, religious faith was an essential influence: a Lutheranism, strongly influenced by pietism, which emphasized obedience to God in all aspects of daily life, a personal devotional life nourished by Bible reading and prayer, and the strong imperative to bring the Christian Gospel to every race and person. For Friedrich Albrecht, it was a religious foundation which was to be integral to his life.

The eldest of eight surviving children, he was by nature a happy and sociable child, and might almost have become totally absorbed in the life of his village. But a fall into a cellar at twelve months had left him with one leg slightly shorter than the other, resulting in a permanent limp. Being unable to join in the normal games of childhood caused him acute distress as he was growing up. Nor could he find any compensation in school. The work did not come easily to him, particularly with the intermingling of three languages—German in the home, Polish in the playground, and Russian for some of the school subjects. His results were indifferent and he was aware that teachers and others around him regarded him as a person of limited ability.

Albrecht's mother was his primary strength. Helene Eva Albrecht was a gentle, devout woman with a special empathy with her first child and his difficulties, and she encouraged him to trust that God had a purpose for his life. Reading became his great consolation, and the door to a world beyond the village. He read voraciously, anything he could lay hands on, including the mission tracts distributed at the annual mission festivals at the district church in Kamien. He was about ten years old when he first conceived the idea of becoming an overseas missionary. Achieving it was to take Friedrich Albrecht another twenty years. He struggled to overcome academic difficulty and the continuing opposition of his father who assumed the eldest son should carry on the family farm. Finally, in Easter 1913, at the age of eighteen, he began preliminary studies in a missionary institute in a small village in northern Germany called Hermannsburg, some thirty miles north of Hannover.

He had successfully completed the first year and started a period of medical training when World War I erupted. Pressured by the German authorities to volunteer for the German army, he joined a Red Cross unit and was sent to a field hospital on the eastern front. The rapid sweep of the German army across Poland in 1915 meant a constant state of crisis for the field hospitals. Hundreds of wounded Russian soldiers were brought in daily. Typically dirty and lice-infested, and poorly equipped with arms and ammunition, they were frequently left behind by the rapidly retreating Russian forces. Because of his knowledge of Russian, Albrecht frequently had the task of crawling among the wounded, often under battle conditions, to determine medical priorities. As the German army pushed deeper into Poland, he contracted cholera.

Obviously expected to die, he was left with other cholera victims at a Russian farmhouse and barely attended to. But his condition gradually improved and, learning that his field hospital was getting close to his home village, he managed to return to his unit and to visit Kroczyn in the middle of June 1915. Strangers were living in his former home. The Albrecht family had been put on a train for Siberia ten days earlier.

The removal of the Albrecht family from the area in eastern Poland which they had occupied for two generations was a small detail in just one of the vast resettlement programmes instituted in eastern Europe and Russia during the war. Viewed as uncertain security risks by the Russian authorities, thousands of German and Polish families were sent deep into Russia. It took two weeks for the railway cattle-truck carrying Ferdinand and Helene Albrecht and their seven children to reach Kustany in Siberia, beyond the Ural Mountains. The small schoolhouse where they were dumped was appallingly crowded. When cholera broke out, there was no doctor and no medicines. Five of the Albrecht children died in a month—Emilie, fourteen, Rudolf, eleven, and the younger ones, Augusta, Hulda and Eduard. Ill themselves, the parents were too weak to dig graves. With hundreds of others, the bodies of the dead children were left outside in the snow. This news reached Albrecht in a brief Red Cross message almost a year later.

After he recovered his health, Ferdinand Albrecht secured a position as manager of an agricultural estate on the Volga River. Two years later, in 1918, the family received permission to return to Poland, and made the long return trip across Russia in a cattle-truck, arriving in Kroczyn in June. Late in December of the same year, with his discharge papers and the highest order of the Iron Cross awarded for bravery in rescuing wounded under fire, Friedrich Albrecht travelled back to Poland and was reunited with his family on the first day of 1919.

After an initial period of helping his family to restore their neglected farm, Albrecht wanted to return to the seminary at Hermannsburg. But Poland in 1919 was in a state of turmoil and confusion almost greater than during the previous four years. It was occupied by British, American and German Freicorps troops engaged in offensive and counter-offensive action against the invading Soviet army. The border with Germany was closed and armed forces were stationed along its length.

Civilians required special permits to travel even within Poland itself. Albrecht's identification papers had been stolen, and he could see no alternative but to try to cross the border illegally. Twice he said goodbye to his family, but was not able to get on a train. On the third attempt, on the pretext of looking for work, he managed to board a train going via Lublin and Warsaw to the north-west border town of Rypin. He carried no luggage. In his pockets were a birth certificate (the only identity paper he could obtain), a little money borrowed for him by his father, and a Bible which his mother had carried with her to Siberia and back.

Crossing the border was something he remembered all his life. In Rypin he had been warned of impending arrest, so he set out on foot, walking as rapidly as his lame leg would allow. As he approached the border he could see a factory with gun slits in the lower walls on his right, and armed border guards to the left. Machine-gun fire rang out on both sides in the late afternoon. The way across the border led beside a rye field for a distance. Beyond that, a bare hill stretched away, its pasture completely eaten out. Seeing no alternative, the young man crossed a dry stream bed at the end of the rye field and started up the exposed slope of the hill, in full view of observation posts on both sides. He limped up a sandy furrow, his heart beating violently, watching for any sign of bullets hitting the sand near him. Eventually he reached the other side of the hill and the shelter of another rye field.

When he reported to German soldiers on the other side, he was viewed with suspicion and locked up for the night. In the morning, two men interrogated ahead of him were taken outside and shot. When his turn came, the lieutenant questioned him closely, then spoke in a low voice to one of the men with him. 'He's only a cripple. He's not worth a bullet', was the muttered rejoinder. Eventually he persuaded them to phone his former base in Hannover to confirm his identity. Evidently satisfied, the officer issued a travel permit to *Der Deutschpole*, Friedrich Wilhelm Albrecht, to continue to Hermannsburg.

Forty miles north-west of the Hermannsburg Mission Institute was a small village called Wesseloh. One of its farmers, Wilhelm Gevers, and his wife Katharina were strong supporters of their village Lutheran church. They also had a keen interest in missions, regularly attending the annual mission festivals at the Hermannsburg institute, and supporting the mission society financially.

Most Lutheran pastors in Germany were trained in theology at universities and subsequently took up positions in the State Church. Such students typically came from well-to-do families since poorer students could not aspire to a university education. Their only hope lay in gaining admission to mission institutes like Hermannsburg, Leipzig, Basel and Neuendettelsau which had been founded in the first half of the nineteenth century. From these seminaries, pastors and missionaries had gone to many parts of the world, not only to bring Christianity to indigenous peoples but to provide teaching and nurture to German Lutherans wherever they were. Since students were supported after the first year of study in the *Missionhaus*, the institutes constituted the only avenue of ministry training for poorer families.

For Wilhelm and Katharina Gevers, responsibility to the poor was a central aspect of faith. In late 1919 Wilhelm heard that a German-Pole refugee had arrived at the institute with virtually only the clothes he stood up in. Bringing some lengths of seasoned pine from his Wesseloh cellars, he arranged for a set of bookshelves to be built for the new student, particularly requesting that they be able to be easily dismantled for shipping overseas when the candidate had completed his training. He might have hesitated a little before offering his help if he had known that in a few years the same student would be wanting to marry his only daughter.

At that time, Minna Gevers was twenty. Born on 11 December 1899, she was the middle child in a family of six boys and had grown up something of a tomboy. Riding on a wagon to one of the further pastures, she would drive the horses rather faster than her father approved. One day they almost ran away from her, and he lectured her severely. Yet Minna was deeply drawn to her father, with his high forehead and serious expression. His skill in farming, his hard work, and his almost inexorably high standards in everything he did were qualities which left a lasting imprint on his daughter.

Minna worked in the fields outside school hours, helped her mother look after a hundred fowls, and did most of the milking of their six cows. She also helped her mother in the house, sweeping clean sand across the cobblestone floor of the smoky kitchen, preserving fruit in summer. At fourteen, her village education was completed, and she was sent to a *Haushaltungsschule*, or finishing school, for further training in household management. Not long after, she contracted tuberculosis. In the long months of enforced inactivity in a sanatorium, she pondered the directions of her life, and her favourite verse in the Psalms: 'Take delight in the Lord and he will give you the desires of your heart'. Her decision to become a nursing sister in a missionary service overseas prompted little encouragement from family or church. No mission society would want a nursing sister with tuberculosis. When she was well enough, she took a position in the household of a lecturer in the seminary at Hermannsburg and before long she had made the acquaintance of Friedrich Albrecht.

Albrecht's studies were progressing satisfactorily, but two issues troubled him deeply. He asked himself if his first duty should not have been to stay with his parents after their horrifying war experiences. Secondly, he had crossed the border illegally. Obedience to secular law, provided it did not conflict with God's law, was a strong principle of Lutheranism, and something he would be teaching as a missionary. His doubts were compounded by the news of his mother's death in 1922. It was a profound blow. He realized for the first time the extent of the suffering caused by the war and the loss of her children in Siberia. And she had been a mainstay of his life.

Gradually the confusion was resolved. A letter came from his father telling him to stay where he was. His friendship with Minna Gevers was also deepening. She saw his desire to become a missionary and quietly affirmed it. Then, in November 1923, a letter came from across the world inviting him to be the missionary at the Finke River Mission at Hermannsburg in the centre of Australia. Hermannsburg had been without a missionary since the death of the Reverend Carl Strehlow in October 1922. Seven calls had been sent out by the mission board, all unsuccessfully. The isolation of the mission and the lack of medical facilities were critical problems both to older people and to younger men with families. For Albrecht, then twenty-nine, the call was the confirmation he had been seeking. When he asked Minna if she would go to Australia with him, she felt that her own prayers had been answered.

Nobody else approved of their decision to marry. His fellow students thought her health made her unsuitable and that she did not have enough education for a missionary's wife. For her parents, it was more the prospect of permanent separation from their only daughter. They had already lost one son in the war. Yet their own faith would hardly permit refusal. After the completion of his final year at the institute, Albrecht spent some months at Wartburg Seminary, Iowa, USA, for further study and to improve his English. In June 1925 Minna farewelled her family at the seaport of Hamburg and travelled by ship to Quebec, then by train to Winnipeg where they were married on 14 September. They continued to Vancouver and boarded a ship for Australia.

By 1925, German-speaking communities such as Bethany, Hahndorf, Langmeil, Klemzig and Tanunda were part of the fabric of South Australia. The first Germans to settle in South Australia in 1838 had been a large contingent of four hundred Lutherans fleeing religious harassment in their native Prussia. Later, German settlement spread north and east into the fertile valleys behind Adelaide and into the drier areas in the Murray Valley and beyond.

Inherent in the religious convictions which had brought the Germans to their new land was the command to take the Gospel to others. They supported missionaries from the Dresden mission society in Germany who were contacting Aborigines in the settled areas in the first few years of the colony and, by 1866, two Lutheran synods were supporting a joint missionary venture to the more remote Dieri tribe around Lake Killalpaninna in the Lake Eyre region of South Australia. The difficulties were intense. The general aridity of the region combined with droughts made sheep-raising doubtful and agriculture impossible. The Aborigines exhibited minimal interest in the new teachings, and their nomadic ways were confusing to any European understanding of a stable community.

By the early 1870s the centre of the continent had become the focus of Australian colonial ambitions. The Overland Telegraph Line was completed in just under two years, crossing Australia from north to south over two thousand miles of virtually unexplored country, and the first leases for cattle stations were issued. Having withdrawn from the mission effort at Lake Killalpaninna in 1874, the Evangelical Lutheran Synod of Australia (ELSA) approached Surveyor-General George Goyder about land for a new mission in Central Australia. As at Lake Killalpaninna, missionaries were to be provided by the mission society in Hermannsburg, Germany. A lease was granted eighty miles west of the telegraph repeater station at Alice Springs, or Stuart as it was then known.

The land included part of the Finke River whose permanent water-holes made it likely that Aboriginal people would roam in its vicinity.

The South Australian government, which then had responsibility for the Northern Territory, promised rations for the Aborigines, and two newly trained missionaries from the Hermannsburg institute, Hermann Kempe and Wilhelm Schwarz, arrived by ship in September 1875. On 22 October the large party comprising missionaries, laymen, wagons, thirty-three horses, fowls, sheep dogs, food, tools, medicines and other supplies set out on the thousand-mile journey to Central Australia. With three thousand sheep from the mission at Lake Killalpaninna, drought conditions forced a long halt at Dalhousie Springs, and it was almost two years before they reached the mission lease on the Finke in June 1877. They chose a site on the north bank, naming it after the small village in northern Germany in which Louis Harms had founded the Hermannsburg mission society in 1849.

The first time my grandfather saw the missionaries, it was morning time. He was hunting kangaroo, and he saw this dust coming. And he run to high hill, look down, something coming here, hide in the bush. He don't know what's coming. Then run back to the camp and tell everybody, they went to the sandhill and stopped there, crying and frightened. Sheep and white people coming, but they don't know what that is. After that they saw the people, Aboriginal workers, they brought with them. They come to Henbury, stop there, two, three days. Kill six sheep for them people, give them flour, they throw it away, they don't know tea and sugar. Then they boil tea, show them how to make tea. They never drink it, frightened. My grandfather was young fella. They thought they was debbils, they don't know whites. They reckon this white is a ghost one, come from the dead. And the Aborigines said, those ones from further south, no, this not debbil, only the skin different. From Henbury, they come to Hugh River, come to Owen Springs, then to Hermannsburg.

A third missionary—Louis Schulze from Saxony—with lay helpers and the fiancées of Kempe and Schwarz, arrived in April 1878, having spent five months on the journey from Port Augusta. Though the Lutherans were not the first Europeans to come to Central Australia—the cattle stations of Henbury, Owen Springs, Undoolya, Idracowra, and Glen Helen had been stocked, and the telegraph station was open for traffic—they were the first to establish a permanent home there. Other Europeans came temporarily, often at the behest of large pastoral companies, with the intention of eventually returning south.

To Friedrich Albrecht, pondering it in 1950, it seemed that only something like 'the simple faith of Abraham' could have prompted and helped them to do such a thing. With the wisdom of hindsight, it was easy to see the mistakes—beginning the journey in early summer, taking sheep rather than cattle which would have been hardier and less susceptible to the scant water supplies. And yet, thought Albrecht, with faith, God often turns our very mistakes into blessings.

Contact with the local Aborigines, the Western Aranda tribe, was slow at first. But distributing the government rations encouraged their proximity, and nearby Aboriginal children were gathered each morning to learn reading and writing. By 1880 the number of children attending lessons had grown and a school–church was built of local stone, lime and timber. By 1883 mission workers, wives and children numbered twenty-one, and much effort had gone towards making the community self-supporting by planting cereals and vegetables and sinking wells.

But within Central Australia generally, other tensions were developing rapidly. By 1879 much of the better land in Central Australia was occupied by cattle stations, and active Aboriginal resistance to the European intruders was escalating. The Aboriginal attack on the Barrow Creek telegraph station in 1874 marked the end of a conciliatory approach by Europeans and the beginning of almost two decades of active conflict. Aborigines frequently speared the white man's cattle, both for food and to drive them away from the waterholes on which they depended. Europeans retaliated with large-scale raids and reprisals on Aboriginal groups. About one hundred Unmatjera who had gathered for a ceremony were shot at Italinja—'Blackfellows Bones' as it became known to the Europeans—on the northern edge of Harts Range.

The Lutheran missionaries were quickly embroiled in the conflict. They held that both police and graziers were killing Aborigines unjustly, and feared for the survival of Aboriginal tribes. Graziers for their part accused the mission of harbouring cattle thieves, 'spoiling' their potential workforce by providing rations, and sometimes administering severe corporal discipline to the Aborigines. The fears of the missionaries about the future of Aboriginal tribes were well founded. In 1894, Charles Winnecke of the Horn Scientific Expedition to Central Australia said that the Aborigines had greatly diminished in numbers and were 'still passing away'. Baldwin Spencer, Professor of Biology at the University of Melbourne, noted in 1901 that the Unmatjera were nearly wiped out by drought and dispersion. The multiple impacts of European diseases, shootings, destruction of food resources by livestock, and rough treatment resulted in increased Aboriginal deaths and fewer births.

Contact between the Western Aranda people and the Lutheran missionaries had evolved rather differently. Unlike many of the settlers, the missionaries had not come believing the Aborigines were doomed to extinction, or unduly treacherous and murderous. With their more conciliatory approach to the people, they had not encountered the open resistance experienced elsewhere. There was no Aboriginal attempt to drive the missionaries from the reserve, and the Aranda people took advantage of the resources offering in the new situation. In May 1887 seven Aranda teenagers at Hermannsburg asked for baptism, and were baptized after the long period of instruction usual in the Lutheran church. Another group was baptized in 1890, among them a boy of twelve, Tjalkabotta, who in accordance with mission custom chose a Christian name for himself, Mose (Moses).

Yet the difficulties were immense. A severe drought between 1888 and 1894 wiped out crops and gardens and, by the end of 1896, every cattle station in the Centre except Erldunda had been abandoned or had passed into other hands. The missionaries were suffering health problems, and the adverse effects of an open break between the mission society in Germany and the South Australian church, which withdrew its support from the mission in Central Australia.

Other expectations, too, were undergoing painful reassessment. The missionaries had hoped to convert Aborigines, assimilate them, achieve a self-supporting agricultural base for the mission, and transform these roaming people into a settled community. But the Aranda people, like the Aborigines at Killalpaninna, joined the community only sporadically and worked intermittently. Nor had their theological training provided the missionaries with any approach by which they might begin to unravel the encounter between two such different cultures. Louis Harms's mission society, isolated in a small rural community from winds of intellectual and doctrinal change, was conservative even in the context of

European Lutheranism, and uncompromising in its attitude to all native customs which could not be clearly reconciled with Christian faith.

And the degree of hostility and conflict between Aborigine and European in Central Australia was in itself deeply disturbing. It seemed it would only be a matter of time before the Aboriginal tribes there experienced the same destruction as their brothers in Tasmania. In a letter to the church newspaper *Der Lutherische Kirchenbote fuer Australien* in July 1891, Kempe pondered with great perplexity the meaning of the biblical story of the curse on the descendants of Cain: in every period of world history, it seemed that 'the further the white people advance, the further the black people retreat or vanish'. Looking at the history of 'Red Indians in America, South Sea Islanders and Africans', he could only believe that the pattern was repeating itself in Central Australia. Since it seemed to him hopeless that the material situation of Aborigines in Central Australia could be improved, he concluded that teaching them the Gospel was the only way in which the mission could help them:

> All worldly education is of no use to them. It would not be difficult to teach children to read and write English. But what would be the use? If they leave the mission and go to a station they would not be paid one penny more than other blacks, they had to be satisfied with their keep, clothing and tobacco, although they might have had a better education than the whites.

Discouraged by deaths in their families and severe health problems, the missionaries gradually left for the south.

After a period of uncertainty of almost three years, the mission was sold to the Immanuel Synod, and Reverend Carl Strehlow was called as missionary in 1894. The next year he married his fiancée, Frieda Keysser, when she arrived in Australia from Germany. Strehlow was an exceptionally able and determined man. Over the next twenty-five years, the settlement acquired a church, a school, four houses for mission staff, sleeping dormitories for Aboriginal children, a store, a blacksmith shop, a wagon shed, and a central eating house for the Aborigines which in 1920 constituted the largest single room in Central Australia. Strehlow's methods of religious instruction were no less thorough. He implemented in full the Lutheran intensive instruction periods for adult baptism and confirmation, admitting Aborigines to church membership only when he felt they were ready, though some church members criticized the conservatism of his approach. During his twenty-eight years at Hermannsburg, a Christian community was firmly established, with almost two hundred Aborigines baptized.

In his first years at Hermannsburg, Strehlow tried to suppress traditional ceremonial life, but later came to develop a deep interest in Aboriginal culture. While he consistently refused to attend traditional ceremonies himself and discouraged ceremonial life for Aboriginal Christians, he pursued his studies of traditional culture and language through tribal elders from neighbouring groups. Many of his evenings were spent in his study with its whitewashed walls and stone floors, working on a monumental seven-volume anthropological and linguistic work, *Die Aranda und Loritja Staemme in Zentral-Australien,* written partly in reply to Baldwin Spencer's historic work on the Aranda-speaking people.

Nothing approaching this kind of exploration of Aranda traditional culture was to be undertaken again in Lutheran mission work in Central Australia for another fifty years. Albrecht, who was to dominate the mission approach for several ensuing decades, had different pressures and priorities. Yet Strehlow's work, at this formative time in the development of anthropology as a discipline, was also lost to the English-speaking world as a whole. Strehlow wrote in German and his work was published in Frankfurt. Though a member of the British and Foreign Bible Society strongly urged the Finke River Mission board in the 1920s to have the work translated into English, reiterating the burgeoning interest of anthropologists throughout the world in the Australian Aborigines, the step was never taken.

Strehlow also developed a solid base of Christian materials in Aranda. He revised and greatly expanded the dictionary and grammar begun by Kempe, produced other worship materials and a school primer, and in 1919 completed the task of translating the New Testament into Aranda which he had started in 1913.

By 1920, the Strehlows badly needed rest and medical attention. They also wanted to return to Germany to visit their children who, apart from the youngest, Theo, had been taken there in 1910 for their schooling and were then cut off by the war from returning to Australia. The mission board sought a replacement missionary without success. Finally, a severe deterioration in Strehlow's health forced a hurried departure in October 1922. He set off in a buggy with his wife and fourteen-year-old son to try to reach the railhead and medical help at Oodnadatta four hundred miles away. Despite heroic efforts by Hermannsburg Aborigines and European station owners on the way, Strehlow died at Horseshoe Bend on the tenth day of the gruelling ride down the sandy bed of the Finke in heatwave conditions.

Yes, I remember Pas' Strehlow, he baptize me. I was born in 1916, December 23, just before Christmas. I was little bit bigger boy, I was six [when Strehlow left Hermannsburg] and I walked with my mother, Pas' Strehlow was in the buggy. A lot of people followed him, because he was someone that's been with them all the time. And they knew he wasn't going to come back. They followed as far as they could. Old Station, Henbury, Idracowra, they had to go with the water-holes. I went to Henbury. My mother went to Horseshoe Bend.

That Carl Strehlow had died in his missionary task had its own impact on the Aboriginal congregation at Hermannsburg. Moses, the twelve-year-old who had requested baptism in 1890, was now a mature man, though blind from illness in early adulthood. He helped the teacher, H. A. Heinrich, in confirmation lessons, and took turns with Heinrich and others to preach on Sunday mornings.

Moses was also urging his fellow believers to take the Gospel to other Aborigines, 'especially as we have had the Word of God for over fifty years'. In the middle of 1923 three Christian Aranda made a short trip to the west to make contact with tribal people, and Moses started to visit Aboriginal people at Alice Springs and the cattle station of Deep Well. It was with relief and anticipation that the Aboriginal congregation awaited the arrival of the new missionary and his wife early in 1926.

DROUGHT TIME
1926~1928

*I remember the day that Pastor Albrecht arrived. He came middle of
the drought, seven year drought. He was a stranger, he was coming
here. A truck bring him, pull up over there. All the congregation
was there, everybody. His wife too. No kids. Only young feller.
I remember him stay here, start his work.*

Since the Northern Territory had been a Federal Territory since
1911, the Hermannsburg mission, like other Territory missions,
operated under the auspices of the Commonwealth government of
Australia. Relations between the government and most Territory
missions had been ill-defined and often uneasy, partly because
successive Commonwealth governments had not developed any
coherent Aboriginal policy, and were niggardly in their approach to
funding: missions with their supporting churches and sometimes
dedicated personnel became a cheap and convenient surrogate. The
government simply wanted to see Aborigines working, living in
reasonably hygienic conditions, being trained to become useful
citizens and learning to speak English. How to achieve these ends
and how to finance them was the business of missions, apart from
meagre annual subsidies. The general attitude of government
towards Aborigines still living traditionally was that they were best
left alone, if possible in large reserves.

The Hermannsburg mission had actually incurred considerable
Commonwealth disapproval, partly through its German associations

and the resultant hysteria during World War 1. Baldwin Spencer, in particular, whose visits to the mission had occurred in periods of uncertainty and lack of leadership, had reported unfavourably on the Lutheran mission, and recommended in 1923 that the Commonwealth government take over the station. A number of other government reports had also been critical of mission management, its failure to achieve financial viability through cattle grazing, the apparent lack of employment opportunities for the Aborigines, and poor standards of hygiene and sanitation. The result had been an unhappy relationship between mission and government. Annual subsidies had been successively reduced, eliminated and haggled over, and by 1926 the government was insisting on reviewing the mission lease on a yearly basis, despite a positive report on the mission by Reverend John Sexton of the Adelaide-based Aborigines' Friends' Association in 1925, and a strong recommendation that the Lutherans be granted security of tenure.

The mission's financial outlook was also bleak. Debts had mounted even in Strehlow's time, difficulties only to be expected for a small institution with scanty resources attempting to respond to the physical needs of a fluctuating Aboriginal population. The droughts common to inland Australia meant not only stock losses for the mission run but an increase in the numbers of Aborigines from other stations and outlying areas coming to the mission for food and refuge. Extra food had to be brought from the south, incurring the disproportionately high freight charges to Central Australia. In the beginning of 1926, debts amounted to more than £4000, despite a sum of £1600 raised by the South Australian church, and an £800 loan from a board member, Albert Graetz. In his annual report to Federal Minister for Home and Territories, the Honourable G. F. Pearce, the chairman of the Finke River Mission board, the Reverend J. J. Stolz, described the predicament:

> If we turn to the problem of financing the work we are at our wits end, how are we to get rid of our debts [and] at the same time supply the wants of an ever increasing native population. We need now from 2½ to 3½ tons of flour alone per month. The annual upkeep will not be under £3000. On top of these difficulties a terrible drought is upon us . . . It's quite likely that the end of this year will see us with hardly any stock left.

The recent South Australian District Conference, Stolz wrote to the Minister, had responded to these 'hard facts' by voting to raise an interest-free loan of £5000 for the mission over the next five years. But any chance of effecting long-term station improvements required greater security of tenure:

> Then we feel compelled to put the straight-out question to the Government: is it right that the burden of feeding and employing the natives should rest on the shoulders of a small section of the community: the South Australian District of the United Evangelical Lutheran Church in Australia, which is almost solely responsible for the maintaining of the Finke River Mission, numbers 6,700 communicants. Surely others should help too ... We are quite willing to employ the natives and pay them their due. But ... if we would employ only such as are urgently required—as other stations do—we would have to turn away the greater number of our natives, and this would mean under the present drought conditions to turn them out to starve. Shall this be done? We dare not do it. Yet on the other hand where are we to land with our finances?

His plea that the Australian government accept more responsibility for the original inhabitants of the continent was to be reiterated in successive mission correspondence and elsewhere for another decade and a half before substantial change took place. For the young missionary and his wife travelling north by train in April 1926, there was no real assurance that the mission would even continue. The mission at Lake Killalpaninna, they had been told by the board, had been finally closed only a few years before, even though there were still twenty-five Aboriginal children in the mission school. Hermannsburg might also have to be closed if the financial difficulties could not be resolved. The prospect was unthinkable to the pair who had come so far towards their goal. Both felt strongly that if Carl Strehlow had lived there for twenty-eight years and built a Christian congregation, they had to do everything in their power to continue the work.

The railway ended at Oodnadatta, four hundred miles to the south of Alice Springs. Albrecht and Minna were met there by Gerhardt Johannsen, a Danish immigrant whom the mission board had appointed manager of Hermannsburg in 1923 following Strehlow's death. The board had hoped that a lay overseer would run the station more efficiently and develop employment opportunities for the Aborigines. Despite Johannsen's efforts, however, debts had continued to increase. From Oodnadatta it was a three-day drive into the tiny township of Alice Springs, or Stuart as it was still named. It was all strange country to the newcomers—the jagged

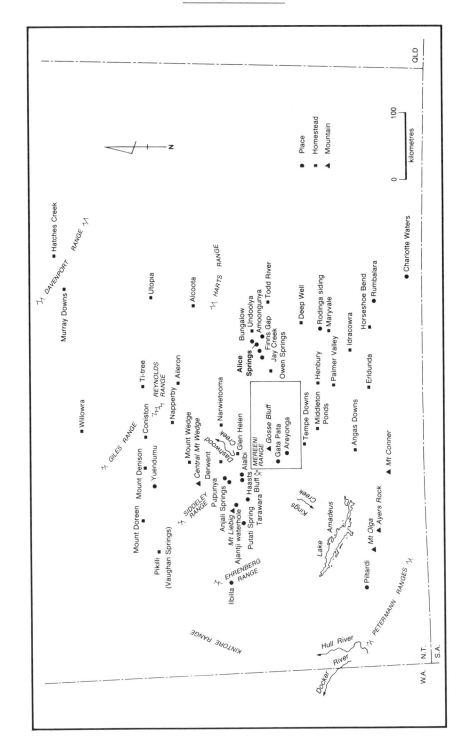

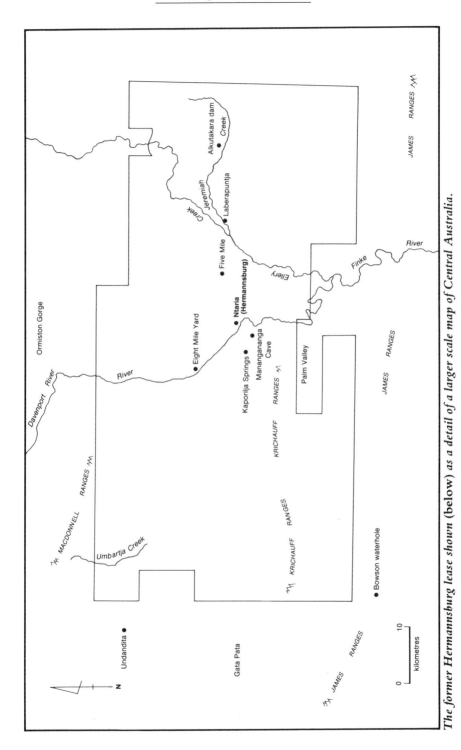

The former Hermannsburg lease shown (below) as a detail of a larger scale map of Central Australia.

cliffs rising up on either side of the track as they drove through Heavitree Gap on the southern side, the austere beauty of the surrounding ranges, the surprise appearance of the tall gum trees growing out of the dry bed of the Todd River which ran through the settlement.

In Central Australia, as elsewhere, large numbers of Aborigines had drifted to the fringes of European settlements. Albrecht had the impression there might have been 100 or 150 people around the small settlement. Some worked in town in the day, but they were required by law to leave at nightfall. Many were diseased. The township itself was tiny—a hotel, Wallis Fogarty's store (an off-shoot of the larger store at Oodnadatta), a police station, a saddler's shop, a Chinese baker, and a café where one could have a meal. Scattered around the town area were the camps of Afghan camel drivers and their animals, a few Chinese, and a number of white drovers.

Albrecht and Minna stayed overnight in the home of Mr and Mrs Ernest Kramer, itinerant missionaries to Aborigines, and supported by the Adelaide-based Aborigines' Friends' Association, and in the morning the new missionary was taken for the necessary round of official introductions in this small outpost of European civilization—the head Commonwealth government official in Central Australia, Government Resident J. C. Cawood; the police sergeant; and the manager of Wallis Fogarty's store. They started for Hermannsburg late in the morning, driven by Johannsen. There was no real road, only a two-wheel track which ran beside a spur of the craggy Macdonnell Ranges for a couple of hours, then turned south through a gap. Late in the afternoon, Johannsen pointed out a mountain whose slopes and shadows stood out from the surrounding range—Mount Hermannsburg—and a little later they came to the crest of a rise overlooking the station.

The broad valley of the Finke lay before them, the sandy watercourse winding through river gums, the far side stretching away to further ranges. On the near bank, buildings nestled among the trees, faintly glowing in the last rays of the sun. A moment or two later, the car pulled up in the middle of a sandy compound encircled by whitewashed stone buildings, with dark figures running from everywhere to crowd around them. Some of the older men waited more reservedly and were then introduced—Jacobus, Nathaniel, Rufus, Martin. Moses was led up and put out his hand, saying simply in English, 'I am glad'.

Their first Sunday service was led by the teacher, Heinrich, with Moses preaching the sermon in Aranda. The men of the congregation, some of them old and grizzled, sat on one side of the church. Children overflowed the aisle between the two rows of wooden forms, and mothers with babies and some adults who had not joined the church squatted in the sand outside. Albrecht, reflecting that this was his first experience of a congregation consisting partly of converts from heathenism, felt a certain awe.

Their house had been a pleasant surprise, especially to Minna, who had been preparing herself for a mud hut. It was quite large, with thick walls of stone smoothed over by many coats of white lime wash. Rooms were a good size and some even had linoleum over the flagstone floors. Ceilings had been constructed by inserting smaller mulga branches between the main beams, and covering them with clay mixed with grass. Hessian had been tacked underneath and also washed over with lime. At the back of the house, twenty or so stone steps led down to a garden of large date palms planted by the first missionaries. Beyond was bush and the sandy river bed of the Finke.

The station itself was a semicircle of whitewashed stone and lime mortar buildings built over the previous three decades. To the right of their own residence was an even older house occupied by the stockman Phillip Henke and his family, and beside that the blacksmith's shop and the wagon shed. Immediately across from the missionary's residence was the church, two tall gum trees in front of it. The little school stood close by the church, the scene each weekday morning of a prompt line-up, following the teacher's whistle, of forty or fifty children who then marched into school. As the morning progressed, various chantings of the alphabet, numbers and the times tables attested to the efforts at instruction in mathematics, and reading and writing in Aranda and English.

A small meathouse, an eating house used for communal eating in Strehlow's day, and the Heinrichs's house completed the buildings in the central area. Further on were two separate whitewashed buildings used as segregated sleeping dormitories by the school girls and boys. Further towards the river was the main Aboriginal camp, a mixture of mud and grass huts outside which people built their fires and did their cooking.

It was not until that first evening in April when he climbed out of Johannsen's buckboard into an excited but unintelligible clamour of voices that Albrecht fully realized the magnitude of the task of learning Aranda. It was not that the idea of foreign languages was new. He had grown up with several. But in Central Australia, his task was to preach the Gospel, to communicate about deep issues of life and faith with a people obviously very different in background and thinking—a task which extended language to its limit. But he started immediately, learning individual words as he became acquainted with the people and the organization of the place. He soon had an offer of help. Each morning at sunrise, Moses appeared on the verandah, and for half an hour Albrecht read to him from the Gospel of St Luke which the British and Foreign Bible Society had printed in Aranda the previous year, using Carl Strehlow's translation. Moses listened intently, correcting the pronunciation word by word. The two men talked, too, during these sessions. Together with information from Mr Heinrich, the new missionary gradually pieced together something of the life of this man in his late forties who, despite his blindness, held immense authority among the Aranda people.

Moses (Tjalkabotta) had been born at Labrapuntja, ten miles east of Hermannsburg, about the time that the first missionaries arrived. His father was a man of knowledge and influence among the Ntaria and Ellery Creek people, and master of the *tnurangatja* or witchetty grub totem. He was one of the first Aranda people to make contact with the newly arrived missionaries, and initially helped them in their attempts to learn the language. Because of this contact, Tjalkabotta joined the small school of nine or ten children. He found it irksome, and sometimes ran away. Once he was away nearly a year.

As he grew older, he felt increasingly confused about the different teachings he was receiving. The missionary message about Jesus and God was ridiculed by the old tribal men, who also impressed upon the boys that unless they were circumcised they would always be classed as women and children and could not take part in the decisions of the group. Tjalkabotta also had his own questions about the new teaching. Why did the missionaries urge the children to disobey their parents in these matters of belief, when God's commands told them to obey their parents? Yet slowly he began to feel that the new doctrine was a better way than the Aboriginal sacred stones and their stories. What attracted him most deeply was the picture of Jesus on the cross, and he repeated to himself, '*nukaguia*' (for me), 'Jesus died for me', feeling happy to think he was included. At twelve years of age, he asked for baptism, and was given the biblical name of Moses.

Some time after his baptism, he and three other boys were taken forcibly by some of the men and circumcised. In accordance with Aranda custom, they were then taken to a place north of Hermannsburg, in the Macdonnell Ranges, and kept in a secluded spot. The elders told them that the stone *tjurungas*, the sacred objects, had come from the Dreaming and were to be treasured above anything, and the heavy slabs of stone wrapped in paperbark were handed over to the boys. Later, Moses and the other boys took the stones out of their wrappings to examine the maze of lines and circles engraved on the surface. Unlike the Bible, Moses thought, the stone carried no picture of the beings from whom it had come. It also seemed to him that the engraving had been recently done. How therefore, he asked himself, could it also be old and sacred?

Not long after, he suffered a heat stroke while looking after sheep near Ellery Creek, and his vision was impaired. By this time the first missionaries were leaving, and the newly baptized young people were subjected to a lot of ridicule. He was overjoyed when the Reverend Carl Strehlow and two other men arrived in 1894 to re-establish the mission. In 1903 he married a woman called Sofia, and a couple of years later he lost his sight totally in a severe illness. As he could not do outside work on the station, he began to help teach the baptism classes, and worked closely with Carl Strehlow in his translation and anthropological work.

Though active opposition to the new way continued during Strehlow's time, many of the Aranda-speaking people in the mission area accepted Christian teaching and were baptized. The strength of traditional culture was also being steadily undermined by other contact with European civilization, as the cattle stations were built up and a small township grew up around the telegraph station. Strehlow's death seemed to mark a further stage in Aboriginal attitudes to the new faith. Much of the previous enmity of other Aborigines towards Aboriginal Christians seemed to disappear.

General station work was soon absorbing much of Albrecht's attention—medical sessions twice a day at the little dispensary at the western end of the verandah, organizing tasks on the station. Maintaining adequate supplies of food, tools, and other station requirements needed careful thought and planning: orders were compiled twice yearly, and had to be sent well in advance. The buying was done in South Australia by a member of the mission board, and goods were dispatched by rail to Oodnadatta, and then by camel train up the Finke valley. The monthly camel mail also travelled through the stations along the Finke, driven by a small thin man whose name was Harry Tilmouth but who was referred to universally as 'Bony Bream'. Minna was also settling into her new life. Soon after she had arrived at Hermannsburg, a part-Aboriginal woman named Mariane (Marianna) approached her. She had worked in the Strehlow household, and now offered her services to the new missionary and his wife.

In late July, three months after their arrival in Central Australia, the local Presbyterian minister, Reverend John Flynn, drove out to the mission with Alf Traeger, a talented young radio ham from Adelaide on whom Flynn had pinned his hopes of developing a radio link to remote areas. The Albrechts had met Flynn on first coming to Alice Springs. Flynn had already travelled widely in the bush, visiting cattlemen and their families, seeing at close hand the hardship that accompanied the isolation and immense distances of the inland. In April 1926 he had begun to build a hostel in Alice Springs which he hoped would be the centre of a medical service to the inland. Urgency and frustration were written all over his face as he showed the newcomers over the site. 'As a Christian minister', he said to Albrecht, 'I'm supposed to run a Sunday School and conduct services. But I don't have a hope! On Sundays I have to plan the work for the whole week ahead, order materials, then go out to the blacks' camp to get people for cutting timber for the lime kiln . . .' Albrecht had listened to him quietly, seeing a man who had found a task he could not ignore, even if it meant neglecting the work he had been sent to carry out.

The small buckboard in which Flynn and Traeger drove out to Hermannsburg in July carried a wireless set, a number of glass jars, and a Morse keyboard. Traeger had been able to establish radio contacts over short distances but now wanted to carry out a test over a longer distance. They left equipment at the mission and the next day managed to send a signal to the mission at a prearranged time. It was the first long-distance signal to be successfully sent and received over what later became the pedal wireless. For the Albrechts, hearing the signal was a major step in breaking the intense sense of isolation they had previously felt.

Flynn's new hostel was completed, and in September Minna went there to await the delivery of their first child. Albrecht was preparing to join her a week later when two telegrams came through on the wireless. The first told him that a daughter had been born in Tanunda in the Barossa Valley, South Australia. The other indicated that his wife was very ill, and asked him to come south urgently. Then a third telegram arrived. 'Very unnecessary. Minna.'

The contradictions were puzzling, but he concluded there was no need to rush south.

The two nursing sisters who had examined Minna in Alice Springs had found a high percentage of albumin (water-soluble proteins found in blood) in her urine specimens, implying a serious kidney condition, and they had advised her to get to Oodnadatta to catch the fortnightly train south. After the baby was born in Tanunda, she became very ill with a kidney infection. When the initial crisis was past, she sent a telegram to reassure her husband, but a mistake in transmission changed her original message, 'Worry unnecessary' to 'Very unnecessary'. The mission board had given permission for her husband to come south for a month, and Minna could not understand why he did not arrive.

With the camel mail coming only monthly, weeks went by before the separated pair could exchange letters and clear up the misunderstanding. Minna wanted to return north, but doctors told her she would never survive the journey in summer and would have to wait for the cooler weather in February or March. She named her new daughter Helene Katherine Frieda—Helene in memory of her husband's mother who had died in Poland, Katherine for her own mother, Frieda for the baby's two godmothers, the widowed Frieda Strehlow and a special friend, Frieda Roehrs. A photograph was taken on the baby's baptism day in December— Minna looking at the baby in her arms, radiant with happiness; Frieda Strehlow watching her, a gentle smile overlying the habitual sadness of her face. Other friends shared the moment including the two bright-eyed children of the Roehrs family.

The drought in Central Australia was steadily worsening. The last good rain had been in January 1925—more than a year before. And 1924 had been the second driest year on record. There were showers in April and May of 1926 but not enough to replenish waterholes or grow any real feed for the cattle. June, July and August were dry. What water was left in the waterholes in the Finke was becoming brackish, and the wells near the station were lower than anyone could remember. More cattle were dying.

Albrecht missed his wife acutely as he struggled with language study and the management of the station. He was also beginning to learn something of Aboriginal ways. A man who said 'my father' might not necessarily mean his own father, but rather his father's brother. What to a European would be an uncle was, in the Aboriginal kinship system, another father, with the same kinds of responsibilities as a real father. The complexity of tribal kinship and its network of obligations was a strange world to the new missionary. He was worried, too, by the degree of petty theft on the station. Every week brought complaints from one or another that someone had stolen a shirt, or his tea and sugar. His remonstrances that this was forbidden in God's Word had limited effect. A more serious incident arose when the stock camp killed three bullocks in a week instead of the usual one, and a large group of non-workers moved out to claim the extra food. Albrecht knew that this would have been normal in traditional life: all food was treated communally. But the mission was struggling for its very existence. With a debt of more than £4000, the bank had refused to advance any more money, and only the large loan from Albert Graetz had enabled them to continue buying essential foodstuffs. There was no money to engage another European stockman, so the run either had to be worked by the Christian Aborigines or not at all. He wrote in his diary:

> We have not as yet made much progress with our 'Station Rules', it will take much effort before we have established something like law and order. Of course, everything would be much simpler if we would not be compelled to scratch and save at every turn.

If 'Station Rules' were having little effect, Albrecht felt it imperative that Christian Aborigines exercise more responsibility, though he had the impression that Carl Strehlow had run the mission as a 'patriarchy'. The New Testament concept of congregational elders was in his mind. But perhaps, he thought, this could be built upon existing tribal authority. He called a meeting and tried to explain the responsibilities of congregational life in the New Testament, mentioning that Paul had appointed elders, with tasks of discipline and care for the people. He also pointed out the good things that God had given them in their traditional tribal organization, and that they should not neglect their older men, like old Petrus. This aroused definite interest, and elders were elected.

Their authority seemed to be recognized by the congregation, and the level of thieving and fighting gradually diminished. Not that the system always worked smoothly. Sometimes an elder, conscious of his new position, would call a meeting of the whole congregation to settle a personal grievance. It was years before Albrecht felt they understood fully that the institution of elders was there not to settle personal grudges but to deal with matters that involved the whole group. Their presence was also important for him. He was glad to be able to discuss issues with them, and let them take a significant share of the responsibility for resolving disputes, or exercising discipline. The mission was an almost closed community, isolated from wider support by distance and poor communications as well as by the ignorance and indifference of the majority of Europeans in Central Australia. It was a practical necessity that most problems had to be settled within the community itself.

The finances of the Finke River Mission continued to be a major issue for its supporting church. With only about thirty-two congregations large enough to have their own pastors, the entire annual offerings of the South Australian church amounted to no more than £8000–£9000 each year. Yet the annual running costs of the mission were about £3000, and only in good years did the sale of cattle make any substantial contribution. The government subsidy still stood at £250, though Stolz had pleaded vehemently with the Minister in 1923 that the cost of maintaining the children, the old and infirm, and the teacher's salary—in his view clearly the minimal responsibilities of government—amounted to £550 per year.

In early 1927, the annual synod of the South Australian District of the United Evangelical Lutheran Church in Australia (the result of a merger of the two previous synods in 1921) was held in the little town of Nuriootpa, South Australia. Pastor John Riedel, who had replaced Pastor John Stolz as the mission board chairman, was pleased to report that the Commonwealth government had finally granted the mission a twenty-one year lease and had also offered a £500 loan to carry out improvements provided that the church could find another £1000 for the same purpose.

Riedel had also to inform his listeners that no cattle had been mustered for over a year because of the dry conditions. Without good rain, suitable European workers, and the necessary improvements, there was no prospect of the mission getting on its feet financially. A year earlier, Riedel had issued a strongly worded challenge to his church to 'dip into our own pockets . . . for the Finke Mission'. Now he reiterated his plea, warning them against 'letting this work of the Lord perish by sheer indifference'. Discussions were protracted, but the synod resolved to continue to support the mission, and to try to clear its debts and raise the extra £1000 required for the government's £500 loan.

Late in March 1927, Minna and her baby returned north on the train, almost seven months since the September morning she had left for Alice Springs. As the year wore on, the station grew drier and dustier. Aboriginal men were sent routinely with shovels along the Finke, deepening the remnants of waterholes. The station itself had no running water, the only water supplies consisting of several wells and two rainwater tanks on the staff houses. Once a day, women from the camp walked a quarter of a mile down the sandy bank of the Finke, returning with four-gallon tins of water balanced on tightly wound circles of towelling on their heads. Some of this was kept for tea and drinking water. The rest was poured into forty-four gallon drums at the camp and at the eating house to be used for laundry and washing up. As the water in the river soakages grew more salty, they began using a small spring of fresh water about half a mile upstream from the mission. The Aranda people called the spring Ntaria, the name also designating the general locality of the station.

Albrecht was worrying about the diet of the people which was becoming more and more restricted to flour and a little meat, along with the inevitable tea and sugar. Apart from the meat, these were bulk foods sent up from South Australia by rail and camel train. He regularly sent people out to scour the surrounding areas for the small onion-like bulb, *yelka*, and other bush foods. But bush tucker had not been plentiful even in 1926, and with so little rain since then, not much had sprouted. Albrecht wrote again to ask the mission board to let the congregations know that gifts of barley or other grains would be welcomed.

No [government] rations that time, only from Oodnadatta on the camels [food purchased by the mission]. Pastor Albrecht tell all the men, bring yelka, paraltja, *to eating house, all ladies send to get the rabbit, cook them and bring them in here. Not enough kangaroo in drought, no cattle here in drought, few skinny skinny. Pastor Albrecht work very hard.*

He was also trying to make the available food go further. In Johannsen's time as manager, the workers had been paid a wage, from which they were expected to support their families. It seemed a logical and convenient system, particularly to European thinking, but in practice there were problems. Workers purchasing flour, tea and sugar with a month's wages would be besieged by a host of relatives claiming their share. After a number of occasions when women came to Albrecht as superintendent saying they had nothing to eat, he thought it would be best to provide food daily for the most vulnerable groups, and reverted to Strehlow's system of feeding the sick, the aged, and the women with children at the little eating house, three times a day. And most workers were paid in food rations rather than money. Some of the mothers, too, were bringing their babies to the house each day. Minna felt the infants would have a better chance if they had some regular powdered milk, and she wanted to see for herself that they got it.

Results in the mission school were improving as Heinrich had been relieved of outside responsibilities. Albrecht also went frequently into the little schoolhouse, taking Scripture lessons and testing the children in their other work. Language instruction in English and Aranda had always been a part of mission schooling, though the government had showed little interest in whether they learned to read and write in Aranda. Baldwin Spencer, commenting on the state of education in 1922, had reported that though some of the children could write in Aranda, he did not see that this could be of much use to them.

Albrecht felt strongly that these children should grow up bilingual. He felt they needed English to help them find a place in the general community, and wanted them to learn good English, not merely a broken pidgin version. But he felt equally strongly that they needed to retain their own language, not just for speaking but for reading and writing. It was especially important that they could read the Scriptures in their own language. It reached to their deepest feelings in a way that English could not.

He had continued diligently with his own language study, and one Sunday morning in May, a little over a year after their arrival, he took his place in the pulpit, Moses beside him. Instead of speaking in English for Moses to translate, he began his sermon in Aranda. A sense of expectancy came over the congregation and the silence deepened as he struggled on. Outside afterwards, an excited chattering enveloped the groups of people walking back to the camp.

Government Resident Cawood paid a visit to Hermannsburg in late December. He seemed preoccupied with the worsening drought and the complaints by European settlers that Aborigines coming in from the bush were becoming aggressive in their demands for food. They had to be taught a lesson, he told Albrecht, before they drove the whites off the land in Central Australia. Cawood issued instructions that pure poison was not to be issued to Aborigines for dingo trapping, and that no Aborigine was to carry a rifle without permission.

Early January 1928 brought sixty-two points (0.62 inch) of rain, falling in a narrow strip from the Eight Mile paddock across to the station. There were other small showers toward the end of the month, and the rain records for January showed a little over an inch, the only substantial rain for that year. Central Australia settled to fine weather, blue skies, and a landscape which dried out more and more as the weeks went by. In Alice Springs cattle were coming in to the telegraph station springs in search of water, and dying by the score. Extra horses had to be brought in to drag the carcasses away.

My mother came from the country south-west of Mount Olga. They used to go out hunting, go from one place to another. If they saw big rain, they would go to that place, to save the food round their country. That's how they used to do it. They would come to Mount Olga and live round there, then halfway to Hermannsburg and live there, then to Ayers Rock and live round that country. In the seven year drought, they went to every country. It was very hard, just found little bit to keep them alive. My mother was little girl then, and she told me about a lady who killed her own son and ate him before the other people came along. Her husband came along, and saw her track and he knew straightaway—she has killed my son—and he tracked her and killed her then. That was drought time.

Early in the year there was an outbreak of whooping cough at the station. Soon forty were ill, most of them children, and among them the Albrechts' sixteen-month-old Helene and the Heinrichs' baby, Dennis. Riedel wrote sympathetically. His homeopathic book, he said, defined whooping cough as a lengthy illness, usually lasting sixteen weeks. Arnica, copper, ceratrum and album were the main medicines, and he had ordered some to be sent with the next mail. By late February Albrecht wrote that the epidemic was abating, though the medicines had not yet arrived:

> Yesterday we dug the ninth grave here this year. That speaks volumes in a congregation this size. There were eight children, and a woman, Bertha, the sister of Rufus. Her baby died a week before she did . . . We tried to console the relatives as well as we could, but the Lord is the only one who can really console us, and He did. Our native people often speak about having visions. It's something quite strange. Now that we know them a little better and can communicate more easily, we are told all sorts of things.

A five-year-old boy called Amos was one of those who died. Despite Albrecht's efforts to help him clear his congestion, the boy had choked in his arms. His foster parents told Albrecht that the

F. W. Albrecht with Minna on their honeymoon in Banff, Canada (photograph by a passing photographer), and late in his life.

Minna Gevers with her parents at Wesseloh, northern Germany. Albrecht served in a medical unit in the German army in World War I (seated at desk on left).

previous night he had told them Jesus had called him and would soon come and take him. There were angels around him too, he said, singing beautiful songs. 'Perhaps', wrote Albrecht in the same letter, 'the Lord speaks to these people through visions more than we are inclined to believe'.

The Albrechts had been fortunate not to lose their own child. Early on a Sunday morning, three weeks earlier, Helene's condition had deteriorated. Her eyes were dull and, as the morning passed, she grew colder and colder. In the afternoon, they felt the end was near. Thinking that there was nothing to lose, they packed her into wet towels and then wrapped her up in blankets, a treatment that Albrecht had read about in the medical book he had brought from the mission institute in Germany. After some time the child began to perspire and seemed a little more responsive. She continued to improve over the next few days and was soon out of danger. But Albrecht's heart was heavy for the loss of others. Four men were still away, travelling with the camel train of an Afghan man, Ali Mohammed. Three of them had each lost a child, and Laurence his wife as well. 'They are going to find it hard when they come back and find out what has happened', he wrote to Riedel.

At the time he was writing, the weather had changed. Cool southerly winds blew for weeks. It was a welcome relief from the summer temperatures, but boded ill for the chances of rain. Dust storms began to blow up, covering with a fine layer of sand the young grass which had sprouted briefly. Work on two underground water tanks continued. Albrecht had been surprised on coming to Hermannsburg to find what little rainwater storage there was. Visiting Yorke Peninsula in his first months in Australia, he had seen underground tanks for the first time. He understood the construction method, and could supervise the work. They were being built near the staff houses to catch rainwater from the roofs.

The mission board had managed to secure the services of a Lutheran farmer from Eden, Mr Gus Droegemuller, for some months to do repairs and improvements on the mission, and he arrived in the middle of the year. Though no longer young, he was a tenacious worker, and took on the gamut of tasks needing attention—making cattle yards, building fences, sinking wells, repairing staff houses. He worked slowly but doggedly, and was sometimes impatient with Aboriginal workers who did not meet his exacting standards. Yet, on the whole, they respected the old man they privately referred to as 'Pipe' because of his constant smoking.

The apparent lack of capacity of many of the Aborigines to work consistently was a recurring frustration to the superintendent. Few people seemed to be able to work independently, and often tasks were simply left undone. In one episode, Droegemuller had been obliged to leave his well-sinking at a part of the cattle run called Umbartja to come into the station to make some iron implements. The Aboriginal workers left behind to continue preparing timber for the walls of the well did minimal work while he was away. Albrecht spoke to Moses about it, and was still more frustrated when Moses conveyed the impression that the issue was hardly worth commenting on. That in itself preyed on the superintendent's mind for days: how could the future of these people be assured if they were so little interested in making an effort themselves? It was not only that it interfered with projects like the well-sinking that he thought were vital. He also felt that such lack of responsibility was a serious impediment to progress in their Christian faith. The biblical injunction that 'he who does not work does not eat' was deeply embedded in his own cultural and religious background.

He was teaching a baptism class for older people. They had been coming three times a week for the previous eight months. It was often trying. Everything had to be repeated over and over and, even then, they often could not remember what was just said. Sometimes, as he visited people in the camps, he was appalled by the sense of inertia and unresponsiveness which seemed to surround them as they sat 'dreaming and doing sweet nothing', as he wrote to Riedel. Sometimes he felt it was a dreadful dullness or stupidity, at other times he asked himself if it was an active resistance to what he was saying. But two from his class seemed to take it seriously and remained. At the end of the lessons, he always gave some time to teaching them to read, hoping it would open God's word to them.

Moses was also actively involved in Christian teaching. He travelled by donkey down the Finke and visited Aborigines living on cattle stations. There was little interest at Horseshoe Bend, though he had attracted a big congregation there last time. But some Loritja people from the west had been in contact with them in the meantime, and one of their elders had warned the people against Moses' teaching. At the railway siding of Charlotte Waters, by contrast, a lot of Aborigines had come over on camels and horses for the services, though they had been told to stay away from the railway construction gangs by the authorities who wanted to discourage begging and prostitution. In general, the Christian teaching seemed to be gaining ground among the people along the Finke, and people knew of Albrecht even if they had not met him. Most referred to him as the lame pastor, *ingkata inurra*.

I used to go mustering cattle. I knew about Hermannsburg . . . that's what I knew about Hermannsburg, the good word. Hermannsburg was good word country. My father used to bring me here, sit down here for a while, [when] Strehlow was here. Stay for a week, two weeks sometime, go back to Henbury. That time I was heathen, and I know nothing much. Then I was married, and I come to Hermannsburg altogether, because good word there.

Carl Strehlow's Aranda translation of the four New Testament Gospels had been printed by the British and Foreign Bible Society, and a consignment of the books had been sent to the mission. As there was no money to pay for them, it was decided between Albrecht and the elders that the people be encouraged to bring an offering. The response astounded the young missionary. Spears, boomerangs, shields, stone axes, stone knives, strings of human hair, red bean necklaces and some sacred artefacts were brought in as the days passed, and many people expressed their happiness in being able to bring such an offering to God. Several cases were packed and sent by camel train to Oodnadatta and then by rail to the Bible Society in Adelaide.

With the winter of 1928 rapidly approaching, Albrecht was worried about the scarcity of blankets for the people, and wrote to the mission board. Chairman John Riedel contacted the Liberal Member of Parliament for Angas, Langdon Parsons, about the possibility of a government issue of blankets. Blankets had traditionally constituted one tangible compensation for the dispossessed Aborigine in every Australian colony from the days of first contact when the blanket had been a diplomatic gift. Along with issues of clothing, it was decreed that such blankets could not be sold or exchanged, and remained 'the property of His Majesty'. In this case, the seemingly inevitable issue of blankets for Aborigines was not to be. The Secretary of the Department was directed to inform Parsons that though it had been ascertained from the Government Resident of North Australia that the Bathurst Island, Goulburn Island and Millingimbi mission stations had each been supplied with twenty-five blankets (since 'in these cases, the Missions are practically agents of the chief Protector of Aboriginals') he had been advised by the Government Resident of Central Australia that 'no grants of blankets are made to Missions in Central Australia'. Such were the constraints on government spending on Aborigines in Central Australia in 1928.

Faced with people who had practically no covering in the rapidly dropping night temperatures, Albrecht wrote urgently to Riedel asking the board to purchase blankets. 'Bob Buck from Middleton Ponds station had been able to buy some of reasonable quality for 7/6 each for his people.' One hundred were dispatched from the south. Such governmental neglect could only occur in a context of widespread public indifference to and ignorance of Aboriginal people, particularly those living in the Northern Territory remote from the major centres of European population. Yet sometimes the mission was encountering not only indifference but clear antagonism. Two southern reporters visiting the mission the previous year had criticized the mission policy of supporting people who were not working, and accused the mission of doing more harm than good by its charitable generosity.

Such charges were additional stress for Albrecht. It was now his third year of work without a break, since he was due three months of furlough only at the end of each three-year period. He was also well aware that these kinds of opinions were shared by many local station owners. But he felt he should make some public reply, and wrote a long letter which was translated into English for the weekly magazine of the Lutheran church, the *Lutheran Herald*:

> I wonder if the author of the article ever tried to live with his family on 10/- a week, which would not even be paid regularly ... The white graziers do not permit the blacks to hunt on their land, and the land where herds are grazing are off limits to the blacks. Black labourers are looked after at most of the stations, but what is left for the others? In most countries people who cannot earn their living get unemployment benefits. These poorest of the poor are denied this ... Should the Mission now also take the attitude that the 'niggers' are not worth living and turn their backs on them ... We try to help them as much as possible with their meagre livelihood and try to make it possible for them to have a family. But one cannot expect these people to work all day for three meals a day consisting of flour soup or barley broth. The mission lacks the funds to employ these people properly and the personnel for supervision ... Above all, we pray and hope that God will send us rain. Then we will have more work ... Until then the question is not to create for the blacks a different livelihood ... but how to keep them alive at all. If we want to achieve this then the Mission Station cannot do so on its own.

Even graziers with only up to ten black workers to care for went bankrupt and were forced to give up their station, caused by the great drought . . .

Perhaps the worst charge, as far as Albrecht was concerned, was that the mission tried to coerce the Aborigines into becoming Christians by giving them food, shelter and clothing:

The mission wants to bring the Gospel to these heathens, the decision is theirs whether they want to take the final step to Christianity. We never bribed anybody, and the handing out of rations never depended on their conversion to Christianity. We have to help them and ease their burden, because nobody else does.

Sometimes he had to struggle enough with his own doubts about whether it was all worth it, reminding himself that only the Lord could make that judgement.

The mid-year order of foodstuff, tools and clothing which came up with the camel train of Ali Mohammed arrived well past the expected time. The new railway being built between Oodnadatta and Alice Springs had now reached Rumbalara, but Ali's camels were so emaciated that it was taking fifteen days, more than twice the normal time, to travel the remaining distance up the Finke. With the loading so overdue, there had been virtually no food left, and the previous day Albrecht had risked sending Aboriginal men out hunting with guns. He wanted to avoid sending the stockman Phillip Henke to Alice Springs in his truck for supplements because prices there were high, and the costs for Henke's truck additional. The mission itself had no vehicle. Albrecht had been offered a truck as a gift not long before, but had declined it. With the mission struggling to find basic food for the people, he felt the costs of petrol and maintenance could hardly be justified.

Included in Ali's return load south were over fifty cattle hides, three euro hides, and a number of snake and goanna skins, all of which could be sold in the south. Mrs Heinrich had also parcelled up sixteen pounds of completed fancy work to be sent for sale. These materials were ordered from department stores in the south —doyleys, traycloths, and tablecloths in Irish linen with printed designs of scrolls and flowers—and given to the Aboriginal women to complete in lazy daisy, stem and satin stitch. The women often took their work home to the camp, and by the time it was finished it was usually thoroughly dirty. But it was washed, starched and ironed to perfection before being sent away. Any money gained from selling these articles could be used for medicines, food or other mission necessities. From the beginning the board had impressed upon Albrecht the importance of creating job opportunities for the Aborigines. But it was not an easy task. He had tried brush-making, using horsehair from the horses' tails. But between the lack of interest in the finished product in the southern congregations, and the disinclination of Aboriginal workers for the monotonous work with brace and bit, it had not been a commercial proposition, and Albrecht had finally reverted to the former practice of sending the horsehair south for sale.

By early August bush tucker had completely gone, and even kangaroos and euros were dying in the ranges. Several groups of emaciated bush Aborigines came in from the country west of the station.

Yes, big mob come in during the drought. All the nekkids, no trousers, dress, no anything. They were little bit frightened, some have not seen white people before, reckon somebody might kill him . . . They used to come in on this side of the river, five or six hundred yards away, where that grass is, people here used to go down and talk to them, friendly. When they were quiet, they would come to eating house, for devotion, nekkid. Native people and Pastor Albrecht gave them clothes. They were frightened, given clothes. People showed them how to put them on.

The drought conditions were aggravating other deeply rooted tensions. In August 1928 one hundred miles north of Alice Springs, an elderly European station-hand by the name of Fred Brooks was riding westward to trap dingoes. While camped at a soak west of Coniston station called Yurrkuru by the local Warlpiri people, Brooks was killed by two Aboriginal men, apparently over his dealings with an Aboriginal woman. When the authorities heard about it, a revenge expedition set out from Alice Springs, led by Constable William Murray and including some settlers and an Aboriginal tracker called Police Paddy. They travelled north and west of Yurrkuru, riding into native camps and shooting indiscriminately.

Murray later reported that about thirty people were killed. Two Aboriginal men were arrested and taken to Darwin to be tried for Brooks's murder, though there was no evidence that they had been the actual killers, and they were eventually acquitted. No other prisoners were taken. At the trial in Darwin, the constable was asked why so many people had been killed outright rather than suffering wounds. Murray replied that he had shot to kill. 'What use is a wounded black feller a hundred miles from civilization?' he asked, doubtless sincerely.

... From Yimampi [Coniston station] the whites set off by truck for Alice Springs to get more whites including policemen. They all came with lots of horses to attack the Aboriginal people ...

They then split up into two parties; one went south and the other west. There was a camp to the south where the ones responsible for killing the white man had been camping. The whites coming from the north were then ready to attack towards the south. They shot all the people they found. They attacked in the late evening. Many people ran away to hide during the fighting. The whites sent away two old men, one of whom was a blind man called Rdakamuru and another called Wantapurrupurru from Yarrungkanyi in the west. The whites told them: 'Go away and take the women with you'.

Meanwhile the ones who had killed the white man were still alive and making their way through the rocky hills ... A lot of old men walking around south of there were all shot. Many others travelled at night and some were shot as they arrived exhausted at the watering place. These were drinking when they were shot ...

Some Warlpiris had made a bush fire to the north and when the whites saw it they headed that way to attack whoever might be there. A lot of Warlpiris were camped by a waterhole. The whites came there and shot them all. There were really a lot of people living in that camp. They didn't even know about the trouble and killing of the white man ...

What became known as the Coniston massacre was not an isolated instance. The killing of Europeans by the Aborigines resisting the invasion of their lands and resources, or for any number of injustices according to tribal law, and large-scale retribution by European settlers and sometimes European authorities, formed a pattern of frontier violence in every Australian colony. Aboriginal people from the Hermannsburg area knew of local killings. In one case, ten or twelve men had been shot for the killing of a milking cow.

The evident lawlessness of the law-keepers in the case of the Coniston expedition might almost have been hushed up had it not been for a Methodist minister, Athol McGregor, who was visiting Central Australia. He hurried to Darwin to alert national newspapers. The national furore which resulted from the publicity forced an inquiry into the expedition and the murder trial.

The inquiry tribunal was hardly impartial. The three members were a police magistrate from Cairns, a police inspector from Oodnadatta, and J. C. Cawood, Government Resident and also the Police Commissioner for Central Australia. As the official who had authorized the expedition, he could be presumed to have been deeply implicated. After hearing many witnesses and investigating the conditions of Aborigines in Central Australia generally, the board found the shootings were 'justified'. For the moment, the matter was quashed. But the ripples that had begun in response to what, fifty years later, a white historian would term 'spectacular injustice', could not be so easily dispersed. Along with the more widely publicized events in Arnhem Land in the early 1930s, the Coniston killings provoked the first nation-wide stirrings of conscience about Aborigines in twentieth-century Australia.

Minna was expecting her second child late in 1928. Wanting to avoid the confusion and worry which dominated Helene's birth, she decided to go south well ahead of the birth. Taking the two-year-old Helene and accompanied by Marianna, she boarded the train at Oodnadatta in October. Albrecht was to join them later for his first furlough.

'THE CHRISTIANS ALL DIE'

1929

He was up late at night, he couldn't sleep too . . . people call him. He walked slowly, he couldn't walk fast. The very sick ones, they bring them up near the house in that little hut, carry it on poles. But the other people, they were in the camp, and he walk down there.

*I*n January 1929, the mission stockman in Central Australia sent a telegram to board member Albert Graetz on his farm in Sedan: too dry to muster. It had been more than three years since the last general muster, and conditions on the run were worse than Graetz had ever known. He was writing to the Henbury Todmorden Pastoral Company, trying to acquire more land for the mission. Part of the Henbury lease had been rented for some years, but the new owners did not want to continue the arrangement and had offered the land for sale instead. Since the government had declined to purchase the land on the mission's behalf, Albert Graetz resolved to borrow money and buy the block himself. It could be rented to the mission until a more permanent arrangement could be made.

The Albrechts and Marianna were staying with the Roehr family at Bethany, and a son was born on December 10—Theodor Johannes Wilhelm. The fair-haired, strong baby quickly became a delight to his father—at least for the brief times the missionary spent with his family. He was taking the opportunity to visit parishes up and down the Barossa Valley and elsewhere, speaking at mission festivals, talking with anyone and everyone about 'the work' in Central Australia.

'The work' was rapidly acquiring new dimensions. As the new railway slowly pushed north from Rumbalara with its accompanying cortège of equipment, food supplies and construction workers, the government deemed it inadvisable that camps of indigent Aborigines be allowed to remain in its vicinity. In part, this was considered a matter of 'protection' for the Aborigines. In every Australian colony, Aboriginal groups in contact with Europeans had suffered depopulation and disease, and rapidly gravitated to a detribalized indigent existence on the fringes of European settlements. An increasing number of part-Aboriginal children and the rising incidence of venereal disease only deepened prevailing pessimism about the capacity of the Aboriginal race to survive contact with European civilization. Resulting government policies emphasized protection and segregation, often in institutions.

But the federal Minister and his advisers in this case were doubtless also conscious that the all too public spectacle of detribalized and undernourished people begging along the Central Australian railway line reflected little credit on the Commonwealth Government's handling of the original occupants of the land. More than one hundred people living in camps south of Alice Springs were 'removed' west to the Lutheran mission at Hermannsburg. Government Resident Cawood agreed that 4s 8½d would be paid for each person per week, and board chairman Riedel again requested that government assistance for mission Aborigines who could not support themselves (children, the aged and infirm) be placed on the same per capita basis.

Riedel also asked for help with water. Already pitifully low with the drought, water levels in the wells and soakages had dropped dramatically with the arrival of so many extra people. Five miles from the mission, in the hills on the southern side of the Finke, were the Kaporilja Springs from which over 10 000 gallons of clear fresh water flowed daily. If the government would supply the materials to build a pipeline, the work could be carried out by the mission community. Other people were also asking questions. In the Federal House of Representatives, Langdon Parsons put formal questions to the Minister about the scarcity of water at the Finke River Mission and the reported severe illness in the mission community. The only tangible result of these representations was the authorization of one government camel and three water canteens for the mission's use in carting water from Kaporilja Springs.

Half-way through March 1929, the Albrechts with Marianna and the two children boarded the train at Tanunda, South Australia, for the long trip home. Huge stacks of wheat bags stood in many of the little stations along the line. But by Quorn, only two hundred miles further north, there was not a wheat bag to be seen, and the country looked dry. The second day of the trip saw the train rumbling across dry gibber plains south of Marree, and by the next morning they had left the former train terminus of Oodnadatta. The blast of hot air through the open windows was a forcible reminder of Central Australia. They were met at Rumbalara by the mission stockman, Phillip Henke. As they drove out to Hermannsburg, the country became more and more desolate. The last eleven miles from Jeremiah Creek were an expanse of porcupine bushes, a few remaining live trees, and sand. There was not a vestige of grass or undergrowth, though there were many carcasses of kangaroos and rabbits staked in the lower branches of trees where they had leaped up trying to reach the last vegetation. When they reached the house, they found the floors covered in sand, in some places several inches deep, though Mr Heinrich said he had carried out several buckets full only fourteen days before. '*An die veraenderte Lebensweise werden wir uns erst wieder gewoehnen muessen*', wrote Albrecht in his first letter south:

> We will have to become accustomed to the different way of life here. There is no fresh meat available, and fresh vegetables are out of the question altogether, as well as milk and butter. This might do for adults when they are well; but whether children can grow up under such conditions without endangering their health is hardly likely.

Nor could the Aborigines now supplement their rations with bush food and game. Plants of food value had long since disappeared, and they were prohibited from using firearms for hunting. Most mission people had lost the art of hunting with spears and, since they could no longer be issued with poison, even dingo hunting was impossible. The government bounty for scalps had been a steady if small source of revenue for many Aborigines. Now they were wholly dependent on mission food.

More bush people had walked in from the west, some of them very thin and weak. Several were Warlpiri people who had walked down from the Reynolds and Giles Ranges, two hundred miles to the north. Those distances were not unusual in normal times. The trade store at Hermannsburg had long been a stopping place for Aborigines travelling along the Finke and northwards to trade scalps for food and items like tomahawks. But many Warlpiri had scattered in 'the [Coniston] troubles' of the previous year and, still afraid to return to their own country, were suffering because of the scarcity of bush tucker and animals.

First time to Hermannsburg. Old man [Albrecht], we heard about him. We bin get the clothes like this, and rations. Big mob Aranda there, safe there, all right to go there, oh yes, old man bin there. Other people used to walk there, bring news back. People came back and said there was soup, mana *soup, flour soup. If they were hungry, they could go there and get soup. First time I went down I had a few whiskers, go by self. Country very dry.*

By April Albrecht was writing to Riedel:

I've come to the stage, where I say to [ask] the people here on Monday, who will be away for the week. Usually about a hundred people respond to that, and they receive flour for one day, though the old get a little more, and tea and sugar. Then they go off to forage for lizards and other animals. Some arrive back by the middle of the week, driven by hunger. But in general they do stick to the instruction. I send no one away, but whoever wants to go walkabout may not come back and receive food before Saturday morning. How else can I deal with this flood of people descending on Hermannsburg? And they like this system too. Of course the women and children stay in any case . . .

Illness in the Aboriginal camp had been increasing for most of the year. Many of the sick were complaining of loose teeth and abscesses in the mouth, some of pain all over their bodies. Others, like old Salome, had had trouble breathing, and Albrecht attributed her death to influenza. But he thought that beriberi, which he understood was caused by vitamin deficiencies, was a likelier diagnosis for much of the illness.

The older children continued to look reasonably well, but mothers, babies and the elderly were painfully thin. The babies were underweight and undernourished at birth, and their mothers had little or no breast milk. Minna continued her programme of special feeding for the babies and the sick. Under her direction, babies were fed three times a day, and the sick had as good a midday meal as she could devise. Yet more babies continued to die than survived, and the burden of caring for the sick grew heavier. Night after night saw the small winking light of Albrecht's hurricane lantern moving around in the camp. He administered what medicine he could, but knew in his heart that the greatest need was not for a doctor or medicine, but for better food—indeed for rain. Often he prayed with sick people with a heavy heart, feeling he would be burying them in a few days.

Seventeen people died in the space of four weeks. One burial seemed hardly over before they were gathering for the next. A small one-room building at the back of the church became a makeshift morgue, and the body, wrapped in rough hessian or sometimes placed in an empty tea chest, was taken in procession from the church over to the cemetery on the east of the compound. In addition to Albrecht, elders usually spoke at the graveside, especially Moses and Abel, and often the missionary marvelled at the steadfastness and certainty with which these men spoke of the resurrection, and of a future reunion with the one who had died. Standing beside his dead son, Frederick, Moses told the congregation that this was the fourth child God had taken from him, and his last son. 'But', he said, 'I thank God that I can believe they are saved'. 'To be able to give thanks in such dark hours is a special grace of God', thought Albrecht. 'This is Light in all the darkness surrounding us.'

Not everyone had such faith. '*Jakkai, Kristarinja inkaraka iluma*' (the Christians all die), said one of the women to Albrecht one day. And Mortana, one of the old people from Alice Springs, told him that people who got sick in Alice Springs were only sick for a few days, then they got better. At the mission, where there was God's word, they had to die. He told Heinrich to pray in English, not Aranda, so that God would hear. Jampijimba, one of the Warlpiri people who had come in earlier, decided that the mission had been 'sung', and left.

By mid-April fifty people were ill, twenty of them too weak to get up. Langdon Parsons again raised the matter in parliament, pointing out that the nearest doctors were in Cloncurry, four hundred miles away by air, and Hawker, South Australia, a rail journey of seven hundred miles. He also spoke at length about the responsibility of the Commonwealth government for the physical welfare of the Aborigines. An aged pensioner in a charitable institution, he reminded his listeners, cost the government 10s 6d a week to maintain. Yet at Hermannsburg, government assistance for the children, the sick and the elderly was only one shilling per week. The small Lutheran mission was carrying financial burdens which rightly belonged to the Commonwealth.

At the end of April Cawood's secretary, Vic Carrington, drove out to the mission with a Dr Howley from the railway construction camp at Rumbalara. Howley made no new suggestions about nursing the sick, but prescribed fluid strychnine, and ordered that brown rice and split peas be provided for the sick instead of flour, and that the babies be given condensed milk. The government would pay some of the costs. Seeing the dismal state of so many old and sick people, Vic Carrington drew Albrecht's attention to a section of the Aborigines Ordinance which provided that any European person in Central Australia was entitled, within certain limits, to employ an Aboriginal of his camp in hunting. Albrecht needed no further prompt. Though he kept a strict eye on ammunition, he sent a few people out to hunt for whatever game might still be alive in the drought-stricken countryside. Occasionally an animal was brought in. Albrecht always ordered this meat to be prepared for the sick, but it didn't necessarily reach them. People carrying meals to the patients would help themselves and, even when the meal did reach the sick person, there would be pressure to share it with relatives. Reproaches and even punishments availed little. Nobody directly challenged Albrecht's authority, but it was obvious they did not feel as he did that the sick should have first priority.

Nursing presented similar problems. People seemed to get tired of caring for their relatives. One old woman was always without water when Albrecht visited her in the camp, and even Christian men seemed glad to leave sick wives and go hunting for the week. People without close relatives were very neglected. For Albrecht, going the rounds of thirty or forty people each day was tiring, since his lame leg made it difficult for him to walk in the loose sand.

The exact nature of the illness was still a puzzle. Some people remained ill for months, even after more food became available through the extra government supplements and the many large consignments of dried fruit and peas from Lutheran farmers in the Barossa Valley. Even younger people sometimes succumbed. Albrecht found one of the schoolboys sitting with grossly swollen feet and hands, and beside him several of his teeth which had fallen out. He died a few days afterwards. Many people had bleeding gums and sore mouths, some of them so bad that all they could swallow was a paste of flour and fat.

The nights grew colder as winter came on, and the shortage of firewood became acute. Not everybody had huts, and the rest found what shelter they could behind windbreaks in the sand. With blankets still in short supply, people depended on their fires for warmth. It was impossible for the weak donkeys to cart wood enough for everybody, and people who were well enough to go and bring in their own had to collect some for the eating house as well. As a result the sick were often left without enough wood to last the night. Some of the babies would have lived, thought Albrecht, if they could have been near a fire all night.

When he could he visited the group of people who had been shifted from the railway line near Alice Springs. But he often came away with a sense of futility, feeling that years of living on the fringes of European settlement only brought Aborigines the worst of both worlds. Old Jack Norton was always complaining, and one of his first complaints to Albrecht was that he could not sell his woman for two shillings a night. 'Where can I get'em two bob now', he asked.

In June, the Federal Minister for Home and Territories, C. L. A. Abbott, came on a tour of Central and northern Australia, but he did not visit Hermannsburg. Riedel and Albrecht met him in his hotel room in Alice Springs, and Riedel again put the mission's case before him. In August, Riedel received a letter from the secretary of the department. It confirmed government support at the agreed rate for the people shifted from the railway line. But every other request was refused. The department was of the opinion that 'the mission must accept responsibility for the maintenance of all able-bodied lubras and men, and the mission children'. For the aged and infirm, the annual subsidy was 'more than sufficient'—there was to be no per capita basis for assistance. The water problem brought a summary refusal:

> Consideration has been given to your request that piping should be supplied to the Mission to carry water from Koprilya [*sic*] Springs to the station. The Government has no funds available to meet the cost of supplying this piping and the Minister considers that work of this nature is the responsibility of the Mission.

Neither did the government have funds to provide extra land, nor for part of the teacher's salary. In view of the difficult times, however, there would be a special grant of £250 in addition to the usual subsidy for 'this financial year only'. The special grant could only have been a grudging admission both of the unique circumstances created by the drought and of some degree of government responsibility for the survival of Aboriginal people. But it was only a stopgap measure, putting off any clear commitment of policy concerning Aborigines and those involved, not only with their Christianizing, but with their feeding, educating and 'civilizing'—functions which the federal government of a few years before had been pressing very heavily on the Lutheran mission.

A few days later, another brief epistle came to Riedel from the secretary in Canberra, returning an account of £42 10s 7d, which the mission had claimed for sundry expenses. The letter reminded Riedel that the Commonwealth had already supplied the mission with a camel and three pairs of canteens for carrying water. 'In the circumstances, therefore, your claim for reimbursement of various items of expenditure cannot be admitted as a liability of the Commonwealth.'

The long-awaited rail link from Oodnadatta to Alice Springs was completed in August, and one of the first trains brought a scientific expedition from the University of Adelaide. Arriving at the mission, Professor J. B. Cleland immediately diagnosed the epidemic as scurvy. The response from Lutheran congregations and the public to an appeal for citrus fruit was prompt and generous. In the next few weeks 132 cases arrived. Oranges were cut into pieces, and the worst sufferers were fed one slice every two hours. The improvement was dramatic. Within a day or two, most people reported that bleeding from the gums had ceased and they were beginning to feel better. Other donations of food were prompted by the publicity. Many came from individuals, and the Sydney-based Association for the Protection of Native Races sent two consignments of brown rice, each of two tons. Not everybody recovered—some had been ill too long. But the whole station was seized with a new spirit of hope.

The leaders of the university expedition later reported to the federal government on the nutrition and general health of the Hermannsburg community. They considered that the people showed remarkably good general nutrition apart from the scurvy, and the eye troubles like conjunctivitis and trachoma caused by dust and the smoke of camp-fires. Fresh fruit and vegetables and some fresh meat were essential to prevent more scurvy, and yeast supplements were suggested to prevent beriberi. Bush people were continuing to come in from the west, most almost starving. One boy of about ten arrived with his younger brother. Both were very weak and bleeding from the mouth. They did not know where their father

The Albrechts' first child, Helene, was baptized at Bethany, South Australia, in 1926. From right, Frieda Strehlow (widowed and working in Adelaide), Minna holding Helene, Agnes Scherer, Frieda Roehrs; Walter and Herma Roehrs in front.

Silver wedding anniversary of Reverend Carl and Frieda Strehlow in 1920 at Hermannsburg (two years before his death). Carl Strehlow second from right, Frieda beside him, son Theo (T.G.H.) behind.

Paul Johns (of Lasseter expedition) attending people at the 'dispensary' on the front verandah of the Albrecht home.

Hermannsburg community with a group of tribal Aborigines (front row) who walked in to the mission from the west during the 1920s drought. The tribal people are wearing large handkerchiefs provided by the mission as makeshift loin cloths (the people used the first issue as headbands, so a second assortment had to be found).

was, but their mother had died on the other side of the Macdonnell Ranges, and they had walked more than one hundred miles to the mission, living on little snakes and worms they found on the way. Dismal conditions in the bush were also reported by Hungarian anthropologist Dr Géza Róheim and his wife when they returned from the west in September. They had advised eighteen people to go to the mission, but over forty finally arrived, many of them children without parents.

There had been an unexpected sequel to the August visit of the university expedition. One of its members, Dr Harold Davies, Director of the Elder Conservatorium of Music in Adelaide, had wanted to record authentic Aboriginal music, especially singing, and offered to pay people a shilling to perform a song, or part of a song. Men and women from nearby areas were also invited, and turned up in considerable numbers.

At the time of the recordings, Albrecht was in bed with a high temperature. After the singing had gone on for a day or two, some of the older men of the congregation came to the house to ask the superintendent—*ingkata* (pastor), as they called him—if he had given permission for the non-Christian Aborigines in neighbouring areas to come up and sing corroboree songs at the mission. Yes, he told them, the songs were not being sung as worship, but for a scientific purpose. Albrecht had the feeling, as the men left, that they were not satisfied with his explanation, but nothing more was said. The recording went on for two weeks, and Dr Davies was surprised that none of the Christian people participated. They were so poor, and it was such an easy way to earn some money.

Some months later, some of the elders came to Albrecht complaining that corroboree dancing had taken place not far from the station. Participation in ceremonies had been forbidden to Aboriginal converts by the first missionaries, for whom traditional Aboriginal belief and ritual was clearly heathenism. The same stance had been continued by Carl Strehlow, and the older Aboriginal Christians who had received their basic teaching in Strehlow's day also supported it to a large degree. For Albrecht, arriving in 1926, the same opposition between the Christian Gospel and indigenous religious belief had been fundamental to his own Christian background and missionary training, and he had continued the existing prohibitions.

Pursuing the elders' complaints further, Albrecht found that dancing had taken place, though no Christians had participated directly. But tension was plainly running high in the Aboriginal camp, so he called for a meeting. Eighty-three people came and sat down in the sand in front of the missionary's house. Albrecht addressed the large group, reminding them of the terrifying time they had been through and that, despite everything, God had not forsaken them. There had always been some food, especially with the help of Christian people in the south, and then there had been the wonderful advent of the university expedition. Through the doctors' advice and the quick action of the board and other friends, the suffering had come to an end. 'For all this, we should thank God—not go and honour idols by arranging the dances at night', he said. He asked who had started it.

For a moment or two, there was dead silence. Then one of the men pointed at Albrecht and said, 'You did it'. A chorus of other voices immediately followed. 'Yes, yes, you started it all.' The missionary was stunned. It was obvious the matter had been smouldering for some time, had been much discussed, and had engendered considerable resentment. He asked them what he had done. They replied that he had allowed Dr Davies to record corroboree songs. He was still puzzled. 'Yes', he said. 'But I did that to show our gratitude to the scientists for the help they gave us. And the singing was not done at night in a ceremony but in the daytime. The recording is important so that future people will know how their ancestors expressed themselves.' Still they were not satisfied and insisted that he should have told Dr Davies to go to Glen Helen station to make his recordings. 'Here we praise God', they said, 'not *tjurungas*'. There was another vehement interjection. 'We understand difference between corroboree singing and singing for Dr Davies. But these ignorant people from west, they don't know difference. Sing'em daytime, sing'em night-time. Sing'em station, sing'em garden, him all same to them.' They were clearly affronted at the thought that Aborigines from other districts would assume that corroboree singing was going on at the mission.

Both sides looked at each other for a few moments as Albrecht quickly deliberated whether he should try to defend his decision. But he felt he would hardly convince anyone in the present atmosphere and, from a certain viewpoint, they could be regarded as right; his decision to allow the singing had not been understood by some of the congregation, and had been offensive to them. After a few moments, he spoke soberly. 'Friends, I'm sorry to have offended some of you, and I want to assure you that as long as I am at this place, this will never happen again.' He led in a brief prayer, and the large crowd dispersed in an atmosphere that was almost solemn.

For the thirty-five year old missionary, the experience left an indelible impression of their reverence for God, and the strength of their conviction that the old beliefs could not be mixed up with their faith in the true God. In a way, it had been humiliating for him, but he felt happy. The atmosphere had cleared, and he felt the cause of the gospel had gained.

Perhaps Christian reverence was not the sole factor in their protest. Group pride may also have contributed. The Aranda people had always considered themselves superior to the 'ignorant' Loritja to the west of Hermannsburg, and their relatively new identity as a Christian congregation would only have fanned this sense of superiority.

In the last days of December 1929 it rained, and the Finke River flowed for the first time in five years.

CONTACT WITH THE WESTERN TRIBES

1930~1931

It was the first time they had met a white man they could trust. They were quite surprised, he shook their hands, and they thought, must be good white man after all.

More than eight inches of rain fell in the first two months of 1930, and the country came alive. Choruses of crickets and frogs sounded almost deafeningly along the river, and stretches of sand and stones became waving vistas of lush green grass. Wild-flowers that Minna had never seen appeared and, as the first floodwaters receded, small fish appeared in the waters of the Finke. As the donkeys gained strength and condition to carry materials, repairs began around the neglected station. Verandahs on the stockman's house and the schoolchildren's dormitories were rebuilt and improvements made to the eating house. Men began to shift the drift sand which had swept up almost uncontrollably around station buildings in the huge dust storms in the last months of 1929. Small vegetable gardens were started.

Food was still short. From the three thousand head of cattle on the run before the drought, only a few hundred had survived. Restocking the run would be a long and expensive process. Only one bullock a week could be killed for meat, though four had been standard before the drought, and that had served a smaller number of people than now. Neighbouring stations also had little stock, and Aboriginal men who in better times would have been employed as stockmen continued to drift in to the mission. Numbers varied between 250 and 350.

In July, a farmer from South Australia, William Mattner, came north to bring up 575 sheep bought by the mission board, and to work for four months at the mission. He started on three more underground tanks. There was heavy rain in early October, and the first tank filled with rainwater from the roofs.

Albrecht continued to send people out to look for bushtucker, though little larger game was available. It would take a number of good seasons for kangaroo and euro to replenish. But millions of grasshoppers had appeared after the rain, making up for the shortage of meat to an extent. Mice were also plentiful, though this addition to the food supply was somewhat offset by the amount of newly sprouted *yelka* they were eating.

General health improved slowly, though some people still suffered after-effects from scurvy, and several cases of tuberculosis had been diagnosed. Albrecht was convinced that the only long-term solution was a diet with more fresh fruit and vegetables— something that could only be achieved by Kaporilja water and a large garden. In family prayers in the Albrecht home, and at the community devotions held each day near the little eating house, there was constant prayer that a way would be found to bring the water to the station.

The essential poverty of the community had changed little, since there were few opportunities for the people to earn money. A gang who went road-building north of Alice Springs were returned on a truck after a week—European workers had objected to jobs going to Aborigines. Some of the older men earned a little money collecting or making Aboriginal curios for sale to museums and tourists, and the women's fancy work continued. Cattle hides salted and sent south for sale were a minor source of income.

Well there was not much to eat, that's why people sell those things [tjurungas] to the store, so old man Albrecht can send them away, or sell them to some tourist people coming in, collect the money. Money for tucker, tea and sugar, bit tobacco too. They were happy to sell it—twenty or thirty shillings—make money for medicine for sick people.

Visitors were increasing. Board member Pastor F. J. Lehmann reported to the *Lutheran Herald* that 'since the opening of the line to Alice Springs, Hermannsburg has been frequented by tourists of all descriptions from Governors to prospectors and tramps; from Catholics and other divines to Moses Gabb, M.P . . .' With the countryside returning to normal, European Australians were becoming interested in the remote heart of their land. Palm Valley was attracting attention—a dramatic red gorge of sandstone, clustered with hundreds of a species of palm found nowhere else in the world. The government authorized a better track to be cleared from the mission to the valley, and a gang of men had work for ten weeks. Visitors typically had a cup of tea, sometimes a meal, and were usually interested in buying Aboriginal curios. Told about the need for water, one man left a donation of £50 'for Kaporilja water', and others made small donations.

Alf Traeger had finally developed an instrument by which people in remote areas could make radio contact. The new set was reasonably small and portable, and a smooth flow of power was generated by the operator pedalling something like bicycle wheels. This left his hands free to tap a message in Morse. The set was installed in a small room off the centre hall in the Albrecht house. The base was Cloncurry, four hundred miles away in western Queensland, where Flynn had established the headquarters of his medical service. Hermannsburg had to transmit its message in Morse, but could hear the reply by voice from Cloncurry. It was the mission's first permanent radio contact with the outside world.

Many of the 'wild ones' who had come in from the bush during the drought began to leave, and Albrecht felt it was time to initiate some regular contact with tribal people living on Crown lands to the west. The idea appeared to be supported by the older Christian men, but some hesitation always surfaced. Albrecht felt that underlying it were unresolved ties to their former beliefs. Avowed Christians though they were, he knew there were still sacred places where no woman, child or uninitiated person was permitted to go, under pain of severe punishment or even death, and felt that such ambiguity was bound to hinder their progress as a Christian congregation. 'We are finished with all this, but we don't go there because of the heathen people nearby. If they find out we had been there with women and children, they will come and raid our camp at night', was a typical answer to his questions. Albrecht knew there was truth in this, but said that Christians had to be prepared to suffer, if necessary, as witnesses to their faith. 'And if we are afraid here at the station, what will it be like if we go out to the heathen, and become involved in a dangerous situation?'

Manangananga cave, he was dangerous place, you know, kill one another, not allowed for women go there, or men. Only old man who had to look after the place. Titus Rengkareka, his father was in charge, his brother also, two men in charge. He might be Christian, but still in charge of the place ... look everywhere around here, look for the track, somebody might go there. If anybody go there, he had to kill him.

Fights were another area in which traditional tribal laws frequently seemed to Albrecht to conflict with a Christian approach. Fighting still went on in the camp, and the use of weapons like knives, spears or pieces of wood sometimes resulted in serious injuries. But typically he found that as a quarrel developed everybody took sides according to tribal relationship: nobody had any choice but to join his side, right or wrong. Sometimes it happened that someone who seemed clearly in the wrong might get off scot-free, with an innocent party badly hurt.

Finally, a particular incident brought the issue to a head. After a fight in the camp one Saturday evening, a man was brought to Albrecht, his thigh cut to the bone with a sharp butcher's knife. Fortunately, the main artery was not severed, but it took a heavy dose of ether and eighteen stitches to draw the two sides together, and the man was very ill. Malicious gossiping had caused the trouble, and the man who started the stories was not hurt. 'Before God, we are not excused of our wrongdoing by tribal relationship', Albrecht said to the elders. 'If this man dies tonight, it will not only be the one who used the knife, but everybody who supported him because of their tribal relationship that will be guilty of murder.' He spent a troubled night, and went to the elders early on Sunday morning. Instead of the usual church service, they sat down in the sand outside and for more than two hours discussed the incident and others like it, trying to apply the insights of Scripture. In the end, Albrecht told them he would not have another communion service unless the congregation clearly showed that they were prepared to put God's Word before tribal law. 'God cannot and will not bless you unless you are prepared to do that', he said. The man with the knife wound gradually recovered. But the leading men, after much talking among themselves, reached a decision. The sacred cave of Manangananga in a dry gorge running back into the nearby hills would be opened to everybody.

On the day before Pentecost Sunday, the women baked cake, and several men put a large copper on a donkey cart. Then, on Sunday afternoon, the whole community walked the three miles out to the cave. The day was sunny and warm, with not a cloud in the sky. They filled the copper with water from the sacred rock-hole, and lit a fire.

We had a service there. Mr Albrecht decided. Yes, old men mob decided too. All women, man, children, go there and have a service. Go inside that gully there, make a big fire in creek outside the cave, put the copper there, boil'em tea, bread, cake, meat. Everybody was watching, man and woman and young girls and young boys. We was children, everybody watching for the cave, little bit frightened. Before service, took stones out and put them on the ground. Everybody sat in big circle, and stones were put in the middle. Kids were scared! First time we bin see that stone. Old man [Albrecht] start those opening words, In the name of the Father, the Son and the Holy Ghost, then everybody relax, we start to sing hymn. Then he preached about Moses and Aaron and the golden calf. Tjurungas were like the golden calf. Old man preach, and everybody look up, yes, that's really true. We bin think about God make this free. Yes, stones very frightening for Aboriginal people, that's why Pastor Albrecht go there, 'Come here, everybody, come near, sit down here'. People touched them, children, everybody. Moses preached too. People feel free altogether afterwards. Still tell stories, but never bin frightened.

Albrecht had proceeded with his plan to trek west to contact tribal Aborigines, and preparations were completed in mid-September. As well as the riding camels, there were five pack animals to carry food, tents, blankets, and three eight-gallon canteens of water. Minna had spent days packing large wooden boxes with salted beef, tinned food, jars of preserved vegetables, flour, baking powder, powdered milk, dried fruit and sweets. She also included a few of her husband's favourite foods like sauerkraut, sausage and potato salad. The jars of fresh foods were wrapped in wet towels to keep them cool. The towels would be redampened each camp, and the food would last a few days. She packed his clothes too, putting the smaller articles into separate sections of a gaily coloured hussif she had made. Martin, Hezekiel and Lewis were going as guides and camel men.

They were pitching tents for their first camp when a young

Warlpiri man called Meranano appeared. He had come into Hermannsburg during the drought, and now wanted to return with them to his country to see if his parents were still alive. They camped the next night at the foot of the Macdonnell Ranges at a place where they could be crossed by camel, and the following day saw them winding up the range forming the main watershed of Central Australia. It was evening of the fourth day when they reached Anjali Spring beyond Haasts Bluff, and continued northwards into country untouched by cattle. It was strange to them all except Meranano. Following fresh human tracks, they came on half a dozen wurlies, evidently made by breaking shrubs in the centre and bending them downwards, with the gaps scantily filled in with smaller branches. Nearby were two women gathering *paraltja* or sugar gum—a sweet white substance produced by an insect on gum leaves. Both women wore tattered men's shirts, and one carried a small child in her coolamon, the basin-shaped wooden dish typically used for carrying.

Soon four men came up, the first an old grey-headed man, two spears in his hand, and wearing only a small apron slung around his hips. He readily accepted the damper offered to him, so it appeared he had seen Europeans before. Five others, he said, had gone down to the mission station, or Ntaria as they referred to it. Another man returned near evening. He wore a *memba* on his forehead, a small decoration of emu feathers sewn together with a string of human hair. He had been at the mission eighteen months before with an ill child. He greeted the party warmly, and fetched his child, now two years old and quite healthy.

As the women came up, one of the men threw a stone on the ground and the women sat down in the place indicated. Speaking through Meranano, Albrecht greeted them and asked them to bring their children. Soon there were sixteen children gathered, and he took a bag of lollies out of the packs and shared them round. The women also looked eager for something, and Albrecht gave them each some dried fruit, thinking they looked thin. He wondered if it arose from their tribal rule which obliged women to share with the men whatever food they had collected in the day. As he understood it, men only passed on from the day's hunt what they did not eat themselves.

The men had put their spears aside and, after the evening meal, Albrecht and his companions sang some hymns. He asked the people if they had heard the new message that was told and believed in Ntaria. We know something but not enough, they said, and the four Christians tried to explain the Great Spirit who loved all men, and his Son, Jesus. It was difficult to tell how much they understood, and the missionary was conscious what little connecting link they had to the new ideas. But they seemed to welcome the suggestion that an Aboriginal Christian from the mission could come and live with them and teach them. They would treat him well, keep peace, and try to learn Aranda.

When they were ready to go next morning, the grey-headed man brought some *paraltja* and 'cake' sent by the women. Prepared from certain grass seeds and baked in hot ashes, it had a strong oily taste, and Albrecht thought it must be most nourishing for any stomach that could tolerate the taste. They went off with a strong sense of this group at Ilapakutja as their nearest neighbours—seventeen women, sixteen children and eleven men lived here.

Their journey led northward through the range, the long tiered rampart of Mereeni Range on their left. They planned to go as far as Pikilli Springs, two hundred miles to the north-west. These were large springs, and it was likely that people would be living there, unless they had totally scattered in the aftermath of the Coniston revenge killings of 1928.

From the waterhole Arebelango in the Siddeley Range, they headed north-west across a waterless plain fifty-five miles wide. Meranano grew quieter and quieter as they rode, though an inner restlessness was evident. He had left his home country soon after the police expedition had gone through, shooting a number of his friends and relatives. He lived in much fear, and also dreamed at nights of men coming from the west to spear him. Around the same time, he had heard of a place to the south-east where people lived peaceably together. He was also told they had recourse to one in heaven. That had started him on his journey to Hermannsburg late in 1928.

The approach to the Pikilli hills ran beside a small grassless plain covered with little stones. Meranano told them that his father, Old Tumuna, went there every year to 'make' *langkua* fruit. Dismounting from his camel, he demonstrated the ceremony. On the ground he made small enclosures with stones, and taking sand from the centre threw it into the air. Where it fell, the fruit would thrive. Albrecht watched him with interest, and a certain poignancy. How pitiful, he thought, not to know Him who still provides for men, even in this solitary landscape.

When they were only six miles from Pikilli, a column of

smoke rose to the north-east. Shortly after, another column went up, then more, one after another. According to Meranano, they were likely to find at least thirty men here, without women and children. With the recent shootings in the area, Albrecht was apprehensive. His men had no explanation, so it was decided that Martin and Meranano would go ahead and try to contact them peacefully. A long time went by. Albrecht continued to wait and pray, fearing that the men had been speared. Then Martin reappeared, a naked boy of about twelve on the saddle in front of him, and a man with spears and another boy walking beside him. A little behind were two women, one carrying a small child. They all looked afraid. 'Ntakanerakai? Iwunaka unta kuta indora juraka?' (What happened, what took you so long?) exclaimed Albrecht in great relief. Martin explained that the people had run away from them, forcing them to give chase. Then the people had crawled under some huge spinifex bushes, and refused to come out for fear of being shot. Finally, they heard Meranano's voice, and his message that the visitors had come from Ntaria. The earlier smoke signals had only been a message to their friends that they were going to the springs.

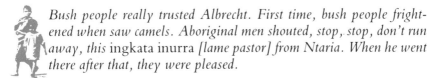

Bush people really trusted Albrecht. First time, bush people frightened when saw camels. Aboriginal men shouted, stop, stop, don't run away, this ingkata inurra *[lame pastor] from Ntaria. When he went there after that, they were pleased.*

The people were very thirsty and, when offered water, the women quickly cleaned a coolamon for filling. The father and his two boys drank first, kneeling and bending their faces to the water rather than scooping it up in their hands. The women followed. Albrecht was intrigued by the usefulness of the coolamon and the skill and ingenuity in its making. Unlike spears, it was made from a piece of soft wood about two feet long. The inside wood was carved out by stone knives, and the edges left standing over slightly at the top to reduce spilling.

The group continued with the camel party, and they reached Pikilli shortly before sunset. It was a beautiful large waterhole in a wide gap of rock. Reeds and rushes grew round the edge and large gum trees created a haven of shade and coolness. As Albrecht sat by his fire, the smoke-signaller, Palanbangu, approached. On his spear-thrower were two cooked yams, which he offered to Albrecht. The European was deeply moved, knowing that the yams were the better part of the man's food for the day. He accepted them warmly and gave him beef and damper in return.

Three days later, almost twenty people returned, among them Meranano's parents, and that evening saw the first meeting with the men of the district. It was not long before they asked Albrecht bluntly why the white people in the Coniston expedition had killed so many of their tribe. They told him that the two Aboriginal men who had killed the dogger Brooks were living in the hills not far away. 'If you people had asked us, we would have handed them over for punishment, and the rest could have been left alone. They should not have killed innocent people.' Albrecht looked at them, deeply ashamed that such a thing could have happened. Talking about it, it seemed to Albrecht that the number killed would have been nearer to a hundred than the thirty reported by Constable Murray. He told them he would do everything he could to prevent anything like it again.

From talks with the people, Albrecht thought there must be two hundred people roaming in the area. At present it was still 'unoccupied' Crown land, but he knew that a European had been exploring the area with a view to starting a cattle run. Once it was stocked, what would become of these people? Leaving on the final morning, he shook their hands and repeated his promise to try to help them. As the line of camels rode off, children followed them excitedly for the first few miles.

Ilbilla in the Ehrenberg Range was eighty miles to the southwest. For most of the next two and a half days, they could see their destination ahead—a low blue range on the southern horizon. Their water supply was quite depleted by the time they approached a gap in the range and saw ahead a growth of low tea-trees and smaller foliage. Birds were all about, and the air reverberated with the humming of dragonflies and other insects.

A few Aborigines approached, led by a tall well-built man wearing a pair of trousers and a shirt hastily put on back to front. His name was Kamatu, and he was a leader of this group. Albrecht thought him one of the finest looking Aboriginal men he had met, and later reflected on the sense of contentment he had felt in the camp. Late in the afternoon, he noticed a mother with three small children. They were pushing and pinching her, obviously wanting food, but the mother was reluctant in the presence of strangers. He urged her to feed them, and she immediately squatted down with seeds and a grinding stone. Putting some seeds on the stone, she poured a little water on them with one hand, and with the other rubbed them with great speed and dexterity. Within seconds there was a paste, then a little ball the size of a dove's egg. The three children had sat down opposite her and, at the precise moment, the first opened his mouth wide and the mother skilfully landed the morsel right in the little opening. In another moment, she had another ball ready which went into the next mouth, followed in a moment by the third. Albrecht watched in delight, thinking this was a mealtime with one of the oldest families of the land. Again he could not help wondering how long these people were likely to remain like this. As more became acquainted with the new life that Europeans had brought, they would drift into settled areas and remain there. It was also likely that this land would eventually attract someone with the idea of grazing. First there would be a grazing licence, then a lease, and the Aboriginal people would simply be pushed out.

Kamatu showed them some rough huts made of brush and spinifex. One contained tools and food supplies and a message signed 'Das Lasseter', which indicated that he had left the supplies there to use on his return from the Petermann Ranges. There had been a lot of publicity about Harold Bell Lasseter. The man had sought backing to search for gold in the Petermann Ranges west of Ayers Rock, maintaining that he had been through the area earlier in his life and knew of large gold deposits, and the Sydney-based Centralian Gold Exploration Company was formed. From Alice Springs, the expedition was to proceed to Ilbilla by truck, then south-west across desert country to the Petermann Ranges. According to Kamatu, the Europeans had left Ilbilla on camels and proceeded in a westerly direction, after failing to get any of the Aboriginal men to accompany them as guides.

In the following few days, Albrecht and his companions learned more about these people at Ilbilla—how far they roamed for food, who was living further west. The group seemed pleased that mission people might visit again, and the camel party prepared to return east.

First time Albrecht went, some of them, Pintubi mob, never seen white men, they were frightened. Loritja people had contact with white people because they used to spear white people's bullocks. But Pintubi mob never saw them before. For a lot of them, he was the first white man they saw, didn't know why he came, most white people came for trouble.

They couldn't understand flour, what this one, might be ashes . . . Tea and sugar, people tell them this way. You get a billy can, make tea and give it to drink, and if mix it up with flour and bake it, you can eat, it was good, other meat is from bullocks. Pintubi liked it [flour] straight away, wasn't ashes after all.

For the first time in the trip, they were not crossing sandhills. Here the sandhills ran east–west, and they could ride along them. A little west of Mount Liebig, they reached Potati Spring. Being the only waterhole for miles around, it was a popular stopping place for roaming Aborigines. Everywhere around it stones had been piled up to form windbreaks a foot or so high, where people could lie down for the night. Several more days of riding brought them to the eastern end of the sandhills. Before them was the plain which lay between the Macdonnell and Krichauff Ranges, extending well over a hundred miles eastward to blue ranges floating on a distant horizon. The sky was a dome of light, and Albrecht was conscious of the vastness of the land.

They turned south and into a valley of the Krichauff Ranges to get to the cattle station of Boatswain's Hole. Albrecht also wanted to visit the Aborigines living and working on cattle stations to the south, to see if it might be feasible for Aboriginal Christians from Hermannsburg to keep some regular contact with them. Boatswain's Hole was picturesquely situated among surrounding hills. Beyond the stockyards the newcomers could see a separate kitchen of whitewashed masonry and a one-room cabin made of split wood plastered with clay. Not far away were several Aboriginal huts which seemed to be small heaps of bushes spread over with an old flour bag or piece of canvas. The station owner was out on the run, but Albrecht and his companions talked for an hour with the ten or twelve Aboriginal people who were there. They appeared to appreciate the time, and said they would welcome regular visits.

South of Boatswain's Hole, the river seemed to force its way into the range, and the line of camels entered a large rocky gorge. The valley grew more beautiful as it proceeded, the gorge gradually widening to waterholes, cool and beautiful beneath tall stately gums. Albrecht thought he had never seen such a growth of trees in Central Australia. One could ride for miles in their shade. As they finally left the valley behind, they saw ahead of them the glimmer of iron roofs in the sun—Tempe Downs station.

Tempe boasted two stone buildings, one a bedroom and sitting room for the manager, and the other a kitchen where

Albrecht had a cup of tea with the station cook. Later he talked with the small group of Aboriginal people, including a woman from Hermannsburg, Grace, who was visiting her son. Only a small number of Aboriginal people lived at Tempe. Bush people were not allowed to come in, as Tempe had suffered badly in the past from Aborigines spearing cattle. Being on the outer edge of the pastoral land, and bordering the great central reserve, it had suffered more than most stations from Aborigines still actively resisting European settlement.

Many Aboriginal groups on the reserve were still notorious for their hostility, not only towards the European pastoralists, but to each other. Several killings had taken place recently, and twenty people had arrived at Hermannsburg to try to escape a further round of retaliation. Albrecht had sent a message to the likely avengers, asking them to come to the mission and make a peace, though he felt in his heart that lasting peace would only be possible when they had found a way of love rather than mutual fear and hostility. This would mean treks into the Petermann Ranges and the great reserve, and the way necessarily led through Tempe Downs. Albrecht knew the Tempe Downs manager, Bryan Bowman, as a friendly man, and thought he would have no objection to mission Christians visiting his workers.

At Middleton Ponds station, which had been started only recently by Bob Buck, the travellers met more than twenty Aboriginal people, none of whom were familiar. Among them was 'Erldunda Bob', by reputation an important ceremonial boss and a man of considerable influence among the Aborigines in that area. Albrecht was therefore pleased to meet him, and had the impression that Bob was also glad to make his acquaintance. The two men talked for some time and Bob assured the missionary that he no longer possessed any of the traditional objects and would like to hear the Gospel. That is only half true, thought Albrecht. Yet he felt that the mission had gained much as long as Bob did not work against them. Middleton Ponds would be the third station, he pondered, that an Aboriginal itinerant preacher would have to visit regularly.

At Henbury, they were invited to lunch by the manager's wife. It was probably the first time that a European woman had lived there. Henbury had been established about the same time as the mission. Sited near a beautiful deep waterhole in the Finke which did not dry up even in the great drought, it had quite a number of buildings. Most were of split log construction, though the manager's house was stone, with a ceiling of empty flour bags. The men were glad to stretch their legs out under a proper table, and Albrecht, as often happened when he visited stations, was asked to say grace. He appreciated the gesture, feeling that the way he and his companions were received by station owners was important for the religious work with the Aboriginal workers. The camp for the Aborigines was on a sandhill a little distance away. Albrecht was surprised to find about eighty people there. He later learned that the influx of people had come from Horseshoe Bend and Charlotte Waters, where the drought had not yet broken. He limped slowly from one hut to another, speaking to anybody he found. Many seemed to know who he was and, since almost all spoke Aranda, conversations were easy. He always asked about their families, and noticed they appreciated his interest. In many cases, it seemed that the Gospel was not unknown to them. They had liked Moses visiting them, and a number said they were coming up to Hermannsburg for a visit. Henbury station had about three times the land of the mission run, so there would always be quite a large number of Aborigines employed in normal times, together with their relatives.

From Henbury, it was sixty-five miles up the Finke River to home. After five weeks and over five hundred miles of riding, there was enormous relief on all sides when the camels finally went down in the sand in the main compound at Hermannsburg in late October.

A few days after his return, a wireless message came from Alice Springs that the pilot of the Lasseter expedition was to land at Hermannsburg the next day. Albrecht was never to meet Lasseter in person, but circumstances were bringing him into more than passing contact with the ill-fated expedition and its confused tangle of misfortune and complicity.

Earlier in the year, a young man named Paul Johns, who had been briefly employed at the mission in 1929, had approached Albrecht to purchase or hire a camel team. Johns planned to meet the Lasseter expedition at Ilbilla, believing that their truck would be unable to negotiate the fifty-feet sandhills south of Ilbilla. He would offer the camel team and his services. His opportunity came as he had anticipated. By the time the eleven-man Lasseter expedition had reached Ilbilla, there had been serious mishap, and misgivings about their leader's stated experience of the country were growing rapidly. Turning south from Ilbilla, they encountered the sandhills, and ten of the party abandoned the expedition. Lasseter hired Johns and his camel team and headed south-west into the dry sandhills,

Some of the many Hermannsburg visitors in the decades of
isolation, when no facilities
existed beyond Alice Springs.
From left, Vic Carrington
(government official), Lord and
Lady Hore-Ruthven (Governor
of South Australia), Minna
with Helene, Paul Johns, Aide-
de-camp to Governor, Phillip
Henke (Hermannsburg stockman), Mrs Henke and children.
(Burns-Albrecht Collection,
South Australian Museum)

Family holiday to Palm
Valley, c. 1929. Minna and
Marianna at front of donkey
waggon with Helene and
Ted.

In October 1930, the elders of the Hermannsburg congregation decided with Albrecht to hold a Christian service to 'open' the traditionally sacred cave of Manangananga in the nearby hills.

Concerned at the continuing depopulation of Aboriginal tribal lands and the disappearance of many Aboriginal groups, Albrecht from 1930 established regular contact with tribal Aborigines to the west, and stationed Hermannsburg Christians with Aboriginal groups to encourage them to stay in their home districts. Here, tribal men around Haasts Bluff listen to his gramophone.

leaving behind the supplies which Albrecht and his men had seen in the hut at Ilbilla.

Plans for the Lasseter expedition had included the hiring of a plane and pilot to provide backing for the main party. When pilot Errol Coote landed at Hermannsburg in November 1930, he was on his way to meet Lasseter at the Petermann Ranges. But first he was to land at Ayers Rock and meet a camel party with petrol supplies for the plane. As the plane landed on uneven ground, the propeller hit a small shrub and cracked. It was temporarily repaired by the mechanic accompanying the petrol party, and Coote returned to Alice Springs, without attempting further contact with Lasseter. He was then ordered by the company to fly to Sydney.

At Ayers Rock, the petrol party also left, leaving behind the mechanic and a Hermannsburg Aborigine called Rolf to clear a larger landing area. Soon after the plane had left, the mechanic's tent containing all his clothes and food supplies caught alight while the two men were away from their camp. By the time they returned, everything except Rolf's blanket was reduced to a heap of ash. 'All gone', said the Aborigine philosophically, assuring the mechanic he would look after him. He was as good as his word. He walked the three hundred miles of rough bush country between them and Hermannsburg, allowing the mechanic to ride the one remaining camel. At night, he gave the European his blanket, saying he was used to sleeping beside a fire without a blanket. Each day he managed to find a little water and some food for them—an odd lizard, a rabbit, some edible plant—even though the country was strange to him. A week brought them to Middleton Ponds, and another two days to Hermannsburg. Albrecht immediately wired the Sydney company on the mechanic's behalf.

The company had dismissed Errol Coote, hired two new pilots and had the plane refitted with extra petrol tanks. Their return message to the mechanic instructed him to proceed with Paul Johns to Ilbilla to await the arrival of the plane on December 10, and signal the landing place with a smoke fire. Paul Johns by then was back in Alice Springs, having explored the Petermann area and returned north to the depot at Ilbilla with Lasseter. But there had been ugly exchanges between the two men, and Lasseter had set off alone to return to the Petermanns.

Paul Johns and the mechanic proceeded as directed to Ilbilla. But on the crucial morning, they had fallen asleep waiting for the plane, and heard nothing. They waited for ten days. Realising at last that lives could be at stake, Johns started urgently for

Hermannsburg. Again Albrecht went to the radio room to contact the company via Cloncurry. The Morsing was slow. Words often had to be repeated, sometimes many times. With the continuous pedalling of the set, he was soaked with perspiration by the time it was finished. Two Air Force planes from a base near Melbourne were soon on their way to Central Australia to search for the missing aircraft. Search flights from the mission went on unsuccessfully for a week until one of the planes broke a wing tip landing on uneven ground at Ilbilla. Another long message—three hundred words—had to be Morsed through. The reception to Cloncurry was bad, and it took over three hours to transmit. Another two planes were sent, and the company plane was finally sighted near Dashwood Creek.

The two pilots had survived for almost four weeks near a small claypan of water filled by a shower of rain. With nothing to eat except tadpoles and a few roots, they were extremely weak but alive—preserved almost miraculously, it seemed to Albrecht, by the hand of God. The Sydney company directed the mechanic to attend to the immediate salvage of its plane, and two weeks passed before Johns and the mechanic were instructed to restock with supplies and search for Lasseter. Neither wanted to go, and asked Albrecht to recommend someone else to the company.

Albrecht was deeply perturbed. It was now February. Johns had parted with Lasseter in mid-November, and no-one had heard of the prospector since. Aborigines could not be sent alone, as the local people were not friendly with the Pitjantjatjara people in the Petermann Ranges. Bob Buck of Middleton Ponds set out accompanied by two Aranda men from the mission. They reached a rockhole called Piltardi at the eastern end of the Petermanns in less than two weeks, and found an old Pitjantjatjara man camping near the waterhole. The old man knew nothing about a white man, live or dead. Later, when Buck had gone to sleep, he was more communicative. Was the white fella a catcher? No, they assured him, he was no policeman. Satisfied on this score, he gave them the information they were seeking. There was a dead white man just across the range and a little way west.

It was not far to the place marked on some maps as Winter's Glen. The body looked as if Lasseter had died about a week before. Nearby was a shelter of boughs such as Aborigines on walkabout make for single men. They buried him in a shallow grave and erected rails cut from young gum trees around it.

When Buck and the men returned to the mission, he brought

back papers and diaries which he had found near a cave west of the place where Lasseter had died. Some were addressed to his wife, and these were sent intact to Sydney. The others Albrecht and Buck perused carefully, Albrecht noting that the handwriting matched the pencilled instructions in the hut at Ilbilla. Together with information from Pitjantjatjara contacts, they pieced together something of the last months of the unfortunate prospector.

It appeared that he had reached the Petermanns successfully after parting from Johns, but lost his camels one evening when they took fright. He was left with nothing except a few small bags of food and some writing pads which fell from the packs as they galloped away. He then fired shots in an attempt to attract help. Since no Aborigines came near him, he concluded they must be unfriendly. But as time went by they made contact with him, taking him on trips to collect food, and sharing what they had. He was especially befriended by some of the older women, and directed in his diary that certain ones be rewarded with gifts of tinned food, or a bag of flour. Sometimes he complained bitterly about the men, but it was clear that he survived as long as he did only through their care. He wrote that he had found the reef and pegged claims for the company, but left no map or directions.

As time went by, he began to grow weaker. He developed dysentery and sandy blight, and the illegibility of his handwriting testified to his failing sight. Towards the end was a cry of anguish: 'This is the 78th day without food, but the worst of it is not to know why I have been abandoned here'. When his death seemed inevitable, the Aborigines decided to take him from their country to a place which could be more easily contacted by Europeans. At first he walked, then they carried him. At Winter's Glen, they erected for him the small bough shelter near where Buck found him.

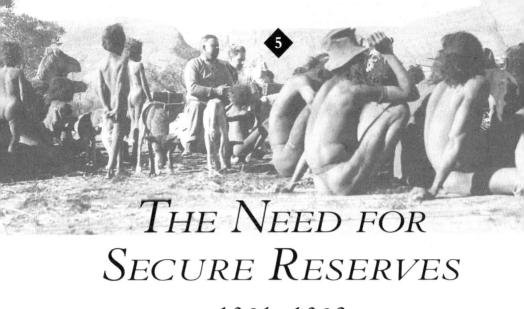

THE NEED FOR
SECURE RESERVES
1931~1932

When the white man came, we rushed like perishing bullocks to the trough.

The camel trip to the west had convinced Albrecht that a way could be found to preach the Gospel among the neighbouring nomadic tribes. Even if the respective groups wandered 150 or 200 miles looking for food, they still had their home waterholes, and it was mainly the young men who went on the longer excursions— women and children usually stayed behind. So it should be possible for an Aboriginal Christian to live with either group and tell them the Word of God.

For Albrecht, it was not only a matter of religious teaching. He felt strongly that urgent action of some kind was needed to counteract the steady depopulation of Aboriginal tribal lands. Everywhere, it seemed, contact with Europeans caused Aborigines to leave their bush areas and come into Alice Springs or the cattle stations, often to live by begging. And even in the most outlying areas, tribal Aborigines were coming into contact with Europeans. The Mackay aerial mapping expedition had been at Ilbilla for some time, and many of the white unemployed of Alice Springs had been given three months' rations by the government and sent out to search for gold. They had traversed the Macdonnells and some had even reached the Petermann Ranges to the south.

Albrecht believed that if nothing was done to keep bush people in their own areas, they would come out in ever increasing numbers, and ultimately disappear altogether. He thought the drift away from the bush might be halted by stationing an Aboriginal Christian among them to give them Christian teaching and to encourage them to remain on their tribal lands. He had read of similar work in Lutheran missions in New Guinea, but as far as he knew, nothing like this had been tried in Australia before. But it would have to be Aboriginal Christians—the mission had no European staff who could go.

He was not without misgivings. Religious teaching would have to be done in Aranda, since a considerable amount of Christian material had already been translated into Aranda, especially the New Testament and the church service book. 'It would take the whole lifetime of a white man to get well into the Loritja language', he wrote to Riedel, 'and the small number of people hardly warrants it. Besides, this Loritja is just one dialect among many others'. So Aranda Christians from the mission would first have to learn the tribal language, in order to be able to teach the people the Aranda language.

But his chief concern were the Aboriginal evangelists themselves, and whether they could continue their spiritual life completely isolated from other Christians. Good intentions and simple faith were obvious among the Christians at Hermannsburg, yet also evident were the innumerable small ties with their old culture. How would Christian evangelists maintain a distinctive Christian witness if they were living right in the centre of the old life? He knew there would be disappointments.

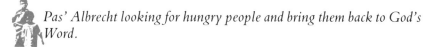 *Pas' Albrecht looking for hungry people and bring them back to God's Word.*

The trek had also given Albrecht a far greater understanding of the impact of European settlement on Aborigines, since it was his first real experience of Aboriginal tribal life in conditions almost undisturbed by the advent of Europeans. He had seen for himself that in normal seasons, Aborigines living in unsettled areas could easily maintain themselves. With their marvellous adaptability to any food a semi-desert could provide, they were able to live in places where even cattle could hardly survive. But it was equally clear that this held good only as long as their country was not used for stock, the tribes stayed in their respective districts, and areas did not become overpopulated.

It was now obvious to him why the mission reserve was regarded as a home, not only by the original occupants of the district, but by many others from the bush and neighbouring cattle stations. People in the bush covered enormous distances in their search for food, even though the bushtucker in unstocked areas was much more plentiful, and included many grass seeds and berries which in settled areas were eaten or trampled by the cattle. But Aborigines whose tribal lands had been taken for cattle raising had been pushed into small areas adjacent to station homesteads. With such restricted areas, it was evident why they could no longer support themselves on bush food and tended to drift in to the mission or Alice Springs. Some of the station owners were reasonably generous with food and clothes for Aboriginal workers and their families, but there was no way they could support large groups in real need. It was not surprising, therefore, that the maintenance of three hundred or more people meant a heavy expenditure by the mission in bringing extra food from the south.

As the winter of 1931 approached, Albrecht planned another trip west. He was keen to see if mission Christians could share the nomadic existence of the bush people and teach them the Christian way of life. The idea was well supported by the elders and the congregation, and a number of men—Titus, Rolf, Albert (who was later to become known to the world as the artist Albert Namatjira) and Abel—offered to go out. On the second day of the trip, Albrecht developed severe pain in the back and abdomen. By the time he got back to the mission he was very ill, and the Flying Doctor at Cloncurry was called. They offered to fly him to Adelaide, assuring him that the cost could be paid later. But a debt of several hundred pounds would have been an enormous burden on a salary that did not always meet their personal expenses. He and Minna and the two children took the train south, he lying on a mattress and blankets in the brakevan.

The camel party continued without him and, as planned, some of the Christians remained at various bush camps—Titus with Rolf and his wife at Potati, Albert and Abel at Pikilli. Each had food rations to last four or five weeks. By the end of that time, it was hoped they would have made friends with the local tribal people and be able to live with them and support themselves. But in a matter of weeks, most had returned—bush life was too difficult.

Their hunting skills were poor, and a diet of grass seeds and other bush food was unpalatable after European food. Albert in particular lost more than two stone in weight.

In the south, Albrecht gradually recovered from what was diagnosed as an attack of kidney stones. Someone advised Minna that barley water would help. She began a routine that continued for years—boiling up barley each day, straining off the liquid, and cooling it. Her husband drank it with each meal, and frequently between, using it as a substitute for tea and coffee. By the end of September, he was well enough for them to return home.

The problem of the bush Aborigines was still paramount in his mind since, as a race, they seemed to be fast disappearing. Only fifty years before, at the onset of European settlement, Alice Springs had been a big centre for Aboriginal people. Now, of that original group, only an old man and his wife and one son were left, and the same was true in many areas. A casual traveller would not understand, since Aborigines were a familiar sight at every station homestead and railway station. But almost all of these belonged to tribes living further out, and had drifted in. It was an inescapable fact that the original occupants of the country and their descendants had already disappeared from many places in Central Australia, and only remnants remained of many other groups. The mission itself was the only area that Albrecht knew of around Alice Springs in which almost all of the families who originally occupied the district were still represented. In the seventy-odd children in the school, there were clear indications that here at least, the people were not dying out. Even Baldwin Spencer, writing his largely unfavourable report on Hermannsburg in 1923, had commented almost with surprise on the large numbers of children in mission families.

Yet many of the factors which had led to such depopulation were still operating. Earlier in the year, the federal Minister had refused an application by the Sydney-based Association for the Protection of Native Races for an additional reserve which would extend from the north-west corner of the large central reserve established in 1920 and include the block of land around Pikilli and the Davenport Range. The grounds for the refusal were that the rights of Aborigines living in primitive conditions were safe-guarded even in areas leased to settlers. He cited a 1927 Ordinance dealing with Crown lands which stated that Aborigines would continue to have full and free rights of access to natural waters and hunting grounds. Asked by the secretary of the association for evidence on the issue, Albrecht spent some hours writing a detailed response. He was also a great believer in firsthand experience, and wrote to the secretary:

> If the actual position of the Natives in C.A. would be better known to their friends, more would be done for them. But such knowledge cannot be gained unless a man goes and sees the people on the spot . . . God willing, I shall be travelling again as from April next year. Should you have a Christian man there, physically fit for a ten weeks journey on camels, and willing to come with me, I should be only too pleased to take him around. He could look into the whole matter as an unbiased person and his observations should be of great value in directing the activities of your Society.

To Albrecht, the Crown lands ordinance rested on an assumption that was fatally wrong—that Aborigines and cattle could go together, that grazing licences could be issued to run cattle on Crown land and the Aboriginal people not be disturbed. Everywhere in Central Australia, the very opposite was true. Life in this arid land centred around the waterholes. Wherever Aborigines lived near an open waterhole, cattle would be frightened and disperse. In practice, Aborigines were always ordered away from waterholes used by stock, and the ordinance never had been, nor could be, enforced. 'It always meant either Natives or the bullocks, and as the protection of the bullocks seems to be of first consideration, Natives have to go.' Even the Aborigines allowed to stay near station homesteads were in a difficult position, since the men who were employed as stockhands could no longer do their part of the food-gathering. Albrecht felt it was only just that a stockman's family should be supported by the station, since stockmen were paid irregularly, if at all. This was done by some station owners, but there were many exceptions.

He recommended to the association that where land was taken up for grazing, a certain portion with suitable surface waters be reserved for any Aboriginal tribe who had been living there. Two areas were particularly in his mind. In the Pikilli area in the Davenport Range to the north-west, tribal organization was still intact, and it was ideal for a smaller reserve because of its waterholes and plentiful bush food. Eighty miles south at Ilbilla, in the Ehrenberg Range, was another centre for bush people. Therefore the central reserve should be extended north from Ilbilla to include Pikilli. Despite pressure from various quarters, the government did nothing on the proposals, and a returned serviceman settler called William Braitling was granted grazing rights in the area around Pikilli. Twelve months later and according to the customary process, the grazing rights became a lease, and almost three thousand square miles of country in the Davenport Range became Mount Doreen station.

Another expedition looking for gold in the Petermann Ranges had set out within a year of the Lasseter expedition. It returned in six weeks instead of the planned six months, and two of the members told Albrecht that as far as they were concerned the Petermann Ranges were not gold-bearing country at all. The men were surveyors from Western Australia. Hearing about the need for Kaporilja water, they took measurements and levels and found that the springs were 133 feet above the wireless mast at the station. It was encouraging news, since the levels had always been disputed. Standing at the springs and looking across the wide valley to the station on the other side of the Finke, one might almost think the station was higher.

But a report late in 1931 by the government engineer in Alice Springs on the feasibility of bringing the water from Kaporilja by pipeline was highly unfavourable. Albrecht was angry. He felt much of the report was based on hearsay and opinion rather than accurate measurement, and that underlying it was a barely disguised antipathy to the mission itself. He continued to make his own enquiries from a variety of private and public sources—piping firms in Victoria and New South Wales, engineers and surveyors visiting the mission as tourists . . .

By early 1932, he had gathered enough information to feel that a pipeline was a practical possibility and that the 25 900 feet of piping necessary would cost about £3240. There were still many details to resolve but he felt it was time to issue a formal appeal for funds. The Appeal for Kaporilja Spring Water was to be separate from general support for the mission. The mission board had not really endorsed the scheme, and Albrecht also felt there would be interest and support from non-Lutheran visitors—'our English friends' as he referred to them. Donations totalled £185 by the end of the year.

Albrecht was to trek west again in 1932. Rolf and Titus were keen to go out again, saying the people from Ilbilla had been really interested to hear more about the Gospel. But they had to have more support with food. He constructed a large box from several old packing cases and lined it with tin. It was large enough to hold two 150 pound bags of flour, a bag of sugar, tea, some medicines, and a few other dry goods. It would be locked up and left with the evangelists who could open it and take out a week's rations at a time. If he went out himself each April and September, and the men came in at Christmas, they would have some contact every four months.

For much of the nine or ten hours of riding each day, Albrecht was absorbed in reading. There was little time for it at the station, so he saved books and magazines for the camel trips. With the camels on nose lines, and the men choosing the route in the front, it was easy enough and helped to pass the long hours of riding. This time, his subject was a medical book. Minna was pregnant, and had made up her mind not to go south for the birth. With the emergency trip south earlier in the year, no furlough was due, and she could not bear the prospect of another long separation.

Her husband was far from happy with her decision. With her bad medical history, the thought of complications in their isolated situation was frightening to contemplate. But there was no budging her, so in considerable trepidation he thought he had better learn midwifery. He read and reread the book until he knew certain pages by heart. He thought of her often on the journey, aware that her delivery was not far away and wishing he could have gone west at a different time. 'But the Lord is with us', he reminded himself. After visiting as many groups as possible, Titus and Rolf were left at Putati, and the camel team returned home. Three weeks before the expected delivery, a double-certificated nurse visiting Palm Valley agreed to stay until the birth. A boy was delivered without complications, and was named Paul Gerhard Ernst.

The mission board had been seeking another missionary for Hermannsburg for some years, and a young pastor from Victoria, Werner Petering, took the train north in the middle of July 1932. Alice Springs had grown in the three years since the coming of the railway. The main street included Kilgariff's hotel, Wallis Fogarty's store, the Australian Inland Mission hospital, and a group of official residences for the Deputy Administrator of the Northern Territory, the police sergeant, government engineer, and a resident medical officer. The post office was adjacent to the railway station, and a boarding house, gaol, and several streets of houses made up the little township.

After Petering was met at the station by Albrecht on a Saturday night, the two men stayed overnight with the Aborigines' Friends' Association missionary, Ernie Kramer, and on Sunday morning attended his service in the little bush church not far from the railway station. It was built of assorted materials—walls of sun-dried bricks and a roof of spinifex grass and opened-up oil drums.

The congregation of Aboriginal people straggled in gradually, having walked the mile or so into town from the camps beyond Heavitree Gap.

Monday was a business day for Albrecht—taking reports in to Vic Carrington, consigning boxes of curios and fancywork at the railway station for freighting south, arranging with Fogarty's store for a truck to take them and some goods to Hermannsburg the next day. On the Tuesday they started the eighty-mile drive to Hermannsburg in a truck without a cabin. Albrecht shared the open seat with the driver and a woman tourist from Victoria called Una Teague who was on her way to Palm Valley. Werner Petering sat in the back on a stack of flour bags, nursing the cello he had brought north.

It took most of the morning to drive the thirty-five miles to Jay Creek where Harry Freeman came out to invite them for lunch. He was the superintendent of the small building and group of tents called the Half-Caste Institution. For years it had been the Bungalow, a part-Aboriginal children's hostel at the back of the Stuart Arms hotel in town. But in 1928, the government moved it out to Jay Creek to get the children away from contact with railway construction gangs. Jay Creek was a dusty spot with no permanent springs. Water was obtained from a few wells which in dry times almost failed. Boys of ten and twelve were lowered into it night and morning with jam tins to scoop water from the sinkhole in the bottom into the windlass bucket. In 1932 it was the sole government institution catering for Aborigines, part or fullblood, in Central Australia.

At Hermannsburg, tensions had smouldered between mission staff for several years, first between the Heinrichs and the Henkes, then between the Heinrichs and Albrecht, and in 1932 the mission board accepted Mr Heinrich's resignation. Werner Petering took over the school, assisted by Abel, and helped in the mission store, which Albrecht had made into a cash store in addition to the trading store it had always been. He believed that a cash store gave Aborigines a chance to handle money and, even with modest pricing, it was a small means of income for the struggling mission. Station owners along the Finke used it to supplement their own supplies, and the small trickle of tourists coming through to Palm Valley or Kaporilja Springs were always interested in the odd array of goods for sale. Aboriginal people from the mission, and sometimes other areas, brought in handcrafts like curios or fancywork, sometimes ceremonial objects, and the mission received a small percentage of sales.

Poker work was a new style of curio—carved wood orna-mented with black dotted designs or texts using a heated fencing wire. Albrecht had seen similar work on his last trip south, and had brought some pieces back. Several men took it up, bringing in mulga logs in the donkey wagon and sawing them roughly into slabs in the deep sawpit near the smithy before the last stage of finer carving and poker work. Albert became the most skilled, and also the most persistent worker. Three shillings and sixpence was the usual charge for a piece of mulga wood.

By the end of July, Albrecht had finished his annual report for the financial year ending 30 June 1932. He noted that more than 300 people had been living around the station; food requirements had included 70 998 pounds of flour and wheat, 6050 pounds of sugar, 702 pounds of tea, 2676 pounds of dried fruit, 920 pounds of field peas, and 2453 pounds of white and brown rice. Clothing, blankets and medicines were additional. Private individuals had made gener-ous donations, one man sending 15 hundredweight of brown rice and 24 gallons of olive oil, and the government had contributed its subsidy of £320. But the annual costs of running the mission were well beyond £2000. There had also been new efforts to employ people. Donkey and camel teams run by men on the station now did most of the carting of goods from Alice Springs. Other men were employed on the run. A dozen men were currently employed outside the mission. Six were stock riders at Henbury, two were yard and fence builders, two were away droving, and two were police trackers.

The diet of the community had continued to preoccupy the busy superintendent, seared as he was by the deaths in the drought. He was energetically promoting the use of whole wheat—a recom-mendation of Professor Cleland and Dr Fry of the 1928 university expedition, who thought that the persistent eye trouble among many of the people was due partly to an unbalanced diet. Albrecht set up hand grinders on a little bench in front of his house, and supplied whole wheat instead of white flour to people who were not working. Some of the people felt it rather an affront, preferring the white flour they were used to. But Albrecht persisted, pointing out that his own family also used the whole wheat. Some of the Aborigines still managed to avoid the grinding by sending their children to do it, and it was some time before Albrecht realized that the wheat was not being ground properly, thereby losing much of its nutritional value.

Two of the winter visitors were artists from Victoria, John

Gardner and Rex Battarbee, who with Albrecht's permission spent several months living in a caravan and painting in the mission area. Before returning to Melbourne, Battarbee offered to exhibit their paintings for the staff. Albrecht agreed but suggested that the Aborigines would also be interested, so the seats were taken out of the schoolroom and the paintings set up. As the people began to see the familiar scenes and places of their own country translated into paint on a canvas, bedlam broke out. They dragged each other from one painting to another, excitedly pointing out this or that.

One man seemed apart from the general excitement. Albert went around the room, studying them carefully. Then he asked Albrecht what the artists were paid for their work. Perhaps between two and twenty guineas. Albert was silent for a moment. 'I think I can do that too', he said. Albrecht was taken aback. He explained that the two artists had trained for many years in an art school, after a good general education. The man walked away, and Albrecht immediately regretted his answer. He felt strongly that it was very wrong to discourage an Aborigine. Later Albert came up to him again—he still thought he could do it. Albrecht was relieved, and assured him that he would get some brushes and paints for him. He added that Battarbee wanted to return to Central Australia, and suggested that Albert offer his services as a camel man in return for painting lessons.

At the end of the year, the youngest son of Carl Strehlow, Theo, came out to the mission to spend a few weeks at his old home. He helped prepare Christmas parcels and, as an accomplished organist, spent many evening hours helping Werner Petering train the men's choir in four-part arrangements of the Lutheran liturgy and special Christmas hymns. Ten years had passed since he had left as a fourteen-year-old in the buggy with his mother and dying father. He was now twenty-four, and had graduated from Adelaide University the previous year. He had returned to Central Australia earlier in the year with a £100 grant for linguistic studies and ethnology, and in that time had roamed over thousands of miles of Central Australia, mostly with an Aborigine called Tom Ljonga, whom he had known at Hermannsburg as a boy. The experience had affected him deeply. Disease, undernourishment, squalor and hopelessness seemed to him the common conditions of life for most Aborigines. Whole groups in the Aranda- and Loritja-speaking areas were apparently doomed to extinction, many consisting only of a few aged survivors, with the remaining women past child-bearing age.

On Christmas Eve afternoon, Theo, or Ted as he was often called, helped to hand out presents at Hermannsburg and, as he looked into the bright faces of scores of Aboriginal children excitedly untying their bandannas, he felt some measure of hope. Here were children—children whose eager faces carried the sense of a future. As he watched them, he thought bitterly of a succession of governments which had based their opinions and policies on scientists such as Baldwin Spencer who had reported so disparagingly on the mission in earlier days—its lack of sanitation, its unbalanced diet. Yet, he thought, it was chronically starved for funds and maintained for decades only through its own meagre cattle sales and the gifts of a few hundred earnest men and women who felt it their Christian duty to help their fellow men.

What had men like Spencer ever done, he thought caustically, to alleviate the position in these doomed areas not under mission control? What scientists had ever interested their learned friends in establishing a single centre which was properly sanitized? Not that he felt the mission's record was one of unqualified success. Nevertheless, it had saved the people on its lands from extinction and given them some hope and confidence. He had only to look around him to sense the bonds of a community life, still with its own language and living on its ancient group territory. Where the wit and wisdom of scientists and policy-makers had failed to solve 'the native problem', love and practical human sympathy had overcome a problem considered insoluble for generations.

The young man's opinions were strongly felt, born out of idealism and perhaps some of the hurts of his father's life. Not only had Baldwin Spencer criticized his father's administration, they were also intellectual rivals, holding different and in some ways opposing anthropological views. Partly through his co-operation with longtime telegraph stationmaster Francis Gillen, Baldwin Spencer had become the acknowledged authority on the Aranda people, a recognition which Ted Strehlow felt belonged rightly to his father. Ted Strehlow's own work was just beginning. But the return to Hermannsburg in 1932 helped to crystallize feelings and attitudes which were to shape much of his life. It was also the beginning of a longstanding relationship and co-operation with the pastor who had followed his father, though it would be difficult to conceive of two more different personalities.

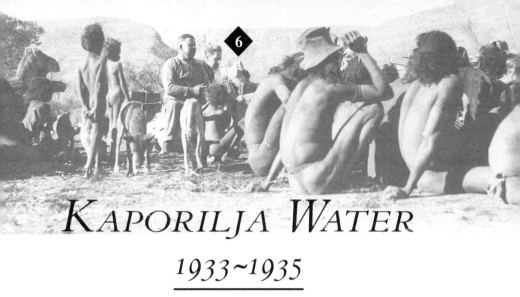

KAPORILJA WATER

1933~1935

My parents' country was Napperby, I think they came to Alice Springs when they was young, people used to travel around . . . I bin working in Alice Springs, for a builder and training race horses. Lived in camp across the river. Big mob there, maybe two hundred. Many people had work. They could also get government rations there, for old men and children and sick people. They would share it with their families. Too many gambling things, that's why I didn't want to stay there, lot of fighting. People went to pictures, this made trouble sometimes, mix'em up in the head.

Early in 1933, many of the Hermannsburg people made a trip into Alice Springs. Young and old, men, women and children made the exodus—some walking, some by donkey wagon, a few by camel. Many had not been there before, and were keen to see 'the big fella snake', as they called the train, and other emblems of town life. Alice Springs was a potent attraction for Aboriginal people from the mission and elsewhere. The government now handed out better rations than the mission could provide, and it was an easy way to escape the irksomeness of work routines or community discipline.

Albrecht thought it better that they experience the 'wonders of civilization' as a group and with his approval, since there was no real way to keep them totally away from Alice Springs. But he felt that the town environment was becoming a worse and worse influence for Aboriginal people generally. Drinking, prostitution and venereal disease were increasing, and normal tribal and family cohesion disintegrated at an alarming rate. Albrecht often had the impression that Europeans regarded the instability and prostitution among Aborigines in Alice Springs as insignificant, remarking that in their old state, Aborigines often exchanged wives or changed marriage partners after a quarrel. He felt, however, that under traditional law such things might be accommodated within the marriage class system, and the basic tribal organization remain intact. But in the settled districts, all tribal organization was broken down, and he felt strongly that if family life was not protected there, the Aboriginal community would cease to exist.

Even the early part of the year was busy. A seven-man expedition from the University of Sydney under the leadership of Professor H. W. Davies arrived. They were studying Aboriginal needs for water. Albrecht felt he could not refuse their request for accommodation and camel teams for a six-week period, though he knew that feeding them would be difficult. It was the height of summer and there were no fresh vegetables. Trying to provide for everyone was difficult for Minna. Every nook and cranny seemed to have someone sleeping in it. Not long after that group had left, members of the Mackay Aerial Survey expedition arrived to carry out aerial mapping flights in the south-west of the Territory. The planes refuelled at Hermannsburg, so Albrecht had to arrange delivery of fuel supplies from town.

He was not feeling particularly well, and his increasing insomnia was becoming a problem. Overwork was probably the underlying cause. Werner Petering was enthusiastic, and the school children were enjoying *ingkata kurka* (little pastor) as they called the strapping young man who stood well over six feet in his socks. (Although Aboriginal nicknames often played on physical idiosyncrasy, doubtless the 'little' in this case was a recognition of the greater authority of the superintendent.) But until Petering became more fluent in Aranda, he could not help substantially with religious classes and preaching, let alone the work with the bush people in the west.

Tourists were also increasing, usually hiring mission camels or horses to go to Palm Valley. This was extra work, but brought in a little money. Rex Battarbee also returned in the winter of 1934, and Albert took him with a camel team down the Finke. It was a dramatic landscape, red cliffs rising precipitously from the sandy river bed. Battarbee taught him the essentials of choosing a subject,

*Albrecht visiting tribal people
in the Haasts Bluff area,
c. 1935. Albrecht seated in the
middle, camels to left.*

*Arrival home from the camel
trek west in 1936. From left,
Albrecht, Dr Charles Duguid,
Reverend David Munro.*

Helene and Theo Albrecht with Aboriginal friends at Hermannsburg. Helene and Sylvia McNamara (far right) remained lifelong friends. Photograph. Rex Battarbee.

preparing the paper and mixing colours. Albert had tried water colours in the intervening two years without much success, but Albrecht had noticed the development in his poker work, and the increasing self-consciousness of Albert's approach to his craft. He was also a more persistent worker than the other men. Sometimes he and Henoch worked together to saw up the slabs of mulga, and invariably Albert would end up grumbling at the other man to pull his weight.

Sick Aborigines from the bush still came in sometimes. They suffered from a variety of ailments—the tropical disease of yaws, boils and other sores, eczema, kidney and bladder troubles—and Albrecht administered what treatments he could. The extra numbers stretched food supplies at the still struggling mission, since people rarely came without their relatives. But they were never turned away, and Albrecht was pleased they could go back to their tribes in better health. He never encouraged them to stay permanently.

In early winter, he went west again himself. Last year's experiment with the tuckerbox had been a mixed success. Rolf and Titus had remained in the bush, but feeding themselves was difficult. However he was relieved to find that none of the hundred tribal people around Potati had left the area. Watching Titus in the camp, Albrecht had the impression that for the tribal people he was a bridge between two worlds. He could satisfy their curiosity about the white man and answer their questions. He could also indicate some of the disadvantages of becoming involved with the white man's way of life—the loss of personal freedom in having to work, the interference with families, and the loss of their own social life. He noticed that the bush people regarded Titus as invulnerable to spirits. His shotgun, which Albrecht had given him partly for self-protection and partly to help him with his food supply, was doubtless part of this. But it went deeper. One night, Titus told him, the whole camp had been trembling with fear of evil spirits. Titus took a piece of wood and went around their camping place, hitting all the trees and bushes. Then everyone settled down.

Albrecht often pondered how few European Australians realized that even bush Aborigines had been decisively affected by the advent of European civilization. Curious about the white man's food, clothes and way of life, they were inevitably drawn toward European settlement. He thought it entirely natural that the white man's life would seem easier and more desirable to these Aborigines who had to struggle so hard at times to wrest a living from their arid environment.

In those days, people didn't thought about that [their land], they didn't thought anything about the country. They just thought, we got European here, we'll get feed from them. Everything start to change, they start to forget everything—bush tucker, everything, because they learned for flour, tea, and sugar, and all that bullock meat.

But Albrecht also felt that the impact of European civilization went deeper than curiosity, or the attraction of food. He had seen whole tribes leave their area, and thought that their observations of the European and a totally different life had undermined their social organization and shaken their religious belief. They saw the European as having a different kind of magic, perhaps a stronger control over his environment. Once this doubt was introduced, he sensed a fear in the people that finally would drive them away from their old places to seek protection from Europeans.

Even people as far away as these at Potati lived in an ethos which was partially shaken. Titus pointed out two children in the camp, a boy of ten and an older sister, who had been found in the bush by Pintubi people, not far from the bodies of their murdered parents. Albrecht was distressed. He had sometimes seen people go raiding and killing when they had a grievance they could not resolve themselves. He knew that killings like these in the unoccupied areas west of Alice Springs were frequently ignored by the authorities, yet ineffectively dealt with by tribal and cultural laws fast losing their strength and cohesion. European justice was not necessarily the answer, let alone action such as the Coniston police expedition which Albrecht regarded as 'an entirely lawless act'. But he thought that properly administered native courts, under magistrates with an understanding of Aboriginal culture, would play an important part in helping bush Aborigines remain on their traditional territories.

He felt strongly that the prevalent idea of simply leaving them alone in large reserves, when their own social and spiritual orientation was threatened, was unutterably wrong—like leaving a blind man without a guide in the midst of city traffic. He voiced similar sentiments in replying to a letter from a Sydney man expressing his concern for tribal people in the Petermann Ranges in case of a gold discovery. Albrecht wrote in detail of the need to establish an inviolable reserve, with some organizational support in food and sympathetic guidance in establishing contact with the wider community.

It was not only the western people who were occupying Albrecht's attention. Dealing with everyday life in the mission community itself was frequently a daunting task for the superintendent. Disputes within the life of the Christian congregation often presented him with dilemmas—problems of a congregation which was 'partly Christian and partly heathen', as he sometimes expressed it One of the men, Epafras, was currently asking for reinstatement in the congregation after a long estrangement. He had been at the centre of a number of contentious issues over the last year—a liaison with a woman at Ilbilla which he later denied, stirring up discontent about the whole wheat ('only birds are fed with that'), arguments about wages. The man was adept in pursuing what he wanted—particularly, thought Albrecht, in playing staff off against each other, like the time he wrote a letter of complaint to Riedel which accused Albrecht ('unlike Pastor Strehlow') of letting people die of hunger. Albrecht found it difficult to believe the man was sincere in his plea to rejoin the congregation. He pointed out to Riedel that no-one had died that year, and that Epafras found it convenient to blame him and the whole wheat for all the deaths in the drought. The complexity of Albrecht's role in the mission community added to the difficulties. He was not simply a spiritual guide and pastor to Epafras, but responsible under the government as well as the church for the management of the large mission community. As such, disruption over food supplies and work arrangements was a serious issue, especially where food and money were chronically in short supply. Writing to Riedel:

> ... about Epafras and Victor. I would not have bothered you with this if I was only the Missionary ... But here I am also the head of an institution for the people who has to care for their keep and physical wellbeing, in other words, a very worldly business. I called on you and the Committee as my superiors and asked for a decision regarding a man [Epafras] who quite openly works against the existing order at the Station as much as he can ... On the other hand, I don't want to stop him from returning, I shall ask all the other people in a general meeting ... then it is a matter of the congregation.

Victor was another difficult case. He had left his wife, Amanda, spent a time in gaol for stealing stock, and lived with several other Loritja women. Now he was with one wife and wanted to work at the mission and rejoin the congregation. It put Albrecht in a quandary. Lutheran doctrine had interpreted Christ's words about marriage and divorce very literally: marriage was fundamentally indissoluble, divorce could be granted only in the case of adultery, and only the innocent party could remarry. Which of Victor's unions was legal? And what kind of contradictions would be created by allowing Victor and his present wife to rejoin the congregation of which Amanda was still a member?

In early October, an influenza virus brought from Alice Springs broke out among the people. Many of them had high temperatures, and some developed pneumonia. One woman died. Albrecht went to the camp twice a day to visit the worst cases. Many were so weakened by the fever that they could hardly sit up to eat, let alone prepare their own food. He found that some people were very neglected. If the patient was a relative either by blood or according to the class system, he was helped. Otherwise, he was often ignored. Albrecht found it discouraging to reflect that even with many of the Christians, traditional values were still a stronger influence than the Christian motive to love and serve others.

He felt the same way sometimes as he sat with old Loritja men to write down the stories connected with the *tjurungas* they sometimes brought to the store to sell, noticing the eagerness in their eyes and voices as they explained the stones and their engravings. Sometimes they became so unconscious of their surroundings that, in the midst of speaking Aranda, they would lapse into Loritja without realizing it. As he gently reminded them to tell him the story in Aranda, he asked himself if they would ever be so gripped by Christianity as to speak of it with such zeal.

Sometimes it was the accumulation of trivial incidents that he found most harassing. Old Thomas and his wife were living in a small stone house with a chimney and an open fireplace, to which a stone floor had been added to encourage cleanliness. Visiting them during the flu epidemic, Albrecht found them almost unrecognizable with ashes and dirt. In the age-old way, they had lit their fire in the middle of the room rather than the fireplace, and in the night their blankets and some empty flour bags had caught fire. Strangely enough, the old couple had escaped with negligible burns. But they were full of complaints and requests for new blankets, and extra tea to recover from the shock. As the superintendent left, Thomas called him back and asked for dripping. Albrecht reminded him that he had given him some only the day before. Apparently it had been eaten by camp dogs. It was a typical episode. People were often indifferent that their eating utensils were shared with the dogs, and only became concerned when the dogs took the best share of the food.

For the weary superintendent, such everyday incidents some-times accumulated into an aching inner question. Was it worth-while to carry on with mission work? What real progress was there? Work problems came up constantly. The milking girls would leave a cow half milked, or pass by others without even touching them, though to a superintendent harassed about community health it was so obvious that the milk was important for babies and the sick. Even skilled people rarely worked well for more than a couple of months. Then they would slow up, seem dissatisfied and lazy, and finally become impossible. Anybody knowing the signs would send them bush for a while, and later they could return to work.

Albrecht's worrying was not simply about running the mis-sion more efficiently. He constantly pondered the future of the Aboriginal race as a whole. Would they survive the advent of Europeans? Was the mission effectively preparing them for life in the wider community? Confronted constantly with behaviour he could only think of as irresponsible, he gloomily reflected that people like these would never survive in the modern community which expected every man to stand on his own feet. Even worse there were many Australians, even church people, who thought that by helping the people, the mission was doing them a disser-vice — 'spoiling' them. Yet, as he wrote in a report to be published in the *Lutheran Herald*, he could find no other path to pursue:

> When we spend so much time, energy and money to help them, to earn them a livelihood, and to make useful members of the commu-nity of them, we do it . . . to right the wrong which was done to the natives by the settlement of their land, and when no other means of existence was provided for them. Should there be anyone who . . . says that the race is not worth being kept alive . . . we cannot but tell him that it is committing a sin to pass such a judgement of life and death over a race. With exactly the same right someone might deny us or others the right to live — we see it happening in Russia at the present time!

His encounter with traditional Aboriginal life in the western camps made him feel even more strongly their need for the Gospel. Some aspects of traditional life he found deeply repugnant, and could only attribute to 'dark heathenism' accounts of infanticide, or the treatment of women, some hardly more than children. In the same letter he wrote:

What the women have to undergo ... is indescribable. Today a woman may belong to Kamatu, and tomorrow, when she is out seeking food by herself, she is robbed by Monkey. When Monkey takes ill, she runs away from him back to her relatives. As soon as Monkey has recovered, he approaches Kamatu. Now, Kamatu has other wives, and after this episode he is not very anxious to keep this particular woman, so Monkey receives a spear-wound in his thigh for his first robbery and may then drive the woman away with him.

In his own mind, he thought of Aboriginal traditional life in two quite distinct aspects. One was their basic religious belief, the ancestors' stories, the belief in magic and spirits. From this they gained their whole understanding of their origins, and their view of life and death. The other he thought of as a lighter side including sexual excesses. He thought the first and deeper part had been destroyed by the contact with European civilisation:

> ... it is simply impossible for the Native to coordinate his religion with what he hears and sees from the white man. Since he cannot otherwise but trace everything back to a spiritual origin, he concludes that the white man has access to great spiritual powers that give him his superiority. For him, therefore, it is a matter of finding out how he can gain this access himself, not of keeping his old belief, in which he has lost faith completely. In this way the real part of his religion has broken to pieces long ago, but he still retains in many cases the lighter side, especially sexual pleasures, which often uncontrolled, bring him down to a beast. What I have heard about this side of their lives among people out West, has shocked me. I simply fail to see how this form of life can have the slightest bearing on their struggle to maintain their integrity.

Another official party visited the mission in June, this time the new Federal Minister, J. A. Perkins, and his wife. The group was greeted by the whole congregation outside the Albrecht house, and the schoolchildren sang 'Advance Australia Fair'. After lunch, the Minister inspected the station. Albrecht explained the urgent need for the Kaporilja pipeline, but sensed the Minister's opposition. He also told him of the indications in Alice Springs that there was grazing interest in the land right out to Mount Liebig, a good thirty miles beyond Haasts Bluff. He'd had a number of discussions about the need to enlarge the central reserve with Carrington, the police sergeant, and the government medical officer. The Minister asked him to put his ideas on paper.

Late in the winter, a visitor of the previous year, Una Teague of Frankston, Victoria, returned with her sister. Violet Teague was horrified to hear of the sufferings of the drought, and astounded to learn that a community of over three hundred people drew their water by hand from wells and soakages. 'Why, pastor, this is ludicrous, you must have water!' she exclaimed. Violet Teague was a tiny lady of around sixty years of age. But where church and a succession of governments had decided that nothing could be afforded, this woman made up her mind that something would be done. She enlisted the support of fellow artists in Victoria who each donated a painting to an exhibition to raise funds for the pipeline scheme. The cause was given good publicity by Melbourne newspapers, a number of prominent writers sold signed copies of their books in support, and public interest and enthusiasm was aroused.

Yet controversy over the scheme continued. The government engineer in Alice Springs thought a holding dam at the springs would be necessary, and that the pipeline should be brought across the Finke on high cement pillars. Stockmen in the area, using instinct and eyesight to determine the levels, talked disparagingly about the mad missionary who wanted to make water run uphill. A positive report by water diviners from Appila, South Australia, about the chance of finding underground water close to the station, raised another line of argument—that the funds collected in Melbourne should be used for boring and well equipment rather than a pipeline. The cost of a supervising engineer was another obstacle. The standard fee was 10 per cent of the cost, yet the funds collected so far did not even cover construction. Albrecht approached Commissioner A. Kenyon of the Victorian State Rivers and Water Supply Commission, who had been a guest in their home. Kenyon introduced him to their chief engineer, who promised technical advice and planning for the scheme on an honorary basis. Another hurdle was to choose the type of piping. Violet Teague sent up samples of fibrolite piping recommended by Kenyon. However, because it was quite heavy, mission staff were apprehensive about breakages and the cost of freight. Wooden pipes were unsuitable, given the white ant pest in the Territory. Then a director of Broken Hill Proprietary recommended two-inch galvanized piping. The Teague sisters were adamant it was to be fibrolite pipes or none at all.

By August of 1934, Una Teague was writing to Pastor Riedel as chairman of the mission board, informing him that £1900 had been collected in the Victorian appeal, and strongly urging the board to proceed with the scheme. Writing in her strong flowing handwriting:

> Anyway we and Mr Kenyon feel that the Pipe Scheme is now ready for you and your Committee to say if you will send it forward, and start at once by ordering the pipes (Fibrolite Asbestos Cement High Pressure) without further delay ... we still require about £600 to complete the scheme, and we feel quite certain that you and your Committee will feel prepared to begin your work and that this amount will be able to be raised within a year in South Australia and perhaps a little in Sydney ...

Hearing of a promising well site near the station, mission friends in Loxton, South Australia, resolved to send up a man called Arthur Latz to do the sinking. William Mattner, the carpenter and handyman who had come up again to work at Hermannsburg, continued to argue that Finke water would be adequate. Whether the mission board was confused or bemused by the variety of approaches to the water problem, it continued to mark time for several months. No decision to order the pipes was made and, when Albrecht asked if Arthur Latz could stay on and supervise the laying of the pipes, they refused.

Albrecht had thought initially that he could supervise it himself. But time factors were ruling that out. Albrecht and his family would leave for furlough in December so as to be able to launch the appeal in South Australia early in the new year. He felt it impossible that the laying of the pipeline be delayed until he returned. Writing in mid-August:

> ... the drought has got so bad that I consider it my duty to do anything in my power to get some variety in the food for the natives. Now the water is so near and we should do everything possible to get it ... Now we have to dig about 5 to 6 feet deep through a small hill. Our people could do that but I know from experience that it is much cheaper if a white person is there supervising it ... Mr Latz would be the right man for it. If we don't get rain soon, then we will have a very difficult time again ... This letter the doctor will take in with him who visited Alwin who had pneumonia badly ... The day before yesterday we buried the old Emilie who also had pneumonia. Everything points to the same symptoms like before the big drought. *Das ist so bedrueckend* ... it is depressing.

The year was becoming very dry, and a medical examination by the government medical officer in Alice Springs showed that forty people at Hermannsburg were tubercular to some degree. He issued stringent instructions against letting people congregate in enclosed places, and warned Albrecht that the mission would face closure if the disease was not brought under control. In July of 1934, he asked a prominent Adelaide doctor who was visiting Alice Springs to go to Hermannsburg and give his opinion.

Charles Duguid was a tall man in his early forties. Born in Scotland, he did his medical training at Glasgow University where he also won honours in the athletic field. He emigrated to Australia and, after war service in Egypt, established a city practice on North Terrace, Adelaide. In the late 1920s, he began to pay attention to disquieting information about the state of Australia's original people. His disquiet was fanned to a burning anger with the publicity given to the Coniston killings in 1928, and the trial and sentencing of an Aboriginal called Tuckiar in Arnhem Land in 1933. In the middle of 1934, he went to Alice Springs to see for himself.

The weeks in Central Australia were a turning point in his life. He saw the Australian Inland Mission hostel—run and supported by his own Presbyterian church—refuse admission to sick people of Aboriginal descent. He learned of the incidence of venereal disease among Aboriginal women, and knew the effects on their babies. He visited a number of cattle stations around Alice Springs and, with some exceptions, felt that the Aboriginal people, especially the old people, were undernourished and lethargic.

At Hermannsburg, Albrecht took him immediately to some of the sick in the camp. Duguid looked askance at the older huts, their thick clay walls, and poor lighting and ventilation, and told Albrecht it was imperative to raze these to the ground, as they would carry the tubercular infection. He thought that the incidence of the disease put the future of the Aranda people into serious question. In ten years there might not be many left. Telling Duguid of his attempts to help tribal people stay on their lands in the west, Albrecht raised the question of the Musgrave Ranges in northern South Australia. 'Nobody knows what's going on there', he said.

Duguid returned to Adelaide, but Australia's Aboriginal people had gained a powerful friend. Duguid was a keen, intelligent observer, highly articulate and totally fearless. And he moved in influential circles. He could hardly have been more different from Albrecht with his humble village background, his physical disability, and the suffering that had marked so much of his experience. In 1934, it meant that Albrecht, who had been standing virtually alone in his efforts to gain some measure of justice for tribal Aborigines in a Central Australia dominated by Europeans and grazing interests, had gained a valuable ally.

Like most visitors to the mission, Duguid was interested in the array of goods in the cash store. He took away items worth £3 12s 6d including a snake skin for 5s, two stone knives at 2s each, one wallaby tooth (commonly used to engrave *tjurungas*) at 1s 6d, a message stick for 6d, and two ceremonial beaters for 2s 3d. He also bought some of the women's fancywork for 19s 6d and three stone *tjurungas* for 15s, together with their stories which Albrecht wrote out for him.

> *Old man [Albrecht] take the camel one day. We was kids. We say, what you doing, old man, heh, what you going to do with this mirror? Old man said, I want to have a look Kaporilja, water come from Kaporilja to Ntaria. How can you do that?* He said, karalai unta kala 'ritjina *[wait and see]. Anyway, we go out with him to the sandhill, have a look from here to Kaporilja. Then we say, heh, old man, how you going to reach the water from Kaporilja to here? You got the engine? To start the water?* Anma, *he said,* anma *[later] ...*

Not until early December of 1934 did the mission board agree to hire Art Latz to supervise the digging of the Kaporilja trench. It had to be dug by hand with picks, shovels and crowbars across five miles of limestone country. They had to blast in places, especially through a small rise where the trench had to be dug to a depth of six feet in virtual rock.

The Albrecht family went on furlough at the end of 1934, three years after their emergency trip down in 1932. For Albrecht, it was hardly a holiday. Most of his time was spent in preaching and lecturing assignments as he strove to interest southerners in the mission work and the Kaporilja scheme. He went to Victoria, consulting with Commissioner Kenyon and his engineers, the Teague sisters and others. Returning to Adelaide, he spent weeks organizing the South Australian appeal. The Lord Mayor was asked for the use of the Adelaide Town Hall for a major meeting in early February to launch it. The Governor was invited, Duguid would chair the meeting, and a number of prominent people had agreed to speak—Professors Cleland, Harvey Johnson, Harold Davies. Ted Strehlow would talk on 5CL radio.

Most of the newspapers were helpful, though the chairman of directors of the *News* told Albrecht that he was 'interested in the blind and deaf and dumb but not in natives' (despite a letter of introduction from Duguid). A lot of material had to be prepared for the papers and radio station to keep the appeal before the public over a period of time. Posters were made and distributed by students of the Lutheran Immanuel College. Individuals also agreed to help—Hans Heysen, a member of one of the Lutheran congregations, would donate the proceeds of two paintings. In March 1935, Albrecht went to Melbourne again to complete the buying of the pipes and fittings, and on the return journey to Central Australia managed to win a further railway concession in freight which would save several hundred pounds.

A governess had been engaged to supervise correspondence lessons for Helene and Ted. Minna was too busy. In addition to running the household, she spent many hours a day supervising women's work on the station—needlework, soap-making, patching the schoolchildren's clothes. She helped oversee the gardening, and kept a close eye on the water supply in the well. She also felt her English was not good enough to supervise the children's education. The new governess was Ruth Pech of the large Pech family at Appila. She boarded in the Albrecht house and quickly fitted into daily life at the mission—helping with the daily sessions on the pedal radio, duplicating for the superintendent, and a dozen other tasks.

The new Minister for the Interior, T. Paterson, visited the mission in the first half of 1935. Again, Albrecht raised the question of the Haasts Bluff block as a secure reserve, asking the Minister directly if he thought that one white man was worth more than two hundred Aborigines. Paterson gave no firm reply. Albrecht liked him, but feared he would not be strong enough to stand against the permanent officials of his department. He had the impression that some of them had very little sympathy for the Aborigines. Albrecht felt strongly that no federal government in Australia had yet been willing to look at the whole issue of Aborigines and the land. Writing to Duguid, he pointed out that, if an individual white man taking up Crown land for grazing was required to feed the Aborigines previously living there, he would have to leave the place at once—it simply would not be an economic proposition. Similarly, if the government was required to support displaced Aborigines with the rent paid for the land, they would not consider granting the lease. 'Now, if this is so, have we a right here to dispossess the Native?' He continued:

Years ago, when Mr Braitling was to take up the country around the Davenport Range, I wrote a sort of a pamphlet and sent it to the Sydney Society for the Protection of the Native Races. They first asked my permission to have it printed, but a little later I received a telegram saying 'owing to the change of Government it is not thought advisable to have it done now'. Here the matter ended, and today—the poor Ngalia people who have lived as long as can be remembered in their old myths, near their Pikilli water hole, they are scattered everywhere ... I believe the number of people affected there was also in the vicinity of 200. My statement is supported by Mr T. G. H. Strehlow, who has done a lot of travelling in that district. There, too, the one white man was worth more than all the Natives who lived there before.

In July, Albrecht set off for Alalbi, the new camp near Haasts Bluff, to which the people had moved from further west. The spring at Ilbilla had been dry since the search parties associated with the Lasseter expedition had been through. It was easy for large groups of people, especially with larger animals like camels or stock, to damage small water supplies. The situation at the Alalbi camp did not please Albrecht at all. The food supplies which had been intended to last the two Christian men from Hermannsburg, Titus and Gustav, until the beginning of September had already run out, and the men had sent back messages to various people at the station, reminding them of their tribal obligations and asking them to send food.

Albrecht was further irritated by the sight of a few odd goats near the mudhole. The year before, he had sent out a number of goats with strict instructions that males which were born could be killed for meat, but the females had to be kept to build up the herd. Now Titus had slaughtered all the goats born that year, including eleven young females. The herd which had increased to twenty was reduced to four. It had been proved so many times, he thought to himself in exasperation, that the mission Christians could not stay in the bush without some backing in food, and he had done his best to provide that. But they were not doing their part. He asked them how they could do their teaching if they didn't have rations and had to hunt all day, and come back tired at night.

He had the impression that Titus had some regret about what had happened, but that it did not go very deeply. Albrecht felt he was looking into a strange world where his standards were acknowledged, but only partially. These men had rations, and their friends had none, and so according to their tribal law they had to give. Whether their friends were actually in need, or simply too lazy to find something for themselves as in this instance, was of little importance. 'But why did you kill all the goats?' he asked. 'We were meat hungry', they said, 'and the people, too, wanted to eat them'. Albrecht gathered that the goats sent out from the mission were regarded as mission property and had not been touched. Those born out there were regarded as theirs and treated accordingly. His plan, which in time would have given them both a meat and a milk supply, had come to nothing—for them, the idea of a future benefit had no deep appeal. Try as he might to see their side, he was unable to feel that it was satisfactory, so he told Titus and Gustav to come back to the station at the end of the month. He would try others.

Two days later, the camel party went on to visit another camp further on in the hills with thirty men and a good number of women and children. There were interesting talks at night, after everybody had eaten their meals and were chewing *pitcheri*, a native tobacco. Monkey, who had spent some time in Alice Springs, told how some whisky had nearly killed him, and how much better he felt to be back with his people.

In the morning after devotions, most of the men went hunting, and the women and children to collect bush tucker. Most were in good health, except for a girl of about eight or nine whose lips were almost totally eaten away with yaws. At first, she refused to come over for the injection and, when Albrecht approached her, she ran away into the bush. A number of younger women ran after her and eventually brought her back. He felt deeply sorry for her. Ashamed of her disfigurement, she was too sensitive to face strange people.

After devotions on the last morning, the men asked him to wait. About twenty of them stood round him in a circle, preventing him from moving. Was it true that Titus was to go back to Ntaria? Yes, said Albrecht. Would he come back? He didn't know. An agitated babble of voices broke upon him. Monkey with his smattering of English planted himself in front of the missionary, saying fiercely, 'Him look after all men, lubras, and piccaninnies. Can't tak'em Titus away, must stay here all the time'. Old Ngalibilala, who a couple of years earlier had thrown a spear at Titus, kept shouting, '*Kulbandaku, kulbandaku*' (Must come back). They would not move until he promised them that he would write to the 'old men' down south and then talk it over again with them.

Their outburst was an unexpected shock, but it put his differences with the evangelists over rations into better perspective. The people around Alalbi obviously felt secure in their present situation, and told him they would not return to Ilbilla even if the water came back. They had become apprehensive about returning to Ilbilla after an Afghan travelling in the Kintore Range further west had taken one of the Kintore Aboriginal men as a camel man. Those people might well assume that the Ilbilla people had killed him, and raid their camp in revenge. With Titus at Alalbi, they had peace and a leader, and were obviously contented. The season had been good, and there was plenty of bush tucker. But deeper, Albrecht felt their tribal life had not been undermined. The clash with civilization that had proved fatal to so many had here been minimized. It seemed to him that the four years of experiment offered some insights into solving the problems of contact.

He could see that the Gospel message, too, was having some influence. The very fact that two groups of traditionally hostile people, Warlpiri and Pintubi, were co-existing peacefully was in itself significant. While he knew that the Christian message was only partially understood and often mixed up with other things, he didn't think it was his task to interfere in that process, feeling that one had to wait as the power of the Holy Spirit gradually made itself felt in their lives.

On this trip he had noticed again how much more native game there was than in the settled areas. A group returned one evening after a day's hunting with thirty-two rock wallabies, all killed with sticks, and in three days they brought in over eighty skins which Albrecht paid for with flour, tea and sugar. He thought it important not simply to give them things, apart from expressions of good-will, but rather to help them understand the white man's system of bartering or sale of goods. That night he could hear them making dampers, and drinking gallons of tea. He had also brought along a portable wireless transmitter bought out of contributions from the Lutheran Young People's Societies in Victoria and South Australia, and one night he invited the bush people to come and listen in to Adelaide radio. About a dozen came, and listened with rapt attention for over an hour, despite the coldness of the night. As they proceeded further inland, they lost contact with the station even by Morse, but the contact via Cloncurry was maintained throughout the trip. Everything seemed less strained, and the intense feeling of isolation that had always marked the earlier treks had gone.

Albrecht's contact with Aboriginal people around Alice Springs had also been increasing. In earlier years, itinerant missionary Ernest Kramer had kept contact with many of them. He spent half of each year visiting Aborigines on the cattle stations of the district, going about in a van with a calico hood on top, a Bible text painted on the side, and two goats named Faith and Charity tethered to the back for a milk supply. In the hotter months, he concentrated on the work in town. Kramer had been directed by the Aborigines' Friends' Association of Adelaide to preach the gospel, telling the people 'the old old story' but not baptizing them. Later Albrecht came to feel this was a pity. He thought they would have had a better foundation for their faith if doctrine had been taught in a more definite way.

With the coming of the railway, the town had grown rapidly, even if only with a shifting population, and the burgeoning numbers of detribalized Aboriginal people around Alice Springs were arousing debate even in government circles. Around 1934, the Roman Catholic church began to work among the Aboriginal people of the town, and attracted many who had previously attended Kramer's church. Kramer became discouraged and went south, and the Aborigines' Friends' Association asked the Finke River Mission to take over its work. Most of the Alice Springs area was originally Aranda country, and the board agreed. With his heavy round of station duties and the commitment to the western tribes, Albrecht felt the best he could do was to station his best evangelists in town. Moses and his son-in-law, Johannes, and Martin had gone in earlier in the year, and he tried to go himself every second month. Since each trip meant ten days of travelling by camel or donkey wagon, more frequent visits were impossible.

Church services were held under large gum trees on the bank of the Todd River. Over a hundred people attended, sitting on the river bank or spread out in the dry sand of the creek bed. In June, Albrecht spent a week in town conducting daily Bible classes as well, and found it heartwarming to see all the people gathered about under the trees and feel their response. Many seemed to have a real hunger for God's word. Aranda people were in a minority, but most understood and spoke the Aranda language. Ernie Kramer had often said there were too many Aboriginal languages around town to preach in one, but Albrecht disagreed. A sermon in Aranda was more understood than one in English, and several old people expressed their pleasure at being able to understand him.

He estimated that about two hundred of the people now around Alice Springs had come in from further west, and thought that about 30 per cent of these had even come from places near the central reserve. He wrote again to the Minister and to Charles

Duguid, reiterating that unless something was done for people living in the unoccupied areas, there would soon be none left. Apart from not letting cattle people push further into these areas, he felt it vital that the reserves have some organizational support. But after less than ten years in his missionary role, he had moved considerably from the traditional 'station' model of mission work. As he stated to the Minister:

> . . . establishing a station directly among natives still living their old tribal lives is, at present at least, not in the interest of the natives. Even establishing a permanent camping place will require much wisdom and experience to do it in such a way as will not prove to be detrimental . . . It is very easy to throw a myall native out of his old ways of living, but it is not as easy, in fact very often impossible, to bring him back again . . . Fullest attention should therefore be given to avoid anything that would tend to weaken their lives as nomads.

He felt that such work was best done by other Aborigines. And again he urged the appointment of a patrol officer who could monitor movement of people to and from the reserve, explaining that, prior to the advent of Europeans, Aborigines could not leave their home districts without the risk of being killed. Giving them total freedom immediately was likely to cause them equally serious trouble, even if it was not so obvious.

The first pipes began arriving in Alice Springs in April 1935 and were carted out to the mission on a special desert train vehicle made available by the government authorities. Unfortunately Vic Carrington was away when the pipes arrived, and the resident engineer authorized them to be taken only as far as the mission. Albrecht was irritated. It meant that ninety tons of piping had to be laboriously carted the extra five miles to the springs by donkey wagon—at least a month's work. He felt sure Vic Carrington would have given permission to take them the whole way.

Art Latz and his workers made good progress on the Kaporilja trench, and by late June were beginning to lay the pipes. Albrecht rode out on his camel as often as he could, and others visited the workers on the pipeline. Dora Pech, a sister of Ruth Pech, came north for a holiday, and was sometimes sent on the donkey wagon up to the pipeline workers with a message or some equipment. She sat on the pipeline, waiting for the morning tea billy to boil, writing letters to her boyfriend in the south, or describing the novelties of 'camping by camel' for a country newspaper in South Australia. Details of campfires under moonlight, the ancient cycads growing out of the cliff faces of Palm Valley, and the idiosyncrasies of camels must have carried a picturesque and exotic air to her distant readers. She was also very fond of 'Mrs Albrecht', as she called Minna. As September wore on, and the pipeline grew nearer to the Finke, the two women began to work in the large garden area which had been marked out beyond the cemetery. Minna ordered seeds from Yates in Sydney.

D. D. Smith, resident government engineer in town, arrived with a parliamentarian in early September. Albrecht went out with them to where the men were working on the pipeline. It was now barely a quarter of a mile from the station. The engineer was sceptical. 'That water will never get to the station', he declared. He thought the little water that did flow from the springs would be absorbed by the fibrolite pipes. Albrecht said little. He had always felt that the engineer had little sympathy for the mission and indeed had specifically advised against the water scheme. But it wasn't easy to hear Mattner's prompt agreement: 'Yes, you can call me a flying Dutchman if that water gets to the station'. Mattner had always maintained that nothing would flow beyond the first limestone rise about a quarter of a mile from Kaporilja springs.

Albrecht was finding it difficult to sleep at nights. Sometimes he would get up and walk to try to calm the turmoil inside him. Over the last five years, he had put his utmost effort into the water scheme, believing it was essential for the survival of the Aboriginal community at Hermannsburg. Yet the nearer the day came of its completion, the more the obstacles and opposition piled up in his mind, and the more alone he felt in the responsibility for its success. Even his mission board had not supported it, believing it was the government's responsibility, and had specifically forbidden him to approach Lutheran congregations for donations. Further, Albrecht was conscious that he had chosen to ignore the advice of the government engineer, advice which even his fellow worker supported. What if the whole scheme failed? Three thousand pounds worth of material was buried, and could not be retrieved. He thought about the engineer who designed the pipeline for the Kalgoorlie goldfields in Western Australia. Before the water arrived, he had found the anxiety intolerable, and killed himself. Albrecht had no intention of following his example, but the desire to escape was strong. If the ground opened in front of me, he thought to himself, I'd be glad to disappear.

There were still insufficient funds to cover the costs of reticulation from the pipeline to the garden, and the Teague sisters made no move to help further. Albrecht felt there was nothing for it but to borrow the money. It had to go in. As the pipeline grew closer, men were sent out to cut desert oak for posts for a garden.

Some of us started the garden then, pipe going this way, that way, ready for the water. Some of us working there, others on the pipeline. All night digging.

The weather warmed up as September wore on, and the men worked into the night when the air was cooler, building fires along the trench for light. Some of them had worked the forty weeks from December without a break. The superintendent's tension was evident to his family, though he said little about it. In the last week of September, the men worked in the dry bed of the Finke, laying pipes on bedrock deep below the sand. The lights of their fires were obvious from the back of the Albrecht house. 'You should not have sent away for those seeds', he said to Minna. 'Couldn't you at least have waited until the water came?' '*Selbstverstaendlich*' (Of course, it will come), she said firmly. She and Dora had been planting radish seeds in expectation.

The finishing touches were made late in the last day of September. Up at Kaporilja springs, Mattner was to divert the water into the pipeline at six o'clock in the evening. Albrecht calculated it should reach the station around ten o'clock. Minna was tired, and went to bed. Albrecht said he would stay up for a while as he had some work to do. At two in the morning, there was still no sign of the water. He went to bed, saying his prayers. God must have a plan about the water, he thought.

A little before sunrise the next morning, there was a great outcry from the women going to the milking. *Kwatja! Kwatja!* (Water! Water!) The valves at the end of the pipeline had not been shut tightly, and a stream of water was shooting up twenty feet into the air. Within a few minutes, the spot was overrun with people. The din was indescribable. Adults and children ran through the water, laughing and shouting uncontrollably. Water! Water everywhere! The unbelievable had happened.

Albrecht said we want to try to get the water here, hard to believe that one, very hard altogether. Everybody bin say, I don't think water's coming out of that, white people too say that, Lutherans too, station people too. Yes, everybody bin say, I don't think we'll get the water. When we saw that one, the water, we said, old man, your word is really true. I'll get it, he said. He did! Pastor Albrecht's word was true altogether.

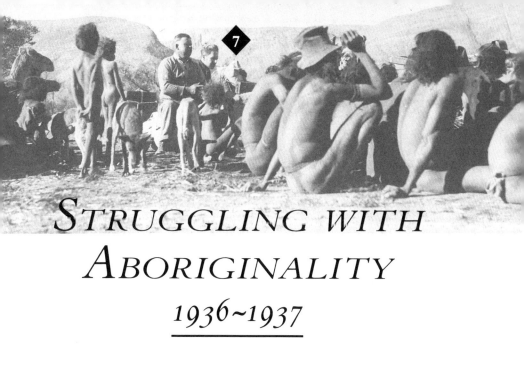

STRUGGLING WITH ABORIGINALITY
1936~1937

Old man Albrecht, sometimes he take the big school kids to Ellery Creek, one week's holiday. He used to ride that donkey—that donkey's name is Box! The boys and the girls used to carry a little swag on the back for rations. In the wintertime, the cold time, they went, took tents, blankets—Box used to carry them things. Helene went, and Ted. Old man used to tell them stories, around camp fire after tea, singing, hymns, devotions. Morning they would walk around. Old man used to sit in the shade, watch all the kids, count all the kids—number for the girls, number for the boys. If anyone away, tell the big kids to get them back.

Early in 1936 Albrecht was obliged to go south to give evidence in a court case brought against Werner Petering by the former mission teacher, H. A. Heinrich. Though the formal dispute lay between Heinrich and Petering, allegations were brought against Albrecht that he had been implicated in severe corporal punishment of two Aboriginal women in 1932. One incident had involved a pregnant woman whose husband had told Albrecht he was going to beat her for some misdemeanour. Thinking that he should not interfere too far, he told the man not to hit her above the knee. Subsequently she had lost the baby, and Heinrich had maintained that Albrecht had authorized the husband's mistreatment. The other incident involved a woman called Karma, whom Heinrich claimed had suffered permanent injury from being hit. Albrecht had told Riedel about it when Heinrich had first complained to the board in 1932:

> Karma and Serena had a fight. Heinrich of course had to interfere, he locked Serena up in the girls house. Then Karma took a stick and tried to break open the door and the verandah. I was working on my camel boxes for the trip last year that I got sick . . . This happened after midday, I went over a few times and told Karma to go to her house. When I was there, she went away, but as soon as I started on my work again she went back, banging against the door and the verandah. I told her she would get a thrashing if she did not stop. I was hardly back at my work when I saw her running over again, and I told Theodor [Karma's husband] who was with me to go and calm her down, but he said he couldn't handle her when she is mad. So I took a piece of greenhide and went over to her and gave her a few on her behind and locked her in her house. She broke the door and followed me, complaining that I had hit her although she was sick. Theodor took her back then, and the incident was finished . . . For me and also Karma everything was forgotten long ago. I visited her after I came back from south and she told me that she'd got much quieter since she was sick, she was always far too excitable and God had punished her because she was a bad example to her children . . .
>
> I can imagine that people here are looking for something against me because I am not only missionary but also police. Mr Heinrich could have gone to the police in Alice. But I managed so far without help from the police, but that works only with strict discipline . . . I don't mean to say that I am perfect, only God knows how much I still have to learn and how much I try to do everything right. I don't want to cover anything up, I would be quite pleased if somebody came here to investigate and tell me what could be improved regarding the management of a partly Christian and partly heathen population in Central Australia.

Evidently, Heinrich's resentment against his former superintendent and the mission board which had supported Albrecht had smouldered for years, despite protracted efforts to resolve the differences within church structures and disciplines. Many in church circles believed the root cause of his longstanding antagonism lay in the fact that, in the four years following Carl Strehlow's death, Heinrich had been virtual superintendent of the mission. Such authority would be difficult to relinquish to a newcomer.

The case was heard in a civil court, and attracted considerable publicity in the press. Largely on the evidence of a doctor who had examined one of the Aboriginal women concerned, Albrecht was cleared. Returning north in early April, he felt it was essential to talk openly with the mission community about the case. It was almost Easter, and a service of Holy Communion had been planned. If there were tensions or undercurrents, they must be resolved. He told them what had happened in Adelaide, what had been alleged, and asked them what they had said at the time about the incidents. They said repeatedly that they had not discussed them at all.

During the same evening he saw through the window of his study some men approaching the house. Then more came and waited for him on the verandah. They brought up the case of Gerhard who had brought a girl from Alice whom he wanted to marry. Albrecht knew that this was only a preliminary. Then they said that after his resignation, Heinrich had told several of them that the business of the two women was not finished for him, intimating that he intended to pursue it further. But they had not broached the subject with Heinrich or discussed it amongst themselves. Albrecht felt grateful they had come and spoken so simply and directly about it.

The question of corporal punishment on the mission had also been raised by Duguid the previous year after public accusations that an Alice Springs policeman called McKinnon had thrashed two Hermannsburg young men. Albrecht gave Duguid some of the background. Both of the boys had been difficult. One of them attacked Mattner with a stone on a building job and, despite several warnings from Albrecht, tried to assault a young girl. Albrecht felt he could do nothing else but dismiss him, telling him that if McKinnon was there to give him a hiding, he would probably be a good boy afterwards. 'As a rule all such offenders are handed over to the old men and they deal with them. Percy, however, had been in their hands on several occasions, but it seemed as if he became unmanageable.' McKinnon had come to the station while Albrecht was away and, at Mattner's complaint, had administered the punishment to the two boys. Corporal punishment at the mission was rare, Albrecht told Duguid. Nevertheless he felt it was sometimes appropriate in an Aboriginal community:

> My opinion about this is firstly: whether I would have called on McKinnon to fix up these two boys, I don't know. I certainly said before, I should hand them over to McKinnon if he comes along. However, during the time I have been in charge of this place I have neither sent anyone in to jail, nor handed them over to the police for punishment. I always managed to straighten these things up with the advice and aid of the old men at the place, and there has never been

a need to touch anyone myself or call on other members of the staff to do so.

At the same time, knowing how Natives react to corporal punishment, I cannot believe that the punishment meted out has been to the disadvantage of the Natives concerned ... Simeon ... told me joyfully he had received his just punishment, the first time I ever heard of the incident. And now he, in return, expected me to forget and give him another chance. This I did. He is just now away with some camels to take rations out to Titus. This treatment is in accordance with their feelings and understanding and therefore has the desired effect ... Here at the Mission we have [sometimes] ... had no fight for over two years. I know fully well that this is above all the influence of the Gospel. It is very seldom that a Native receives corporal punishment here, in fact very rare exceptions. But I cannot deny that it has some effect on the community life here, and a very beneficial one at that. If anyone, even from Government quarters, comes along, I shall make no secret of this my opinion, even if severe criticism should follow from people who don't know anything about Natives.

He was glad he had not been away longer. Mattner had been overworking and was quite ill. For months, he had been working with Art Latz and a dozen Aboriginal men on a large storage tank for the water from the pipeline. The walls were two feet six inches thick, and made of concrete and river stones. Over a ton of cement had been laid in the foundations alone, and all the work done in the hottest months. Many a time Albrecht had noted temperatures of 111 degrees F (43.9 degrees C) in the shade of the verandah, while the men at the tank were working on concrete under a tin roof.

The tank was now finished, and usually kept at least half full by the spring water. In the garden, fifty beds had been planted with cabbages and other vegetables for winter. '*Da kann man auch sagen, dass man auf Schritt und Tritt den Fuss-spuren Gottes folgt*' (When I go through the garden now I feel as if I'm following in the footsteps of God), he wrote to Riedel. Apart from the main garden which he planned and supervised, he hoped that some of the Aboriginal people would take the opportunity to have garden plots of their own. The response so far had not been particularly heartening: 'nothing had happened so far, they said "too much trouble", they carry a dreadful burden of laziness'.

By June, two newly married couples had arrived back on the station. Art Latz had married Dora Pech, Werner Petering a girl from Victoria. The Peterings moved into the large eleven-room house previously occupied by the Heinrichs, and the Latzes took up residence in the eastern house across from the church.

Albrecht and some Aboriginal camel men left for the west in early June. He had also invited Dr Charles Duguid and the Moderator of the South Australian Presbyterian church, Reverend David Munro, to come on the trip. He knew Duguid's commitment to the Aboriginal cause, and his proposal to the Presbyterian Church of Australia to found a medical mission in the eastern Musgrave Ranges in South Australia. The trip was Duguid's first experience of tribal Aborigines. He was interested in everything—their weapons, food grinding implements, cooking, the way many of the boys in the camp could count European style. Later he found they often spent time with Gustav, one of the Hermannsburg evangelists, and he had taught them. Heading north-west towards Central Mount Wedge gave him his first experience of the long red sandhills. Running east—west and parallel to each other, they seemed interminable, and the long hours of slow difficult climbing and descending was tiring to men and animals alike. Even Aborigines crossed this desert only in the wintertime.

At Ajantji waterhole and Potati, they found large groups of people. Some were treated for yaws, one man with sores so severe that his nose had been eaten away entirely. With each group, Albrecht held devotions. Many of the people had learned some Aranda, and the evangelists translated into Loritja and Pintubi where necessary. 'Do you think they understand what you are saying about God?' Duguid asked one night. Though a staunch Presbyterian himself, he was not really at ease with the direct teaching of the Christian faith to people of such a different culture. 'It is my job to give them the Gospel', the Lutheran missionary said simply. 'God will open their ears.' He explained that the evangelists did little in the way of directly opposing corroborees, circumcision and polygamy. But they presented the Bible teaching, and found that with these ideas and example, the way of life was gradually altering. Nothing had been heard of revenge parties for about two years, and the women were getting better treatment.

First time he had service here, we didn't understand. Different story. Titus had pictures to help, different pictures for the different Bible stories. We gradually understood more and more and said, this sounds really true.

The question of reserves dominated campfire discussions. Even in the country they had just traversed, they had met over 120 people living in tribal conditions. Obviously they would be scattered if the country was taken up for grazing. Duguid promised he would see Paterson, the Minister for the Interior, about securing Haasts Bluff as a reserve, and resolved to press on even more urgently with the medical mission in the eastern Musgrave Ranges. Such a centre would keep European doggers and prospectors from intruding more and more into tribal territory, and be a buffer between tribal people and the encroaching European civilization. Like Albrecht, he considered that contact was inevitable, but was angry that nothing was being done to prepare the Aboriginal people. The kind of contact he had witnessed between the Hermannsburg Aboriginal evangelists and the tribal people seemed to him ideal. In his brief stay at the station before returning south, Duguid noticed a new look of health in the Hermannsburg people, evidently due to the mission garden and its vegetables.

There were other visitors in the Albrecht home when they returned—Pastor W. Riedel and his wife, two seminary students from New Guinea, and two other church women from the south. Rex Battarbee had also been staying for the last four weeks, painting in the area close to the station. The number of visitors to the Albrecht household was sometimes daunting. In the previous year, 170 people had passed through their home in five months. Not all stayed overnight, but everybody at least had a cup of tea. With the widespread publicity given to the drought and more recently to the water scheme, Hermannsburg was becoming known in the eastern states, and many influential visitors to Central Australia were keen to include a visit to the mission on the Finke River. The Governor of South Australia had come in 1935, as well as the Minister for the Interior with an entourage of fifteen people instead of the expected seven. So there was a flurry for Minna, but everyone was made welcome, and the superintendent spared no effort in showing people around and trying to broaden their understanding of the Aboriginal situation.

Minna and her husband had decided early in their marriage that their home would be open to anyone. Both were naturally hospitable, and they also believed it was important for the better understanding and support of the mission that flowed from it. But Minna sometimes thought that some visitors did not understand the effort necessary to accommodate extra people. Marianna and the Aboriginal girls who worked in the house were an enormous help, but someone still had to organize the work and see it was done. However she knew and accepted that her husband felt it was important to welcome people. Charles Duguid took a different view. He told Albrecht bluntly that his wife would wear herself out if they kept up all the hospitality to church people.

There were others who questioned Albrecht's approaches. Pastor W. Riedel was brother to John Riedel, chairman of the Finke mission board, and a lecturer at the Lutheran seminary in Adelaide. He had served for a time on the mission at Lake Killalpaninna, and had very different ideas from Albrecht on the proper tasks of a missionary. They often argued about it. 'Preaching and teaching' was Riedel's idea. He didn't much approve of the energy and effort that was going into the question of the reserve for Haasts Bluff. According to what Albrecht had been told on first coming to Australia, Pastor W. Riedel had reported to the South Australian synod in the early 1920s that the work at Killalpaninna could not be done because the Aborigines were going away, and were being interfered with by Europeans. To Albrecht, a missionary was there precisely to stop such trends—he could not necessarily expect a ready-made congregation. He had always thought of Killalpaninna, or Kopperamanna as he referred to it, as a potent symbol of church failure, and from his first days in Australia had passionately committed himself to preventing a similar closure of Hermannsburg.

Inevitably, he thought, a missionary would have to wrestle with the whole social and physical environment of Aborigines, whether he liked it or not. Otherwise, there would be no-one left to teach or preach to. 'Deal thy bread to the hungry' was a Biblical injunction which constantly came to his mind. He had used the verse as title to a pamphlet he had written for 'mission friends' the previous year, explaining his conviction that the mission should do everything possible to provide an adequate diet for the people. This held even where it was apparent that health was suffering because some of the mission people were disinclined to grind the whole wheat properly and sent small children to do it instead, or simply cooked the whole wheat without grinding it. As he wrote in the pamphlet:

> From our point of view, we could have said: if they are too lazy to prepare their own food if given a chance, they may just as well go hungry. But this would not have done justice to the native as he actually is. He is a Stone Age man trying to find his way into a strange world: from a collector to a food-producing way of living. It was up to us to help him . . .

Sometimes he tried to explain to the board chairman and others that what appeared to a European as pure laziness had to be interpreted by different standards: 'This "laziness" is made up of a lot of factors which we should not overlook.' Even going out to hunt for bushtucker was something they would avoid; as he put it, 'They [would] rather beg or starve, we cannot change them, we have to take them as they are'.

As always, there was a multitude of matters to be organized. Camels were in very short supply. Some had sore backs, and the rest had gone with Bert Nananana and two other Aborigines to collect salt from Lake Amadeus, two hundred miles to the south-west. This was done only in winter. Even then, daytime temperatures on the bare surface of the lake made the work difficult.

Bags of rock-hard salt were brought back by camel, and women ground it fine, usually sitting on the ground outside the eating house. But the round trip took a month, which meant that at least one loading of goods would have to be carted out by Fogarty's truck rather than by camel—more freight costs.

We carry one bag at a time, and follow the hard patches on the salt lake. Have to wear boots, or feet would get burned from the salt. Then travelled back. We went for one taia, *one moon [one month].*

Albrecht was also preoccupied with equipping the new well on the western side of the Finke. He had been writing about it to Riedel for over a year, as he had always known that Kaporilja water alone would not grow enough food for the whole community. Trying to communicate all the details of secondhand equipment and different pumping systems to the chairman by letter was a cumbersome process at best, and worsened by Albrecht's feeling that the board members thought he was wanting to incur needless expense at a time when there was still a debt of almost £400 on the Kaporilja pipeline. Even more frustrating was the fact that they were a thousand miles away and not really in a position to assess the matter. He, on the other hand, did not have the authority to make the decision.

Ted Strehlow was having difficulties with some of the Aboriginal workers. He had asked Albrecht to suggest two Christian men to travel with him in his new appointment as government patrol officer. Albrecht sent Henoch and Rolf, and Strehlow had bought them new clothes and boots, and paid them the five shillings a week wage customary for Aborigines in government employment. After two weeks, the men had refused to continue, saying the wage was not good enough. Strehlow was frustrated. 'What is the use of trying to do anything for the people when they are like this?' he asked Albrecht.

Albrecht thought that Strehlow's appointment as patrol officer represented for the government a significant departure from the old policy of police Protectors. It was part of the federal government's gradual progress towards a new Aboriginal policy for Australia though, ironically, the same government was implementing a commitment to indigenous people with far greater vigour in the more visible international arena of Australia's mandated territories in New Guinea. Strehlow, a cautious and reserved personality anyway, was far from confident that government officers in Alice Springs or Darwin would give him much real support in his efforts for Aboriginal justice and welfare. He felt their first loyalty was to the Europeans of the Territory. Partly because of this, he and his wife had settled at Jay Creek rather than Alice Springs. No government funds were provided for their housing, so some large tents became their home for several years.

By virtue both of his position as patrol officer and his own experience and knowledge of the Aranda people, Strehlow could bring a measure of judgement and authority to situations which clearly called for disciplinary measures, and Albrecht was glad to be able to call on him at times. Strehlow had dealt with Lukas, who had beaten his wife with an axe when he returned to the mission after working at Owen Springs station for a month, and found her wearing a short skirt. He thought she was trying to attract other men. Strehlow listened to both parties, all speaking in Aranda, then gave Lukas the choice of being picked up by the police or having a beating. Lukas chose the latter and was given ten lashes with a whip without his shirt by one of the Aboriginal men.

Despite the younger man's reserve, Albrecht felt he could trust him, and that he would be a blessing for the Aborigines. Strehlow had been travelling in the Petermann Ranges area and told Albrecht that the central reserve was now almost empty. Albrecht had been fearing this for years, and at Christmas a newspaper had reported that two hundred tribal Aborigines from the southern Musgrave Ranges had congregated around Ooldea on the eastern Nullabor. He wrote again to the Reverend John Sexton, secretary of the Aborigines' Friends' Association in Adelaide:

> Strehlow has returned from his extensive trip to the Petermanns. He did not find any evidence in connection with the reported shooting, but what is worse, he hardly found any Natives; some of them he met near Oodnadatta. It appears that already the majority of the

people who lived there before are gone. What I have tried to convince the authorities six years before has come to a sad climax. This is a direct result of the old leave them alone policy. As if these people could be left alone as long as there is a community of white people surrounding them, or as if spiritual influences could be stopped by a reserve boundary ... At the same time our experiment West from here proves definitely that something can be done.

He again urged Sexton to apply pressure for action on the Haasts Bluff land, pointing out that at any time a grazing licence could be granted for the area. The block had changed hands four times in recent years, and with every good season, interest would grow. He went on:

Mr Braitling was allowed to go to the Davenport Range with the Pikilli waterhole, sacred to the Ngalia tribe. Not a word was said, and nothing at all done for the Natives who lost their Corroboree place, their spiritual home. Now they say they can't remove him because he has paid rent for a number of years. This very same fact could be established at any time at Haasts Bluff. As the lives of so many Natives, yes, the existence of the remnants of two tribes, the Pintubi and parts of the Ngalia and Loritja, are at stake, nothing should be left undone to have this whole area, if possible including the Davenport Range, declared a reserve.

Early in November, he received a somewhat testy letter from Riedel, questioning the purchase of a boiler for the pumping plant and the generally mounting costs. Could any money be saved on food? Albrecht's reply was as frustrated a letter as he had ever written to the chairman. He had been hoping to pay the initial costs of the boiler and pumping plant from some money given by Ted Strehlow in appreciation for months of hospitality. And he was prepared to pay freight costs for the boiler out of his own salary if necessary. He wrote:

All my endeavours are for the mission and not my private interests. And all the trouble I take to get the gardens going is to reduce the food orders from south without risking the health of the people we look after ... at the moment we cannot save with food without leaving the way open for T.B., I could not take the responsibility. To reduce cost for food there is only one solution, plant more. But this can happen only if we have enough water. Otherwise I do not know where I wasted or where I could have saved.

He finished the letter with a final plea about Mattner. With the old man's increasing rheumatism, the board had decided to put Art Latz in charge of the stock work. Mattner was incensed with the proposal that his salary be reduced, and the implication that his work was not as highly regarded as Latz's. He would leave, he told Albrecht, on the first of January. As Albrecht explained:

> This is the most difficult problem for me at the moment. If Mr Mattner goes, I am again where I always was, my whole life one big hurry and haste ... We have nobody here who could, even partly, take over Mr Mattner's duties. Nobody else here has this essential mixture of authority, work knowledge and understanding. I am therefore pleading with you not to let Mr Mattner go. Is it really impossible for the mission to leave him his salary?

Some of Albrecht's exasperation undoubtedly came from his state of health. A few days before, he had been unable to urinate, and by the next morning was in extreme pain. Urine finally came, bringing a lot of blood with it, and they knew it must be kidney stones again. He and Minna and Paul went south in late November, leaving Helene and Ted in the care of Ruth Pech and Marianna. He was treated for a few weeks for 'gravel in the kidney', then returned to be at the station for the busy Christmas period. Minna and Paul were advised by their doctor to stay longer.

In those early days, Aboriginal people often frightened, because they didn't know what might happen to them. Well, people still think that. Sometimes people when they go through a cattle station, they still think today they might be shot because station owners might get greedy of the country. They know themselves they are traditional owner for those countries, and it's still in these people's mind today when they go through the country, they might get shot too, people might start fight over country. They go through, but not really confident, not underneath ... They feel safe in Hermannsburg, outstations too, bit frightened in cattle stations, bit frightened to meet station owner, because they don't know what sort of man that station owner is. Very important to know what sort of man is on the station. But today, people not sure, because they have left their country, don't work for them.

Albrecht resumed his daily instruction classes for baptism when he returned from the south. He often had mixed feelings about them. More than half of the older people attending had never answered a single question. If only he could deal with them individually. But where could he find the time for that? Sometimes they surprised him. One old woman who had been very ill came to class a few days later, saying that God's Word was precious to her. And a man who returned to Hermannsburg after an absence of three years had not forgotten any of the Catechism articles he had memorized, even though he was elderly and could not read. Albrecht was taking extra time for daily lessons with Moses, Martin, Titus and the other evangelists who had returned to the station for a month after Christmas. Paul's letter to the Romans in the New Testament was the topic for one session, and he was happy to feel they grasped much of what was discussed.

In the last week in January 1937, the Methodist minister, the Reverend Harry Griffiths, arrived at the mission, bringing with him a young man who was introduced as 'the new owner of Haasts Bluff'. Albrecht was stunned. They argued for some time, Albrecht trying to explain to the young man that stocking the block, as was intended, would mean the virtual end of the two hundred people living there now, since they depended totally on the land for their livelihood. As someone in the prime of life, Albrecht told him, he could find a job anywhere in Australia. But pushing these people off their hunting grounds was tantamount to signing their death warrant. He would not be intending to support several hundred people in compensation for taking over their country. The man was unmoved, and Albrecht felt hopeless. The terrible cycle of dispossession that had taken place so often—the European came in and the Aboriginal moved out—was to be enacted yet again, and he was powerless to stop it.

Later, a thought came to him. It was the beginning of a verse in Proverbs: 'Open your mouth for the dumb, for the rights of all who are left desolate'. Much of the very grain of his thought had come from the Bible. 'Open your mouth for the dumb', he thought to himself. You at least have the chance of writing and protesting—something these people do not. The same day, he wrote an eloquent letter of protest to the Deputy Administrator at Alice Springs. He pointed out that, through the mission contact started six years before with the tribal people in the Haasts Bluff area, the so-called myalls had been kept away from Glen Helen station and from drifting in to the settled districts. No prisoners had been brought in from that district for years, and some who had left earlier had even found their way back to their old hunting grounds and tribal life. He went on:

> But above all, being humans as we are, they should not be denied the very simplest form of subsistence. But if Haasts Bluff is allowed to be stocked, about 200 natives will be forced on the first step to total extinction, and all this just in order to provide a means of livelihood for one white man. History in Central Australia will once more repeat itself in its most dreadful aspects.

The Pintubi people could no longer use the Ilbilla area, and the allotment of the Davenport Range area had forced a number of Warlpiris down to Haasts Bluff. 'And in addition ... all the remnants of the Loritja people are living here, even those who used to have their hunting grounds on what is at present Glen Helen station.' Giving some rations to the aged and invalids could not be considered recompense since this was never aimed at maintaining the whole tribe, which as a result faced extinction. He wrote in similar vein to the Minister for the Interior, the Assistant Chief Protector, John Sexton, and Charles Duguid. 'When Titus heard about it', he wrote to Duguid, 'he became very distressed, and now he is asking the people here to keep praying that God may prevent the worst.'

Duguid could not have been more incensed by the news and wrote immediately to the Minister. An indefinite reply came back; Cabinet was not presently in session. Duguid contacted him again, telling him that an immediate decision was needed: once the block was stocked, it would be almost impossible to do anything. Again the Minister reiterated that he could do nothing until the various Cabinet ministers had returned to Canberra. Duguid and his wife were about to go to England. He wired the Minister that he would go to the Home Office in London about it unless something was done immediately. The Minister wired him to stay his hand—he would come to Adelaide to see him.

For the Minister's visit, Duguid spread out on a large table all the photographs taken on the camel trip the previous year. 'These are the people you are going to kill', he told him. The Minister seemed genuinely distressed. The Territory administration in Darwin had the power to allot land for a twelve-month period without reference to the federal department in Canberra, and had used it in the case of the Haasts Bluff block. 'It must be stopped somehow', he said, and asked Duguid in detail about the people in the area. Duguid explained that the Pintubi and Warlpiri people had been displaced once already. The final outcome was a telegram from the Minister to Darwin, cancelling all grazing licences in the Haasts Bluff area.

Minna arrived back in early March with the five-year-old Paul. But her happiness at being home was abruptly cut short with a letter from her father in Germany. Her mother had died on the last day of January after a brief illness. The news was all the more painful as, only a few weeks before, they had received a letter from Germany offering them the extra money they needed for a trip home. It was thirteen years since she had kissed her mother goodbye on the wharf at Hamburg on her way to the United States.

Early in 1937, Albrecht dispatched to Riedel a large box of goods made on the station—tanned goods, goat and cow hides, boomerangs, and a good range of mulga work. They sold well in the Lutheran congregations, and orders came in. Tanning had been in Albrecht's mind from the beginning. Even in Germany, he had visited tanneries to learn the process, as he was already aware of the need for employment on the mission, and the availability of the bullock hides.

The first experiments had been made in 1933. There was no money to spend on concrete vats, so Albrecht had directed a part-Aboriginal man called Manasse to cut and hollow lengths of gum tree for soaking the hides. At first the hides went putrid in the strong sunlight. It was better when the gum tree vats were shifted into the shade of the large pepper trees near the Latz's house. The next year, euro skins and some cow hides had been tanned fairly successfully, though there were high freight costs on the South Australian wattle bark used in the tanning solution. Manasse and one or two other men gradually learned the process, scraping the hides each day to allow the tanning solution to penetrate. Even if the product was not good enough to be sold on the open market, it was quite strong and could be used for mending donkey collars, renovating horse saddles and plaiting stockwhips.

But tanning on any larger scale had had to wait for Kaporilja water. Even in the hectic months in the south organizing the Kaporilja appeal in early 1935, Albrecht sought out more technical information. Always one to research a project as fully as possible, he read whatever he could find and looked for people with expertise or experience to talk to. The Hardie Pipe Company put him in touch with one of Melbourne's leading tanners, and they kept up correspondence after he returned to Hermannsburg. The product improved gradually and within a year or two, cow and bullock hides were being tanned in quantity as well as hundreds of euro and kangaroo skins brought in during the winter months. Skins tanned with the fur left on were used at first as rugs and mats for floor and bed coverings. Some of them went to the boys' and girls' dormitories. They were cheaper than blankets, and lasted better. But Minna designed a saleable product as well. Decorative rugs were created by cutting the skins and hides into suitable shapes which were then sewn together with strips of hide. Minna was very skilled in handcraft, and took care matching the colours and finding the most economical way to cut the hide. Mission visitors were always interested in such articles, and sometimes a kangaroo rug became a gift to someone who had been of special help to the mission. One was packed up and sent to the Teague sisters early in 1937.

As Albrecht did his monthly financial statement for July 1937, he felt encouraged as he added up the receipts for curios, fancywork and leather goods. It seemed they were finally achieving something of the task given to him in 1925 to develop industries for the Aborigines. He sent Riedel a sketch plan for workrooms which would make it possible to produce more. They would be built next to the smithy and behind the church—adjacent rooms for tanning, hides, pokerwork, saddles, a carpenter's shop and a display room. Economy determined most of the details. Timber and stones were available on the station. Some old iron left over from the big tank would serve for the ceiling, and other iron originally bought for a bath house for the camp could be used. Most of the windows would have to be bought, though they had one secondhand one.

Yet his efforts for economic progress were often undercut by recurring problems about work. People would not arrive for work, or they would leave early. In one incident, not one of a group of men sent out to kill a beast had gone. The next morning, when Mattner refused one of them meat in his ration, the man had told him to go and hobble the camels himself. Even Gustav, who had come in from the west because of a child, was negligent and shouted at Art Latz. When Albrecht told him to be quiet and go to work, Gustav walked off for a day or two. Gustav told Albrecht later that the people respected his authority, but did not regard other staff as having any more authority than themselves. Albrecht felt that, particularly in the case of Art Latz, there was no excuse for rudeness. Mattner could be grumpy at times, especially when he had rheumatism, and he was too set in his ways to compromise his work standards. But Art Latz was a gently spoken man who was patience itself. Albrecht's fortnightly letters to Riedel often sounded a note of discouragement:

> When we started with our work, all the confirmands and baptism pupils wanted boots. I told them they did not need them at the station, and the mission did not have enough money. They did not like it. Then they wanted full weekly ration, even if sometimes they only work three hours.
> Maybe our Natives think it is enough if they work a bit now and then. But they expect food and clothing to be provided all the time. Educating them to work is a major problem.

No uniform wage system had existed from Albrecht's early days at the mission. Individual people had very different abilities and inclinations as far as work was concerned, and he did not feel it was possible to pay everybody alike. As a general rule, people were given rations and clothing and expected to do some work in return, though wages were paid in cases where greater skill or regularity was evident. Articles made for sale at the store were paid on a piece basis.

If people became too recalcitrant about work, the frustrated superintendent felt his only recourse was to dismiss them from their jobs. But this brought no real pressure to bear. They simply obtained food from friends and relatives, while their wives and children were fed by the mission. Albrecht wondered if he should send the families away, but felt this only caused suffering to innocent parties:

> Vagrants are a big problem here. Some come with dingo scalps and stay on because the garden provides something to eat. For everyone who works, we have two who don't. Some of our Christians have not worked since Christmas, and they still even ask for clothing . . . Others are lying around the sheep camps . . .
>
> Because of their communist past, they cannot understand that a Christian cannot be a parasite. I explained that the other day in detail, but I don't think I made any impression. I told them if they prefer hunting to working, I fully understand, and that is right also for a Christian. But nobody is listening. Especially on meat days they come forwards to get a share from our workers and beg for clothes.

Sometimes traditional demarcations would interfere with what appeared to be a clearcut task. During his last trip to the west, Albrecht had left one of the most responsible men in charge of watering several rows of young cabbages in the garden. There was piping for one row, and he told him to get one of the other garden workers to help him shift the pipe every couple of days to water the rest. He had gone straight to the garden when he came back, hoping to find them thriving. One row had flourished. The rest were shrivelled and dead; they had never been watered. When he remonstrated with the foreman, the man told him that the other worker was, under tribal law, a father to him. So it would have been insulting to give him orders.

Old Albrecht, he didn't understand life of families, not really. He was just telling people what to do, and not to do such thing. That's all he realized, and that's all he told, one way. I don't think he understood everything, like inside feelings, or inside work with the community.

Some people he used to pick for work, for a job—like that man picked to look after the cabbages, he couldn't do much, or tell his father, because he wasn't game to tell his father to do this. Lot of different ways happening. Maybe two men working, that man might be his brother-in-law, or son-in-law, well that still happening today. They can't talk each other. Old Albrecht didn't understand that part, he tried to force them all the time, he didn't understand all these other ways. All the time he thought, why this man not working, or telling that man. But that was the reason.

Work problems were culture problems, and that time people weren't game to go his place and explain all that. They missed it, to tell him, what's happening, how the system works in the community.

Albrecht was aware, or became so, of some of these cultural complications. And doubtless there were more adjustments than he sometimes realized.

There was not too much trouble. Because they only bin listen one boss, and that boss listen Pas' Albrecht, then Aboriginal boss told the others. When Albrecht give orders, they watch one another, because boss got to tell something [give instructions]—Aboriginal boss, not old man. They worked it out between them. Albrecht was alright. What he wanted done, we tried to do, even if it made a bit of trouble. That's why we like old man, because old man do right thing for us, so we do good for old man. Mistakes don't matter. He tried very hard, he had to learn everything.

But it was frustrating for Albrecht when issues that seemed obviously important for the community were treated with indifference. It seemed so obvious that better diets were important, and now there was a chance for it. But the people did not necessarily share his priorities. Four of the milking girls had repeatedly added water to the milk to save themselves work. After several warnings, he had dismissed them. Now they were spending weekdays sitting in the camp, getting food from their relatives.

He was disappointed too, because some of the girls had refused to marry young men on the station, which had resulted in several young men making doubtful alliances with girls from elsewhere. Gerhard had found a wife at Alice Springs, a girl who had refused to help bring in wood. Arthur married a schoolgirl on the station who had not been baptized, and Jeremias had wandered off with a schoolgirl only ten years old.

Beset on all sides with ambiguous responses to his authority,

Albrecht reflected ruefully that he had interfered too much in the early years with the traditional marriage laws. He had thought it wrong that the old men should be able to force the girls to marry certain men, and had taken this authority away from them. What he should have done, he thought now, was to appeal to the old men to act as Christians, but otherwise leave them their authority. The old system where the girls were married off when they were thirteen, seemed after all to have been the best for the community. 'I try to do two things', he wrote to Riedel.

> Firstly I point out to the young people that it is God's will that they act according to the wishes of their parents when choosing a spouse. Then I explain to them that they should ask themselves whether the road they choose is God's road. May God show us the way out of this impossible situation.

Another round of marriage entanglements in the Aboriginal camp was erupting. They were a recurring source of harassment to Albrecht. Some were resolved by the elders but, when that process failed, they came to him. That did not mean that his advice was followed. And even when it was, he often felt that he merely became responsible for whatever went wrong.

Tourists were contributing to the increasing restiveness. Albrecht felt that the Aborigines looked at the busloads of tourists and felt that Europeans had a life of ease and comfort while they did the work. Yet he could hardly stop the visitors. Many who came had contributed to the water scheme, and they always immediately asked to see the garden.

Early in June, a second daughter, Minna Lydia Ruth, was born. This time there was no sign of kidney infection or other complications. The birth took place in the Australian Inland Mission hospital in town. Because of his wife's imminent delivery, Albrecht had not made the winter camel trip to the west. The Peterings went instead, riding up the Finke Gorge to Glen Helen, then west to Haasts Bluff. Werner had had little success in mastering Aranda, so he had to rely on Titus as interpreter. Each morning, the two men went and sat in the sandy bed of Alalbi Creek and talked over lessons from the Old and New Testaments, and other issues concerning the people. In the usual evening devotions, Titus would pass on to the people what they had talked about. It worked to a degree, but Petering was conscious of the limitations. If a call to ordinary parish work came, he might accept it. His wife, Marjorie, was something of a rarity for the tribal people. For some, she was

only the second white woman they had seen. The women in particular were shy yet curious. After a while, they came up to her and
rubbed her skin gently with their fingers. After the initial surprise,
she realized they wanted to see if the whiteness came off on their
hands.

More than 15 000 plants had been planted in the large mission
garden which now covered more than three acres. There were
cabbages by the hundreds, marrows, silverbeet, kohlrabi, and other
vegetables. With her husband so engaged with the big garden and
station responsibilities, it was Minna who took charge of their own
vegetable garden at the back of the house. She was a good gardener,
and the work was a pleasure to her. She thought it was important
too, since it was the only fresh food they could get. Sometimes
Minna felt her husband was too unconcerned with the household
and family. But time had only brought increasing pressures for
him, and he was glad enough to leave family matters to her.
Knowing she had Marianna's help also reinforced the sharp division
of roles between them. But it was his interest that she missed more
than the physical help. She would have liked to talk things over
more—the things she was concerned with—the children, their
lessons, his advice on the garden. Most often she was the listener, as
he talked over his questions and worries. She was the one person to
whom he could really unburden himself. Late in the evening was
almost the only time of the day. '*Komm zu Bett, Papa?*' (Won't you
come to bed?). If he did not stay working in his study, they would
talk in bed, the low voices a background murmur to the younger
children as they slept in the other end of the long sleepout at the
back of the house.

As ever, Albrecht was worrying not only about the mission
but also about the whole situation of Aborigines in Central
Australia. Change was in the air, but no-one knew quite what form
it would take. Strehlow had been pressing for action on the Haasts
Bluff block. He also wanted a small reserve at Jay Creek, where
unemployed Aborigines could live away from town and receive
their rations. The reserve was declared in July, but there was no
sign of the necessary buildings or the truck he had been promised.

Stirrings of concern were starting in government circles about
the people on unoccupied Crown lands. Scalp depots—where
people could buy rations with dingo scalps—were discussed for
Ilbilla, Ajanti near Mount Liebig, and the Petermann Ranges.
Albrecht was pleased to feel that at long last something might be
done for the people in these areas. But he also felt it was crucial that

these depots be supervised by suitable people. Strehlow agreed, saying that the government had no-one suitable and that it would have to be someone from the churches.

As board chairman, Riedel was cautious about the new possibilities, wondering if the government would foot the bill for staff at any new depots. His concept of Christian mission was still largely traditional—compact mission stations where work could be provided, women and children protected from interference, and intensive Christian teaching available. He distrusted the idea of the large reserve, an idea which had been pushed for years by groups like the Aborigines' Friends' Association, thinking it was more realistic to accept that in the Australian community European interests would always be paramount. One might as well bow to the inevitable, and let land go to grazing and mineral interests, since it was impossible to police a large reserve properly.

His opinions were shaped by logic, caution and the always limited finances, as well as by faith, and in many ways they were far in spirit from his man in the field in Central Australia. Albrecht still worked under the board's authority. Yet at a deeper level, he was now operating out of his own ten years of experience among European and Aboriginal in the Centre. There were people in the southern churches who felt he was too concerned with the physical welfare of the Aborigines. Albrecht knew it, but most of the time it did not trouble him. 'You can't preach to people if they have nothing in their stomachs', he would say, pointing to the fact that Jesus fed people as well as taught them. 'You have to deal with the whole person. You can't separate body and soul.'

Winds of change were stirring, yet much remained unchanged. The mission on the Finke still received an annual government subsidy of only £360—around one tenth of its operating costs. The £400 debt on the Kaporilja pipeline was finally paid off only because the editor of the Melbourne *Argus* rather reluctantly agreed to Albrecht's request—underlined by the gift of a boomerang—to run another subscription. In Alice Springs, a mission friend from South Australia called Koschade tried to stimulate interest and funds by a public slide show of photographs he had taken on a camel trip west. Every Aborigine around town turned out to see it. The only Europeans present were the Johannsens and the Reverend Harry Griffiths.

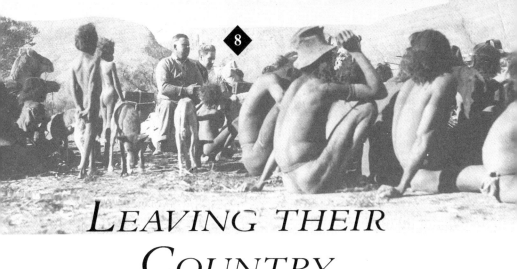

LEAVING THEIR COUNTRY

1938~1939

There was spear-throwing, shot putt, tug of war, high jump, obstacle racing—you know, had to crawl under these big camp sheets. Billycan racing, billycan on head and weren't allowed to spill any water. Kids did racing for different ages. Hop, step and jump, high and long jump. Mr Latz and all the staff arranged it. Aboriginal people used to come from all over the place.

Christmas of 1937 brought some rain and a cooler change, which was especially appreciated by the competitors at the sports on Boxing Day, or 'Third Christmas Day' as people called it, after the traditional German celebration. An eclectic mix of forty to fifty events were contested. Spear-throwing was popular. In one kind, competitors pitted their skills by throwing spears at a wooden target. The other tested the skill of a human target to jump and dodge spears coming at him from a number of men. Titus, who had come in from the west for Christmas, won easily.

Albrecht had always encouraged the sports days, feeling they were some substitute for the loss of their past ceremonial life. Sometimes he had suggested that some of the non-secret ceremonies ('play-about' corroborees as he termed them) be revived for this purpose. But the elders had been against it implying that, even

117

in these, there were still connections to their former beliefs, and Albrecht guessed that Carl Strehlow's injunctions were still important for the older Christians. Even so, the issue of traditional ceremonial life was never completely clear-cut. Some degree of ceremonial activity (especially initiation) obviously went on even among the Christians, even if it was not explicitly discussed with him. Albrecht's theology could not support it, but he was also a realist, and felt he had to accept it to some degree. But he never lost an opportunity to urge people toward another way.

When I was a boy at Hermannsburg, my uncle take me away for mak'im man. When I finish, come back night time, I think he [Pas' Albrecht] might be know this, me like his son. He turn around and say, Oh, you man now eh? You man in the bush, eh, your culture, but what does God say? You got to be a man in the Word of God!

Eighty people attended the Christmas services at the Jay, and over two hundred in Alice Springs. Albrecht duplicated a special order of service and sent copies to the evangelists. He hoped that some people would learn the Scripture passages and hymns by heart, and thereby the deeper meaning of the celebrations would take root in their hearts. It was a busy time, and the number of services he had taken in town and at the Jay was only possible because of a Chevrolet utility truck which had been given to the mission by southern friends earlier in the year.

By early January, the evangelists who had come in for Christmas had to return to their places. Moses and Martin had little to carry, since they received weekly rations in Alice Springs, supplied partly by the mission and partly by the federal government. William, who was going to Henbury to help an older Christian stockman called Gamaliel, managed to put his supplies on one camel, but four beasts were needed to transport Titus and Gustav, their supplies for six months, and the Christmas treats to the western camp at Alalbi. Titus had told Albrecht at Christmas that he considered some of the western people had developed sufficiently in their faith to receive baptism. Albrecht was cautious. Those in question were still young, and he felt that the tribal conditions in which they had to live and prove themselves as true Christians after baptism were very difficult. He felt it would be wise to wait.

The Albrecht family plans for their three-year furlough were disrupted by an outbreak of infantile paralysis in Adelaide. People

were strongly advised not to bring their children south, so Albrecht
went alone for brief consultation with the board. When he returned
in early March 1938, he was accompanied by the new governess for
his children. Elizabeth Rohde was the daughter of a Lutheran pastor
in Freeling, on the edge of the Barossa Valley. Aware of a certain
restrictiveness in this staid rural background, she jumped at the
chance in her sixteenth year to go to the mission station in Central
Australia.

Even the ride north on the train called 'The Ghan' after the
Afghan cameleers of the inland was an experience. Sitting at the
open window to catch any movement of air, however hot, she
noted the steady build-up of soot on the once white cuffs of her
navy college uniform. At Port Augusta, they changed trains, and
she noticed with curiosity that the pastor put on khaki clothes. She
had never seen a minister in khaki before. He had a box of food
with him as there was no diner on the train and, when the train
stopped at stations for mealtimes, he went up to the engine for hot
water to make a pot of tea for them.

The governess's first months in her new post were not easy.
She was cordially welcomed by Minna, but her German was rusty,
and she found it difficult to join in the household conversations in
German. But she admired Minna also, sensing the difficulties she
faced in not being fluent in either Aranda or English—feeling at
the same time her adaptability, the way she could welcome anyone,
the genuine rapport with a Governor-General's wife who spoke
German with her and came into the kitchen to help with the meal.

Sundays were their own form of trial. To Minna, religious
teaching was an essential part of her children's upbringing. When
they were dressed and ready for church, she sat them in the lounge
room and read to them from a collection of sermons by Louis
Harms. The language was already archaic, and the content hardly
geared for children or their sixteen-year-old governess. But it was
important to Minna, and she persisted. Sunday afternoons were
nice, and it was a time when Albrecht also relaxed. He often went
out on to the swing on the front verandah, and it was rarely long
before some of the older Aboriginal men appeared and gathered on
the verandah to talk. Often Moses held the floor, telling stories out
of his prodigious memory, his listeners rapt with attention.

Bryan Bowman's mother had been a guest in the home. Bryan
had moved from his position as manager of Tempe Downs station,
and bought Glen Helen station. Bowman was an intelligent man
who learned bushcraft from the Aboriginal people in his area and

treated them with respect, though a total lack of sentimentality. He got on well with Albrecht, respecting his competence, his obvious commitment to Aborigines, and his wide-ranging intelligence. They could talk about almost anything, and Bowman appreciated the missionary's capacity to take a joke against himself. 'The ways of God are beyond understanding', Albrecht told him one day. It was obviously raining at Glen Helen, but the sky at the mission was clear, though the run badly needed rain. 'Ah, Mr Albrecht, you see the devil looks after his own.' They both laughed. It was a relationship of respect more than close friendship. Partly, it was customary to treat ministers with a degree of formality. And doubtless there was in Albrecht, for all his genuine friendliness, a certain reserve, further reinforced by his awareness of the implications of being superintendent. The complexities of that role both within the mission and in the outside world allowed little scope for the totally personal. That was reserved for Minna.

There were other staff changes early in 1938. In view of his difficulties in mastering Aranda, Werner Petering had accepted a call to the parish of Hahndorf, South Australia. Ruth Pech, with her command of Aranda and general competence, took charge of the school following the departure of William Raatz, who had taught at the mission for several years. An older man called Hermann Vogelsang was appointed to run the store and help with the garden.

The mission had received a small government contract to make the Palm Valley track fit for a vehicle. The Administrator of the Territory, C. L. A. Abbott, and the wife of the Victorian Governor, Lady Huntingfield, were to pay a visit to the mission and to the famous Valley of Palms, and it was thought more suitable if Lady Huntingfield could go in a vehicle rather than the donkey wagon. Lady Huntingfield proved a cordial visitor. She was interested to meet the Aboriginal artist, Albert, who with continuing encouragement from Rex Battarbee was becoming skilled in capturing the Central Australian landscape through traditional European techniques of water-colour and canvas. Like most visitors, she was very interested in the large mission garden. Albrecht's efforts since the middle of 1935 to bring water from the well on the other side of the Finke had finally been successful. A Mrs Shaw from Grassdale, Victoria, who came on a tour and stayed a few days in the Albrecht home, donated a Macson pump; the Melbourne firm of A. H. Macdonald sold the mission a Diesel engine at half the usual price, and Mr Lange of Appila gave another ten-foot windmill. The efforts had been rewarded by an ample supply of vegetables for months.

A farmer at Greenoch, South Australia, called Erhardt Materne had come with two other mission supporters to Central Australia in July 1938. They camped with Albrecht in the dry creek bed of the Todd River adjacent to the Aboriginal reserve, joined the Lutheran church service under the gum trees, and stayed a few days in the Albrecht home. Returning to the south, Erhardt Materne took with him a collection of Aboriginal curios and articles made on the mission, a sense of gratitude for hospitality enjoyed, and a lively awareness that 'Missionary Albrecht' and his staff were taxed to the limit, and working sometimes without the barest essentials. The result was a cordial letter of thanks and an offer from his father to pay for the building of a church and goods shed in Alice Springs. It was for the old man a thanks offering to God for his recovery from a serious illness. For Albrecht, it was a gift from heaven.

The need for a church in Alice Springs had become more and more pressing, and he had written about it to Riedel several times earlier in the year. He thought the Aboriginal people could hardly feel that the Lutherans had much interest in them, with not one building, and still holding services in the creek bed. It was most unsatisfactory anyway, with wind, dust storms and camp dogs to contend with. Inexplicably, Riedel and the other board members had not been particularly encouraging. They quashed his suggestion to a mission friend in the south that a special building fund be designated, and cautioned him about the costs of corrugated iron for the roof. They eventually approved his suggestion to purchase a block of land opposite the Aboriginal reserve, but remonstrated when he bought an extra area himself in order to include a shed, which he thought would be useful accommodation for anyone coming in to town. Riedel with his usual logic told him that if the extra land and shed were necessary, the cost was a matter for the mission board. Albrecht replied with considerable chagrin:

> You wrote that you cannot understand that I bought a block of land to build a shed: if that is necessary, then it would be up to the mission to do so. I fully agree. But after the question of building a little church in Alice found so much opposition, you should understand I was not game to ask for a room. On the other side, as I point out to you before, I am sick of camping in the creek. I work so hard and when I arrive in Alice I am quite exhausted and need to have a rest. But in summer there is no peace because of ants and dogs. Then I never know whether my tent will not be washed away by sudden

floods, or at least, I get rather wet. I don't want to complain, I put up with a lot of unpleasant things—if necessary. After I worked myself to a standstill at the station, then attend to all sorts of things at the Jay, I think I am entitled to an undisturbed night's rest at Alice.

Albrecht's typed page of specifications and materials for the new church was simplicity itself. The building would be 30 feet long, 20 feet wide and 12 feet high. There were four windows, each 6 feet by 3 feet 1 inch (measured outside the frame); two doors, one 4 feet wide, the other 3 feet wide, both of 'ordinary height'. The sides would take 66 sheets of corrugated iron, the ends 38 sheets, the roof 66 of 6 foot iron . . .

Seven Aboriginal men supervised by Mattner finished the church and nearby shed in mid-December, and the bell that had been kept from the little bush church of Ernest Kramer and used for years to call people to the services in the creek was erected in front of the new church. The buildings were sited opposite the Aboriginal reserve. Albrecht had come to feel that building on the reserve itself would make the mission forever dependent on government, and subject to the whims and vagaries of its policies. A week before Christmas, about two hundred people met for a last service under the old gum tree, then formed into a long processional to walk to the new church for its dedication.

Two weeks earlier, in the Fine Arts Gallery in Melbourne, the first full-scale exhibition of Albert's water-colours had been brought before the Australian public. Rex Battarbee arranged the exhibition, and Lady Huntingfield agreed to open it. All of the forty-two paintings sold in a week, and Albert received a cheque for £140. It was a far cry from the response only eighteen months before when Albrecht had taken ten canvases priced at five and ten shillings each to the church synod at Nuriootpa to try to sell them. Only four sold, one lady from Victoria telling Missionary Albrecht she could not possibly hang the paintings of an unknown black man in her living room. Disappointed for Albert, Albrecht bought two himself, and others in the following year. Several he gave as gifts to individuals who had been particularly generous to the mission. Prior to the Melbourne exhibition, it was suggested to Albert that it might be fitting to include a surname in his signature. His first paintings had simply been signed 'Albert', since Aborigines at the mission and elsewhere in the Northern Territory had no European-style surnames. Albert chose the Aboriginal name that his father had before he took the name of Jonathon at baptism, and Australians heard for the first time the name of Albert Namatjira.

Late in 1938, Albrecht was planning the four months of furlough due in the new year. Already he had received many requests for preaching and speaking engagements. He asked Riedel if there might be an old car available for his use. It was not absolutely essential, he emphasized, but reducing his travelling time would give him more time with his family—and he was unable to resist the equal pull of promoting the work of the mission:

Also with a car I could visit friends of the mission which I could not do otherwise . . . I think personal contact means a lot to our friends. I have taken recently a lot of photographs which I would like to show . . .

Doubtless it was inevitable, as he sat at his old typewriter in the study in Central Australia, that he would cherish the hope that four months in the south, plus the use of a car, would enable him to do the impossible—maximize the opportunities with mission supporters and also spend time with his family. Not surprisingly, it did not work out like that. Speaking requests came from all sides, and even Riedel had trouble finding a time that the missionary could speak to his congregation. Pastor W. E. Wiencke observed privately to Riedel that the missionary was far too busy, and was unable to have any real holiday. Minna herself felt that the family was neglected. Their third son, Martin, born on the twelfth of April, was baptized several Sundays later, and she was nettled to find that speaking engagements had been arranged for that day as well.

Albrecht was also researching tanning, as he believed they would have to move into boot production if the tanning of bullock hides was to be stepped up. He had brought a part-Aboriginal man called Manasse to South Australia with him, and arranged for him to work in R. M. Williams's tannery at Prospect. Manasse was progressing well in the work, but he was very homesick and Albrecht wondered how long he could tolerate the strange environment. His peace of mind was not aided by a letter in early May from Ruth Pech, informing him that she would resign if he was not back by the end of June. He knew that she was simply overworked.

The mission was approaching a staffing crisis. Mattner would be seventy in October, and planned to return to his family in September. Art Latz could manage the stock, but Mattner had been invaluable for building and repairs around the station. Petering's departure the previous year had required Ruth Pech and Albrecht to assist Hermann Vogelsang in managing the store. And Ruth's family wanted her home by the end of the year. Riedel had been looking for staff, but there were no immediate prospects for a handyman or a teacher, let alone a second missionary. Nor was it easy to find suitable people. It was not enough that people had a strong Christian faith, it was virtually essential that they master Aranda. And they needed to be adaptable. Albrecht told himself he would rather do without staff if they could not work with other people.

Albrecht had made a trip west in July of the previous year, 1938. As usual on the return journey, the camel party carried dingo scalps, curios, and kangaroo, euro and wallaby skins collected by the people around Haasts Bluff. They would be turned into cash at the store and provisions bought which would be sent out on camels. Albrecht felt this arrangement gave the western people a feeling of belonging to the larger community, and satisfied some of their curiosity about the new foods. At the same time, they could live their own lives.

He was still very uneasy at the government's failure to act decisively on the Haasts Bluff block. The ministerial action in 1936 had merely ensured that the current grazing licence over the area could not be renewed. There was no reason why others might not be issued, and the present lessee of the block had recently sent out a man to dig for water, with the apparent intention of stocking the block with sheep. These activities had not gone unnoticed by the tribal people, who sent Albrecht several messages and letters, asking if they would be driven out of their country. Albrecht felt it cruel and deplorable that nothing had been done to remove the uncertainty hanging over them.

His views were very close to those of the patrol officer, Ted Strehlow, who had received little official response to a number of comprehensive reports he had written, the first almost two years before. Writing again in early August 1938, he argued in the strongest terms that no other white civilized country had annihilated its indigenous population as thoughtlessly as Australia. Now, 'the whole future of the natives in Central Australia balances upon the decision of the present Federal Government: a wise and immediate decision of the Government alone can still save the balance of the native population in Central Australia . . .' He had pushed vigorously for two extensions to the large reserve. However, like Albrecht, he felt that the mere existence of the reserve served little for its inhabitants, since 'the policy of isolation is impracticable. The vast majority of the natives, employed or nomadic, are in close and constant touch with the white settlers, and will not consider going back to the culture of the Stone Age'. Most of the officially estimated 1200 inhabitants had left to settle around cattle stations and ration depots. Doggers, prospectors and travellers had made them familiar with European food and clothing, and life in the reserve was relatively insecure.

Strehlow argued that the history of the Hermannsburg mission proved that, with positive action, Aboriginal groups need not necessarily 'peter out' at the contact with white civilization, as was often assumed. Where the other Aranda groups that came into contact with Europeans soon after the opening of the Overland Telegraph Line were now on the verge of extinction, the Western Aranda group had survived to the present day with the same approximate numbers of sixty years before. With numbers of the third and fourth mission-born generations now increasing, the continued existence of the group seemed assured. They had had significant advantages with the continuing access to traditional territory, protection of family life, medical help and some employment opportunities. And he also felt that the mission teaching had been a helpful influence, especially for the younger people in their inevitable transition to a new culture.

The general principles successful at Hermannsburg could, he argued, be applied to the central reserve. A ration depot should be established in the heart of the Petermann Ranges for the benefit of the Pitjantjatjara people, and another near Mount Liebig for the Pintubi tribe but, apart from cases of illness, rations should be given only in exchange for trade articles like dingo scalps, Aboriginal implements, or ceremonial objects. With these depots established, the existing ones at Alice Springs and Charlotte Waters could be closed, and any old and infirm Aranda people in Alice Springs transferred to the Jay Creek reserve. He felt strongly that the ration depots along the railway line had had a disastrous effect on the life of the tribes living adjacent to them.

Knowing the urgency for government action on these questions, Strehlow had kept touch with Albrecht on furlough in the south in the first months of 1939, warning him that the Director of the newly created Department of Native Affairs, E. W. P. Chinnery, was coming down from Darwin for consultation. To Albrecht and Strehlow, as well as to many others concerned with Aboriginal issues, Chinnery's appointment was a hope for a new era in Commonwealth Aboriginal policy. Chinnery had worked in the Australian administration in Papua and the mandated territories within a very different ethos and attitude towards indigenous peoples. In early June, a message came that Chinnery had arrived, and the Albrecht family took the first train north.

A starting point for the discussions with Chinnery had already been established in an earlier comprehensive report which Albrecht had prepared at Chinnery's request. It outlined the extensive efforts to provide employment and to create industries. At the same time, Albrecht emphasized that these industries at best helped some individuals to make a little better living for themselves, but could not provide basic support for families. The continuing existence of the whole Aranda group had only been possible through the special efforts of Lutherans in South Australia and Victoria. He asked that government support of the vulnerable groups—women, children, and the aged and infirm—be put on a per capita basis, suggesting a figure of four shillings a week per person. He also requested specific items to assist the industries, and the list itself was a telling comment on the paucity of resources: a little cement, tanning tools and some machinery to boost leather production; a lathe and a small power plant for the mulga work; corrugated iron for the workrooms which were still not built ... For the overall situation in Central Australia, Albrecht stressed the need for action on the Haasts Bluff block, and for the Alice Springs ration depot to be transferred to the Jay. Like Strehlow, he felt it could not be more urgent. 'Of most of ... the tribes of Central Australia, there are only remnants left ... We hope that you, Sir, will be able to see that our Natives are not disappearing of necessity, but only as a result of neglect and indifference.'

The meetings with Chinnery went well. The Director seemed convinced of the need to declare the Haasts Bluff area a reserve, promised government assistance with a number of items, and told Albrecht to submit quotes for the cement, corrugated iron and machinery he had requested. The declaration of Haasts Bluff as a reserve would be sufficient for the people there for a time, since a degree of supportive contact already existed by virtue of the mission outpost. But the question of the Petermann Ranges area was still unresolved. So many Aboriginal people drifting around the southern stations seemed to be Pitjantjatjara from the Petermanns that it was obvious they had been leaving their home area in considerable numbers. There was no likelihood they would return unless it was made more secure for them, and positive support provided. Worse still, a letter had been received at the Lands Office in Darwin suggesting that, since the Aborigines had virtually left already, the reserve be thrown open to pastoralists.

The landscape watercolour paintings of Rex Battarbee created a sensation among Hermannsburg Aborigines and attracted the interest of Albert Namatjira when, at Albrecht's suggestion, Battarbee first exhibited them at the mission in 1932. (above) Tribal Aborigines around Haasts Bluff look at paintings by Rex Battarbee during his early visits to that area in the mid 1930s. (below) Albert Namatjira and his father, Jonathon. Photograph by the late Reverend S. O. Gross.

*Mission staff in the 1930s.
From left, Werner Petering
(second missionary) and his
wife Marjorie, Art Latz
(stockman) and his wife Dora,
William Raatz (teacher) in
front. Photographed at Palm
Valley by Rex Battarbee.
(Battarbee Collection, South
Australian Museum)*

*Minna and Friedrich Albrecht
and children, c. 1939. From
right, clockwise, Min, Helene,
Theo, Martin, Paul. (Fehlburg
Collection, South Australian
Museum)*

Petermann people frightened at an aeroplane, women and children ran into bushes to hide. Witch doctor thought it was big debbil, and tried to bring it down with woomera. They left their country then, and came to Tempe Downs.

Pressed on the matter, Chinnery was noncommittal. It was decided that Strehlow and Albrecht would undertake an expedition to the area to provide a first-hand report. They could find out what Aboriginal people were still there, and if there were sites with enough water to establish a depot with a European overseer. Charles Duguid, and the Reverend Harry Taylor from the infant Presbyterian mission at Ernabella in the Musgrave Ranges, were invited as informed and interested parties, and Oswald Heinrich, a farmer on Yorke Peninsula, would come as mechanic. The Europeans would travel by truck to Piltardi on the eastern end of the Petermann Range, and proceed from there by camel. Going by truck they would miss places where Aborigines walked about and camped, and contacting them was the aim of the expedition.

A five-hundred-mile round trip to the Petermanns could not be undertaken lightly. Extra canteens were constructed for carrying water, since much of the territory was unknown. Two wireless sets would be taken—the old mission one which had to be pedalled, and a new Traeger battery transceiver which would have its first testing on the trip. Several weeks in advance, the team of twelve camels with its supplies of flour, salt, meat and sugar was sent with three Aboriginal men on the two-hundred-mile journey across country via Ayers Rock to Piltardi rockhole on the eastern end of the Petermann Ranges. The Europeans of the party met up at Ernabella mission, and started west in two trucks towards Piltardi. The country was mostly open, apart from small patches of mulga. Looking across the undulating spinifex plains to the north, they could see the huge monoliths of Mount Conner and Ayers Rock on the horizon. The trucks gave no serious trouble apart from dozens of punctures from dry mulga stakes broken off near the ground. Piltardi, about eighty miles due west of Ayers Rock, was a beautiful hole of clear deep water almost surrounded by steeply rising cliffs—a natural reservoir for rain falling on the range above.

From Piltardi, they set off by camel along the northern side of the range, guided by an Aboriginal man called Tjointjara whom they had found with his son by a small fire the evening before. Good rains had fallen very recently. The gum trees were showing fresh young tips, and green shoots were everywhere. But it was obvious that a severe drought had ravaged the area in the last year or so. There was not a kangaroo or wallaby to be seen and, without the larger game, Albrecht felt a stillness, almost an eeriness, such as he had rarely encountered in his camel trips in the west. In the first few days of travelling, they saw no sign of people, though they came across many old camp sites. In some, as many as a dozen hollows indicated the number of people who had slept there. To the Europeans, it was difficult to imagine sleeping naked in the freezing winter nights. Aborigines typically kept themselves warm by building some kind of windbreak for the head, scooping out a little hollow to lie in, and building a fire between each person. With another fire at the foot end of each, some degree of warmth spread across everybody. From the number of these large campsites, all of them old, it was obvious that a large number of people must have lived there not long ago, and had either left or died. For all their thick clothes and blankets, the Europeans were cold at night; in the mornings, the tarpaulins under which they slept were white with frost. Even the days were cold, despite heavy clothes and coats. Sometimes a bitter wind blew all day.

About fifty miles west of Lasseter's grave, they came to the cave where he had lived for several months. A little way up the bank of the Hull River, the cave entrance looked out on dry creek sand and mulga scrub stretching away on the other side. It was here that he had written his journal and the letters to his family. Thirty yards from the cave was a good soak in the bed of the river, and it was clear that Lasseter must have got his water from there. The party was out of water, so Ted Strehlow set to work digging a deep hole in the sand. There were shells on the walls of the hole, and gradually the water began to trickle in. They needed at least twenty gallons, and it took two and a half hours to fill the water canteens.

A few days later, they met an Aboriginal man called Paling-kana. He was a tall man, perhaps about sixty-five years old. He went with them as they continued west to the Docker River, a permanent spring of water in a flat expanse of rocks not far from the Western Australian border. Fifty or sixty miles to the south, a low outcrop of ranges was visible on the horizon, and the party debated whether to go there. Perhaps there were people there. Asked about it, Palingkana's response was a firm *Wia* (No!). When he understood they might proceed without him, he responded more vehemently still. Gradually, an explanation emerged. On the distant range were the bones of many people who had died there. They had never been buried, and he did not want the European people to see them lying about. The party was silenced. Palingkana accompanied them as they started back east, and more of the story was pieced together. There had been a very long drought, in which all the temporary waters in the district had dried up. The water in that range had been expected to last until it rained again. When the last water turned into mud, the stronger members of the tribe went north to the permanent spring at the Docker. But mothers with small children and the older people could do nothing but remain there.

Two men had walked into the camp at the Docker River. They carried no spears, showing they were unafraid, and later they brought their families. Another man with a wife and child and an old woman also appeared. They had recently given their dingo scalps to some European doggers in the reserve in return for food. The party had seen the tracks of a camel buggy the previous day, and Strehlow made a report by wireless to Perth of this illegal entry of the reserve. The two men were fined when they returned to civilization, but the fine would have been negligible compared to the government bounties paid for the scalps.

Several other family groups were contacted on the return journey to Piltardi. Some made the journey back with them, vigorously striding ahead of the line of camels and their riders. They had no food apart from the bushtucker they collected each day. But extra damper had been baked on the last day at the Docker, and everyone shared in the camp meal each night. There were several babies amongst them, and the Europeans, especially those from the south, observed with interest how the mothers handled and carried them. From a very early age, the babies became used to being carried on the back, and spent much of the day asleep, despite the miles of walking. Babies too small to grasp their mothers' necks or shoulders were slung around the back of the waist, and held loosely in position by the mother's joined arms.

Women on the march also carried pitchis—large wooden containers in which they put food collected on the way—balanced on circular wads on their heads. Even with these loads, and striding along with digging stick and a lighted firestick for warmth, they kept a lookout for edible roots, or any little track that might lead to a lizard or other small animal. As Albrecht had often sympathetically observed in his trips to the west, it was often the women who kept the family going, supplying not only their children but often their husbands as well. Even when game was about, the hunters were not always successful, and in calm weather could come back empty-handed for many days. But they also noticed that, in the faster travel with the camel party, the men took turns in carrying the babies.

Duguid noticed a well-built lad of about sixteen who travelled somewhat apart from the group. He was not circumcised, which seemed unusual for his age. Each night a girl of about twelve went over to his camp two hundred yards away. Duguid learned later that it was his sister, and that she took him food. Since ceremonies could take place only when food and water were sufficient for a large number, the prolonged drought had probably delayed the initiation for several years.

Both Heinrich and Duguid had cameras with them, and the photographs they took must have been among the last obtained of Australian Aborigines in virtually undisturbed bush life. Albrecht stood beside Ossie one day as he photographed two women. The older one was resting. Her breasts and limbs were thin and scrawny, and she looked tired as she sat on the ground, digging stick in hand. The other woman stood by her side waiting, two pitchis on her head. To Albrecht, the scene signalled danger. The older woman could no longer keep up with the younger women. If it happened repeatedly and the progress of the group was hindered, the old men would eventually decide that she had to be left behind. A little water and some firewood would be left her as a last act of grace. 'The older people know this is the sign that they should stay behind, and they do. The early explorers reported finding old people like this from time to time.'

He recalled a little family he had encountered on a camel trek in the country around Mount Liebig. The man had lost the soles of his feet through some disease. With the flesh underfoot like raw meat, he could not walk with the tribe and had been left behind. His wife was with him and two babies, one about six months and the other about two years old. She was scouring the whole area for what little she could find in roots, lizards, mice and other small fare. She was terribly thin, but still breastfeeding her two infants. The camel party left what food they could with them, and learned later that they had survived. But it was obvious to Albrecht why Aborigines, given a chance of greater security, would leave their home areas. A sense of the hardship inherent in bush life was very deep in him.

Cultural curiosity was not only one-way. One evening meal of tea, salt beef and damper was concluded on a festive note with Ossie Heinrich playing his piano accordion and Charles Duguid dancing a Highland Fling, to the great amusement of the bush people. On the final day, the Aborigines were paid for their scalps, and a last meal was shared together. Ossie Heinrich had been wondering what they could give the people as a gift. He thoroughly cleaned a gallon oil can, and fitted it with a wire handle. Tjointjara was very pleased. It was ideal for carrying water.

But the Europeans were subdued. Only twenty-six people had been found in the five weeks of travelling on both sides of the Petermann Ranges. Plainly, many more had once lived here, perhaps the five hundred estimated by the Mackay aerial mapping expedition of a few years before. Most had either left or perished in the drought. Each of the party felt privileged to have shared briefly in their tribal life, but could feel only a deep uncertainty about their future. Nothing stood in the way of increasing European intrusion into their land and way of life, and no provision existed to help them in the event of another disastrous drought.

As soon as he could after his return, Albrecht wrote to Riedel and to Reverend John Sexton of the Aborigines' Friends' Association. What he had seen in the Petermanns had not surprised him, but the rapidity at which this depopulating process had proceeded had shocked him deeply. It was absolutely urgent that something be done there before the last remnant of Pitjantjatjara were scattered, and the hundreds now drifting around settlement were totally dispersed.

Albrecht tried to account for the numbers of people who must have been there only a few short years before. Donald Mackay had reported in 1936 that his camp at the Docker River had been visited by between 150 and 200 people, and had estimated the total number in the area as around 500. Later there had been reports that many had gone south to the East–West railway. Albrecht himself had noticed Pitjantjatjara people from the Petermanns everywhere. About 70 were near Kings Creek on Tempe Downs station, and William had counted 64 near Middleton Ponds station the year before. There were well over 100 in Alice Springs and another 80 near the Finke Siding. Twenty or so had even found their way north to the people at Haasts Bluff. Writing to Sexton:

It is obvious that they cannot be left under present conditions: within a very short time, the last trace of tribal cohesion will be gone, ordered family life cease to exist, and these homeless and aimless wanderers will have died out, as has happened everywhere where they have been left to their fate. Also it is a fact that these people would develop gradually and on sound, natural lines, only in their home district. Here they have their sacred waterholes, their caves, it is here where their spirit world lives, and where they find all the places dear to them from their fathers. For some considerable time they will find life worth living only here. It would be possible to congregate them elsewhere and see that they would not suffer want. But is not the price these people would be asked to pay far too much? Should it not be within reach of our Government to see that the future of these people is safeguarded: even if it costs more. The many wrongs they have suffered in the past should be a further inducement to do the best that can be done for them. And this is nothing less but that they should be brought back to their home districts and allowed to live, also by supporting them to such a degree as to assure their wellbeing.

Seeing Ernabella had convinced him that it was unrealistic to hope that the Presbyterians could initiate work in the Petermann Ranges. As a centre, they were barely established themselves. If anything was to be done, it would have to be done through Hermannsburg, despite the difficulty of distance. With typical pragmatism, he sketched out a rough proposal to build a shorter motor route to the area, and a rations shed and small room at Piltardi. The depot could be looked after by an older man, with the mission sending two Christian Aboriginal families to live there and work among the people in the area. If the government would provide the overseer's wages, clothing and rations for the families, and a truck to carry out rations every four months, it would be enough to get the scheme working.

Riedel's response was tentative. He was cautious about the financial commitments and afraid the depot plan might end up as merely another 'feeding station'. Writing in the first week of September 1939, a few days after Britain declared war on Germany following Hitler's invasion of Poland, he ended the letter on a more personal note:

> Brother Vogelsang mentioned that you are not well. Please, don't let us know only how all the others are, but also how you are yourself. This is most important. Now we have to tolerate in our lifetime another war ... How would your people in Poland be faring?

A second missionary had been appointed, and Pastor Sam Gross and his wife and three children arrived in early October. With Mattner gone, the station was busier than it had ever been. The weather was dry, and Art Latz was working with a team of men to reopen some of the older wells. The big garden and its workers needed a vigilant eye. The store, managed for the most part by Hermann Vogelsang, was steadily increasing in its annual turnover. Tanning work was stepping up, and the first boots to be produced on the mission were being made by Manasse who had returned from the south in June. As December drew near, the busy superintendent and his staff began to prepare to celebrate Christmas with the largest number of people ever in contact with the mission. With folk at Alice Springs, Jay Creek, the cattle stations to the south, and the outpost at Haasts Bluff, as well as the Hermannsburg community, almost a thousand people would be involved.

After the initial discussions on the Petermann area with government officers, Albrecht had heard nothing. He felt he should be doing more to pressure them, but he really had no time. He thought that the government officials appreciated the fact that the people would be better off brought back to their home districts, but the war was beginning to dominate every discussion about finance. 'May God show us the way to help those poor people', he often thought. There was one positive outcome from the journey. Given the clear advocacy of every member of the expedition, the question of throwing the reserve open to pastoralists was quietly put aside. The Petermann Ranges would remain Aboriginal reserve land.

STIRRINGS FROM GOVERNMENT
1940~1942

Titus became boss for people around there. Other people were the bosses of each group, the landowners, Aboriginal business. Titus kept out of that. He was only boss in the life of the congregation, he helped fix up fights between groups, helping keep people separate, like Warlpiri from Loritja, like umpire. He was ingkata, *trying to get people to live in peace. People lived in different groups, came together for devotions. Sit 'em down different groups, talk together to stop fights.*

The boxes of 'Christmas cheer' arriving from the south towards the end of 1940 were weighed, noted in a store book, and the contents carefully unpacked by Minna, Dora Latz and Else Gross with the help of Aboriginal women. A parcel was prepared for each person at the station, for visitors and for Aboriginal people living elsewhere who were in contact with the mission. Ruth Pech, with the help of Elizabeth Rohde, made parcels for the schoolchildren and held choir practices almost every evening in preparation for Christmas services. Pastor Gross and Art Latz arranged the sports for Third Christmas Day. Old Abel roamed the sandhills for days looking for Christmas trees, and there was a last-minute influx of leather articles, fancywork and mulga work to be sold to the store. People liked to have a little money at Christmas to buy extras.

The great hour finally arrived and 382 people at the station were handed parcels on Christmas Eve afternoon. It warmed Albrecht's heart even more to see that many had saved a little money for a special thanks offering to send to the British and Foreign Bible Society which was planning to print the whole New Testament in Aranda. The collection came to £3 2s 1d. 'What an expression of gratitude', he wrote in a January newsletter to mission friends. 'It is one of their weakest points not being able to keep anything for the morrow. But in this case they succeeded admirably.'

An Aboriginal stockman called Gamaliel who had become an important Christian influence at Henbury station arrived the day after Christmas with ten other people. Gamaliel had come to Hermannsburg some years before to get married. His wife-to-be had married someone else, but Gamaliel had remained and become a Christian. From being an acclaimed rain-maker in his district, he had turned his considerable personal energy and talents towards teaching and encouraging the Christian way among people at Henbury. He could not read or write, but he knew by heart many Bible stories, several hymns, and the entire contents of Luther's Small Catechism. The people with him were eager to show Albrecht their considerable knowledge of the Small Catechism. Bible history was a different story. They were well acquainted with all the events surrounding Christ's birth, suffering, death and resurrection, but questions about Moses posed a problem. 'I don't know him too well myself', remarked Gamaliel.

Albrecht had taken the morning service in Alice Springs on Christmas Eve. Afterwards a number of old men came up to talk. One man had met him and Minna at Deep Well in 1926 on their first journey north. 'I'm only one left of that mob', said the old man. 'Others all pass away.' He had no children. To Albrecht, it seemed all too common a fate for Aboriginal families, and he thought with gratitude of the hundred or more growing children at Hermannsburg. Outside the church, gay red handkerchiefs full of lollies, dried fruits and the coveted honey biscuits were passed out. Two hundred and twenty pounds of 'cake'—bread dough with added dried fruit—had also been brought in, as well as a salted bullock, and forty pounds of mixed tea and sugar.

Hermann Vogelsang was relieving Ted Strehlow at the Jay, and took out a similar stock of food and gifts. But the celebrations there had included more than the Christian festivities. Old Papatjukurpa had a boy of twelve whom he considered old enough for the 'mak'im man' circumcision ceremony, and had persuaded a number of the Haasts Bluff people to come in to the Jay—for Christmas, as they told Moses, but really for the circumcision corroboree. The singing and dancing went on for a week before Christmas, and then they had stayed on to attend the Christmas services. 'They had Christmas with a sideshow', wrote Albrecht in his newsletter He understood the importance of the ceremonies in the former social and religious life of the tribes, but thought it was impossible to reconcile them with a Christian understanding. With his strong sense of the essential disintegration of their former ethos, he felt strongly that their best hope lay in a total grounding in the new faith, fearing that a mingling of old and new would leave them uncertain. Disappointed and a little angry at the holding of the corroboree at Christmas, he prayed nevertheless that the love of Christ might still have been communicated through the services and distribution of gifts.

He wasn't interested in those stories!! That's only rubbish!! You got to believe God! Like witch doctor, he not believe that one, tell them run away. Only one way, he preach to people God's way, he didn't know about this Aboriginal culture. He wasn't interested, so we didn't talk about it to him. Kept that part by ourselves.

In the first week of January, Titus and the evangelists from the other centres returned to the mission for their refresher course. The new missionary, Sam Gross, took part as well, though he had to speak in English. Titus had recently married for the second time, his first wife having died many years before. His new wife was a Pintubi woman from Haasts Bluff and, after a class in the Gross house, Titus stayed behind to ask if he could bring her to see the Christmas tree. When they returned, the blinds were drawn and the tree lit. Beneath, candles illuminated a tiny manger tableau. The shy tribal woman looked at it in wonder as Titus, excited as a child, explained everything, especially the figures depicting the Bethlehem scene.

When Titus and his helpers were ready to return to Alalbi, Albrecht asked him to travel via a new camp of 140 Pitjantjatjara people at Undandita, forty miles to the west. Earlier in the year, Albrecht had received a letter from the manager of Tempe Downs station asking him to shift a large number of bush people who had come into Tempe Downs country. There had been a fight and the manager felt they were interfering with the Aboriginal workers on the station. Manasse and another man went over to investigate, and led the Pitjantjatjara to the Undandita area, a few going further north to Haasts Bluff. Their language was relatively close to that spoken by the Warlpiri and Pintubi people, so communication with Titus and his friends would not be difficult. Titus in particular had proved himself very gifted in his ability to pick up new dialects in the years in the west.

Sam Gross spent the first months of his missionary calling in Central Australia in an eclectic round of tasks. In addition to preaching on most Sundays, he helped with carpentry, gardening, storekeeping, blacksmithing, plumbing, masonry, furniture and floor repairing, servicing the truck, pumping water and attending to dingo scalps. Writing south in January, he mentioned that the Latzes had bought themselves a refrigerator. 'Our experience so far convinces us that a refrigerator cannot altogether be considered a luxury here, with a summer that has so few cool changes and lasts for practically six months.' The Albrechts did not have a refrigerator so they rented a small space in the Latz refrigerator for sixpence a week.

The new schoolteacher, Hilda Wurst, arrived in early February. Her first months were difficult. The children whom Ruth Pech had said she could rely on were the worst, their allegiance still being with their 'Rutapeka'. The school had pitifully few resource materials, and her only assistant with sixty-odd children was Old Abel whose help was limited to keeping discipline and assisting with rote learning.

Albrecht left by camel for Haasts Bluff in the middle of May. The situation there was changing. A number of young people had left and he thought the time was fast approaching when more facilities would have to be established there—a ration depot at least, which could also take their dingo scalps. He also thought that gradually some form of employment had to be provided through which they could earn enough to obtain the amenities of civilization they would inevitably want as they compared their living conditions with those of their people in the settled areas.

But the area was not yet formally a reserve, and that issue had barely left his mind all year. Mealtime conversations revolved around it constantly, and rumours and counter-rumours kept him in painful suspense. Albrecht liked Chinnery personally, but found it hard to understand what was preventing a decision on the block. 'It is very, very hard to understand how anyone with sympathy for the Natives could possibly let a thing like this slip out of his hands', he wrote to Duguid early in August 1940.

He was heartened by what he found at the camp at Alalbi. Over a hundred people were there, only a mile or two from the foot of the Bluff which rose up from the plain like a giant human figure lying on its side and stretching away to the south. Four tribes were living in close proximity—the Pintubi to the western side, Pitjan- tjatjara to the south, Warlpiri on the north, and Loritja and some Aranda on the east. A number of years before, Titus had managed to stop a payback killing between two of the groups. Since then, they had lived peacefully and travelled through other tribal areas without fear.

Albrecht was particularly pleased to notice that there were four newly married young couples in the Alalbi camp. He'd had many discussions with the old men in which he had tried to convince them to modify their marriage customs. In former tradi- tional life, young girls were promised to the old men from a very young age, and the young men were obliged to wait a long time to marry. This had served well in the old days, because the women, as food gatherers, provided security for the old men when they were too old for hunting. In the changing times, however, Albrecht felt the old system did more harm than good. As they became more aware of life elsewhere, the young people were less inclined to respect the dictates of the old men. If a young couple ran away together, they no longer had to return to the tribe and accept whatever punishment was meted out. They could take refuge at cattle stations or other European settlements. Thus the tribe lost its young people and especially its hunters in the young men.

Albrecht had come close to open conflict with the old men on the subject a year or so before, after coming upon a large group with a number of people with spear wounds in their buttocks, and one man with a very severe knee wound—the results of a dispute over the allocation of young girls, most of them not more than eleven or twelve years of age, as additional wives for the old men. Around a campfire after the evening meal, he asked if they couldn't try a different way of arranging marriages. He suggested that since they had been busy distributing young girls to the old men, they should concede the same right to their older women by allowing them to take some of the young unmarried men as additional husbands. This would create a better balance in the community, and they would no longer lose their young hunters.

He was well aware that, under their strict marriage laws, this proposal sounded atrocious. He was told not to talk like that, it was utter rubbish. He replied that he knew that, but reiterated that what they were doing was worse: they only had to look at the fighting and injuries. For a time there was dead silence, then a rustling of spears among some of the men at the back. He explained that he was not trying to ridicule them, but to show them where their present arrangements were leading. Conditions had changed. Why couldn't they have a general meeting before allocating marriageable girls? And let the girls and the young men have some say in the discussions. They would be more content to stay with the tribe, and the whole community would benefit. To his surprise, several spoke up in agreement, and the atmosphere relaxed. Later they finished the meeting with a prayer and Albrecht rolled into his swag quite late.

The camel party departed in the morning after he treated a number of sick people. But he particularly noticed that a large group of women came to say goodbye. It must have been the first time, he thought, that anybody had spoken up for them.

Albrecht used to bring all the people together, have big talks, with young people, young womans, old people, old womans, all the people. Things got to change. They got a bit upset. How come that bloke wants to break our Law, very important Law, and it's all tied together, with the land, and the tjurunga, *and the promise system. And they didn't like it, because it was their Law and a very important Law. So they got really wild. This bloke's coming in, and he's going to change our Law.*

Usually the meetings were after devotions in the evening, and all the people sit around. He might say, what do you people think, now that you're Christians, what about leaving the young women for the young men? They talked between themselves, argued, like they say, the Law is all one piece, can't take a part out, otherwise it will fall down. He never told them they had to do it, he would ask them, what do you think about changing your ways . . .

They could see that there was sense in what he was saying. They tried also to reconcile it all with their gradually emerging awareness of the Christian way, and God's Word—that too had a ring of truth about it. The younger married couples now in the Alalbi camp was evidence that they were realizing that some changes might be for the better.

He also counted eighty-six children in the entire area around the Bluff. Partly this was due to the younger marriages. But he felt it also bespoke a security in their camp life, something he felt had come in part from the years of Christian influence from Titus and the other evangelists. Titus had always been an influence against inter-tribal killings and quarrelling. And he had urged the men to treat their wives better. Sometimes he used the Bible to make his point; at others he was simply pragmatic. 'If you hit your wife too hard', he told one man, 'she might die, and if she does, police will take you away'. But the change in the lives of Aboriginal women was also evident among the Hermannsburg people. Moses sometimes said it was the women who benefited most from the Gospel.

It was ten years since Albrecht's first trip west, and he thought much had been achieved. Where most tribal people left their home areas and lost any spiritual background as well, the people at Alalbi were gradually coming to a faith in God's word. He noticed that many prayed to Jesus in sickness instead of going to their own *ngangkari*, or medicine man. 'Jesus is stronger than the devil' was a statement he had heard more than once. To him, it was proof that the fear of evil spirits, so pervasive in their old life, had largely disappeared. They seemed to feel more safe and secure. But he still thought baptizing any of them was a risk, feeling that only a full-time missionary at Haasts Bluff could really consolidate the teaching that had been started.

The day after his return to Hermannsburg, an investigation of the mission was ordered by the military authorities in Alice Springs after accusations had been made in the federal parliament that Hermannsburg mission staff were Nazis. The investigating officer, a Captain Balfe, inspected the garden and the wireless room where he removed the key for the short-wave transmitter. He declined Albrecht's offer to inspect papers in his study, and reminded him that they had met before in the editor's office at the *Argus* in Melbourne in 1935, when he had written a number of articles about the Kaporilja water scheme in support of the appeal for funds. 'I didn't think', he added quietly, 'that a man who spent his vacation working for the Aborigines would be a Nazi'. He was interested in Albert's paintings, and purchased one and some mulga work before he left. To Albrecht, the search seemed little more than a formality (although the Attorney-General had also questioned Duguid about Hermannsburg) and he hoped the inquiry would set any doubts at rest, at least at an official level. He accepted that the German associations were bound to incur hostility at times, especially from anyone whose financial interests were in conflict with the mission. Comments about 'burning down that bloody German mission' had come from one local person with an interest in the

Haasts Bluff lease. But the original accusations in parliament he felt were little more than a joke.

By the end of August, the Administrator had finally written to Canberra to ask that the Haasts Bluff block be bought for £50 and added to the central reserve. And an unexpected offer of assistance for a church building there had come from Lou Borgelt, a Lutheran garage proprietor from Adelaide. He was raising money for the project by showing home movies of Central Australia and the mission to Lutheran congregations in the south.

But the protracted decision-making in government circles over the ration depot also proposed for Haasts Bluff continued to absorb much of Albrecht's time and energy for the rest of the year. The idea was slowly gaining acceptance but he felt that time was running out. The Bluff area was very dry, and bushtucker was becoming scarce. He feared that if supplementary food was not provided soon, the people would leave the area and move in to town. In the drawn-out negotiations, Albrecht sometimes felt trapped between the government and his own board. The government men had made no firm commitment to funding the ration depot, and he knew they could easily renege on the whole plan. Board members, on the other hand, were also cautious about further financial commitments, and distance isolated them from the tide of events in Central Australia. To Albrecht it was clear that the Aboriginal cause was on the move, however reluctantly in some circles. Some kind of welfare initiative had become a political necessity. And he judged that the government was prepared to work closely with missions, only reserving the right to an overall control.

In the end, he took the initiative. He and Ted Strehlow worked out a proposal for managing the depot which would minimize government costs and leave most of the work with the mission. Rations would be issued to old, sick and indigent people, the government deciding who was eligible. The mission would administer the depot, and be paid 3s 8d per week for each person receiving weekly rations of eight pounds of flour, one pound of sugar, three ounces of tea, some baking powder, and basic medical needs like Aspro, cough medicine and ointments. Obviously surprised at its economy, Chinnery approved the proposal in principle.

For staffing, Albrecht thought that Ted Abbott, a part-Aboriginal man at the mission who had proved himself reliable in work, could be put in charge. His wages would be the usual weekly food ration plus £1 a week. He was a member of the Hermannsburg congregation, and most of the Haasts Bluff people would know and respect him. If a mission staff member went out every second month to check, it should be an adequate arrangement for the present. Albrecht was authorized to proceed, and worked out a tender for the building of the shed with old Gus Droegemuller. A track to the Bluff would be graded at government expense. The horse-drawn grader was worked by two European men from Alice Springs. Bert Nananana from Hermannsburg and another man from Haasts Bluff went with them to show them a route around the back of the Mereeni Range which Albrecht and Titus had worked out in July. Nananana had been a camelman with Albrecht on some of his earlier camel treks, and knew the country west of Haasts Bluff. It was slow going—felling the trees with axes, levelling off the stumps with an adze, and finding the best places to cross the creeks.

Long way round, make a road through all those countries, white bloke gave a few bob wages, long way round, through Tarawara, Wayutakata, Irranti . . .

It was late April when the new storekeeper handed out the first rations. Apart from this duty, he also had to look after a small mission store selling supplies sent out from Hermannsburg. These could be sold for cash or bartered against dingo scalps and animal skins. It was a means of support for the younger people not eligible for rations, and Albrecht hoped that thereby they would feel less inducement to go to the settled area to buy tea, sugar and flour. He thought it would also encourage them to spread over the whole reserve in search of skins and scalps.

Heavy rains had fallen by the time Albrecht and Strehlow drove out again in June. In some places there was waving green grass taller than the truck, and the track was not always easy to find. The store had taken £16 in the ten weeks it had been open, and the rationing was correct. Ted Abbott was a little confused about the dingo scalps, but he had written everything down, and it was sorted out easily. A sense of gratitude welled up in Albrecht:

> It was a nice experience for me when the whole lot (about 58 at the moment) came to get their rations. They were all old people, blind, lame, sick, and orphans. They have now a centre where they can come to get help in sickness and also listen to God's Word. For the young people we have the store. We ask the same prices as in Hermannsburg. They can pay for their tea, sugar and flour with dog hides and other hides.

Scarred by the trauma of the 'seven-year-drought' in the 1920s when scores of bush and mission Aborigines died of malnutrition and scurvy, Albrecht struggled for years to raise money to bring water from Kaporilja Springs to Hermannsburg. The five-mile trench for the pipeline was dug across limestone country by Hermannsburg men under the supervision of Art Latz. The mission vegetable garden made possible by Kaporilja water covered several acres from 1936 through the 1940s. Community health improved as a result. (Burns-Albrecht Collection, South Australian Museum)

In 1939 Albrecht and T. G. H. Strehlow (then patrol officer) were authorized by the government to undertake an expedition to the Petermann Ranges to determine how many Pitjantjatjara people were still living there. (above) Two women on their daily walk for food. (below) Sharing a meal with Pitjantjatjara people on the last evening. On view are some of the water canteens and camel boxes containing supplies for the five-week trek crisscrossing the ranges. Photographs by the late Ossie Heinrich.

It had been eleven years since the first camel trip through the Haasts Bluff district in 1930, and ten years since his evangelists had started work there. For him, it was all-important that most of the people he had met then were still in the area. Writing to the Reverend John Sexton later in the year, he felt bound to express his strong feeling about the work of Daisy Bates at Ooldea, South Australia:

> It is my opinion that Mrs Bates through establishing a camp at that place and attracting Natives there away from the bush, has done incalculable harm . . . If the people living there at present continue to attract Natives away from bush life without . . . doing anything to bring them very slowly but surely into a healthy contact with civilized life, they are clearly an agency for the Native's destruction . . . Not Ooldea but the Ranges should be their place, so that the Natives who cannot be employed and taught work of some sort, could continue their old life with their station as a centre where they could come for guidance and in case of sickness.

Albrecht appreciated that the ration depot at the Bluff was only a first step. In the longer term, it would not be possible for the growing population to continue to gain a livelihood entirely in the traditional way. Characteristically looking ahead, he thought that, if water supplies were improved by cementing rockholes or boring, some people might start keeping a few goats or sheep or even cattle of their own, which they could sell or barter for food or clothing. And if the watering places were not too far from each other, people could move around to some extent, satisfying their age-old wandering instincts yet also having access to the amenities of civilized life they had come to expect.

He was especially thankful for the new spirit of co-operation he was sensing between the mission and the government. 'God still answers prayers', he wrote to John Sexton on 12 March 1941, 'this is our feeling in viewing this development, as it has taken place in spite of the war, and all that this means'.

Board chairman John Riedel was still anxious about Albrecht's health. In June 1941, he wrote 'I would like to ask you not to forget your health with all the planning and building and your refusal to take your holidays at the right time. Please don't carry on until you break down.' The government subsidy had been increased. Unfortunately for Albrecht, it also meant more paperwork. Chinnery wanted separate accounting of costs for the keep of the old, the sick, women and children, and some of the labourers. He had also indicated that some funding might be given for administration, but only if exact figures were provided. Trying to work out a new system and get the books up to date kept Albrecht up late at night. When he did get to bed, he often slept only fitfully.

Their third child, Paul, was a few weeks from his ninth birthday in September 1941, when he came to his father complaining of severe toothache. Following extraction of the tooth—Albrecht frequently performed this service for people around the district—inflammation and blood poisoning set in. Despite a visit from the government medical officer and a second extraction, the boy grew worse. The poisoning spread through his body, and his temperature rose dangerously. The doctor drove out again, but the best he could offer was a prescription which had to be ordered from Melbourne. In desperation, Albrecht thought they must try the tepid baths from his old medical book since they seemed to have helped the other children through their worst illnesses. Every two hours, day and night, the parents held him in tepid water. For almost two weeks, the parents hardly got out of their clothes. They kept Paul in the bed between them and scarcely slept, feeling his fiery body and vividly aware of his irregular breathing. The crisis came ten days after the extraction of the second tooth. The boy's pulse grew weaker, and finally they could not find it at all. His father thought he had gone. Minna continued to pray and, in a little while, there was a small stir, and he managed to swallow some water. A corner seemed to have been turned. The medicine finally arrived from Melbourne, and had some benefit.

But progress was slow. His heart had been strained, and even small movements caused his pulse to disappear. As summer came on and the weather grew hot, his father carried him out each day to a bed on the verandah. Weeks turned into months, and his temperature went up every afternoon. The swelling in his head subsided ever so slowly, and finally the infection erupted into an open sore on the side of his face, which discharged for months. Riedel again insisted that they come south at the beginning of the next year for a holiday. 'As far as we know, Lenchen [Helene] is ready to go to College next year, so you could combine both—take Lenchen to College, and then have a holiday. And we mean a *real* holiday.'

Even so, there were many times in the intervening weeks when Albrecht felt it would be impossible to go. Chinnery had asked him for a report on the prospects of finding water at Haasts Bluff. Evidently the government was considering implementing the improvements to water supplies he had suggested months before. It surprised him, because they would cost many thousands of pounds. It was the worst possible time for him to go south, he thought to himself. Instead he should be going west for two or three months to check all the details thoroughly. It was no small matter to work out the best plan, and to find the right people to do the work.

It had been a bad year in health on the station. Babies and young mothers seemed the most vulnerable groups. The year before, three young mothers had died, two of them following childbirth, and three babies as well. The government medical officer suggested cod liver oil for the infants and young mothers, and sent some out from Alice Springs at government expense. But Albrecht knew there were other factors, some not so easy to change. Despite all his advice to the contrary, most of the young mothers continued to breastfeed their babies through the next pregnancy. When the second child arrived, they simply continued feeding the two. Since the older children needed more nourishment but were not used to solid food, they often became sickly and susceptible to illness.

It was also difficult to get the Aboriginal mothers to take extra nourishment even when it was readily available. Albrecht had always insisted that nursing mothers had the first priority for milk when there was enough grass for the milking cows, but often the women did not bother to get it. They had access to all the milk from the three hundred goats in the goat camp across the river but, again, they seldom bothered. Damper, strong tea and some meat were what they really valued. He had similar struggles about clothing. Most of the mission people still wore too much rather than too little. It was not unusual to see an infant in summertime covered with a towel, a blanket, and maybe some additional garments on top. Then they perspired profusely, and became vulnerable to chills and illness.

The people's indifference to vital factors of nutrition and hygiene was distressing to Albrecht. Nothing hurt him more than deaths that might have been avoided. And the long trauma of the drought in the 1920s, and the deaths from vitamin deficiencies, had etched in him an acute awareness of the importance of their diet. He was forever grateful to the farmer friends in South Australia who year by year had continued to donate wheat which was gristed free of charge by the Laura Milling Company. This constant source of wheatmeal, as well as the dried fruit, barley and split peas, had been an important food source for the community for over ten years.

Albrecht had been pressing Chinnery for some time for

Aboriginal eligibility for child endowment and other social welfare benefits. The government was finally moving on the issue, but intended initially to pay the money to mission administrators rather than to the mothers personally. However it would have to be spent for their benefit, and Albrecht hoped it would substantially improve the health of mothers and children. He wrote again to Riedel, asking him to advertise for a full-time nurse.

In the wartime conditions in Alice Springs, he was also finding other food supplements. He had mentioned to the military authorities that the mission could always use extra food if it was going to be thrown away, and several lots of foodstuffs had been sent down from the barracks to the shed near the church—six bags of sugar which had been slightly wet, a crate of raisins. It delighted the practical, thrifty part in Albrecht. He hated to see food wasted, and it benefited the people as well. A good relationship was emerging between the mission and the armed forces. Truckloads of soldiers going to Palm Valley on Sundays invariably stopped at Hermannsburg. They were always welcomed, and often bought woodwork or other goods from the store. The money coming in from the handcrafts was steadily increasing, and the military spending was part of it. In the last days of 1941, the Albrecht family boarded the train for South Australia.

Soldiers used to go down to Palm Valley, maybe four or five army trucks on a Sunday, they stop here for visit. One Sunday come here, everywhere soldiers all round, training, came north, south, frightened the daylights out of people. They say, don't run away, don't frighten, we're only come here visiting you people.

In the two years Australia had been at war, Alice Springs had been transformed from a sleepy little hollow into a large-scale military garrison. After the bombing of Pearl Harbor in December, 1941 and the escalation of the Pacific War, the northward movement of troops intensified, and sealed bitumen highways were built between Mount Isa, Alice Springs and Darwin. By the end of 1942, there were 5000 American servicemen and 32 000 Australians in Darwin and the Adelaide River area. The maintenance of these men, and the expanding air forces, strained the cross-continental lifeline to the limit. Thousands of permanent troops were stationed in Alice Springs to maintain it as a staging camp for those passing through to the north.

At Hermannsburg, there had been another search, summarily

announced by the arrival of officers and several men in a military vehicle. Bryan Bowman was buying supplies at the store, and was questioned about the sentiments of the Albrechts towards the war. 'As far as I'm concerned, they're pro-German and anti-Nazi', he replied in his taciturn way. He was thinking particularly of Mrs Albrecht, whom he always thought of as 'very German'. Albrecht, he always felt, 'could have been anything', but he knew both of them were adamantly opposed to Hitler. A thorough search of the staff houses and main buildings revealed nothing untoward, apart from confirming the existence of large amounts of flour and brown rice.

It was rumours about these large shipments of food that had caught the attention of the military authorities. After the bombing of Darwin, the possibility of a Japanese land invasion of Australia loomed large in the minds of northern Australians, and at least a few were ripe for the rumours that the mission was storing food supplies to feed the enemy as they advanced across the continent. Mindful of the uncertainty of transport and food supplies in the war situation, Albrecht had ordered supplies in extra large quantities before leaving for the south. The spectre of inadequately nourished Aborigines had never entirely left him, and he felt his first task was to ensure an adequate food supply for the community in his care.

In South Australia, the Albrecht family felt they were in another world. People in the southern cities seemed, by comparison, hardly aware of the war. The family spent the first part of their holiday at the ocean, and it was some time before Albrecht stirred himself to begin some of the contacts and engagements that had usually dominated his furloughs. He talked several times with John Sexton of the Aborigines' Friends' Association, knowing that future developments with Aboriginal issues needed the support of southern groups. At the request of the association, Albrecht undertook to write an article about the previous missionary, Reverend Carl Strehlow, and another on the natural food supply of the Aborigines.

Letters from the north remained disquieting. It appeared that the military wanted to close Hermannsburg, in case it could be a threat in the event of an invasion, and transfer the people to Alice Springs. Discussing the matter personally with Albrecht in a room in Parliament House, Adelaide, Chinnery said that he had done everything in his power to keep the mission open. But the final decision had to come from the federal Minister.

Albrecht was frequently innovative and, in the present crisis, he suggested that doubts about the mission might be allayed if Rex Battarbee could be stationed there as a resident inspector. He thought that Battarbee's war record in World War I would surely put him beyond suspicion. Nevertheless, a complicated screening process was instituted to check his connections with Hermannsburg.

The arrangements of the Albrechts for returning north were rudely disrupted in late May by a letter informing them that they had not been granted a permit to return to the Northern Territory. Alice Springs was officially a war zone, and civilians could not enter it except under special conditions. Stunned and disappointed, Albrecht wrote immediately to Duguid, Chinnery and John Sexton, asking them to do anything they could to secure him a permit to return on his own.

When schoolchildren heard the planes, they used to go running out, down the Finke. Hildawush [Hilda Wurst] used to try to stop them, that's not German plane, that's Australian plane. Oh no, that's German plane coming. And we just about get into trouble because my name is Traugott. Do you speak German, major ask me. I can't speak German, I born in Australia. Same with Adolf and Conrad. Army came twice to Hermannsburg, in 1940, searched Pastor's study. I seen it! Go in the house, old man was there, get wireless. Family away for long time, and search in that time also. Old man didn't come back, cos he couldn't get permit. Everybody worried for old man. We had only old Moses, and Gross—he was really Australian, but old man not really Australian. That's why we bin proper worried.

Three months later, Albrecht received a permit to return provided that Rex Battarbee was stationed at Hermannsburg as resident inspector. No indication was given of when Minna and the family could return. Lou Borgelt was granted a temporary permit into the Territory, and the two men left for the north in the middle of August in the new Lend-Lease mission truck which had been purchased for the mission. Albrecht felt keenly the parting from Minna and all of the family.

Good rains had fallen, and Sturt's desert pea and other wild-flowers spilled in red and purple patches across the dirt track. The nights were full of moonlight. At Ernabella, they stopped for two days. The Presbyterian mission was now five years old, and the two men talked at length with the superintendent, Reverend J. R. B. Love, who had served in the Presbyterian missions of

Mapoon in North Queensland and Kunmunya in Western Australia. Albrecht noted his different approach to traditional Aboriginal religion. 'Rev. Love believes that if the Gospel is offered to the native, there is no need to trouble any further about his religion. The two, Christianity and their beliefs of old, can well stand together and be of benefit to the people.' But he felt they were in full agreement about the need to preserve their tribal organization, customs and social life, as far as they were not contrary to Scripture.

The Ernabella schoolchildren were fascinated by the stout fair man who limped into their schoolroom and spoke to them in fluent Aranda. He sang to them, which they enjoyed hugely, as also his best attempts to speak to them in their own Pitjantjatjara. The sight of their glowing faces was a joy to him, and he noticed with pleasure the neat handwriting on the letters they gave him for children in the Hermannsburg school. None of the children wore a stitch of clothing, and 100 of the 150 children on the roll were off on walkabout with their families. But he could not help pondering their prospects upon leaving school. While it would be convenient to think that the mission could leave their parents and tribal leaders to train them in traditional bush life, he felt it was unrealistic and would work 'least with the young people themselves'. Through their observations of the life of Aboriginal stock riders and station workers, they 'have lost interest in the hunting pursuits of their fathers; apart from periodical walkabouts'. Like Hermannsburg, Ernabella would be faced with the problem of providing employment for these young people.

Albrecht felt that many Australians, especially anthropologists, were interested only in preserving Aborigines in their traditional life. He had always felt this view ignored the forces operating within Aboriginal people themselves, following the advent of the Europeans:

> The exhortation to be good boys and remain objects of study of interested white people has nothing positive for the native and is, therefore, meaningless. As long as there are white people in Australia whom the native can observe living on a higher standard, eating better food than he has, being independent of droughts, being better protected and wearing clothing, that desire of the native, to get into the same way, will always be there. It reveals a rather naive mind to say the problems mentioned are just a creation of the missionary; they have developed as a direct result of the cultural clash.

He thought Ernabella was a place where Aboriginal people could make a more considered response to the new situation. They could, if they wished, continue to live in the traditional way. But if they wanted clothing and other amenities, they had the opportunity to work for them. He wrote enthusiastically to Duguid of his impressions, and suggested that both missions would benefit from exchange visits and discussions of policy. On the last leg of the trip home, he and Borgelt called in at the Jay to see Blind Moses The old man stood near the new truck and ran his hand over the name plate on the bonnet, feeling the shape.

Albrecht's return to the station in the first days of September moved him deeply. The eight months in the south had been his longest absence in the sixteen years he had been in Australia. There had been moments in those months, especially when the doors to return seemed closed, that he had begun to wonder if his life in Central Australia were over. To look into all the faces of welcome which surrounded the truck as they pulled up brought a deep feeling of oneness with them that he could not have escaped even had he wished. He told himself that he would serve with all he had until God called him elsewhere.

Soon after his return, he had to tackle the huge task of compiling the first complete census of all Aboriginal people at Hermannsburg. The request had been made earlier by the government authorities, but it had to wait until his return. A lot of information was requested, and only someone with long experience of the community and fluency in the language could attempt it. For the moment no-one knew why all this information was required, but it was soon clear. The army was mobilizing Aboriginal men throughout the Northern Territory into labour gangs for semi-military service presently carried out by the regular soldiers—cleaning, cutting firewood, kitchen work. By November 1942, more than forty men from the mission were working in Alice Springs. Albrecht and Pastor Gross took turns to drive into town each fortnight, pick up the men at the military camp and take them to the church for a service and a meal, returning them to camp afterwards.

As time went by, the first flush of patriotic enthusiasm faded, and the complaints began. Why did they only get the army 'giggle hat' instead of the regular soldier's hat? Why was their pay only women's pay—five shillings a week? Albrecht had the feeling that some were thoroughly spoilt by the other soldiers, many of whom had never seen an Aboriginal before. Others found the discipline hard. Still others enjoyed the relative equality of the army existence.

It was nice, everything is one. One friend white man, close, like this. Have shower every morning. Good time, good name for them. Everything is one, one tucker, one blanket, one play football.

Army bit rough! More tough than Albrecht! He was tough, but he was teaching, got to learn something, God's kingdom good thing. He was tough, but he was trying to teach something, bring them back, to right truth. Some Aboriginal fellas [in army] homesick, run away.

The two missionaries, and Albrecht in particular, spent many hours with the men, sometimes sitting in the sand of the Todd River until midnight. Some became contemptuous of their former life, and told Albrecht he was not their *ingkata* any more—their bosses were in the army. Certainly someone else, not him, was their new work-boss, he replied, but God remained the one to whom they were responsible, and whom they would never escape. Some of the men took to gambling, others as rigorously opposed it. A number contracted venereal disease.

Albrecht could not but be anxious, thinking that in many aspects they were children and, like children exposed to things they were not mature enough to withstand, were drifting into ruin. Selma, who followed her husband into Alice Springs, became an open prostitute and was sent to Tennant Creek hospital with venereal disease. It saddened Albrecht to think of young wives, some hardly more than children themselves, who as a result of disease would never have families. His old sense of European centres as graveyards for Aborigines had never left him.

He and Battarbee had numerous discussions with the colonel in charge of the labour gangs. They pleaded with him to issue boots to the men, but he found the request difficult to understand. 'Why, they all walk barefooted in the bush, don't they?' They explained that no Aborigine would walk about in the hottest part of the day, and in the army they were supposed to work throughout the day. Boots were issued. He was not so sure about regular Army hats and tunics. The request to pay the men ten shillings a week was totally unsuccessful. But after many visits to headquarters, they were successful in having the families of the men working in the military provided for by the military. Albrecht also suggested that non-commissioned officers be appointed from the labour gangs. He had always tried to give Aborigines responsibility.

He visited the Haasts Bluff depot a few weeks after arriving back in the north. The summer rains had washed out the road around the Mereeni Range so badly that he and Battarbee had to use the northern route via Alice Springs which, for the return journey, meant five hundred miles of driving. The rationing and books were in a reasonable state, though no-one had been out for four months. Personal relationships were in more disarray. Ted had been living with a bush girl and they'd had a child, and Ted and Titus were quarrelling. It left Albrecht in a dilemma, as he wrote to Riedel:

> From my previous experience with Titus, I know he has queer ways, and on the long run it is difficult to work together with him. The same applies to Ted . . . Still, it was obvious beyond any doubt that God has used these two men in a very marked way to do good and serve the 'least of our brethren'. In view of this fact I felt it my duty to do all I could to bring things together instead of breaking up . . . I conducted the devotions twice daily and spoke to them on each occasion . . . Titus came afterwards and asked me for the text which he copied with pencil . . .

In November of 1942, Moses lost his daughter, Priscilla. She was married to Johannes, a man from the Dieri tribe at Cooper Creek, and gave birth to a healthy boy in the Alice Springs hospital where she had been taken after protracted labour. Albrecht had been overjoyed at this news. Moses and Sofia had lost nine of their eleven children, several during the drought in the 1920s. A few days later, Albrecht was back in Alice Springs after another long trip to Haasts Bluff via the north road, and was met by Johannes asking him to come immediately to the hospital. Priscilla had had a relapse of broncho-pneumonia, and could hardly breathe. Albrecht arranged for someone to drive out to the Jay and get Moses and Sofia, but the man was delayed, and Priscilla died on Sunday morning, even before he left.

For Albrecht, the Sunday was full of tasks which had to be undertaken despite his heaviness of heart over Priscilla. He took a service in the morning and had confirmation class for several of the labour gang in the early afternoon. Then there was the funeral service, and an English service at night for white Lutheran servicemen and the Aboriginal men from the labour gangs. After the strenuous week at Haasts Bluff, he was exhausted.

The graveside service for Priscilla was almost over by the time Moses arrived. Albrecht had chosen John 13:7 as text: 'Jesus answered, "At the moment you do not know what I am doing, but later you will understand"'. The next morning Albrecht drove back to Hermannsburg, Moses going with him as far as the Jay. The old Aborigine told him he knew he would learn all about it in Heaven, and spoke of the text on the previous Sunday. 'And after that I saw a huge number, impossible to count, of people from every nation, race, tribe and language; they were standing in front of the throne and in front of the Lamb, dressed in white robes and holding palms in their hands.' He thought God was preparing him through suffering for that great day. After dropping Moses at the Jay, Albrecht drove on, feeling that he was the one who had been blessed by their time together.

A SAFE PLACE FOR PITJANTJATJARA

1943~1944

Maybe God might be working this way. When people live in the bush, might run out of water. Think maybe settlement, sit down, more safe.

It was November of 1942 before the application for Minna and the children to return north was approved. She had booked for a sleeping compartment for herself and the four younger children (Helene remaining as a boarder at Immanuel College), but an hour before the train came in to Quorn, she was told that all sleeping berths were occupied by military personnel. So there was a two-hour effort to get the luggage back, take out blankets, and repack. They ended by sitting on their suitcases at the end of the second-class compartment. By the following morning the train was already eight hours late. This meant at least three nights on the train instead of the usual two. As darkness turned into the grey of dawn on the third morning, it began to rain. On the train itself, water ran out. When the train stopped at a small station, Minna filled her waterbag and billycans at the water tank, and railway staff put buckets of water on the train for washing. When they finally reached Alice Springs, Albrecht was waiting at the station. But the Todd and other creeks were in full flood, and it was several days before they were able to drive the eighty miles out to Hermannsburg. It was almost a year since the family had walked out of the long hall with its thick whitewashed walls and flagstone floors for their journey south.

Minna's first visit to the garden assured her she was back in the north. Large tomatoes were almost ripe, cucumbers were setting, beans flowering, and there would be sweet melons ready by Christmas. Beautiful bunches of grapes hung on the vines. As the new year began, Minna and Else Gross were kept busy with station duties and a steady stream of military visitors. For Minna, it was a vast relief to be home and have the family together again. Together, that was, except for Helene (or 'Helen' as most people pronounced it) at college.

Minna worried about her eldest child whose letters home carried almost a sense of bewilderment. Until now, the only world Helene had really known was the mission station—a spread of whitewashed buildings near the wide sandy bed of the Finke River in Central Australia, and a social world that was in some ways amazingly diverse and wide-ranging, in other ways limited. It was a world she had moved in with a poise and confidence that never failed to impress itself on the visitors she showed around the station. At boarding school, she found it was a world neither known nor respected by her fellow students. Worse, she found that her speech constantly attracted attention and questions. Growing up with Aranda, German and English, and Marianna's firm admonitions to 'speak slowly, and one language at a time', her unusually clear enunciation invariably attracted questions about where she came from. 'Eighty miles west of Alice Springs' was an answer which did nothing to secure her a place in a school which drew most of its students from the environs of Adelaide and the Lutheran congregations in the Barossa valley and beyond. At college there was anyway a mentality, surprisingly common in church boarding schools, that children of missionaries and ministers were a race apart and expected to behave by a different set of rules.

The Finke River Mission financial statement tabled at the 1943 church synod showed a healthy balance for the second year in succession. This fortunate state was brought about chiefly by good seasons and successful cattle sales, the latter due in no small measure to the efforts of Art Latz. With finances for once not in a crisis, Albrecht was pressing the board to buy a tractor and scoop in order to build the dams needed for more reliable water for stock. An alternative was to have dams built by a dam contractor. A Mr Parkinson was putting in dams on other stations in the district. But the man had work for months ahead, so it would be necessary to come to an early decision if there were to be dams on the run before the following summer.

Albrecht had always thought that equipment such as the tractor and scoop, which was clearly part of the cattle run and the livelihood of the people, should be provided by the Department of Native Affairs. Realistically, however, he had no expectation that it would be considered in wartime. But he thought there was a chance, if the board could commit itself to a decision, that the department might give some assistance. It was a blend of pragmatism and flexibility that was characteristic of Albrecht's approach to working with government. It also rested considerably on the good working relations he had established with the government men. Inherent also was a characteristic urgency. He could not rest until the economic future of the Aboriginal community was placed on a firm footing—for Albrecht, that meant the opportunity to work and earn a livelihood. The primary source of food and work on the mission was the cattle and, given the vagaries of seasons in Central Australia, security in stock raising depended on improving water supplies.

As usual, the board's responses were slow and cautious. Correspondence on the matter, dragging on during the year, reflected the very different approaches of the man in Central Australia and his chairman in Sedan. Riedel was a clear logical thinker who always wanted a clear grasp of the whole situation before making a decision. Procedures were important, things had to be done in appropriate sequence. Albrecht on the other hand was painfully aware of needs, constantly pondered how things could be developed further, and was more willing to take a risk for a chance of achieving something important. And his sense of responsibility for the lives of the community was fundamental to his makeup. Their livelihood *had* to be more secure.

He had also persevered tirelessly with the other industries, especially the tanning and leather work. Mulga goods worth several hundred pounds had been made and sold before Christmas. But a lot of damage had been done to the mulga trees around the station and the permanent camps. Especially in the early days, the Aboriginal men had often been careless, taking one or two pieces from a tree which was enough to kill it. It was decided that the truck would be used to bring in mulga from places like the eastern boundary. The cattle rarely used it there, and the old mulga trees which were dying might as well be used. Loads were brought in and the logs put through the circular saw. This was working well, and a firm in Sydney took a large proportion. An agent in Alice Springs was able to sell the rest.

Tanning was continuing to develop, and a pair of boots was sent as a gift to Riedel. Moccasins were also produced by the women, with Else Gross and Minna supervising cutting and sewing in the 'rug room', one of a small line of rooms which old Mr Droegemuller had built near the Albrecht house a year or so before. Another had gone into much needed use as a dispensary. For the previous fourteen years, a room on the western end of the Albrechts' verandah had been the dispensary. It had been most unsatisfactory. When a lot of people had colds or illness, there was dirt and spittle everywhere, and it was a place where the Albrecht children often played.

Since the heavy rains had washed out the track around the Mereeni Range, all the inspection trips to Haasts Bluff were requiring the long drive via Alice Springs and the northern route. Albrecht and Art Latz had interminable discussions on whether a more direct route could be found. Bryan Bowman had no objection to a road being made north-west through Glen Helen station, but the ranges which had to be crossed to reach Haasts Bluff had always seemed impenetrable to vehicles. Art Latz, despite his familiarity with the country from working with the cattle, knew of no place where the range could be crossed by a road. Manasse, however, insisted there was a spot where they could avoid gutters and make the ascent. After some deliberation, Albrecht sent him out with the responsibility of surveying and constructing the road. A gang of young men from Hermannsburg and Haasts Bluff was engaged to go with him, and the logistics of regular supplies of dry foods, meat and other needs were worked out. When Albrecht drove out to inspect some time later, he marvelled at the ingenuity with which Manasse had tackled the job. The thick mulga scrub made it difficult to keep the road straight. Manasse managed this by walking to the end of a section and lighting smoke fires to guide the men as they chopped a narrow path through. This was then widened to the necessary width, cleared and levelled. Many miles were made with pick and shovel.

In the last week of May, Albrecht drove over the 180 miles of new track and reached Haasts Bluff in about five hours. He was elated at the success of the project. Only someone who knew the country like a European knows his backyard could have tackled a job like that, he thought to himself. And Manasse had managed the men well too. Returning a couple of days later, he found that he did not even have to use low gear for the descent. Second gear was enough.

But Manasse's capabilities and his reliability in work were unusual. Even many of those who had been baptized and received into the congregation still seemed incapable of applying their faith to this aspect of everyday life. Recently the sheep had been badly neglected. Some had been lost and later found dead. The men in charge of them, the 'sheepee shepherds', had been staying in the sheep camp making mulga wood articles, because these would get them some quick money in the store. If he reprimanded them too sharply, they were quite likely to tell him 'me leav'im job', and come in to the mission to live off the rations issued to their wives and children.

Even the Christian helpers at Haasts Bluff were giving him their share of heartache. Two of them had been living with Loritja women, though one had a wife at Hermannsburg, and the other had lived with a Hermannsburg woman the previous year after the marriage was opposed by her parents. Ted Abbott was still with the bush girl, and they were expecting another child, but there were no plans to marry. Sometimes Albrecht wondered if Ted could be kept on much longer. He was terribly conceited, and Titus complained about him constantly. Yet he had done a good job in the store and in keeping order among that large group of people. When Albrecht asked the advice of the Christian elders at Hermannsburg, they thought that the two helpers should go, but that Ted should be kept if he would marry the girl.

His sense of burden was compounded by a slowly growing frustration with the mission board. Often he felt they were out of touch. Riedel was a busy pastor responsible for six congregations, and it was a long time since he had been up. The war years in particular had seen big changes in attitudes and policies toward Aborigines in the Northern Territory. But while the government was more willing to support new ventures, it still fell to non-government organizations to undertake the initial risk and do most of the spadework. It was something that Riedel did not always understand. Asked on several occasions by Albrecht to look for a Lutheran teacher in case the government decided to support a school at Jay Creek, Riedel was irritated at the absence of a clearcut government policy on the matter and directed Albrecht to 'enquire from the proper authorities their intention of opening a school at Jay Creek . . . We take it for granted that the Government shoulders

(above) *Moses and his wife Sofia. Moses (c. 1877–1954) was for decades the foremost leader of the Aranda community at Hermannsburg, and an outstanding linguist, storyteller, historian and Aboriginal spokesman.*
(below) *Abel, also a stalwart leader in the mission community, had a special vocation with children, assisting in the school and teaching them the Christian faith. (Burns-Albrecht Collection, South Australian Museum)*

Sports days were a highlight of Hermannsburg life. Albrecht actively encouraged them, feeling they provided some substitute to the Aboriginal people for their loss of traditional ceremony. Finish of a race, W. Raatz on left, W. Mattner on right. (Battarbee Collection, South Australian Museum)

Hilda Wurst, teacher at Hermannsburg between 1940 and 1953, and mission children in front of the school, 1940s. (Scholz Collection, South Australian Museum)

all financial obligations connected with such an undertaking'. Albrecht tried to explain a very different reality:

> You are under the impression that the Government will do every-thing in preparation for the opening of the school, and after everything is completed, we are to ask to be given the opportunity of providing the teacher. If the children concerned would be white children, and their parents have a voice in our public life, then this would be correct. Unfortunately we have to deal with Aborigines. From various enquiries it is clear to me that we can get the financial support . . . to start the work, provided we have the right person . . . The money for a building is there but we would have to find ways to do the building. The Government is prepared to pay the teacher, but we would have to arrange [make the arrangements] and claim Child Endowment so as to get the money for feeding the children.

One vital difference between Albrecht and many of the board members had simmered below the surface for years. For many of them, mission work largely meant religious work. They acknowl-edged the very real physical needs of the Aboriginal community, and had laboured faithfully to support Hermannsburg in the long lean years when government help was minimal. But the split between physical and spiritual was deep, and the issue surfaced again and again, especially as the pressures of managing the mission station, ration depots and industries progressively mounted. When Sam Gross wrote to Riedel in late 1943 that he found it difficult to remember he was supposed to be a missionary, the letter touched a sensitive nerve in the chairman. 'Our station or stations have become to a great extent "feeding stations" . . . We have to . . . try to find laymen to do this work'. He suggested that the missionaries were so busy they were going in circles and becoming disorganized.

Albrecht had no disagreement about the need to find suitable lay staff for the station. But he was by now highly sensitized to the inference that much of their efforts were not directed into true mission work. He replied:

> We must not overlook the fact that God has led us into a work where we have to care for the body if we wish to have souls to be cared for. For instance, if we hadn't stepped in at Haasts Bluff in time, today there would be no Natives left to care for; white people with stock would have seen to that. And now there are nearly 400 there . . . You may reply that it is the duty of the Government to provide the means of livelihood for the Natives. However, if the Government does not do it, and we see a possibility, as in this Areyonga case, that we can

do it in co-operation with the Government, can we afford to sit back and let matters take their course saying, we feel not called to do this work? . . . As it is, however, I have no choice, lest I should go away from this place later on with the feeling that I have dodged my responsibility because it meant work so different to what I thought missionary work should be.

In July, Mr Chinnery visited Central Australia, and was brought out to the mission and Haasts Bluff. Albrecht felt he was pleased with what he saw. But his special concern was their discussion about the scattered remnants of the Pitjantjatjara people. Chinnery agreed that the ideal thing would be to establish an outpost in the Petermann Ranges, which would enable them to return to their traditional area. But that would be impossible without a support structure similar to that at Haasts Bluff, which called for a road over hundreds of miles in sandhill country, regular inspection trips, and so on. Given the very limited staffing of the mission in war conditions, this seemed impossible. Government was not prepared to initiate any venture, and there was no-one else who could offer any help.

Later, an idea came to Albrecht. Perhaps there would be a suitable site for a depot somewhere on the old Boatswain's Hole station, which had been abandoned by Bill MacNamara many years before. It lay to the south-west, in the direction of the Petermann Ranges. Asked about water supplies in that area, a former Aboriginal stockman of MacNamara's told Albrecht of a spring at Areyonga, some forty miles from Hermannsburg. Albrecht caught Chinnery before he left Alice Springs and the director agreed almost at once that the government would finance the building of a store and the establishing of a ration depot similar to that at Haasts Bluff, with an Aborigine in charge. 'Nobody else is going to step in', he said, 'and these [Pitjantjatjara] people will lose the last little vitality they show as a tribe'. He was all the more willing because the ration depot on the railway line south of Alice Springs was soon to be closed. The depot had become a centre for Aborigines who begged for food along the line, and of them many were Pitjantjatjara.

Albrecht made two trips with Rex Battarbee and Manasse to inspect the place—a gorge with high cliffs of red sandstone on either side, but there appeared to be more than ten acres of good land around the springs. They took measurements of the flow of water from the springs, and estimated it at about 17 000 gallons a day.

At first Areyonga thought a dangerous place, water snake there. When I was a boy, people say, don't go there. Pastor, he say, oh, he might be asleep, and he left the car that time, and he walk right up to the top, then he come back home, he say, nothing there, I never see water snake, maybe him asleep. He prayed from there, can't go without that.

The place was, however, inaccessible to motor transport without a road. The last mile or so to the springs in particular was very rocky and rough as it descended into the gorge. To make a road from the mission could cost £200, and the government had promised nothing for that. Albrecht felt he had no real choice but to proceed, but he had to tread carefully with the board members who were apt to feel he was overstepping his authority. In early September, the mission board met and approved the idea of managing the Areyonga depot along similar lines to Haasts Bluff. But it considered the road-making the responsibility of the government. In the same letter, Riedel cautioned his superintendent about overwork:

> One of your co-workers wrote about you: 'He is working himself to pieces'. Let me tell you, that I for one will not thank you if you do by trying to force matters overmuch. May God give you all wisdom what to undertake and then the strength to carry it out.

Albrecht had been overworking for months. The bookkeeping required by the Haasts Bluff depot and the child endowment payments needed a full-time bookkeeper. His efforts to get a suitable man, Carl Gehling, released from the military had failed. He saw no other way than to stay up at nights, struggling with the accounts. Under the continued strain, he had lost the capacity to sleep when he did go to bed. The suggestion that he was forcing things was a bitter pill. All of the frustrations of distance, communication problems, their conservatism about 'proper' missionary work, their doubts about 'feeding stations' swept over him. He wrote suggesting again that Riedel and the board secretary, Pastor Lehmann, come up and see for themselves:

> Only then would you be able to see that it is not a matter of forcing things but of being forced. You know the German word: *verpasste Gelegenheiten*, a missed opportunity. I would feel guilty in that respect if I had only once acted differently to what I actually have done . . . Now Mr Chinnery tells me: Yours is the only organisation that can do something for these people, and we are prepared to back you up financially. Could I leave it at that and do nothing because we have enough to do?

Perhaps over-sensitive from exhaustion, Albrecht had over-looked the real concern in Riedel's reproof. But if he had needed affirmation of the direction he had taken, he received it over-whelmingly in a trip he made to the Areyonga springs not long afterwards. Mission people had told him that already fifty or sixty Pitjantjatjara, hearing of the new depot, had gathered at Areyonga. The road (towards which the government had eventually promised £50) was now finished. From Hermannsburg it headed west towards Undandita and Gosse Bluff, then turned south toward Gata Pata, a gap in the line of ranges on the horizon. As the truck approached the gap, they saw in the distance a long string of people running toward them. He wrote about it over thirty years later, and the memory was still vivid in his mind:

> They were obviously in a great hurry, with many falling down. Others, blind and old people, were dragged along by holding to a stick and keeping contact with the person ahead. They were shout-ing, and gesticulating with their spears. It became obvious that they wanted to meet us, and we stopped the truck and stepped outside. Many were at the point of exhaustion, panting and blowing. For days they had been waiting for this moment, and we were soon surrounded by more than 50 people, as well as a number of children. Curious at first, they soon grew bolder, coming up and touching my lips, nose, hair, shirt, and trousers, and then stepping aside to make room for others. It was a very moving experience. This was their way of saying thank you. No solemn reception in a white man's meeting could have equalled in effect what these naked primitives had done. They all felt deeply that they were going to have a place they could call their home, from which nobody could move them, and where they would be protected and cared for.

Nobody asked for food. Afterwards, he and his helpers got back into the truck and drove the remaining distance to the springs.

That story, all run to the truck, I know that one, I was there. When he comin, we all yell, Pastor, we call him ingkata, ingkata!! *and we run all up to say hello, good day. People came and touched him, say hello. Some old ones knew him, some people had met him because he went with the camels to the Petermann Ranges. But everybody understand that the settlement would be here. We know that one at Haasts Bluff, we know he was going to put another one here. People want to sit down, lot of people die in the bush. We want to put a settlement, put sister to look after the kids, for that nursing. Not only kids but big people, more safe, they might have got not enough tucker. [In that time there was] big mob Tempe Downs, and Bryan Bowman said, maybe some people should go to Hermannsburg, and [from] Glen Helen the same. And Warlpiri people coming in too, because Yuendumu was nothing, and Papunya nothing! With the food, it was safe.*

Pastors Riedel and Lehmann came north for three weeks at the end of February 1944. On their return south, a board meeting was held promptly, and some important decisions taken. The board would make another attempt to get Carl Gehling released from the military to do the bookkeeping and some of the store work. Subject to satisfactory tests, the dam contractor, Parkinson, would proceed with dams at two sites in the east and west of the run. That the visit had brought some much needed understanding between the board and its missionaries seemed implied in the way Riedel concluded his first letter to the field: 'Hoping our visit has been of some benefit . . . and sending my very kind regards to *all of you*. I remain your sometimes stubborn J. Riedel'. Albrecht was the last person to hold a grudge, and he must have appreciated this rare acknowledgment from his chairman.

At Easter, Rex Battarbee took Eli, Edwin and Cyril to Alice Springs for the annual sports day. He had spent many hours coaching the young men. Edwin was the best high jumper, practising on the stockyard rails. Eli and Cyril excelled in long jump, hop step and jump, and the sprint events. It was the first time that Aborigines had taken part in any Alice Springs sporting fixtures, and Albrecht was delighted when they came home with prize money. Over the years he also had given time to the sports, though his special pride was the football team which he had started some years before. His portly figure, sitting on a kerosene tin and holding the watch, was a familiar sight at mission football matches.

Albrecht spent much time and effort in 1944 on a scheme to assist some of the most promising Aboriginal men to establish themselves as small-scale pastoralists. He felt deeply that in the new world in which they found themselves, their own economic independence was essential to their self-respect and long-term survival, and he assumed they would be more motivated to work if they were doing it for themselves.

 Pastor Albrecht start a new thing, give me twenty cows, and a bull and few horses, packs and saddles and I bin grow'em up, all that bullock, sell'em back again, get'em money all the time sell'em, branding, take'em Alice Springs, good work that time.

Albrecht felt the cattle industry had proved one of the best environments for Aborigines, offering them an opportunity to live in the bush away from large urban centres, and a degree of flexibility in employment which gave some scope for their roaming instincts. Most stations had a long break at Christmas before the stock camp was formed again. People could go walkabout then, and sometimes during the year. The Aboriginal men were often good with horses and enjoyed the physical life—its risks and its open-air freedom. He hoped that with land of their own, cattle from which to breed, and help with stores and equipment, some of the men would be able to become independent. He explained his reasoning to Riedel:

> Above all, however, this whole scheme is the result of observations showing conclusively that the Native population, once disturbed in their old way of life, cannot be kept on bush tucker only . . . after the desire for European food is aroused they have lost the taste for bush food, and also interest in their old way of living. Whilst it is intended to do all that can be done to encourage wandering about and making use of whatever there is to be collected, we must not miss the chance of providing for the new development among the people.

He spent many hours trying to sort it out with Battarbee and other government officers in Alice Springs. There were taxation and other legal issues in getting a separately registered brand for the men. Using the mission brand with a different serial number underneath was one solution, and an easy way to get the scheme started. But with his usual sensitivity to long-term implications and his general caution in dealing with government, Albrecht felt it would not be satisfactory:

> The biggest drawback, however, is that officials would be led to think it is only a branch of our Mission undertaking, that not the Natives but the Mission owns the stock . . . Also the Natives might not gain that feeling of pride of ownership, so very necessary if they are to give of their best in this venture . . .

Albrecht had continued regular correspondence with the president and secretary of the Aborigines' Friends' Association in Adelaide. After more than ten years of communication and co-operation, they regarded him as a key contact on Aboriginal issues. The previous year, they had printed the pamphlet on the natural food supply of the Aborigines that they had asked him to write in 1942. It was well received and they were using it in their push for a federal inquiry into Aboriginal food supplies in Australia. Two hundred and fifty copies were forwarded to Albrecht at Hermannsburg for his personal distribution. He had written it after his return to Central Australia in 1942. Despite the pressure of other work, he succeeded, as he so often did, in writing something informative and interesting, enlivened by the odd personal detail. Various seeds, plants, insects and trees which were the mainstay of bush food in Central Australia found a place in his descriptions:

> In the Western Macdonnells in return for a little flour, the natives brought me, as an expression of kindness, a damper made of grass seeds. This particular grass remains close to the ground. It has fairly wide leaves beneath which the seed is to be found in ears. When ripe it is collected by the women and cleaned by throwing it in the air. It is then mixed with water and baked in hot ashes. The Aranda called it 'ntanga' . . .

But he had seen too much of bush life not to want to draw out for his readers some of the harder side of life in a desert environment:

> Seasons of drought . . . are times of hardship and frequently of intense suffering to the natives . . . Much is said and written about the emergency water supply of the aborigines. They certainly have shown wonderful ingenuity in making use of roots of trees and shrubs, discovering tiny rock-holes in limestone country, and even found out how to obtain some water from a frog resting in wet mud. While such devices are most valuable . . . in case of emergency, they have little value to a large number of people with their families and other weak members: they cannot live without an adequate supply of water.
>
> Permanent waters are often quite a distance apart, and it happens again and again that a whole group of people, during a drought, has to remain on the one spot until after a rain . . . as time goes on, the food supply anywhere within a few days walk from the water becomes more and more exhausted . . . If . . . the water begins to give out, it becomes a matter of the survival of the fittest when all will try and reach water and safety. As a rule in such cases many members are too weak to walk very far and will lose their lives.

Such dreaded experiences, he said, were well known to Central Australian Aborigines, and were a primary cause of their leaving the bush, given the chance of more secure food supplies in the settled areas. 'Yet the fact remains, that in spite of losses, they always managed to continue as a race, whereas the changeover from bush food to the refined product of civilisation has helped to reduce their number tragically.'

Characteristically, he ended with practical suggestions. The Aborigines should be encouraged and helped to make use of their natural food supply for as long as possible. This could be most effectively done by improving water supplies. Fear of drought and suffering could be alleviated by an assurance of sufficient food in times of severe drought, and any transition to civilized conditions should try to preserve links with their former natural food. The recommendations expressed much of his philosophy in establishing the outposts at Haasts Bluff and Areyonga.

In late August 1944, Albrecht had a letter from John Sexton in Adelaide asking for a detailed evaluation of a Baptist proposal to establish a mission at Pikilli in the Davenport Range. The Baptist Church of Australia was for the first time expressing interest in Christian work with Aborigines, prompted in large part by a Baptist army chaplain stationed in Alice Springs who had noticed Albrecht's contact with Aborigines in the labour gangs. Albrecht had pointed them to the Pikilli area and, earlier in the year, a young Baptist missionary named Laurie Reece, with the help of a camel team and Aboriginal men from Hermannsburg, had undertaken a trek to the north and west to explore the area and see what people were still there.

Laurie Reece returned from the six-week journey much moved, and shocked, by the experience. He had either contacted or been told of almost 470 Aborigines living in the area—considerably more than the authorities believed. Some lived near pastoral properties in what seemed reasonable conditions. Others worked for food and keep in the wolfram mines on Mount Doreen station, though the employment of Aborigines underground was illegal under Territory law. The camel team journeyed through Coniston station, and it was evident that, for the several Warlpiri men who walked with them as guides for that area, the country was alive with the trauma of an earlier time. Even his own men would not camp in the area and wanted to move on. Further west were people with medical problems. Several had bad wounds, some fly blown, and he cleaned and dressed them. One adult had yaws, another woman he guessed had advanced venereal disease. His guides were told that European stockmen were raiding the camps for girls, and that some of the Aboriginal men were planning retaliation. His report on the trip, written with advice and support from Albrecht and Battarbee, sparked a hornet's nest in government circles in Alice Springs, and a police party was dispatched to investigate.

Albrecht responded to Sexton about the mission proposal in positive and definite terms. He strongly believed that Pikilli or, as it had become named by Europeans, Vaughan Springs, was the best place for a mission in that area. It had always been the main corroboree centre for the Warlpiri people, and there were at least five hundred people in the district who regarded it as their centre, which would be reason enough alone to make it a reserve. And the water was suitable for gardening, which was a vital factor. But he also added that one of the Baptist proposals under consideration —a camel patrol operating from Alice Springs—was totally inadequate. What was needed was a centre where people could receive medical help, trade and buy a little, and come and go as they wished

Various approaches to the military authorities had failed to get Carl Gehling released to be the mission bookkeeper and storekeeper. Albrecht could see nothing else but to keep doing the books himself. But his fatigue was very deep, and Minna was not well. They were so short-staffed that for a time Hilda Wurst had to leave the school in the afternoon in order to help with station work, especially in the boomerang and leather store. And Helene, who had come home to do her Intermediate and a bookkeeping course by correspondence, was doing more and more of the medical work. A young South Australian pastor, Philipp Scherer, was coming at the end of the year for five months to enable the Gross family to take their long overdue furlough. But Albrecht, as the only Aranda-speaking pastor, would still carry the main load of services and classes.

Yet whatever his workload, its spiritual aspects were his central concern and caused him the deepest heart-searching. From a physical point of view, the people had never been better off. The last financial year had seen almost £2000 paid out to them for work and scalps, and another £600 to the people at Areyonga and Haasts Bluff, where boomerang and curio-making had been taken up with gusto. There had been some good years with the cattle and, with the introduction of child endowment payments, the government had at long last put its financial responsibility on a sound basis. The success of Albert Namatjira's painting had also been felt in the Hermannsburg community. That year he had received a record £750 from an exhibition in Melbourne. The life of the people had changed rapidly in recent years, and their contact with European civilization was intensifying through the constant visitors to the mission and the experience of the Aboriginal men in the army labour gangs. Yet, Albrecht asked himself, was this material well-being helpful to the spiritual life of the people? Sometimes he felt that the Word of God was less central to their thought than it used to be.

Few things he bin gone pretty strong with the religion you know. People used to play cards, that was a great sin of religion, people used to steal, people used to go with bush marriage, this sort of thing. They were punished by communities, got to move out for six months bush. My old grandfather used to have a hard time with him. One day he told the old man [Albrecht], you get back to Germany where you belong to, I sitting right here where I belong to. Him and old Albrecht had argument over cards. My grandfather like to play cards all the time, not for money, for clothes, blankets, dingo scalps, kangaroo hides. Lot of people thought Albrecht too strict.

Trying to evaluate the progress at Haasts Bluff, Albrecht felt that only Titus's Pintubi wife, Esmeralda, was ready for baptism, despite the fourteen years of religious work, and told himself that the teaching there would never be consolidated without a full-time European missionary. Hermann Pech, a brother of Ruth Pech and Dora Latz, was interested, but he was still at university in Adelaide. Nevertheless, there were times when he glimpsed deep faith in individuals, sometimes at the greatest crises of their lives. A woman called Frieda died at the mission in July. She was overweight and had a weak heart. In her last hours of life, she saw visions. Her mother, long dead, came to her. A great light was all around her, and Carl Strehlow was there, with a large book in his hands. As Albrecht sat with her, he felt humbled. Many of these people seemed on the surface to be misfits, he thought. It was all the more amazing therefore to see what God could do with them.

One issue which had been nagging at him for months was the printing of the New Testament in Aranda. Though Carl Strehlow had translated the whole of the New Testament and used it in his preaching and teaching, only the four Gospels had actually been printed by the British and Foreign Bible Society. Carl Strehlow's work had been a major achievement in its day, but it had inaccuracies and limitations, and Ted Strehlow had begun to revise it some years before. That had stopped when he was drafted into the army. The Bible Society was keen to print the whole of the Aranda New Testament, and many people had given money for the project. But so far only the Epistles of Paul and the Book of Acts had been revised. And to make matters worse, Ted Strehlow had made alterations in spelling, and replaced some letters by internationally accepted phonetic symbols. Clearly, it could not be reprinted unless it was consistent throughout.

Ted Strehlow was in an unique position to carry out such a task. He had grown up with the people and then studied Aranda extensively in the 1930s, his deeper knowledge of the language growing with his recording of their ancient ceremonial culture. But he had given no definite answer as to whether he would finish it. Albrecht was frustrated. He felt that for this work, Strehlow was clearly ahead of him, both linguistically and in his capacity for empathy with the people. 'If it were not the Bible', he wrote to Riedel, 'I would not write another word about it, but for such a translation, only the very best is adequate'.

Eventually a letter came from Ted Strehlow, but there was still no mention of the New Testament revision. It was a thousand pities, Albrecht thought to himself, as he knew he could not do anything like the same job as Strehlow. But he would have to try. Perhaps after Pastor Gross's return from furlough, and if another staff member were found, he could try to go to Areyonga for a month or two with some of the older men, and prepare the manuscript.

His Aboriginal pastoralists scheme was becoming a reality. In early September, a group brand was finalized for the men—TAP. Each man could have a further distinguishing mark or brand which could be put on the cheek—a letter, or some other mark like a boomerang or quartpot. At mission level, the scheme would be administered by a group comprising Sam Gross as chairman, Albrecht, Art Latz, Hilda Wurst, and Aboriginal members Manasse and Conrad. Cattle and necessary gear would be given as a loan, as well as a credit allowance of 30s a week at the nearest mission store to buy their rations, clothing and tobacco. Repayment could be made when they reached the point of selling cattle.

The board had been slow to accept the idea, proposing that only two men be started at first. But in the end, they agreed to Albrecht's strong argument for four. He felt there was enough doubt about the scheme in government circles in Alice Springs. If they perceived equivocation from within the mission itself, the whole thing might come to pieces. The attitude was typical of Albrecht, especially with respect to government. He felt that if something was not pushed strongly, nothing at all would happen.

It was a time of flux in government thinking about Aborigines. The war had highlighted the whole Aboriginal question, especially in the Northern Territory. Thousands of soldiers from across Australia were passing through the Territory, many of them coming into close contact with Aborigines in the labour gangs. The increased concern for Aboriginal welfare was highlighted for Albrecht at a meeting at Alice Springs in September 1944 to which he was invited to speak. Later he wrote to Riedel:

> One thing seems established now and recognised more or less by everyone that the natives even at cattle stations throughout the North are disappearing, and the question begins to worry. how can this be prevented. Even a firm like Vesteys, who own 24 stations, have employed an anthropologist, Mr Berndt, and his wife, to go up, study the problem, and make recommendations. Mr Clough told me they are prepared to spend thousands of pounds in welfare work for the Natives. So it seems that something is going to be done.

He had talked with Ronald and Catherine Berndt. As anthropologists, they were interested in his unsuccessful attempts to reintroduce the non-religious corroborees, his growing misgivings about the impact of tourists on the mission people and consequent caution about unrestricted access to the mission.

The government officers in Alice Springs were beginning to see the need for further development of the ration depots at Haasts Bluff and Areyonga, but were in little agreement as to how it should be done. Sometimes Albrecht felt he heard a different story every time he went to Alice Springs. And some fine ironies were developing. Late in 1944, he found himself in discussions with a government officer about the ration scale. The officer thought that distribution should be extended to all sections of the community, not just the traditional categories of old, infirm and children. Albrecht disagreed. Much as he did not want the Aborigines to suffer undue insecurity over daily food, he felt that indiscriminate distribution of food would discourage the healthy men and women from going out for bushtucker—that, in his opinion, could only have a pauperizing influence on their community life. In reply, the officer pointed out that Aboriginal people at Tennant Creek were treated more generously, also those at the Jay. Support at the Bluff was absolutely minimal. And what would interested parties in the south think if they heard the government was supporting Aborigines at the rate of only 3s 8d per person per week? Albrecht must have wondered if his ears were deceiving him. It was only the sheer economy of his proposal for Haasts Bluff that had narrowly won official approval for it three short years before.

Albrecht himself believed that something more would have to be done at Haasts Bluff. It was fast becoming over-populated. On his last visit, he had driven the last miles in darkness, and he could see camp-fires burning all along the track from Alalbi to the depot, and many more further over in the mulga. At least 438 people were now living there. He thought the situation further north must have deteriorated, and people were coming down to settle in a safer place. Indeed he had the impression that some government officials were in favour of bringing the Mount Doreen people down to Haasts Bluff so as not to have to provide more land in the north.

The next time he saw Vic Carrington, Albrecht suggested that another depot be established at Mount Liebig, seventy miles further west. But Carrington was leaning towards the creation of a large central station with a hospital, workshops to teach various trades, and a central school. 'As you see', Albrecht wrote to Riedel, 'they are going to the other extreme; before, nothing was done, now it is to be a showplace. I told Mr Carrington some of my feelings in this respect. It is impossible to bridge the gap between the stone age man and our civilisation in one generation. If forced upon them, the result can only be disaster.' He had very mixed feelings about such large-scale government moves, though he was deeply thankful that government was at long last assuming some responsibility for Aboriginal people. Only through definite government policy, not voluntary groups and organizations, was their long-term welfare assured. Yet he felt strongly that the assimilation of Aborigines into the larger Australian society would inevitably be gradual.

Albrecht had kept up the baptism and confirmation classes at Hermannsburg as well as he could despite the other work, and on the first Sunday of December 1944 three teenagers were confirmed and five adults baptized, including a part-Aboriginal woman named Joylene from Henbury and her two children. Joylene had come to Hermannsburg as a child in the 1930s after Ted Strehlow had intervened to stop a local policeman taking her away from her Aboriginal mother. Examining her for baptism, Albrecht was surprised and pleased at her knowledge. The following Sunday he went to Haasts Bluff to baptize Esmeralda, Titus's wife, and conduct Holy Communion.

It was raining, and the roof over the main part of the store had blown away in a severe storm not long before. They made do with the verandah on the side, setting up an altar with two camel boxes. Besides the small circle of nine communicants, which included patrol officer Gordon Sweeney who had just returned from a visit to the Davenport Range, and a station-owner and his wife—a large number of bush people also gathered in the drizzling rain to watch and listen. Albrecht began the familiar words of the institution of Holy Communion: '*Ingkata nunaka Jesua Kristala, ingua ekurala Erina jialbmelakala, Era mana inaka'* (Our Lord Jesus Christ, on the night when He was betrayed, took bread). Beyond the intent faces of the onlookers, he could see the large bulk of the Bluff looming through the rain, and was content.

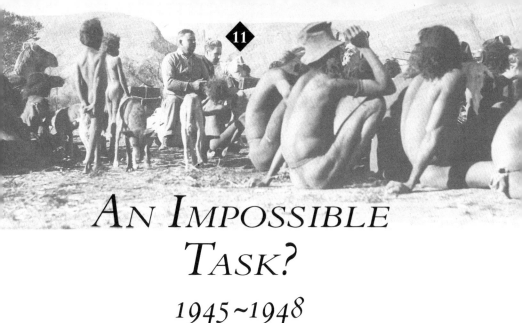

AN IMPOSSIBLE TASK?

1945~1948

*Over a period of time, once the church started here [Haasts Bluff],
people changed their lives. Pastor Albrecht brought a better life, it
was a really hard life before. Gradually they also listened to God's
word, they accepted that, and kept trying to change. Later on, they
had their own church council of elders, and they regulated the
congregation's life. Some of the people were really tough and wouldn't
listen, have to send them away, for a few months or a year, and then come
back again. They would decide that on their own, it had nothing to do with
Albrecht.*

Towards the end of the war, the army began to sell unwanted
goods in disposal auctions. Pastor Gross purchased an almost
unused truck for £140, and later another two, though not so
cheaply. The army also had thousands of 44-gallon oil drums
stacked in huge dumps. Albrecht managed to get five hundred
dumped on the mission block in town free of charge, and later
bought more at 3s 6d each until they had about three thousand in
all. Cut open and flattened, they were a cheap source of construction materials, especially for temporary buildings.

The Albrechts had not heard from their relatives in Europe for
the duration of the war. The first telegram they could send from

173

Australia was sponsored by the Red Cross with a maximum of twelve words allowed. Minna went over it again and again before she was satisfied. News came through gradually. One of Minna's remaining brothers had been killed. Another was missing from the Russian front. In Germany, food was scarce and prices exorbitant, so Minna sent parcels of food and clothing to her family via the Red Cross. Coffee was always included, as it could be traded for food and other necessities on the black market.

Ossie Heinrich visited Hermannsburg from Yorke Peninsula in the middle of 1945, and talked at length with Albrecht about the management of the mission. He felt strongly that the existing structure of decision-making put the superintendent in a difficult position. Albrecht had responsibility without appropriate authority. The difficulties of communication at a distance, and the sometimes protracted processes of the board, exacerbated the issue. He could well see why Albrecht sometimes had to proceed with decisions for which, strictly speaking, he lacked the authority.

The two men spent a couple of days at Haasts Bluff where Albrecht had to check the ration list thoroughly. Rex Battarbee had been there for four weeks issuing sulphanilamide tablets for trachoma. Unfortunately it could not be a complete success, as there were far too many people for one man to manage. Some had come diligently for the medicine, and several men told Albrecht how much further and clearer they could see. But Battarbee also told him that many of the men had lain in the camps the whole week, and only come for medicine on ration day. He had a lot to say about their laziness, and how much a permanent European administrator was needed. He thought that the outpost had outgrown the capacity of an Aboriginal manager and the Aboriginal evangelists.

At the mission, winter visitors were coming and going. Nelson Johnson, the United States ambassador to Australia, stayed for a few days. Like many Americans in Australia during the war, he was very interested in the Aboriginal artists and craftsmen. Sometimes Albrecht reflected how much the American servicemen had contributed to the mission's craft industries. The average Australian before the war was inclined to look down on articles made by Aborigines, as if they might have lice on them.

The open-air hymn singing of the people was another special pleasure to most visitors. Sometimes it was the older men trained by Werner Petering and Ted Strehlow in the early 1930s; sometimes the young people who were also learning the four-part Lutheran harmonies under the guidance of Hilda Wurst and the

T. G. H. Strehlow at Hermannsburg, early 1948, consulting with the older Christian men for his translation of the New Testament into Aranda. From left, Strehlow, Conrad Raberaba, Zacharias, Nathaniel, Jacobus and Moses. Photograph by Reverend P. A. Scherer. (Strehlow Research Centre)

The ration depot established at Haasts Bluff in 1941 with some government assistance was the fruit of Albrecht's efforts through the 1930s to prevent the disintegration of tribal groups in that area. Another depot was established at Areyonga in 1943, and both were later developed into full settlements. (Scholz Collection, South Australian Museum)

After a forced retirement to Adelaide in 1962 for reasons of Minna's health, Albrecht made a number of trips to Central Australia and Hope Vale mission in North Queensland to lead adult education and evangelism classes. The class at Hermannsburg in 1964 included final preparation for the ordaining of the first Lutheran Aboriginal pastors in Australia, Conrad Raberaba and Peter Bullah. From left,

William Ungkwanaka, person not known, Gustav Malbanka, Blind Johnny, Josef, Colin Malbanka, Peter Bullah, Immanuel Rutjinama, Henry Rubuntja, Paddy Panangka, Albrecht, Abel, Nahasson Ungkwanaka, Claude Renner, Conrad Raberaba.

Albrecht and Minna celebrate with family on his eightieth birthday, 1974.

new governess for staff children, Joyce Graetz. Apart from church services, most of the singing went on in the evening as small groups sat in the sand around little fires, the clarity and sweetness of the unaccompanied voices mingling with the intermittent barking of camp dogs and braying of donkeys. Scents of flowering stocks, petunias and other flowers in the gardens of the European women hung in the air in the cooler months.

At the end of January 1946, the Albrechts and their two youngest children, Minnie and Martin, left for their first furlough since 1942. Theo and Paul were at school in Adelaide, and Helene remained to help on the station. Albrecht was long overdue for a holiday. It had been years since he was able to sleep properly. Sometimes he hardly slept at all. They went to Sellicks Beach near Adelaide, where Lou Borgelt had offered them the use of his seaside shack. They swam as always, and felt better. Learning to sleep again was more difficult.

Albrecht spent a week at the church synod in February, and attended a board meeting where he raised an idea that had probably germinated in the discussions with Ossie Heinrich: that some authority be delegated to a field conference made up of staff and an Aboriginal representative. An informal version of this had been in place for a long time, but he felt it was time for it to be constituted properly. He also raised the possibility of a definite wage scale for Aboriginal workers on the mission. Wages were being paid in many cases already, but there were anomalies which only created discontent. He thought higher wages were an important incentive for the better workers, and hoped that a definite scale would help some to accept more responsibility and assume leadership.

Back at the mission in May 1946, Albrecht resumed a full round of work. But he was not at all well. He still had trouble sleeping, and his lame foot was giving a lot of pain. But a bookkeeper, Oswald Wallent, had been found, and arrived with his family. Intensive discussions about further development of the Haasts Bluff outpost were continuing. The government was moving towards transforming the ration depot into a fully equipped settlement, but the lack of a good water supply was still a major obstacle. Albrecht was deeply appreciative of the degree of government support which was now forthcoming. It was evident even in the arrangements with the boring:

> Before at the best we were only tolerated at decisions, or ignored altogether. This time they not only sought our advice, but every bore site was chosen by us and the Works Superintendent, sent out with me by the Department was there only to confirm my suggestion

to the Gov. Boring Contractor. And this time they have sent us the best driller in the NT . . .

Early in July, the boring contractor struck water. Albrecht was jubilant, though it was the start of an even more intense period of decisions and arrangements, since most of the arranging and responsibility still fell to him. He had to find a carpenter, finalize the plans for the buildings, order materials, and arrange transport, food supplies and additional helpers. Around the same time, Reverend Laurie Reece arrived from the south with another Baptist man to negotiate their mission proposal with the government, travelling out to the Mount Doreen area with Chinnery and Carrington. Albrecht had been thinking and praying for a long time about the question of mission–government co-operation. On the one hand, he thought it was inevitable: churches simply did not have the money to provide the employment and training opportunities which the government had come to expect. On the other hand, Albrecht viewed government assistance with caution, fearing that it could effectively become a sell-out to the government—a change in the whole direction of the work the mission had carried virtually alone for years, and which he felt the government with its material and secular orientation was ill-equipped to perform.

In his negotiations with the government officials in Alice Springs, he was feeling his way towards a co-operative structure that might satisfy both sides. He hoped that the government might be willing to appoint administrative, teaching and nursing staff from people nominated by the mission. Hilda Wurst's sister, Ida, for example, had indicated her willingness to come to Haasts Bluff as a nursing sister. Such a structure would keep an essentially spiritual dimension to the work, and yet leave the government with overall control of the secular side of the work.

Little by little, the basic requirements for staff and buildings for the new settlements at Haasts Bluff and Areyonga were negotiated. At Albrecht's instigation, Vic Carrington had a Sydney William army hut allocated as a hospital building for Haasts Bluff. Mission workers were to dismantle it, government trucks to cart it out, and the mission to re-erect it. 'Furthermore', wrote Albrecht, 'I got another two small buildings out of him for Haasts Bluff. Frames for a car shed and workshop we shall take from here . . .' Manasse had taken charge of fencing at the Bluff, but the government would meet the cost and also try to get a school building for Areyonga. By dint of Albrecht's drive, frugality and considerable bargaining talents, along with a government favourably inclined to more substantial help for Aborigines, the settlements were slowly taking shape.

There had been a sudden and unexpected death at Haasts Bluff. Consie, the eldest daughter of former evangelist Gustav and his wife Eileen, died hours after giving birth to a baby boy. A few nights later her husband, Allan, came to Albrecht in his study at Hermannsburg. They sat together for an hour, as the young man talked of his wife and their relationship. Their relatives had not approved of the match, and finally they had run away and lived together. Later, differences were resolved and the young couple returned to Hermannsburg to live. Consie joined the confirmation class where she had been easily the brightest member. Now Albrecht understood that Allan had been teaching her. Speaking with tears in his eyes, the man spoke of how much they had enjoyed each other —there was never an angry word between them. Shortly before she died, she had regained consciousness for a short time, and they had shared a precious time together in which he prayed for her, and thanked God for her faith. Albrecht felt he was looking into a soul deeply grieved, but joyful too, and comforted by God. He could not help thinking of the fights and discord he had sometimes seen in traditional bush camps, especially over additional wives, and felt that their Christian faith was bringing some of the people into a fuller and more conscious life.

For Albrecht and Minna, there was little let-up in pressure. A family from the Point Pass congregation came for a visit, and in late August a party of scientists and their wives arrived in Central Australia after a science congress in Adelaide. Professor Cleland had written earlier to ask if twelve ladies could be accommodated for a night. But with the other visitors, and all the work going on at Haasts Bluff and Areyonga, Albrecht had reluctantly advised him to engage a local man, Mr Tuit, to take them around and provide tents for the party.

Dry conditions were another worry. In September, Albrecht wrote to the board asking for the sinking of two bores on the mission—one past Old Station on the east, and the other near Umbartja in the west. Some of the best feed country on the run was around Umbartja, but the area was hardly used as there was virtually no water there. The western dam had been made, but Parkinson had struck rock, and it was not as deep as planned. And there had been no good rain to fill it. A successful bore would let Art Latz shift some of the cattle from parts of the run that were eaten out. The board decided that, for the present, building needs had to take precedence over boring activities. But at long last, a nurse had been found for Hermannsburg. Saleen Lindner would go up in November.

By September, the Baptist proposal was also taking shape. A new settlement, Yuendumu, was to be established to the east of Mount Doreen station. Major funding was to come from government, and Laurie Reece was to be missionary. Albrecht was pleased. He knew that the Finke mission resources were stretched to the limit and could do nothing for the people in that area. He sometimes thought, too, that there were people in government who felt the Lutherans controlled too many missions. He had a deep sense of disappointment, however, that the settlement was not to be at Pikilli Springs, as Pikilli, not the Mount Doreen area, was the real centre for the Warlpiri people. He believed that if the Baptist Church in the south had made a strong commitment to a mission proposal earlier, government officials would have been willing to secure the land for that purpose. Enough damaging reports had come in for the government to give very serious consideration to cancelling the pastoral lease over the Pikilli area.

Two traumatic legal wrangles had been associated with the establishing of the Baptist mission. Following the initial police inspection and a later one by government patrol officer Gordon Sweeney, station-owner William Braitling was charged in court with causing grievous bodily harm to an Aborigine. He won the case, which was presided over by Judge Wells. But the sweeping allegations by his lawyer, a King's Counsel from Adelaide, that the Administrator, the patrol officer, the police, the Baptists and the Lutherans, and even Dr H. V. Evatt in the federal parliament, had conspired to deprive Braitling of his land, gave rise to demands for a royal commission, and the Simpson Inquiry was conducted in Alice Springs in late 1946. Though the departmental officers and Gordon Sweeney were completely exonerated, the terms of the Simpson Inquiry did not make allowance for challenge of the original verdict, and William Braitling retained his lease of the Pikilli Springs area.

In the years following Albert Namatjira's first major exhibitions, an increasing number of Hermannsburg men had taken up painting, some very successfully. Edwin's exhibition in Melbourne in November 1946 was a great success. Forty paintings sold on the first afternoon, all were gone within three days, and the artist received between £400 and £500.

> *Rex Battarbee take me that exhibition, enjoyed that. Have a look*
> *your exhibition, with the frame. I went there, look through, lot of*
> *paintings, mine. I bin see all of my paintings, my work, I was really*
> *happy that time. Everybody come up and shake my hand, paper,*
> *pencil, sign my name.*

The following week, Namatjira's exhibition opened in Perth, less than ten years after his first major exhibition in Melbourne. Almost everything sold, and his cheque was almost £1000.

Aboriginal water-colour paintings of the Central Australian landscape were becoming a significant, if controversial, art vogue in Australia. Critics viewed with a mixture of acclaim, disbelief and simple puzzlement the phenomenon of full-blooded Aborigines, only a generation or two removed from traditional life, adapting quickly to a Western manner of painting. Some thought it was not authentic for an Aborigine to be painting anything but traditional Aboriginal designs; others felt the work was essentially copyist. An article in the Adelaide *Advertiser* the previous year quoted the director of the National Gallery of South Australia as saying there was little to indicate that the dying Aboriginal race would develop a creative— as opposed to the present representational—school of painting: unless the blacks adopted the white civilization almost fully, there was little hope of seeing much creative work from their hands. Rex Battarbee continued to maintain adamantly that Namatjira and others had the intrinsic talent, and had needed only the opportunity.

The success of the artists was bringing ever-widening ripples of change to the mission community. Namatjira had a truck now, and it was nothing for him to take eight or ten men at a time to Alice Springs, where they would stay for a while, then return to Hermannsburg. His freedom with his money drew an increasing number of people who lived off him and no longer worked.

Both Albrecht and Sam Gross felt that the artists needed some brake on their spending, and art councils were formed to handle local sales and countersign cheques—one for the Namatjira group and another for the Pareroultja brothers, Edwin, Otto and Reuben. At Albrecht's instigation, a non-Lutheran was included in the councils, partly to silence gossip that the mission was profiting by art sales while keeping the men in rations. The mission would receive 5 per cent of local sales and 1 per cent of exhibitions as compensation for the time that staff members were spending on the artists' behalf. Hilda Wurst and Sam Gross in particular had given much time and effort in comment and criticism of the paintings and in preparing them for exhibitions.

With the pressures of mission management and the outpost developments, Albrecht had been in indifferent health for most of the year. In early November it came to a head, and he had a complete collapse in Alice Springs. He was taken to hospital with giddiness and severe pressure in the head, and was there for eight days before Dr L. C. Lum would permit him to be discharged to the mission block in town, strongly advising him to go immediately to the south for at least two months. Albrecht said it was out of the question. The new Director of Native Affairs was about to visit Central Australia, as well as the new Administrator, and Albrecht felt that this visit would doubtless shape future policy on the two outstations. The informal arrangements of past years would be put into permanent form. He tried to explain to Riedel by letter:

> After talking for the best part of an hour, Dr Lum allowed me to go and stay until the above mentioned events had taken place, and then go away. I hardly need to say much about how I feel about the whole affair, to get out of it just now; it could easily mean that most of what I have tried to do over a number of years might be undone, as I am sure the new man will make his decision from the impressions he gains from visiting the place . . .

He said that he was improving, but the letter sounded tired and disoriented. Riedel wrote immediately to tell him to come down as soon as possible, with a hint of reproof that, if he feared to leave the work for a few months, perhaps the mission was still 'a one-man's organization'. Albrecht must have felt his chairman had little understanding of the real nature of 'the work' at present in Central Australia. He replied:

> Very unfortunately, you are not the only one to talk about the 'one man show'. I only hope in future when it will be a 'many men's show', things will go so much better. One thing is quite certain: whether this is largely a matter for one man to push things, or for a number, work among the Natives of this country, at this stage of their development, will only go on if everyone does all that is in his or her power to push things ahead. Otherwise you will hear many excuses and more explanations why this and that could not be done, but with all that things will not move ahead.

By mid-December, the water and feed position on the run was becoming desperate. Only the big dam in the east was holding the situation at all. At the same time, there was an abundance of dry feed in the west, near Umbartja and Gosse Bluff. Late in December, boring operations were begun. In the same week, almost two inches of rain fell. The Alkutakara dam in the east filled to over-flowing and the Finke came down in flood, as well as the Ellery and Jeremiah creeks. Government trucks with twelve tons of loading for Areyonga bogged on the road and remained there for almost a week. When Albrecht went out on the inspection trip with the new director and two officials through Areyonga and Haasts Bluff and back to Alice Springs by the north road, the director's utility bogged three times. At the Dashwood crossing, huge floodwaters had brought down great masses of sand and gravel, and it took almost ten hours of digging and pushing to get the truck to the other side.

It was early February before Albrecht could get away. He had improved considerably, and the slight distortion in his face had disappeared. Once again, his refuge was Lou Borgelt's shack at Sellicks Beach.

I couldn't remember before Minnie and Martin, that was before me. We used to play, Minnie and Martin, and all Aboriginal kids, riding donkeys, swimming. We had good time, went walkabout all day, come back, Latz kids, Gehlings. That was really happy time.

Hermannsburg in the 1940s was a children's paradise. Aboriginal and European children alike had the freedom of large spaces and the run of an entire community. There were rules of course, and daily routines on the station. *Pepa* (the daily devotions) at seven in the morning, handing out rations, breakfast, work assignments, mealtimes. But the regularity of things only meant more autonomy for the children. Everybody understood what was going on, what was permissible, what was dangerous, and Aboriginal people kept an eye out for the European children as well. For a child, it was a large secure environment with enormous latitude for enjoying oneself without the need of constant parental vigilance.

Old truck tyres were a staple ingredient in many of the children's games. Piled on top of one another, they could be jumped on until the whole superstructure collapsed. Minnie and her friends, Ruth and Marie Gross, added a ritual chant to this process, 'damper, damper, damper'. The boys preferred to race them across the compound like trucks. Best of all was to haul them up the steep rough slopes of Limestone Hill to the east, curl up inside them, and be pushed off to roll down the hill. When the tyres finally came to rest at the bottom, the boys staggered out, giddy, the horizon whirling around them.

Saturday was the highlight of the week. Walkabout day. Most children got some raw meat and a handful of tea and sugar, and went off with friends for the day. Bushtucker made up the rest: witchetty grubs cooked on the coals, honey ants. Waterholes along the Finke were favourite roaming places.

After I cleared out from school [at Hermannsburg] I used to hang around down the Finke. That was Strehlow time. Fight with the other boys over the donkeys, with Ted Strehlow too. They used to tease me, here comes that rubbish bloke from down south [laughter]. Ted Strehlow was like any other Aboriginal kid, Paul was like that later on. Old Strehlow don't care, he didn't worry about fighting, not like Pas' Albrecht. He give all the kids a hiding for fighting, Paul and Theo too!

The three eldest Albrecht children had, of necessity, found their companions among Aboriginal children. By the time Minnie and Martin were growing up, there was also a nucleus of European children on the mission. In 1947, when Minnie was ten, Ruth Gross was twelve, Phillip Latz and Marie Gross ten, Martin eight, and Peter Latz six. There were Aboriginal friends as well. Erna, one of Marianna's grandchildren and often in the Albrecht kitchen, was closest to Minnie. To the Aboriginal community, the two girls were relatives, since the Albrechts were regarded as Marianna's family.

Within the freedom the children enjoyed, there were rules. Dinner bells were not something to ignore. Each staff family had its own, which could not be confused with anyone else's. The Albrecht bell was rung five minutes before the meal. It was the signal to go immediately to the house, clean up, and go into the kitchen and see if there was anything to be done. Minna was usually at the stove, stirring a sauce for the vegetables. Marianna handled the big piece of meat—a roast perhaps, corned beef or boiled tongue—onto a platter which was taken to the table along with vegetables and sauces in covered dishes. Everybody helped themselves. With the many visitors, Minna had found it the most practical procedure.

By the time the war was over, truck trips out to Haasts Bluff and Areyonga were also a part of life for both Aboriginal and European children, and the truck never went out in the school holidays without an assortment of children piled on the back. The trips were usually a few days, so swags and extra food were taken too. At the outstations there was plenty to do while the store or rations were being checked and, if the truck broke down or bogged in a creek, it was all the better.

At Sellicks Beach, Albrecht was feeling better, but not dramatically so, and the letter he wrote to Riedel at the end of March was muted, even slightly depressed, in its tone:

> I have had several nights, and especially one, when natural sleep came, and I had that wonderful feeling of being tired. In between there have been occasions when things did not go so well, but even then I have not had attacks again as I used to have before, and I can feel everything has calmed down. Whether I shall regain much more, is probably more than doubtful . . . I am satisfied that I have had all the loneliness one can reasonably bear and put up with, even if everything here has been in my favour and very helpful, even the wireless set, daily mail, and above all this typewriter, without which I hardly think I could have stayed as long as I did.

The typewriter which he had rented for 7s 6d a week from the firm of Chartres Limited in Adelaide had been a lifeline. Ted Strehlow had finally taken up the revising work again, and Albrecht was paragraphing it and providing section headings from the Schofield Reference Bible. The work gave Albrecht some feeling of usefulness to the mission, even if he could not be there personally. Perhaps he felt almost betrayed by his own weakness. In fact, it was only an almost superhuman willpower which had kept him going during the last years of the war.

When Albrecht returned north in early May, he was pleased to see that the new nurse, Saleen Lindner, had settled in quickly and won people's trust. As well as attending to sick people, she had established a clinic for the babies where they were weighed each week and the mothers advised on feeding. Children's health had always been one of Albrecht's special concerns. Wherever he went among Aborigines, he could not help noticing whether there were children, and how they looked. In Alice Springs, he was often haunted by the absence of Aboriginal children. And every infant death on the mission was a nagging question to him. Could it have been avoided? Why had the weakness developed? He was sure that the children's health would improve with the regular monitoring.

Saleen Lindner had had worse injuries to treat while he was away. One woman came in after a fight with her skull laid open to the brain. It was dark, and Mona Kennedy, the new sixteen-year-old teacher of the staff children, was called to the dispensary to hold the kerosene lamp. It was a hot summer's night, and insects buzzed around the lamp. She did her best to hold the light as still as possible, hoping that Sister would finish the stitching before any insects got in.

Lou Borgelt had been working towards an electric light plant for the mission for months. He had raised most of the money by showing his home movies of Central Australia around Lutheran congregations in the south. No direct support had come from the board, Riedel even grumbling a little that Borgelt had not given them an estimate of future maintenance costs. But the scheme proceeded and, in the middle of the year, Monty Rieger and Ted Rieschieck came up for three months to install it free of charge. The old buildings were a challenge to the installers. The beams of very dry desert oak in the old ceilings were hard to drill, and covered with the dust and sand of decades. But the plant was ceremonially switched on by Lou Borgelt, and Albert Namatjira turned on the lights in the church, for which he had given two paintings.

Hermann Pech had been called as a full-time missionary to Haasts Bluff. He was a good student, with special facility in languages—Hebrew, Greek, Latin and German—and he and his wife, former governess Elizabeth Rohde, moved out in the middle of June. A Sydney William army hut was their temporary home. It was one room with no kitchen, and 'windows' were cut-out pieces of the corrugated-iron wall, hinged and propped open with sticks. The nearby well had been equipped with a windmill and tank, but there was no water supply to the house. The young pair set about laying pipes, digging latrines, starting a garden. Two hundred goats were sent out to provide some staples of meat and milk.

Building needs were almost as urgent on the mission itself. Hermannsburg was strained to breaking point. The four single staff members—Hilda Wurst, Mona Kennedy, Saleen Lindner and an older widow, Mrs Edna Teusner, who took charge of the school-children's meals during the week—all boarded with one family or another and visitors had to be fitted in as well. Some of the Aboriginal people were also becoming interested in better housing. Manasse had had a small stone house for some time, and now some of the artists were asking for them as well, saying they would not abandon them if a relative died there. This custom was still strong, and had been a significant obstacle to more permanent housing. Albrecht was pleased at their interest, and the disposal sales were an opportunity for cheap materials, even if a degree of improvisation was required:

I have tried, therefore, to devise some scheme for them, and there are now more than a dozen houses under construction. For 8 we are using the steel canopy frames . . . Such a frame is 12 feet long, and about 7 feet wide. By slightly curving a 10 ft. sheet of corr. iron, a roof is made with 7 sheets placed together. Droegemuller built an 'Isolation' ward for sister like this, and it turned out to be quite good, perhaps a little hot in summer, but with plenty of ventilation this is overcome . . . Then Albert bought a Sydney William Steel building, 60 × 20. Fortunately, we have a complete plan, so I got busy and studied it . . . When finished, our people should all find some shelter in times of rain, which is our biggest immediate concern.

A bakehouse, kitchen and large dining room for the schoolchildren was also planned. Albrecht had felt for a long time that feeding them directly was important for their health. Otherwise they were often compelled to share with relatives.

The first half of 1947 was dry. W. Wurst of Appila, Hilda's father, had offered both time and money to do further boring for water and, when he arrived early in the winter, he and Art Latz took the plant out to Umbartja. It was a good fifty miles from the mission, too far to go in and out each day, so Art Latz came in on Saturdays and returned on Monday mornings. A week later they were down to 180 feet. By then they were running the plant almost continuously, each taking shifts. They reached almost 700 feet without success, and abandoned the hole. Another was started, again in the Umbartja area. This time they reached 585 feet, again without striking water. Towards the end of the year, Wurst had to return to his farm in Appila. Art Latz continued, but the equipment failed in two holes. He shifted to Ellery Creek, where some water was found at 326 feet. He decided to forego his furlough and continue boring while the plant was still available. It was frustrating; the water was so badly needed.

Ted Strehlow came for a few weeks at the end of January 1948 to check certain words and renderings with some of the older Christian men. The old men were as painstaking as Strehlow, reaching into the depths of both their Aranda background and their understanding of 'the Word' brought to their culture seventy years before. Albrecht was surprised at first to see that many parts were being totally re-translated. But discussions with Strehlow convinced him that the new version was superior. The older, more literal translation of the verb 'follow', as in 'the disciples followed Jesus', had used an Aranda word meaning 'tracking' which carried the connotation of following someone to kill him. The new translation had the disciples walking in front of Jesus, to indicate a total trust. Strehlow had also established beyond any doubt that the word '*ltana*' previously used for the Holy Spirit referred only to the departed spirit—more colloquially, a 'spook' or 'ghost'—and should never have been used. '*Enka*', referring to the spirit of the living person, was by far the better word.

And Strehlow never made a final decision on any word unless Moses and the other older men had corroborated the exact meaning with the Greek, Latin and German texts he was following. With his outstanding linguistic ability and his deep feeling for traditional Aranda culture, Strehlow wanted to produce a translation that would incorporate and preserve the highest of Aranda tradition and language. Albrecht was profoundly glad to see the work going ahead. 'What he has done is truly remarkable, and I am glad I never put my finger to it, as it would have been just insignificant compared with his.'

The other Aboriginal evangelists were also at the station during January for their annual refresher courses—*Freizeit*, as Albrecht called it. To him, these times were a delight, and increasingly a highlight of his year. If only there was more time to do this, the really important work. This year the Aboriginal evangelists at each centre were changing. For quite some time, Albrecht had felt that Titus was no longer managing at Haasts Bluff. His wife, Esmeralda, had been unstable since the birth of her baby. And Titus himself was failing. Sometimes he had trouble remembering things, and had lost himself in the bush a few months before. A little galvanized-iron shed had been built for him at the Bluff.

Almost three inches of rain fell at the mission in late February 1948. Haasts Bluff had seven inches, Coniston station nine. The Finke came down in one of the biggest floods they had ever seen, swirling muddy water through the vegetable garden at the back of their house, sweeping parts of the fence downstream, and coming as far up as the date palms. When the water subsided, rubbish was piled up over the plants, in some places four feet high. For the first time in fourteen years, the Kaporilja pipeline coming across the Finke was broken, and it was two weeks before the river went down enough to locate the break. The large mission garden was kept alive by pumping water from the well across the Finke. It was brackish, but it held the garden until replacement pipes could be sent from Melbourne.

At Haasts Bluff, there had been trouble serious enough for Hermann Pech to call in the police. Kamatu, the tribal leader whom

Albrecht had met on his first trip through Ilbilla in 1930, had been speared. The spear was barbed, so that when it was pulled out, the upper leg was horribly torn. By the time Hermann Pech reached the spot, the man had bled to death. He had been accused of sorcery, and the spearing was certainly deliberate. But little information was forthcoming, and no police action was taken. Albrecht was saddened by the news. He had often seen Kamatu in the years at Haasts Bluff, and he had never forgotten the tall well-built leader in the camp at Ilbilla in 1930, and the courtesy with which he had received his rare visitors. He had never sought baptism, but in the last few years he had begun to translate some of the hymns into Pintubi.

Albrecht spent a couple of days with the Pechs, and thought how hard both of them were working. Their garden had more vegetables than they could use, and the surplus went to sick people in the camp, or the older ones. And the people had obviously taken to them. He was also very pleased to see that after only seven months, Hermann was preaching in Aranda. No other European missionary in his time at Hermannsburg had mastered the language. He was having a lot of difficulty, however, with the young men in the camps, and there were similar problems of authority at Hermannsburg. Few were interested in the Christian path, yet they had lost a sense of tribal rules and obligations, and their own fathers exercised no control. Some had been running after the young schoolgirls of thirteen or fourteen. This always distressed Albrecht, and he wondered why they regarded girls of eighteen or nineteen as old. He thought the burgeoning art movement was an unsettling influence for the young men. They saw Albert and the other artists going out painting, with plenty of supplies. Obviously, it was a style of life that appealed to them much more than ordinary life on the mission. Yet he could not but worry how they would find their way back to any regular work or trade. Even more, he believed they would never succeed if they had no spiritual ground under their feet.

The pressures on many fronts were taxing Albrecht to the limit. The building needs and the never-ending difficulties in finding people to do the work were a continuing harassment. The needs of the outstations, too, were always at the back of his mind. Translation work was urgently needed to give the evangelists a few materials. Yet he was tied not only to the administration of the main station but to the greater part of the religious work there as well. While he and Sam Gross shared the Sunday services (Sam taking his in English), confirmation and baptism classes in Aranda fell to Albrecht. He told Minna despondently that as soon as he left Hermannsburg, all the classes ceased. By the time he came back, half of the people would have left for one reason or another. Lately he had begun to wonder if the board should be looking for his successor. Not that he had any immediate plan to leave, but often he had the feeling that his best energies had been tapped.

More and more, too, he was sensing the enormity of the task of helping Australia's Aborigines re-establish themselves in the changed conditions. And the task was so unclear, as he sometimes reflected when he heard Europeans with no firsthand experience of Aborigines championing their cause. Many had no understanding that the most difficult aspect of working with Aborigines was that they simply did not conform to white man's 'ideas and well prepared plans'. It seemed to him that the cultural gap between Aboriginal and European Australians would take generations of deeply committed effort by European Australians to bridge. 'The fact remains that the majority of these boys and girls going through our school cannot as yet take a place in our community life. They have lost their past, but not gained the future.'

Speaking to a congregation at Murray Bridge the previous October, Albrecht had spoken of the way that Christian missions also had played a part in alienating Aborigines from their former cultural foundations. The simple fact of feeding them helped them develop a taste for the European's food. Mission teaching gave them a different understanding of their origins which also tended to alienate them from bush life, since their religion had been an essential part of their sense of mastery over their physical surroundings. Yet how could Christians deny them the truth, especially when their old beliefs were almost always breaking up?

Other factors contributed. Europeans had simply assumed that the dispossessed Aborigines would become workers like themselves. Nothing was further from the truth. Traits of regularity and diligence normal to white man's work were foreign to Aborigines. They were not used to living in larger communities, so many found it very difficult to take orders within an organization. Always haunted by the spectre of the ruins of the Lake Killalpaninna mission, Albrecht had vested every particle of his strength and determination into the Aboriginal work in Central Australia. Yet, he asked his listeners, had even Christian missions done everything possible to assist Aborigines into a new life?

When those Natives, also through the agency of the Mission, had lost their past, was everything done to help them to gain their future? They were expected to come over to us, to struggle and gain a place for themselves, and we had no sympathy for them if they lost. We had helped to create in them an appetite for our foodstuffs and ways of living, but did we really do all we can to help them to gain legal access to it? It has been through our teaching, too, that these people, as pointed out before, have largely lost the feeling of homeliness in the bush, since they no longer are able to believe the tales of their fathers. But what have we really done to make them feel at home under new conditions? If you want to feel at home, you must have a little corner which you can call your own, you must be master of your own way of life . . . Have we really done our duty to achieve such objectives? . . . I have no ready answer to these questions.

I might as well give him thanks anyway, because he's bin done a great many different ways. They had a big drought for seven years, before I was born. In that time, we didn't have even a motor car to bring in food. He's bin working, busting his own stomach to look after this community — seven years drought! He used to go down with people, take all the bush tuckers, feed all the people here, race up to make some garden, get vegetables for people. I got to give him lots of thanks. Us mob born in that time when he was still here, still try to give us good thing.

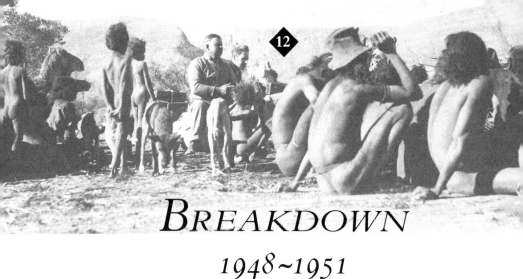

BREAKDOWN
1948~1951

*I was working with Sister when I came back from Henbury, give
medicine for sick people and children, then work in clinic, feeding all
the children. After my children, started do the rugs. And make fancywork. Taught by Mrs Albrecht and Mrs Gross. Then bluchers,
men's boots, from skin. With fancywork, Mrs Albrecht gave it to
you, and you took it away. For the rugs, stay in the rug room, show us how
to do it. You see this little hole, cut this, put little patch, same skin colour,
not different. It was good idea, teach everything, learn how to do things.
I always think that, all the time.*

In May of 1948, Minna suffered a severe heart attack. Helene
came home from her second year of nursing training at the
Royal Adelaide Hospital to care for her mother and help with the
running of the house.

The mission had not escaped the measles epidemic then running
rife on Aboriginal settlments in Central Australia. In the middle of
June, seventy were ill at Areyonga and three had died. Over sixty
were ill at Hermannsburg and the normal routines were completely
disrupted. Many people were on four-hourly penicillin. Helene and
her father did most of the night injections, and were glad of the
electric light. At Haasts Bluff, the church that Lou Borgelt had
sponsored was turned into a hospital ward. Many of the sick and
their relatives crowded into it, lighting their fires on the earth floor
to keep warm in the freezing nights. Again Albrecht was conscious
of a changed ethos:

What a change in the attitude of officialdom. In 1929, when you [Riedel] came up to see the Minister, there were people dying everywhere, and the result of our interview was nil. Now the Acting District Superintendent goes out, he leaves a patrol officer out there permanently to help, and just asks what else they could do.

William Wurst had returned in April and started boring in the Umbartja area again. He put down three holes, all of them unsuccessful, and they wondered whether to continue there. He worked tirelessly, staying out on the job for weeks at a time so as not to lose time in driving, and Albrecht found it hard that there was nothing to show for all the efforts. 'It is a real tragedy', he wrote to Riedel in the same letter, 'God alone knows why we should have to experience this'.

In September 1948 Albrecht went to Darwin for the first time to attend a federal government conference on Aboriginal missions. It was chaired by Sydney University anthropologist, Professor A. P. Elkin, and attended by government officials and representatives from missions all over the Northern Territory. Medical services, education and economic development were discussed, and Albrecht was asked to speak about his experience in establishing industries among the Aborigines. He was interested to see that the Aboriginal incomes that had been developed at Hermannsburg were far higher than anywhere else, though he was at pains to explain that the income of the mission varied greatly according to seasons and cattle prices. A new initiative was taken in government assistance for Aboriginal education. The government would pay missions an annual educational subsidy of £250 for each fully qualified teacher employed to teach Aboriginal children. Twenty years had passed, Albrecht reflected, since he and Riedel had pushed that point so unsuccessfully in the 1920s.

Late that month, Minna had another severe heart attack and was flown in to the Alice Springs hospital. The doctor said there was no question of her returning to the station. She was depressed and not at all her usual self, and they travelled south to Sellicks Beach in mid-November. Despite some improvement in her physical health, the new year brought little real change. Her state of mind was restless and unsettled. Dr Duguid thought she could expect to be perfectly well eventually, but it might take time.

They returned north by train in early April 1950, and Albrecht took up his usual array of tasks. It was Easter, so within a few days he was off to Haasts Bluff and Areyonga for Communion services. Stocktaking at the Bluff store had to be done, and more supplies ordered. New arrangements had to be made about banking accounts and signatures, or else moneys for the cattlemen and artists, as well as for Areyonga and Haasts Bluff, would not be available and difficulties would mount up quickly. Buying for the three stations needed to be streamlined. The bookkeeper, Oswald Wallent, had left in January, and it would be mid-year before his replacement, Carl Gehling, could come. And some building projects were still incomplete. The large schoolchildren's dining hall, built the year before out of flattened oil drums painted over with reflecting silver paint, had no floor so Albrecht organized some men and undertook the job himself. He was reasonably handy with carpentry, and had turned out a few pieces of household furniture when necessary. The floor took two tons of cement, as the building was ninety-five feet long, with a rough kitchen, pantry and bakehouse at one end. He was hoping also to use it for film showings if he could obtain religious films, or others of reasonable standard.

Towards the end of 1949, Minna suffered a severe relapse of depression. Much of the time she was restless and agitated, talking to herself and crying in her bedroom, her distress becoming a constant background to Mona Kennedy's correspondence lessons for the staff children in the room next door. In her unsettled state, even her religious convictions became fuel for depression and self-reproach. The belief that God and His work came first had been the very foundation of her faith, and supporting her husband in his work and helping others had been the cornerstone of all her years on the mission. Now that her physical state prevented her from doing what she had always done, she felt worthless and undeserving of God's love. The daily prayer and Bible reading they continued to share together brought her temporary respite only. Sometimes she could barely be left alone.

Doubtless her illness was exacerbated by the background of the last twenty years. The hard realities of mission and Aboriginal needs, and Albrecht's own unswerving devotion to his task, left little of his attention or energy for family. Visiting Elizabeth Pech and her small baby at Haasts Bluff some months later, Minna asked the younger woman about her household. 'Does your husband pick up the baby when he comes in?' she said. 'Papa never had time for his children', she went on in her still heavily accented English, 'only for the Aborigines'. While Minna's support and nurture had been constantly behind her husband, not enough of a truly personal nature had been returned to her. And she had always been physically frail—tubercular as a young person, renal crises with two births, heart problems. Another person might have been able to accept physical weakness and the limitations it imposed. But for Minna, the exacting standards she had absorbed from her father meant that less was not good enough.

Meanwhile Albrecht's own pressures continued unabated—at the same time that one of the central strengths of his life was only minimally available to him. Writing to the chairman, 'How little we can see through God's ways at times, but we also know He never makes mistakes, and He will be our help also in these times of darkness and suffering'.

On 25 November, Titus died at Haasts Bluff, and was buried there the same day. For Albrecht, the news brought back a flood of memories: unloading the packs from the camels in the creek sand at Alalbi; he and Titus in sober Sunday suits preaching to the naked nomads; Titus going round the camp and hitting the trees to reassure the people that God was stronger than the evil spirits; the old disputes over sharing rations. He sat down at his desk and wrote a piece in Aranda to be used in memorial services. The church at Haasts Bluff, erected through the efforts of Lou Borgelt, had been officially opened by Pastor Reuther of the board only a month before Titus's death. It seemed fitting to Albrecht that the old evangelist had lived to see a church built for his people. He later recorded Titus's death in the annual report for the synod:

> November 25, Titus passed away at Haasts Bluff. He was the man on whom for years past the whole future of this place depended, and if we have a station with a future, we must never forget that it is largely due to the faithfulness of this Aboriginal.

Five months later, Abel died at Hermannsburg. He was another of the older Christian men who were the mainstays of the congregation when the Albrechts came in 1926.

 Old Titus, Rengkareka, he was shepherding sheep in the Ellery, Pastor Albrecht called him to go west to preach the gospel. Titus left the job, and he called a lot of people with their language, speak Loritja and Pintubi, Aranda too. Call a lot of people.

Further developments were precipitated at Haasts Bluff by a report from the government dentist to Native Affairs officials that some older women were in an advanced state of malnutrition. Taking Minna with him, Albrecht drove out to Haasts Bluff for discussions with the government men. It was decided to start a community kitchen, with the cooking done in the open until Albrecht could organize for a shed to be built. The old people would get at least one meal a day. Albrecht also wanted to get some huts for old and sick people, thinking that separate huts would be more suitable than wards. Sick people would be more comfortable since they could have some family and friends with them, yet they would still be close to the main building, to be given meals and medicine regularly. At present, the nursing sister, Ida Wurst, was giving penicillin injections to a patient two miles away. That meant five trips on a bicycle, the last after ten at night.

There had been little summer rain, and the stock situation progressively worsened as Christmas of 1950 came and went. Art Latz and Albrecht conferred about selling cattle. They would only fetch low prices but, if there was no rain, losses would be devastating. These problems were more the worries of Albrecht and his staff than of most of the Aboriginal community. Sometimes Albrecht almost despaired that the people would ever take responsibility for their own survival. Even the cattle scheme which had been started with a few hand-picked individuals had failed to arouse any lasting interest, though most had paid off their loans from the mission through successful bullock sales. For the last few weeks, however, most of the Aboriginal cattlemen had been living in at Hermannsburg and no-one knew if their cattle had any water left, or whether the lot had died. 'It is a tragedy', Albrecht was to write to Riedel:

> Now these men have paid their debts, they have money to enable them to carry on, and they have just lost all interest in the matter. I had always thought if they would be on their own and work for themselves, they would again show the old determination which was so evident in their struggle for existence before white people came and upset the economy. Now I don't know what the next move is to help them.

 I was at Undandita, two or three years. Nanny goats and bullocks. All the time truck'em Alice Springs, get'em money. Yes, good time for me. No water bin one time, sell all the cattle, too much work, get'em money and sit down back in Hermannsburg.

Albrecht went on to detail how the former storekeeper at Haasts Bluff, Ted Abbott, had little interest in his new job as stockman for the cattle the government had brought out to Haasts Bluff, and was always around the camp or in the vicinity of the store:

I am writing about his case fully as in him we can clearly see the whole problem of our Aborigines. On the one hand, they have lost the bush completely, have even raised a family with the backing of the Mission, have a great demand for our living conditions as regards food and clothing, at the same time they are unable to establish themselves in any way to give them legal access to the amenities which they think they cannot live without . . . The question is how can such people be helped. Ted's case could be multiplied so very many times . . .

Early in May 1951, Albrecht received news of serious fighting at Haasts Bluff. Since the Pechs were away on furlough, Albrecht and Minna and the two youngest children, Minnie and Martin, made a three-day trip to Areyonga and Haasts Bluff. Traugott, an Aboriginal child who had grown up in close association with the Albrecht household after his mother had died, also went out as a new evangelist. Several men had spoken at his commissioning service, and Albrecht had noticed in what they said that the work of bringing the Gospel to people at the outstations had become the special responsibility of the Hermannsburg congregation. For years, he remembered, the people at Haasts Bluff were regarded as 'just Loritjas' and hardly worth bothering about. That attitude had definitely gone now. As one man said, 'When the Lord Jesus said, go ye into all the world, he included the Loritjas too'.

The atmosphere was heavy with a sense of impending trouble. Apparently, messages had been sent from Areyonga calling the Haasts Bluff men to a circumcision corroboree. The response was poor, and a Haasts Bluff evangelist, Alexander, was blamed for keeping the people back. Now it was being said he would be killed, and people were waiting for it to happen.

Albrecht asked for a meeting—his usual procedure—at which it was finally resolved who had begun the stories and who was spreading them. They finished with a handshake all round and a prayer, and afterwards the Christian men met to discuss Alexander's behaviour. Unnerved by the tension earlier in the day, he had been involved in a fight. There was no doubt he had been much antagonised, since everybody was saying he would be killed. But Rolf told him that, as a messenger of the Gospel, he should not have been afraid—his body could be killed, but never his soul. Alexander admitted the truth of this, told the men he was sorry, and that he would not fight again. Albrecht said little in the lengthy discussion, but was inwardly amazed at the knowledge of Scripture shown. The incident had also convinced him how much better it was when the older Christians took charge of such proceedings. 'Had I said much, my authority and position would have diminished their feeling of responsibility and clouded the issue'.

By 1950, federal Aboriginal policy included for the first time a substantial commitment to Aboriginal education. Albrecht had attended the first Commonwealth conference on the subject held in Sydney the previous year, and in 1950 a special course headed by Professor Elkin was organized at the University of Sydney for teachers of Aboriginal children. At Albrecht's recommendation, Hilda Wurst had attended with the financial support of the board. The government was clearly serious in its intention to establish schools for Territory Aboriginal children. Previously, only missions had provided education for these children. Albrecht was asked if the mission would rent the school at Areyonga and the old guest-house as a teacher's residence until a government school could be built.

Whether for his own or for Aboriginal children, Albrecht had always considered education an essential tool in fitting a person for life, and he also thought it important in the development of Aboriginal leadership. But he wanted a curriculum developed that was appropriate for Aboriginal children. A European-style schooling, indiscriminately applied to fullblood Aboriginal children, was not enough. And he was deeply concerned at the lack of emphasis on training for employment. In his opinion, the one great danger in recent developments was an undue emphasis on the purely physical welfare of Aborigines, especially on feeding people. It was impossible for him to conceive how any 'spoon fed people' could have a future, whoever they were. Writing to Duguid:

> Wherever the people have to be fed, I think the necessity of employment of some sort cannot be stressed too much; it is just as necessary as food itself, otherwise this free feeding will lead into impossible consequences which will be anything but helpful to the people concerned.

Minna had been considerably better for months, and the Albrechts had hoped for special leave in mid-September to attend Helene's wedding in Adelaide. But she collapsed again into another cycle of depression and misery. Two weeks after she was married, Helene was again nursing her mother, this time in her own home in Adelaide. Then Minna was transfered to a hospital for electric shock treatment. Albrecht returned north alone.

Despite his other work, he found time for extra writing. The

Aborigines' Friends' Association in Adelaide had asked him to write a pamphlet on Albert Namatjira for publication. He agreed, asking the association if they would print at least a thousand extra copies. Tourists were coming to Hermannsburg in large numbers in the winter and would be pleased to buy such a pamphlet. The article was both informative and personal, sketching the man's early life on the mission in 'the patriarchy' of Carl Strehlow's era. Namatjira had clashed with Strehlow, married a Loritja woman from another district, and often sought employment beyond the mission. The article also reflected Albrecht's concern for the impact that Namatjira's increasing income was having on himself and others—his habit of taking men to town for indefinite periods, the continued carelessness with which he handled his financial affairs, the discontent created in the mission community by the disparity in incomes. He thought Namatjira's lack of concern for the material possessions he acquired entirely natural for a man only one generation removed from bush life, but questioned the implications for his future:

> In spite of his achievements, the tragedy of the Australian aborigine hangs over him; he has not found his level in our community in which, essentially, he has remained a stranger. Looking into the future, we cannot conceal a great amount of apprehension; he would have gained very little if through the dazzling lights of publicity and wealth he should lose himself—a wanderer between two worlds.

The art movement had in recent years frequently created problems for Albrecht and his staff as they tried to protect the artists from profiteers and crooked dealers. One man sold Namatjira a crate of inferior paper for the normal price, and the money was recovered only after protracted efforts. In 1948, despite the agreement of the artists that they would sell only through the mission art councils, advertisements appeared regularly in the *Centralian Advocate* for 'choice water colours by the famous Pareroultja brothers and other Aranda artists'. The man concerned was employing the artists at £2 per day to paint pictures under his 'personal supervision'. 'If this continues, it will be the end of any decent art development', wrote Albrecht.

By early 1951, Albrecht was supporting moves to dissolve the former Hermannsburg Aranda Arts Council of which he was chairman, in favour of a new one based in Alice Springs. Albert Namatjira was becoming less and less amenable to advice, and the supposed control over his affairs insisted on by the Native Affairs Branch was in fact non-existent. The artist's own state of mind was unclear. He seemed to be casting about for new directions. Some months before, he had applied to the Lands Department for a grazing block north of Mount Liebig. Albrecht was most surprised when the application was approved but with range country containing essential water supplies deleted from the block. He suggested to the secretary of the Aborigines' Friends' Association in Adelaide that they take up the matter with the Darwin authorities to help the artist get a fair deal. But the ruling was not changed, and the issue lapsed. Around the same time, Namatjira took a sample of copper from deposits near Areyonga into Alice Springs for testing, apparently interested in developing a mine. Albrecht could not help feeling that money was becoming more and more important in the man's thinking:

> One would say nothing against it if he knew how to handle it to his best advantage and for the benefit of others. But the opposite is the case, it becomes more and more a curse to him and to others who associate with him.

Namatjira himself may have agreed. He told Battarbee one night that he used to be happier when he had no money. Yet there were aspects of the man which Albrecht recognized and admired. He had had the courage to risk the new, and in this Albrecht felt he could be a role model for other Aborigines. Writing to Reverend Gordon Rowe of the Aborigines' Friends' Association:

> The average Native if he sees things done by white people he has not practised himself, usually leaves it at that by saying and thinking: that is alright for the white man, but it is beyond me . . . Albert is no exception to this rule, yet he had the courage to attempt something of which he could have never known whether he would succeed or not. I well remember the very first painting he did; it was a picture of one of the Staff dwellings, with a picket fence in front. Since he had never heard of a 'vanishing line', his fence appeared nearly twice as high at the end than in the middle, and the painting made a funny impression. Albert himself could see that too, but instead of giving up, it only made him more determined; he pressed on, and by doing so he paved the way for others of his tribe to follow.

Albrecht had initially encouraged Namatjira in his pastoralist scheme, thinking that it might also assist others. Yet, despite his long commitment to helping the people develop their own economic foundations, he felt that the increased money among the people at Hermannsburg seemed to be creating as many problems as it solved:

There is always money in the camp, through the artists and the cattlemen, and the earnings through our leather industry, and the monthly payments. The men, therefore, know if one has anything, and especially if Albert comes through, the rest are right, and will not go hungry. Also the weekly rations issued to women with children and the old people help to keep the wolf away. It is different at a cattle station where there is nothing to fall back on, and they have to work, or leave.

Nor did he approve of the lenient conditions at government settlements. At Jay Creek, workers were paid £1 a week even though they never turned up for work in the afternoons. In face of seemingly intractable attitudes, he often felt hopeless, and thought the only solution would lie in a better preparation of the younger generation. Even in matters of health, lack of motivation was a critical issue. A medical inspection of Aboriginal settlements for tuberculosis in August 1951 revealed more illness at Hermannsburg than had been realized. Albrecht wondered how they could deal with it in the longer term, since most people were little interested in observing the necessary health measures:

For instance, it is practically impossible to segregate them, even in the slightest. They will insist in using the same drinking and eating utensils, whether the person is sick or not, or swapping clothing with all the dirt and germs on ... Then, we have a vegetable meal for all at midday ... However, for most of them this is far too much bother, they will rather go without, or have a cup of tea, then a good feed of damper at night ... the question of nourishment probably is the biggest one, and I don't know what to do about it ... May God show us a way out of the difficulty.

I got idea about work, this gardening business by Albrecht, all this job, stockman, fencing, building, learned from Missionary Albrecht's time. I want to work and make a business, not bludge on the government. I want to self-develop, make some money. Only few feel that way. Lot of people do nothing, just sitting there. We all born in Hermannsburg, we all see what Albrecht bin doing in the past, and we got to do things. Need job to keep us going, bring up life into this world.

Strehlow's New Testament translation was almost finished. Albrecht thought it an event worthy of special commemoration. Going to his desk early each morning as usual, he produced five closely typed pages entitled 'The Gospel and the Nomadic Aranda in Central Australia'. It was run off on the old duplicator and forwarded to interested people. He meant it as an expression of thanks to the translator, the Bible Society, and the many friends whose contributions had made the printing possible. He commented on some of the issues of such a translation. Much biblical phraseology had little meaning in a nomadic culture. There was no such thing as a permanent house, or a table. Teachings on earthly possessions and financial gain meant little to them. 'Native Christians have occasionally told us that such passages of Scripture refer to white people, not to them.' Nomads had never sowed seed, so there was no Aranda word for 'sowing'. In the new version, the seed was 'rained' on the ground.

Yet in many aspects Scripture had deeply penetrated the inner life of Aboriginal Christians. Moses had often said that the first missionaries found it difficult to explain the idea of sinfulness to the Aborigines, since the tribal elders thought they were perfect and above any law if they were initiated. 'In this respect', wrote Albrecht, 'a great change has taken place; whatever a man does now is judged in the light of the Word of God'. He had noticed how important this factor was at congregational meetings. Much argument ensued on matters which could tolerate a variety of opinions, but for anything on which Scripture was clear, 'the person in question will give in, or promise to make restitution without question'. He ended on a note which sounded his own deepest struggle. Christian conviction in Aboriginal people simply did not result in the kinds of changes in lifestyle and values which European Christians often assumed. Often Christian Aborigines showed little inclination to change from collecting food to producing it:

> ... essentially they continue to live their lives as their fathers did, with the great exception as regards the Word of God ... It has become a great power in their lives and means as much to them as it does to us. We may therefore conclude that if we and our ancestors have received abundant blessings through the Scripture, we may expect nothing less for our Aborigines. Much of our hope for their future centres around this Book.

October 1950 recalled the pioneer Hermannsburg missionaries who began their long trek north from Bethany seventy-five years before. Albrecht wrote and duplicated a pamphlet to remember the occasion, describing the immense difficulties of the journey and the faith and endurance of the missionaries, despite the mistakes made and their ignorance of the country. His generous tribute said as much about the writer as the people he was remembering:

> The dominant factor was simple faith in God. That faith was needed many times in the history of this Mission, both by the Church that

sent them, and the missionaries themselves. But it had its greatest test on this journey. In all their reports, most of which were written under very trying conditions, we never find a suggestion to give up or go back; their eyes were fixed on a very definite goal, and everything had to be done to reach it ... It was, and always will remain, one of the most heroic missionary journeys in Australia.

The last months of 1950 were stressful. A son-in-law of W. Wurst, Vic Modra, had offered to build a new school at his own expense, and the builder he had engaged had levelled substantial criticism at mission facilities and Albrecht's management. Albrecht could not feel that there was real foundation in the statements. But the episode took some personal toll, perhaps because he felt he had heard echoes of some of the same things from others. Sometimes board members intimated that his past hung too heavily upon him, that the traumas of the early years still shaped his approach. In the bright new age of assimilation policy, he seemed over-cautious about the future of Aborigines and their ability to survive in European environments. Sometimes he wondered if there was not some truth in it.

He was drained too, physically and emotionally. The last two years of Minna's illness and its continuing uncertainty had robbed him of much of his primary emotional support. The old reflexes to his work still operated, but some inner mainspring seemed to have snapped. A sense of deep depletion came out in a letter he wrote to Riedel in early November 1950. Riedel had resigned as chairman after twenty-five years, and his place was taken by Pastor R. B. Reuther of Lights Pass. Writing his last letter as chairman, Riedel commented that he felt his official relationship with the mission staff had deteriorated in recent years. Albrecht replied in some detail, affirming that their personal relationship had never been disturbed, but clarifying particular issues in which he felt the chairman's interpretation of his actions had been wide of the mark:

> One was in connection with the water scheme, when I wanted to connect up the Finke wells with the station. On that occasion you wrote to Br Mattner and asked him would he report on what I had done in this matter, and whether he was in favour of this work being done. I thought, after my struggles with the Kaporilja water scheme, that this displayed such lack of confidence that co-operation would hardly be possible again. But thinking and praying over it, I felt I should not do anything; there was too much just started and not consolidated, and after all, I was convinced God wanted me to do a job and complete it as far as possible. Work went on, and grass grew over it ...

Another rift he referred to had been over a staff member, whose reappointment Albrecht had opposed:

> For some weeks I didn't know what to do. But here again, there was the work of the outstations just beginning to take shape, and leaving it then would have brought about a collapse of this side of our activities, and after all the work and anxiety that had gone into it, I again felt I must see it through.

The letter carried no personal bitterness, rather a strong feeling of spentness. The board had offered him and Minna twelve months of long service leave and a holiday in Europe. Though the precise time had not been arranged, it was clear from his tone that he was sensing a watershed in his life and in the work with which he had so totally identified himself:

> I feel, therefore, it will be best if I go out for a while . . . Much will continue simply by the law of 'gravity' and perhaps—a fact that would make me particularly happy—others may find a better way to be employed from now on, building on from the foundation which has been laid. But that will never be achieved except through a lot of selfsacrifice . . . Should everything go downhill, I hardly think I will have the strength to put my shoulder to the wheel and do what I had to do in the past . . .

Minna's uncertain health had so far prevented them from making definite plans for their furlough. Early in December 1950, she was back home. She rested a lot, and avoided anything that might tend to agitate her. Albrecht suggested to Pastor Reuther as chairman that he particularly thank Mrs Gross, who had carried on most of the work normally done by Minna. 'She is always willing, and there is nothing she is not prepared to do at any time.'

And as always, there were tasks Albrecht wanted to complete. Perhaps the feeling was all the more intense, since he did not really know if he would be back. The Aranda service book was still incomplete, since it had to wait for the final form of the New Testament. But he was hoping to see it in the hands of the people before he left. Twenty young people were almost ready for confirmation. And he hoped to finalize the mission–government arrangements for schools as far as possible.

January 1951 brought the evangelists' courses and the annual election of elders. Conrad was out this year, rather to Albrecht's disappointment. Conrad was thirty-four years old, a quiet, dependable individual whose mother had been a devoted Christian in Carl Strehlow's congregation. As a young man, Conrad had asked

Albrecht if he could also be a pastor. At the time, Albrecht had hesitated, explaining that college training was necessary. But Conrad had joined the evangelists' classes, and had served with Titus at Haasts Bluff for a year and at the mission itself. Now, he had been an elder for the last four years. Remembering the first election of elders over twenty years before, Albrecht thought to himself that the mission could hardly have carried on without them. Fighting was virtually a thing of the past. Most arguments were settled at their meetings, which were held frequently, often lasting for hours and never attended by staff. He had not always found it easy to support their decisions, but felt on the whole the men had acted responsibly and as Christians.

Yes, seven years drought. Many people die when I was growing up. My mother pass away too. And my father, he came from Ormiston, he was just ready for baptize, when pass away. My uncle, Abel, my mother's brother, I went into his home. Like another mother take me, grow me up. Yes, it was hard. When I was going to school, I only think about that it's God's will, the drought, this is God's hands, God leading us. When I was little boy, I was thinking too much! My mother was a wise mother, and my uncle show me the way to see Jesus. He's the way, truth and life. Might be eight or nine when I first believed that.

Shortly after the elections, the last surviving child of Moses and Sofia became ill. Klementine was about twenty-eight years old, but small and frail. She'd had yaws badly as a child and later tuberculosis, and she had been very weakened by the birth of her first child. In the Albrecht house and elsewhere, there was much heartfelt prayer that God would spare her. It was not to be. Albrecht was brought the news at daybreak and walked over to the hospital. Moses was outside on the verandah and he and Albrecht went in together to where Sofia and a number of relatives were around the body wailing. Moses was the first to speak: 'Friends, don't cry too much, she has gone to the big light, she sees the Lord now, and we shall find her again'.

Tourists were constantly increasing, many of them brought out by Connellan's Airways and the two tour companies, Bonds and Tuits. Albrecht had always felt it was important to welcome visitors and give what hospitality they could, even if it was only a cup of tea. But the larger numbers were making more and more inroads into his time. 'One does regret the time spent in this way, but there is no way out of it just now, and there will be a blessing in it, too', he commented characteristically to Reuther. The comment was part of his deeply ingrained belief that a Christian had frequently to sacrifice personal convenience to be of service to others. He and Minna had always tried to be available to people whatever the personal cost, and their years at the mission seemed to bear out their belief that God worked through such service. There were innumerable examples, from the Misses Teague taking up the cause of Kaporilja water, to a hundred others. It was still happening. A visitor in June asked how he could help after reading about the mission in Arthur Groom's recently published account of Central Australia, *I Saw a Strange Land*. The outcome was a Southern Cross diesel engine and pump to replace the Finke pumping plant which had broken down.

But sometimes the tourist parties meant problems. The previous September, three of the schoolgirls had spent the night in the vicinity of the drivers' camp at Palm Valley, and the Hermannsburg elders decided there had been misconduct. Rolf and Conrad came to Albrecht and asked him to discuss the matter with the company supervisor in Alice Springs. They wanted the tourist camp at Palm Valley kept under strict control with respect to the Aborigines, and the driver concerned discontinued on the Hermannsburg–Palm Valley route. Albrecht took the matter up as requested, indicating the elders' strong feelings on the matter. He stood firm in the decision, despite pressure from both the company and Native Affairs to allow the driver on the run again. He explained to Reuther:

> The Native Elders would feel their decision is of no consequence and is just brushed aside by me at the request of outsiders. For years now we have tried to hand over more and more responsibility to the Native Elders, and this would mean we would break it all up.

Such experiences caused Albrecht increased soul-searching on the whole question of tourist access to the mission and its impact on community life. Two government officers strongly advised complete closure of the mission to tourists, and most of the staff agreed. Large numbers of visitors every week during the winter disrupted the schoolchildren and Aboriginal workers. On the other hand, Albrecht feared that complete closure could have negative repercussions. Cancellation of existing bookings would create resentment, and he also thought that a closed-shop approach inevitably aroused negative feeling. Always a strong believer in communication, he had tended to encourage people to come and see the place so they could understand it—church people no less than others.

The tourist question was indicative of the increasingly public profile which the mission and its superintendent were gaining. Articles by Northern Territory newspaperman Douglas Lockwood and other reporters appeared from time to time in papers around Australia. Describing in sometimes purple prose Albrecht's struggles in the drought and later years, most lauded a man 'recognised, with Bishop Gsell, as one of the two men who have done more practical work for Territory natives than any other'.

In early September 1951, Albrecht felt he should write something definite to the board concerning their future. Though Minna was quite herself now, the margin to depression was narrow and liable to be stirred up by visitors or other pressures. He suggested that the board consider stationing them at Alice Springs after their return from overseas. If they could no longer fill their positions at the mission as they had done for so long, they were likely to be more of a hindrance than a help. He also felt there might be an advantage in bringing new ideas into station management. 'Perhaps it is true that my past, which was a struggle almost from the beginning to the end, hangs on me.' If they lived at Alice Springs, his experience would still be available to the work, and he could continue to negotiate as necessary with the government officers. Literary work was still sorely needed, such as an explanation of the catechism, sermons, or comments on difficult issues.

> While here at the station, I am now fully convinced I shall never be able to settle down to this. If a drain is blocked, then they come and I have to solve the problem. If the people have a dispute, they are here again . . . I am sure one could do more while living at the Alice . . .
>
> Well, this is what I had on my mind. It is a suggestion only. Very often we make plans, and in the end God has other ways, everything is turned upside down, but found to be better . . . I did not come here to go my own ways, and am still prepared to serve to the best of my ability . . . But we do think a change would be in the interest of the work . . .

The parting was not far off. Train seats to Adelaide for themselves and Martin (Minnie was now at college) were booked for 22 November. Early November was spent packing, sorting and storing personal belongings. Many had been brought from Europe twenty-six years before. Some were pieces of furniture Albrecht had made himself from an assortment of materials—the boards of packing cases used for groceries in the camel days, a little seasoned timber he had brought from Germany. Minna's creativity and skills were reflected in items like the large sofa she had upholstered with kangaroo skin.

Most of the dozen-odd Aboriginal artists appeared on the verandah in the last week with a painting or two. More than once Albrecht felt embarrassed, remembering the many times he had reprimanded these men. But they appeared to hold no grudges. Albert Namatjira also came with a painting wrapped in a hessian sugar bag. Albrecht hesitated, feeling he should not accept such a valuable gift. He and Minna had bought several of his paintings in his first few years, then they had become too expensive. But Namatjira insisted, saying he had not forgotten how much the pastor had done for him. They were formally farewelled a few nights before they left. The whole community sat in the sand in front of the Albrecht home and sang hymn after hymn. Old Moses spoke, followed by Alexander from Haasts Bluff, Conrad, Herbert and Henoch. Albrecht was surprised and moved at their eloquence and the range of their thinking, pondering how well Aborigines could express themselves when their feelings were touched.

Perhaps Albrecht made something of his own farewell in a last letter to the chairman. There were a number of matters to relate: government officer Billy McCoy had been out in connection with a meeting of the Aboriginal Pastoralists Association; the government would like the mission to find a married couple for Areyonga to take over some of the teacher's work; the need for more accommodation. He ended on a personal note:

> We are getting ready to leave here tomorrow, so this will be the last letter from this desk ... It is not easy to make the break, but our hearts are filled with deepest and humble praise for all the Lord has done here with us and to us. May He in His grace cover all our sins, and continue to bless the work as He has so abundantly in the past.

They left late on Sunday, the truck moving away in the midst of a sea of people and faces and goodbyes.

In that time earlier, he brought some people from Ilbilla, from a place called Kintore, and across the south, Docker River, on the Petermann Ranges. He put up that Areyonga mission, that Haasts Bluff mission — Areyonga Pitjantjatjara [people], Haasts Bluff Warlpiri or Loritja, this one [Hermannsburg] Aranda. He had a pretty rough time with the station [owner] mob, they was against him, and the policemen — you shouldn't be doing this, don't worry about Aborigines, shoot them if troubles come.
All these people were saved here.

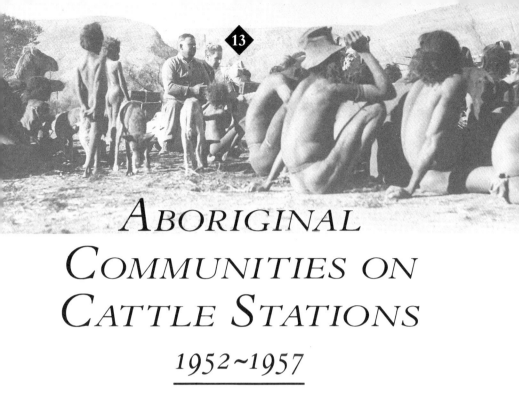

ABORIGINAL COMMUNITIES ON CATTLE STATIONS

1952~1957

Went to Tempe Downs, that's the time I learned to work! Start to teach wash up plate, wash the clothes every Monday, Tuesday ironing, Wednesday ironing, Thursday housework, iron all the clothes, shirts, trousers, pillowslips, dress. Ironed on Tuesday and Wednesday. Hot iron, got maybe five or six on the stove, get cold, put it back on the stove, get another one.

T he return to Europe was a happy time. They went first to Wesseloh, to stay with Minna's family. Several nieces and nephews had delayed their weddings for the visit, and there were several major celebrations, complete with a roasted pig and all the traditional foods. For the younger relatives, it was a first meeting with 'the aunt and uncle in Australia'. But they were familiar figures, even to them. Except for the wartime years, Minna had kept up regular correspondence, and sent a family photograph every year. Minna's father was well in his seventies and in good health. Yet he could not help but be aware of the five grandchildren in Australia whom he had never met. 'If only you could have brought some of them with you', he said more than once.

They attended a number of mission festivals including one at the mission institute in Hermannsburg. A mission society loaned them a Volkswagen sedan, and they used this to tour Germany, camping as they had always done in Australia. They went north to Hannover, where a sister and half-sister of his were living in stringent circumstances after coming from Poland as refugees after World War II. Travel restrictions behind the Iron Curtain made it impossible for them to go to Poland. But his family had been scattered by the wars, and his father had died the previous October. They went to London for a week.

They arrived back in Alice Springs near the end of 1952, a year after their departure from Hermannsburg, and moved into a little house which William Mattner had built for them on the mission block in Alice Springs. Pastor Gross took charge at Hermannsburg, Hermann Pech continued at Haasts Bluff, and a Pastor Leo Kalleske and his wife had been appointed to Areyonga. Albrecht's work was now to centre on Alice Springs (with its dual congregation of Europeans and Aborigines), the Aboriginal settlements at the Bungalow (formerly the old telegraph station just north of Alice Springs) and Jay Creek, apart from literary work and liaison with the government.

It was not long before a new field of work began to open up with Aboriginal workers on cattle stations south of Alice Springs. Albrecht had always had extensive contact with the sixty or seventy people at Henbury, and the Aboriginal evangelists Gamaliel and Peter had lived there and given Christian teaching for many years. As he renewed this contact he was asked to visit the Aboriginal communities on Erldunda and Maryvale stations. In each case, both station management and Aboriginal workers had supported the request.

Maryvale was a large cattle station seventy miles south-east of Alice Springs. The Alice Springs Christian worker, Martin, had taught there for several years, travelling out by train to Rodinga siding, and getting a lift with the station truck that met the train for mail and goods. He had evidently become an important figure to the group. Earlier in the year, the people had taken him down to the creek where they had made a pile of playing cards and corroboree items. '*Nana arai!*' (Look at this!). Then they put a match to the pile. 'We are finished with all this', they told him. 'We want to become Christians.' On his first visits to the station Albrecht found people who knew a good number of Bible stories and parts of the Catechism. Finding a way to provide constant teaching seemed difficult, as no-one there could read or write. But a young man called Paulus Wiljuka offered to come to town regularly for lessons with Albrecht. In under twelve months, he could read and write in Aranda quite fluently. Then he began to learn English, moving quickly through the Adelaide Readers which Albrecht used as a guide.

The immensity of the cultural changes which had taken place in Aboriginal life in Central Australia were also being signalled in Ted Strehlow's work. He was doing research work at Adelaide University and came regularly to Central Australia to record traditional language and ceremonies on film and tape. In July 1953, he was also at Maryvale station, waiting for some old Southern Aranda men to come from Finke siding to perform a major totemic song cycle. With the passing of these old men, some of the traditional ceremonies would be completely lost. He knew he could record the mythology and customs of the Areyonga and Haasts Bluff people more easily, but that could wait for some years longer as ceremonial life there was still active. But the Southern Aranda people had almost disappeared, a fact that both he and Albrecht had been noting —often in reports to government—since the early 1930s. For Strehlow, the close of the ceremony brought a sense of deep sadness. Writing in his diary on July 30,

> It is a strange thought that all is finished here now . . . the time has arrived when the last Southern Aranda, too, are due to pass away. There are only thirty Aranda and Andekerinja names in my list of men today; and of all the Southern Aranda men present only Allen has any children—and both of them are girls.
>
> The sun that set on Maryvale today saw the close of a native festival such as will never again be held in this area . . . My heart tonight is sad—because there is no hope that this fate can be averted.

Older men still alive today, they still talk about [Ted Strehlow], people don't forget that because he was with them on their big ceremony days. That big thing, his connection all his life with that, he was very important man because they choose him to be like a leader for those old men, so they can't forget.
Ingkata inurra [Albrecht], he done a lot of jobs, he done more jobs right through to the big community, from older man to children—he did it more wider. Ted Strehlow did it, but only for man.

Albrecht was attuned less keenly to the past of Central Australian Aborigines than to their potential future, and he was becoming more and more aware of the challenge presented by the estimated

14 000 Territory Aborigines who lived on cattle stations. Until then, almost nothing had been done for them either by churches or government, and their welfare depended primarily on the character and interest of the station-owner concerned. To Albrecht it was not only a matter of religious teaching—he was very aware of their need to find their place in the general community.

Minna had not really been well since her return from Europe. Almost every day, her temperature would rise a little, making her feel listless and miserable. Then the only thing she could do was rest. Marianna had come to town to live with them, and she took care of many household tasks. Minnie, or 'Min' as she was commonly called, was also living at home, studying at the Alice Springs high school for her Leaving Certificate. She usually prepared breakfast, and took a tray to her mother in bed before going off to school. As the time went by, and her father became increasingly caught up in his new sphere of work, she often felt her mother was neglected. He was in and out during the day, and would see if she needed anything. But Min felt that her mother needed more company, and sometimes thought resentfully that her father was always willing to give his time to other people, but not to his wife.

Early in December 1953, Albrecht was invited to Darwin for another government conference with mission representatives from other Christian groups—Catholic, Church of England, Methodist, Baptist, as well as the Aborigines Inland Mission and Australian Board of Missions. Paul Hasluck, the first Minister in the new Department of Territories created in 1951, sent a strongly positive message to the conference about government–mission co-operation:

> Over the past 70 years in the Northern Territory the missionaries have cared for natives at times when many others were neglecting them . . . I wish to assure those present that I know and honour the record of the missions.
>
> Today in the Northern Territory the Government is taking up the question of welfare with a clearer idea of what we want to do and with a stronger resolution than ever before . . . In achieving its aims the Government wants to go hand in hand with the missions.

Under the new Welfare Ordinance, a register of Aboriginal people in the Northern Territory was to be drawn up. Most Aboriginal people would come within the status of 'wards' which did not include normal citizenship privileges such as voting rights, or the right to buy and consume alcohol, but Aboriginal 'wards' deemed to have indicated their fitness for full or partial civil rights could apply for them. For the register, Aboriginal people had to choose a kinship name to be registered as their legal surname. Previously, most Territory Aborigines had been known to Europeans by a first name only.

The Pareroultja brothers are brothers to Namatjira, one great-grandfather. Albert's father and Dad's father were brothers. White man call cousins, we call brothers. One genealogy, [but] names are different, totems are different. Namatjira on totems. Pareroultjas on totems. Didn't pick up Grandfather's name, pick up totem's name. My grandfather went really mad, shouldn't be Namatjira, shouldn't be Pareroultja, should put in great-grandfather's name, this only totem's name. I told lots of things about family genealogy to Land Council mob, they got no sense [couldn't understand].

Albrecht presented a paper on the economic rehabilitation of Aborigines. Hermannsburg industries such as the leather work, tanning, woodwork and needlework were well known, and the economic aspect was an essential foundation of his own approach to Aboriginal development. Economic rehabilitation, he said, was a matter of addressing the fundamental break-up of their former economic system, and therefore a clear question of social justice. 'And yet, charity is about the furthest most people will think about in connection with our Aborigines.'

He had come to feel that cattle stations were potentially a more constructive environment for Aboriginal people than missions or government settlements, since they offered Aborigines an opportunity for training and gainful employment. But he regarded it as vital that the station-owner regarded the Aborigines on his station as a locally rooted, permanent community, not merely as seasonal workers to be pushed off when their services were not needed. A permanent working community made it possible for Aborigines to have children, and the old people to be looked after with food and clothing and in times of illness. To Albrecht, this provided the basic security for them to continue as a race, and was more important at this stage than the level of cash wages.

Henbury was my home, of my grandmother and grandfather. Me and Gordon went back to work there, stockwork and me in house, working all the time for people. Worked more hard on station than at Hermannsburg. But we think, only work, not thinking hard. Hard life all over stations at that time, man workin' the stock camp, didn't see man for months in the bush, must bring bullock from Henbury to

Oodnadatta. People worked hard on the stations—for no money, only for tobacco, trousers and shirt, meat and damper. Not paid anything on station until 1952. Only the relatives of those who were workin' got rations. Daughter work in the kitchen, then mother got rations. If husband workin', woman get rations. Rest lived on bush tucker, looking for kangaroo, emu, bush tucker. If they run out of tucker, they always come to Jay Creek.

Albrecht's own programme of classes and services in town had increased steadily. By the end of the year, he was teaching most week afternoons and for a few hours on Saturday mornings. At Christmas, he organized a special programme for the children, and painstakingly typed out and duplicated a script of readings and verses so all could take part. A large congregation of Aboriginals, part-Aboriginals and Europeans participated.

His interest in children doubtless came partly from the difficulties of his own childhood. His early schooling had not been easy and it had been a struggle to win acceptance for a missionary vocation and a place at the institute in Germany. Despite the hardship, or perhaps because of it, he believed deeply in the value of education in developing an individual life to the full. Their own children had received a clear message throughout their childhood that they were free to choose any career for themselves. The idea of not training for anything was not even mentioned—education for one's walk in life was simply assumed, for girls equally as boys. He had not forgotten his early days at the Hermannsburg institute where he had been shocked to see young women working in households for next to nothing. Only education, he felt, could help women against this kind of injustice.

And still earlier in his life, his experience of the last days of Imperial Russia had left no doubt in his mind that the grave injustice inherent in that society and its sheer disregard for human life in the lower classes—where a man could freeze to death waiting with a carriage outside a ballroom, and no-one think anything of it —had made a revolution virtually inevitable. Albrecht was himself no revolutionary, but a sense of common humanity crossing every colour, class and creed was very deep in him. Finally, it came down to the importance of individual lives, and his deep sense of the God-given potential in any life was especially reflected in the interest and pleasure he found in children.

In particular, he felt the potential—and the vulnerability—in the lives of the part-Aboriginal children with whom he had contact. He thought many of them had the ability for a high school education and a range of employment. But without some broader life experience, they were unlikely to realize that possibility. He had been watching the progress of Nita and Allan Garrett, part-Aboriginal children attending the Alice Springs higher primary school. Both had done well. But he feared they would inevitably lose interest in further education if they continued at the local school and in their close associations with other part-Aboriginal children. Allan had already given up coming to religious classes and told Albrecht that his father couldn't read or write but still made a living. After discussions with their parents and with the help of the board chairman, Albrecht arranged for Nita to live with a family in Nuriootpa, South Australia, while attending high school. Allan went to a family at Keyneton. Albrecht thought that even a few years in a Christian home would give them a wider outlook. He did not think such a plan appropriate for fullblood Aboriginal children, feeling that at this stage they could not really assimilate the experience. When it became known around town that the Garrett children were going south to school, other part-Aboriginal parents spoke to him. Obviously there were others who wanted their children to have wider opportunities.

Perhaps the Australian community at large was awakening to the possibility of broader educational experiences for Aboriginal children. In May 1954, a combined sports day was held in Alice Springs for all 'Centralian Native Schools', and the programme with its list of participating schools illustrated the recent dramatic changes in government initiatives in education for Aboriginal children. Hermannsburg mission school was opened in 1879, the school at the Catholic Mission, Santa Teresa, in 1944. All others —Phillip Creek, Bungalow, Yuendumu, Areyonga and Jay Creek— had been opened or taken over by the government office of education around 1950. The children stayed an extra day or two in town, went twice to 'the pictures', and were taken on a tour of the Alice Springs power house and the railway station to see the mysteries of the goods shed and an engine working under steam.

Albrecht thought that the visit must have been an interesting experience for children who had been roaming naked in the bush until very recently. Yet he was always cautious about the processes of contact, aware that in the longer perspectives of Aboriginal–European contact in Australia, such entertainment had sometimes had unexpected consequences. In the early days in South Australia, Aborigines had been invited to celebrations on national days, like Queen Victoria's birthday, and given gifts like food, tomahawks and tobacco. The Aborigines thought that this was the 'best hunting ground ever', and naturally wanted to stay in order to keep collecting. People brought to towns in this way never returned to their old living places. Something similar had occurred early in the year. Two Aboriginal men from Haasts Bluff who were flown to Brisbane to take part in a corroboree and dancing display for the visit of the Queen and the Duke of Edinburgh had later asked the settlement manager, Les Wilson, for their 'Queen money'. The new clothes, free accommodation, and pocket money of £1 a week provided for the trip seemed to them quite inadequate, and they were waiting for proper pay and a new house each, because they had gone and seen the Queen. 'Instead of helping them to see some responsibility', wrote Albrecht, 'these men had made it an occasion to do a little more collecting, perfectly in keeping with their Aboriginal way of thinking and feeling: this visit had only raised their demands considerably'.

Old Moses was in indifferent health for much of the winter of 1954. Late in June, after a service at the Jay, Albrecht took him into town and they recorded a message from the old man to his people —an American group making Gospel recordings in Aboriginal languages had been in Central Australia for some time. Moses expressed pleasure at the thought that he would continue preaching even after God had called him home, and Albrecht reflected how unbearable such a thought would be to a non-Christian Aboriginal. He died not long afterwards, and was buried in the old cemetery at Hermannsburg where he had so often spoken words of comfort and faith to others.

Albrecht found it hard to realize Moses was no longer with them. He had been part of the Ntaria community for so long, and despite his eighty-odd years was in many ways as alert as ever. Linguistically, he was outstanding. Almost to the end of his life, he would come to light with Aranda words nobody had heard before. He also knew a lot of Loritja, and in assisting with the recent Gospel recordings had often convinced even Loritja men of a better rendition of biblical truth. His memory was also colossal. Only a year before, he had spoken of incidents in his early life, describing details and conversations word for word.

Albrecht was vividly aware of the richness of the experience represented in this man—remembering his graphic descriptions of some of the first Aranda contacts with Europeans, or the account of an early visit to Hermannsburg by the pioneering anthropologist, Baldwin Spencer. Baldwin Spencer thoroughly disapproved of Christian teaching being given to the Hermannsburg people, and took every opportunity to encourage them to return to their traditional beliefs. Moses had painted an unforgettable picture of Baldwin Spencer sitting on the ground outside the little mission church during a Sunday service, his antagonism clear despite his inability to speak the Aranda language. Inside, Moses preached, urging the congregation to ignore the lies of this white man. Albrecht had often said Moses would have been a brilliant man in any circle. Sometimes he thought to himself that this man had influenced him more profoundly than any other person in his life.

If somebody took you to that old cemetery, in that yard, he will tell you, maybe old Traugott, Pastor Raberaba, anybody, he'll say, these people here, in this grave, they are believers, they dropped every-thing, that side ones too [traditional practices]. They were full of faith. In this new cemetery, not sure . . . because people's lives were stirred up with everything, grog and that sort of thing, lot of problems, we're not sure now. But in that old cemetery, a lot of faithful people. That was in Pastor Albrechta's time, people bin passed away. Those people passed away with the songs, with the hymns, with the prayers.

The Hermannsburg community celebrated the seventy-fifth anniversary of the mission school in November 1954, and Albrecht summarized its history for the occasion. It had been started in 1879 by missionaries Schulze and Schwarz. After their time, the Rever-end Carl Strehlow did the teaching himself for more than half of his time at Hermannsburg, besides his duties as missionary-manager, teaching baptismal classes, translating the New Testament, and writing his anthropological volumes. Later, other teachers had come and gone—H. A. Heinrich teaching until 1932, Pastor Peter-ing, Willie Raatz, Ruth Pech and, above all, Hilda Wurst, who had been in charge for the last fourteen years. Now the authorities had said the new school was the largest and most modern Aboriginal school in the Territory.

Albrecht was never content simply to summarize events. He always tried to evaluate, to wrest a deeper understanding to guide future action. What real results had the mission school had in the lives of the mission people? Superficially, there often seemed little. Most Aborigines who had been through the school and could read and write still preferred to live in wurleys, often in unhygienic conditions. At the same time, the Hermannsburg group of Aranda-speaking people had showed a steady increase of births over deaths from year to year. He did not feel this would be so if boys and girls had not been given some sense that life was worthwhile.

I used to work mostly Tempe, Henbury, left children at Hermanns-burg so they could go to school. I could come up and visit them. All the people on the stations would come up [to Hermannsburg] at Christmas and then after Christmas, the whole family would go back to Tempe until school started again. Not until last few years that children on cattle stations had any chance to learn anything, only horse-riding. Bungalow and Jay Creek were only for halfcastes. We sent kids to [Hermannsburg] school for them to hear about the gospel too.

To Albrecht, the art movement, now well known throughout Australia, would not have been possible without some educational background. Neither could the trading stores at Areyonga, Haasts Bluff and Jay Creek have been established and kept going for years by Aboriginal storekeepers. Above all, the large settlements at Areyonga and Haasts Bluff would not have existed without the contribution of Titus who, with other Aboriginal evangelists like Moses, had had a large share in bringing the Gospel to their people. And in the future, education would be even more vital in helping to orient Aboriginal children to employment and a future within the Australian community.

All of the Albrecht children were now away, except for Martin who was finishing high school at Alice Springs. Helene and Ted were married, Paul and Min studying in Adelaide. Albrecht's way of keeping in touch with them was, characteristically, his typewriter. He addressed letters to 'Our dear children', and made carbon copies for each. They were written in English, in which he had long been fluent. Minna's letters, always in German, gave the children home and family news, sometimes snippets about friends at the mission or at church. She was still up and down in her health. Their garden was a picture in the spring of 1955. Minna worked on it in her better times, and people going by often stopped to look. The grape-vines were coming on well and by Christmas they would have as many as they could eat. Albrecht had been working around the house. He had found some cement slabs somewhere, and placed them around the garden seat under the grape-vines in the back garden. Marianna often sat there after her work was finished.

In October 1955, Albrecht was sixty-one. A deep peacefulness and contentment came through the letter he wrote to his children a week or so later:

It is about time I say 'thank you' for your letters, and especially your birthday presents. I really felt like one of the Patriarchs, lovely gifts coming from so many quarters . . . When the figure of 61 is reached, many things one used to think so much about begin to drop back, even out of sight. But not expressions of human love . . . somehow, one remains very susceptible to these . . .

Even in his quietest moments, his thoughts turned almost invariably to the Aboriginal work. He and Minna had expected their time in Alice Springs to be a semi-retirement. The contrary was true, but there was nothing like the intensity of pressure he had felt at Hermannsburg, and he was deeply relieved at the change. He was happy, too, at the continuing influence of some of the Aboriginal Christians on the cattle stations. Gamaliel was still the unquestioned authority at Henbury, and highly respected by the European management although he could not read or write. Peter at Henbury was also a fine Christian worker. Albrecht often thought with dismay how the church, and especially the Lutheran church, had neglected the gifts of its lay people. He had often been impressed by the contribution of Methodist lay preachers. He was less happy about some of the present developments in the Finke mission's work. At the last field conference he had attended at Hermannsburg, he thought how many staff there were now, yet they were still asking for more. He feared that they were simply creating more activities which in the end would have to be run by European staff—a trend of no real value to the Aborigines. It was part of a general trend. Government was spending large sums of money on Territory Aborigines, but not always in a way that would help people to help themselves. At the same time, he was glad there was goodwill and a desire to help.

Ted Strehlow had attended one of the field conference sessions, and Albrecht was interested in his answers to staff questions. Strehlow had emphasized the spiritual life of the desert Aborigines, so often overlooked by Europeans. Despite a hard life, often with little food, they had spent a great proportion of their time on spiritual matters. Modern Europeans lived in plenty but had little concern with the spiritual. He also explained how young Aboriginal men were very strictly trained and guided by the old men until they were about twenty-four years old. It confirmed Albrecht's emerging ideas on the value of an apprenticeship system for Aboriginal boys after formal education. Another staff member asked what attitude they should be taking to corroborees. Strehlow implied that the mission simply had to accept them as a reality, especially since many people from Areyonga went to ceremonies at Ernabella. Albrecht knew that the Ernabella missionary and staff accepted and even encouraged them. Yet even Strehlow, questioned further, admitted that corroborees expressed their spiritual life, and re-enacted phases of the life of some spiritual god-ancestor. If so, Albrecht asked himself, how could a Christian missionary encourage this, without doing harm to the cause of the Gospel?

Since coming to Alice Springs, Albrecht was often called on to attend court cases involving Aborigines. He had been almost thirty years in Australia, and was a familiar and respected figure within the European as well as the Aboriginal community in Central Australia. Sometimes he was required as interpreter, sometimes to give cultural background as expert evidence to certain offences. Sometimes he'd had to explain that a man charged with murder, while he had undoubtedly performed the act, was not the only person involved: his had been the role of executioner, but the real sentence had been passed by others. Judge Martin Kriewaldt in particular was sensitive to the different cultural context and not infrequently requested his services.

Albrecht still felt that European law and law-keeping was sometimes very inadequate in its dealings with Aborigines. Late in 1954, police and Native Affairs officers found the charred remains of a body near Ti-tree station. Albrecht knew from his contacts with Aborigines that the identities of the real killers was common knowledge. Yet because it was a tribal affair, it was not being pursued. He felt it was another form of the old 'leave them alone' policy, an attitude he still noticed sometimes. In reality, it meant that many Aboriginal people in the area lived in fear of the same fate. In a similar case a man had died near Haasts Bluff after attending a ceremony. Concerned that people understand the implications of such 'tribal affairs', Albrecht outlined several of these cases in mission newsletters:

> It must be borne in mind that this goes on in a community where human life is considered sacred and protected . . . It must also be kept in mind that men thus doomed [condemned to tribal killing] are never given a hearing, they have no knowledge of what others have decided against them. As a result, they have no chance of defending themselves. In this case, as far as we have been able to establish the facts, the man had been accused of coming too late for a certain sacred ceremony, and was punished for this. Others . . . state that he was purposely delayed, so that they might have a cause against him, motivated by some grudge. Under any such conditions there is no thought of justice; the individual is at the mercy of some older men

... Under old conditions where there was no outside interference and complete groups of Natives watching and opposing each other, some measure of justice did work itself out in the end. Since the advent of the white man, however, the evildoer so often escapes punishment, with the result that the evil grows ...

Again he advocated, as he had since the 1930s, the need for 'Native Courts under the supervision of a special magistrate. This would ensure that the feeling for justice, which is so strongly developed among our Aborigines, would not be frustrated, but used to advantage in the process of assimilation.'

Early in 1955, an evangelist called Timothy went from Hermannsburg to contact workers on the cattle stations north of Alice Springs. Then Philipp Scherer, who had replaced Hermann and Elizabeth Pech at Haasts Bluff, visited Narwietooma, Napperby, Coniston, Mount Denison, Mount Wedge, Ti-tree and Derwent stations to make some overall estimate of the numbers of people in that area. Over three hundred people were contacted, mostly Unmatjera, but also Warlpiri and Northern Aranda. How to maintain contact with them was another matter. In the end, a series of events spurred Albrecht into regular contact himself.

Driving back from the missions–government conference in Darwin in the middle of 1955, he called at Murray Downs station, three hundred miles north of Alice Springs. The manager there, Burge Brown, was a European who, in Albrecht's opinion, was doing all he could to build up the Aboriginal community. Talking over a cup of tea, Albrecht heard more details of a killing in which Aborigines from Hatches Creek had killed an Aboriginal man on Murray Downs. It was understood that they had others marked, and Brown as well. It appeared that the Hatches Creek men thought the manager had publicly shown pictures of secret ceremonies, and that Aboriginal workers on Murray Downs had also been involved. In any case, Albrecht thought to himself, such rumours are almost always a death sentence, and will be carried out in the end, even if it takes a long time. He was deeply disturbed, knowing the police had no real power to prevent another killing. After discussing it with the Aboriginal Christians in Alice Springs, he and Martin decided to drive up and try to talk to the people concerned.

Most Aboriginal workers in the district had gathered for the races at Hatches Creek. At Albrecht's invitation about a hundred came to a meeting one evening. Albrecht told them what he knew of the dispute, also saying that he understood that under tribal law they had no other choice: they believed their tribe was offended and death was the only atonement. But in thinking this way, he told them, they were acting in darkness. He cited a killing near Alice Springs in 1941. Measles had been rife among the Pitjantjatjara people around Alice Springs, and they were taking their sick people down to the Todd River to bury them in wet sand to bring down their temperatures. In many cases, this brought on pneumonia, and eleven people died in two weeks. They thought the Aranda people had killed them by sorcery, so an Aranda man was killed to break the magic. In reality they had killed their people themselves—it was not Aranda magic. Over a hundred people at Hermannsburg had been ill with the measles, but they were given blankets and medicine and only two died. The Pitjantjatjara people had acted in blindness and darkness, and if someone had shown them the light, they would not have killed an innocent man.

Albrecht reiterated that they too were now in the darkness of hate, and would do things they would regret later. Martin also spoke, telling them how Jesus prayed at the cross for his enemies. Albrecht had the impression that most of the stockmen present had heard of Jesus, and some had a knowledge of Christmas songs. But the old ways still ruled their lives. He could sense the resistance to what they were saying. He tried a different tack, pointing out that there used to be many more Aborigines around than there were now. Some had gone away after the Europeans came, but they were also reducing their own numbers by tribal wars and vendettas. By eleven o'clock, he felt he had to risk a direct challenge.

'I believe I have failed to convince you old men', he said in Aranda. 'But you young men—you are the ones who will be sent to carry out the decision of the old men. Do you still want to go and kill? If not, raise your right hand!' To his amazement, almost every hand went up, even those of the old men. '*Itja kuta*' (Never again), they said. Everyone was quiet for a long time. Then they had a prayer, and Albrecht shared out a bag of dried fruit he had brought. In the warmth of their response, it struck him afresh how these people missed out so much on simple human contact with Europeans. He had always found how readily they responded to a gesture of friendship.

About six weeks later, he drove up again. Meeting one of the original leaders of the vendetta, Albrecht asked him directly if they were still considering killing more people. Charlie looked at him with disgust. 'You destroyed everything', he said. No, Albrecht thought to himself. What really happened was that the people were confronted with God's Word, and the Word won: the magic had to retreat as the night has to retreat when the sun rises. Despite the man's rebuff, he felt that a doorway had opened up for these people. He would try to start visiting on a regular basis, to give them some teaching.

Albert Namatjira's father, Jonathan, died in March 1956 in the Alice Springs hospital. Albrecht was conscious that with his passing went one of the last remaining links with the first Aboriginal Christians, and the missionaries who had founded Hermannsburg. Although Jonathan had already been through the first initiation ceremonies when he had asked for baptism, Albrecht felt he had never turned back on that decision. He pondered how Europeans often assumed that an Aborigine accepts Christianity in the same way as he accepts the European's clothing: it remains on the surface, never gets beneath his skin. Jonathan was one who contradicted such misgivings. He had remained an Aborigine, and was proud to be one. And while in no way an outstanding man, there was always a deep peace and serenity about him—he seemed free of the fears of *kurdaitchas* and evil spirits which seemed to plague many Aborigines. Albrecht had always considered that Albert Namatjira's ability to concentrate his efforts towards his art owed much to the foundation of Christianity his father had given him.

The Alice Springs congregation was steadily growing. Typically, the little church was filled, with many others sitting on the ground outside the door and beneath the windows. The work with the cattle stations was also increasing. A second bush church was opened and dedicated at Erldunda station, an occasion attended by 150 Aborigines and several Europeans. With Albrecht beginning to travel to the northern stations, Art and Dora Latz moved into town from Hermannsburg, and Art took over the running of the store, including stocking the truck for the cattle station trips. The back of the truck now housed a 'store', with specially built racks which could be folded back to display their wares—dry foods, clothes, soap, pannikins and other utensils, blankets—which people could purchase on the six-weekly visits to the stations.

At the end of 1956, Paul Albrecht, now twenty-four years old, finished seminary studies. He married Helen Kuchel and, early in 1957, they moved out to Haasts Bluff. Philipp Scherer had been ill and had gone south on extended leave. The majority of people, particularly Warlpiri, at Haasts Bluff had now moved to the new camp at Papunya, where there was better water.

Minna's bond of friendship with Frieda Strehlow, formed in the first months in Australia in 1925, had continued, and the two women had kept up a correspondence after Frieda returned to Germany in 1932. Minna felt deeply the losses and dislocations of the older woman's life—losing contact with most of her children for more than twenty years, burying her husband in a lonely outpost of Central Australia in 1922. A letter from Germany came to her in March. The nineteen-year-old girl who had sailed from Germany to Australia in 1894 to marry Carl Strehlow was now eighty-two. But she wrote with interest and enthusiasm about the stationing of Aboriginal evangelists on the cattle stations, commenting on the very different missionary task with an agriculturally oriented indigenous people in New Guinea. She had enjoyed news from the last Australian *Lutheran Herald* which included an article by her son, his photograph, and news of Paul's posting to Haasts Bluff. Though she found it difficult to understand why, when conditions were so much better, there was still a shortage of missionaries. In Germany, she said, winter was almost over. Snowdrops were appearing, and primulas and pansies. She sent regards to Minna and her husband, and to any old Aboriginal acquaintances. 'In my thoughts', she ended, 'I am often in Australia. I had to leave too much there.' It was her last letter to Minna. She died six weeks later.

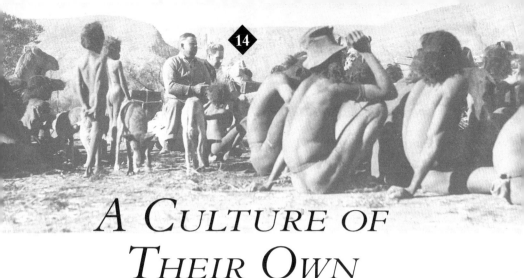

A CULTURE OF
THEIR OWN
1957~1959

Old Albrecht look after all Aboriginal people, government not look after people, nothing. Government come later.

With the increase in the cattle-station work, the mission board suggested to Albrecht that he find an Aboriginal driver. He was well into his sixties and, with the long distances and bad roads, mishaps or breakdowns were always possible. Albrecht sent a message out to Eli Rubuntja who had grown up at Hermannsburg and was now working at Tempe Downs.

I was small when they came to Hermannsburg, I was working with Missus Albrecht in the garden, I was her son. She call me like this, come on, son. She was a good gardener, and she taught me. I was special friend when I was a kid.

I was working station at Tempe Downs, 1957, and he sent a word from here to Hermannsburg, I get that letter, then I went with cattle to Finke, then I finish, and get a lift with stock agent, better go and see him. HULLO, my son!! and gives me big hug, good to see you! He said, when you going to come back? Well, that's why I come up and see you. He want me to work here, so I go back and tell'em boss, work back here. Drive him all the stations, Ti-Tree, Willowra later on, Aileron, Alcoota that mob, Napperby, Utopia, all the places south side, Maryvale, Henbury, Erldunda.

223

Sometimes Minna went also if she was well. Arriving at a property, he would speak first to the owner who would tell them where most of the people were. Aboriginal children jumped on the running-board of the truck as they drove down to the camp. Then a line-up for handshakes, and hugs from some of the women. The bonds of friendship between Albrecht and the cattle-station people were deep, a rapport and respect he had earned over the last thirty years. He was always interested in the details of their family life and their work, and the closeness he enjoyed with them was always evident to the Europeans who sometimes accompanied him— government men, board members, pastors of southern congregations. One president of the South Australian synod told him that he had never experienced a relationship with a congregation of the kind that he had witnessed between Albrecht and the Maryvale people.

Yet for all the closeness, there was an area of reservation. The 'Aboriginal part' of their lives—ceremonies, stories, songs—was something they did not share with him. They knew that for him it was opposed to the Christian way, and that he could not fully receive this aspect of their lives. His very honesty would have required him to say what he felt about it.

If he had something to say, he would tell it straight out, you would not shift him, that would be finished then. He was a straight-out man.

Albrecht went to those cattle stations too, he took everything, things for sale, some were presents. That's why they all loved him, because he took a lot of good things, fruit and things, and he shared to them every time, wherever he went. But they thought, if he hear about their life, what they still doing, they were afraid of that, because he was straight-out man—OK, you're doing wrong thing all the time. That's why they had a strong feeling about him, he was bringing good things to them, he was also growling at them for other bad things. They loved him, but they were afraid of old Albrechta because he was straight-out man, that's why.

Camp was made before dark. After a meal, he might show a Bible film strip, sometimes a film. There were always other things too—lessons in reading and writing, filling out forms for child endowment, cashing the pension cheques that he had brought from town for them. He had found that without help they often did not receive the social service benefits to which they were entitled.

Church then in the morning. They all came, sit down under one tree, clean shirt. It was any day for the service, not just Sunday. Many people at Maryvale, sometimes a hundred. Lot of kids sit in the front, teacher keep them quiet. We sing hymns, proper Lutheran service.

At the end of the service were baptism and confirmation classes, Albrecht asking questions on the material the evangelist had been teaching over the last six weeks. At Maryvale the people were keen, but Paulus was the only one who could read Aranda, so he had to repeat things over and over until the people remembered them. Yet, thought Albrecht, one could only persevere. Something would eventually stick and remain as a seed which would grow. After the services the store on the truck was opened. Albrecht had introduced the store because he had always felt that Aboriginal people should be able to purchase amenities without having to go to towns. Hawkers went around the stations but charged the people exorbitant prices. Sometimes church people voiced the opinion that running a store was not part of a missionary undertaking. Albrecht simply felt it was an essential facility for Aborigines living away from the larger settlements—if it was not provided by government or the station-owner, the mission had to do it. And with his strong instinct to frugality, he thought that even modest profits helped offset the mission's costs in visiting the stations.

The cattle-station work had now been going for several years, and a deeper understanding of it was emerging in his mind. He shared some of this at a joint missionary conference in late 1956 between the Lutheran Finke River Mission, the Baptists from Yuendumu, and the Presbyterians from Ernabella. He thought it was striking that none of the larger Christian denominations in Australia had considered mission work among Aborigines on cattle stations, but had almost exclusively directed their efforts to the European settlers. Yet a missionary could be an important intermediary between management and Aboriginal workers. He had found that his contact with Aboriginal workers had sometimes precipitated other improvements even without direct approach or negotiation. At one place they had been visiting for some time, the owner increased wages by 50 per cent. At Maryvale, the people had started building better huts for themselves, even without much material at their disposal.

However he felt it was crucial to decide whether one was there for the Aborigines or for the Europeans. 'This, of course, is not the ideal; there is only one Christ and Saviour for all men. However at this stage ... one simply has to choose between the two.' In practice, this meant one had to be careful about accepting hospitality from the station owner or manager. A regular visitor would soon become a burden and, if a missionary needed to discuss some obvious injustice with the management, it was much easier if he had not accepted hospitality. But most importantly, if one stayed with the Europeans, one's time would inevitably be spent there and not with the Aborigines, who would quickly feel he was 'just another white person' and shut themselves up against him.

Perhaps it was only someone of Albrecht's cross-cultural experience who could have grasped the issue so clearly. Born into a German family, raised in Poland, and one dominated by Russia, an awareness of differing cultures and loyalties was intrinsic to his background and intensified by his war experience. In the often demarked world of Aboriginal and European in Central Australia he could understand both sides. But he had chosen to identify with the Aborigines as far as possible.

In the final analysis, Albrecht's approach to Aboriginal people was human and personal. A man like Ted Strehlow, or his father, Carl Strehlow, had a deeper and subtler appreciation of the Aboriginal philosophical and cultural heritage. Ted Strehlow in this same period was recording and translating ceremonial songs to be later included in his mammoth *Songs of Central Australia*. With great knowledge and literary sensitivity, he could appreciate them within a cultural context reaching back to Greek epics and song cycles. Albrecht, by comparison, approached Aborigines more on the basis of a common humanity, attuning himself to the practical realities of their everyday lives with their attendant joys and sorrows.

He told his fellow missionaries that misunderstandings between the Aborigines and the Europeans were simply inevitable. Many Aborigines who resented the authority of a younger European boss took a course of passive resistance and avoided work. On the other hand, there were still cattlemen who tried to give their people as little as possible. Sometimes workers lacked the simplest shelters, so that men coming in from a muster in wet weather would find blankets and clothing wet and not a dry spot to spend the night. 'But here again', he commented astutely, 'it is better for the missionary to stay in his tent where the Natives are; this will not only bring him closer to the Natives, but may help to open the white employer's eyes to the need that exists for providing shelter for his people'.

However the real centre of the cattle-station work was the Aboriginal evangelist, and his continuing contact with people between the occasional visits of the missionary. Albrecht's conviction that Aboriginal Christians could best work with their own people was something he had felt since his first years in Australia, and it had only grown stronger over time. Almost thirty years before, he had trusted Titus and others in the teaching of the tribal people in the west and, despite wrangles and difficulties, the Gospel had taken root in the outlying areas. He often thought about the work of itinerant European evangelists like Annie Lock who visited Aboriginal camps in the 1920s, preaching the Gospel. Or Ernie Kramer, who had been in the Alice Springs district for twelve years. As far as Albrecht had ever been able to ascertain, there was nothing left of those ministries, though some Aborigines remembered the people. How different this could have been, he thought, if they had concentrated on training some men as evangelists, and established small churches under their care.

To a casual observer, Albrecht's concerns for the material as well as spiritual welfare of Aboriginal people might have seemed to mirror the government assumption throughout the 1950s that Aborigines could and should be assimilated as quickly as possible. As Paul Hasluck had put it early in the decade, 'Assimilation means, in practical terms, that in the course of time, it is expected that all persons of Aboriginal blood or mixed blood in Australia will live like white Australians do'. Government brochures and other literature pictured Aboriginal women attending health clinics, children seated tidily at school desks, young Aboriginal men working with machinery, and other images of Aboriginal people in the roles and trappings of European Australians.

Albrecht looked to a future in which Aboriginal people would be an integral part of the larger Australian community, feeling that their survival as a race depended on it. But he never envisaged this as a complete blurring of their own identity as Aborigines. And his sense of how to achieve this end was quite different to most government and popular thinking at the time. He actively mistrusted any speeding up of the contact between non-urbanized Aborigines and European civilization, feeling that the longer that Aborigines lived away from European centres, the more breathing space they had in which to adjust culturally. He strenuously advocated schools and training, but wanted them provided as far as possible in the places where Aboriginal people lived and expected to work. His emphasis on working communities underscored his sense of the Aborigine's need for solidarity with his group, and the interdependence of individual and family group so highly developed in Aboriginal life.

Perhaps Albrecht was most at variance with popular notions in his sense of the timetable of change. His perception of the enormous gulf between Aboriginal and European values meant, for him, that change would come slowly. In the sanguine atmosphere of the day, he sometimes appeared conservative, even pessimistic. Albrecht was not by nature a pessimist, but the move into Alice Springs had only accentuated his awareness of the gap between Aboriginal and European values. The theme recurred in personal conversation. Tom Fleming, a young Baptist minister who had come to Yuendumu in 1950, rarely made his two-monthly trip into Alice Springs without calling on the older man, sensing a wealth of knowledge and experience on which he could draw.

It was always a pleasure to Albrecht to share his experience with a genuine enquirer. Sometimes it was the disappointments. He had set up the best of the Hermannsburg stockmen as minipastoralists, only to have most of them sell up when they had repaid their debts to the mission. Similarly, he sometimes felt that the former faith of Aborigines in the efficacy of traditional increase ceremonies had simply been replaced by a faith in prayer to the heavenly Father who would also supply their needs without effort on their part. Another story he told Fleming concerned a diligent Aboriginal tracker who, when the policeman for whom he had worked for years moved away, just 'sat down' and did nothing: his work had been part of a personal relationship, it was not simply a job he would do for anyone.

He was trying to convey to the young Baptist man that he was not dealing with a group of backward Europeans, rather trying to teach people who were simply not motivated by the same things as himself. Europeans, he wrote a few years later, had often not appreciated this:

> There have been times when the white man looked upon the Aborigine as a child, a human being with little brains who never reached maturity, leave alone equality. This opinion, fortunately, has changed, and the majority of Australians have come to realise that we are dealing with a people who have a culture of their own, a social organisation more complex than ours, and have been endowed by the Creator with gifts we had never expected to find with them.

Once, when Fleming commented on his knowledge of Aboriginal people, the older man smiled and shook his head. 'Mr Fleming, in the first couple of years I was at Hermannsburg and became proficient in the Aranda language, I was sure that I knew all about the Aborigines. But after working there for twenty-seven years, and having left and come in here to live, I'm thoroughly convinced I don't know anything at all about them.' Sometimes he compared them to the gypsies of Europe, especially those in Russia. The Communist regime had first assumed they were a dying race. Then they had tried to assimilate them. But the gypsies had never been assimilated, and often he thought the same about the Australian Aborigines—'they find it almost impossible to find a place in our economy anywhere'. 'Yet they are a deeply spiritual people', he went on. Albrecht often remarked that he had never met men with greater spiritual understanding than some of the older Christians— Moses and others. 'These people have a far better spiritual insight than I.'

The serious conflict for Albrecht came from his sense of the gap between Aboriginal thinking and the motivation necessary to survive in twentieth-century Australian life. Nowhere was this reflected more than in his writings on an apprenticeship system for Aborigines. He had proposed this first at the Darwin conference in 1955, and developed it further over the next few years. Partly, it came out of his sense of the larger trends—the increasing numbers of Aborigines in town and many without jobs, the worsening alcoholism. The breakdown was most apparent among the young people, especially the young men who had finished their schooling. He proposed that all Aboriginal and part-Aboriginal youths undertake a period of compulsory apprenticeship between leaving school and the age of twenty. Both schooling and apprenticeship should emphasize practical training for a job, especially for life on a station—yard-building, cattle mustering, saddlery, well-sinking.

In essence, his apprenticeship proposal was an attempt to take into account the very different inner world of the Aboriginal boy finishing school. A European boy of this age would have formed some concept of future work, and seen his life in terms of it. Young Aboriginal men on missions or settlements might comply with the white man's arrangements to get food and clothing, but their deeper goals were directed towards tribal life and its obligations. He had often seen young men, after undergoing the initiation ceremonies, become completely uninterested in their former work:

Not that they lack brains or intelligence: they have quite sufficient of this. But their life is sidetracked, and their real life is lived in a different world, an unreal world ... In the end, he will ... have become an Aboriginal living in two worlds, the world in which he has to earn some living, even if reluctantly, do some work, but in reality live in the past, the past of the fathers.

It was useless, he thought, to give these boys maximum freedom, thinking they could work the problem out for themselves. For Aboriginal boys, 'it is a matter of providing a foundation for their whole life', and traditionally, this period of their lives had been full of tribal training and obligations, as he described:

> Until about twenty or more years of age, these growing lads depend on the old men in every respect. For every little bit of magic disclosed to him, he had to pay with an offering of meat ... He has to attend to the chores in the camp, and his whole life is restricted down to small detail. No wonder the old men succeed where we fail in our endeavour to give him the maximum in freedom he does not know how to use.

If boys were to succeed in European-style employment, they needed a period of practical education and training analogous to this phase of their traditional life. His idea of apprenticeship, he said, was in many ways following the pattern of 'some individual cattlemen, who have had lads with them from early childhood. Many of them have made men of whom they feel justly proud'.

Many of his concerns were shared by contemporary figures such as A. P. Elkin and Ted Strehlow. After visiting Territory Aboriginal schools in the late 1950s, Elkin commented that the European type of education offered had insufficient bearing on the kind of life the child could expect to lead afterwards. If schooling and training did not succeed in securing Aborigines a place in the economic system, he said, their last state would be worse than the first. Getting young Aborigines to value European incentives was a fundamental issue. Like Albrecht, Elkin saw a balance between freedom and guidance as crucial: 'The pressure is to give them freedom, but this can mean bewilderment in a vacuum between two worlds'.

Asked by the Reverend V. W. Coombes of the Presbyterian Board of Missions in 1958 to comment on Albrecht's apprenticeship paper, Elkin expressed general agreement with much of it, and tentative support for the apprenticeship proposal. But he felt that Albrecht undervalued the foundation of traditional Aboriginal life. 'Aboriginal "Mystery" is the central part of the "Dreaming", the philosophical heritage, which we despise or ignore *at peril* to the cohesion of Aborigines', he wrote—though, like Strehlow, he accepted that traditional life would continue to modify as contact with Europeans increased.

Albrecht's conflict about traditional life was present in his language. 'Magic' and 'superstition' were words he frequently used in describing traditional rites and heritage. Tribal training, he had said in his apprenticeship paper, reinforced a different inner world, an 'unreal world'. Unreal it was to Albrecht, both because based on religious beliefs he could not support and because it seemed to do nothing to address another order of reality—their need to work and survive in a changed world.

These Aboriginal men, they were the bosses. Pastor Albrecht, he come from somewhere else, he not a boss. But he bring this good news. He wasn't the boss. This mob, they're the boss.

Yes, if Pastor Albrecht say, do this way, go to work—that was like, white man's things, important for Pastor Albrecht—they do what he want for those things. But this mob, they can do things, dance, take young fella, mak'im man, that's Law, right from there to today, that's Aboriginal law, can't leave that one. Pastor Albrecht, he knows alright! He knows that old Aboriginal story from top to bottom! But he didn't believe it!

The announcement of Queen's Birthday Honours in June 1958 included the name of Pastor F. W. Albrecht of Alice Springs: a Member of the British Empire for his work among Aborigines. It was his second award in Australia—he had received a Queen's Coronation Medal some years earlier. An immense number of telegrams and letters came in, to which Albrecht replied in a duplicated letter in which he drew attention to Minna's part in the honour. Characteristically, the letter was not only a letter of personal thanks, but an effort to distil something of their life's experience in 'the cause ... of the Aborigines':

> When sent here by our United Evangelical Lutheran church in 1925, it looked as if we had been called to render but grave digger services ... However, the men who predicted an end of the whole effort at Hermannsburg, have since acknowledged the change that has taken place. If there are about 140 children at school at present, the foundation for this change was laid in those years when everything seemed to be in jeopardy. The Kaporilja pipeline, opened in 1935, brought about the turn of the tide; it is still flowing ...

The drought years, the deaths, the struggle for the hundreds of bush people in the Haasts Bluff area—he spoke as if they were yesterday, except that they were condensed, the details fallen away, the experience only more numinous with the passing of years.

But the very *necessity* of struggle in a person's life was something Albrecht was reflecting on as he grew older. Both his early life and the years in Australia had involved immense effort— often a struggle against the seemingly impossible. Yet the final fruit of such arduousness, it seemed to him, was a depth of experience otherwise impossible in an individual life, part of their essential 'making'. The theme was clear as he spoke one Saturday afternoon to a group of newly naturalized citizens in Alice Springs. Standing before them, his own origins elsewhere must have been evident—the large round figure, fair full face and broad forehead, the voice with just the slightest trace of a different intonation. 'Ladies and gentlemen, it is nearly thirty years since I walked into the Police Office here in Alice Springs and the station sergeant administered the oath of allegiance. Although I was conscious of what I said at that moment, the full significance of that step only became apparent as the years rolled by.' Australian immigration pamphlets often emphasized the money to be made in Australia. Yet, he asked, is it money that will bind you to a country?

> What is a life lived in much pleasantness, and without the trial of the last ounce ... of one's determination and ingenuity—what is it? It will not reach down to the same depth, will not give the deep satisfaction one experiences by going through such trials and experiences ... sharing in that experience of suffering [the drought years] has left an indelible mark on our lives, there is a tie established which can never again be destroyed. No money can ever buy that.

The volume of letters and telegrams he and Minna received indicated the high level of interest in the Aboriginal question among the Australian public. Yet, he was only too aware that 'we are still far off the point of having found a solution to the problem of bringing a nomadic people satisfactorily into our way of life'.

Drinking problems among Aborigines and part-Aboriginal people in Alice Springs were steadily worsening. In the minds of many local people, the deterioration was directly attributable to the lifting of alcohol prohibitions for part-Aboriginal people some years earlier. Though it was still illegal for fullblood Aborigines to drink, or for others to supply them with alcohol, they had easy access to it through part-Aboriginal relatives. Albrecht was appalled at its impact on women and children, yet drinkers were the hardest to be convinced they were doing wrong. In fact, many Aborigines believed they were not responsible for what they did in a drunken state.

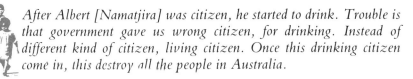

After Albert [Namatjira] was citizen, he started to drink. Trouble is that government gave us wrong citizen, for drinking. Instead of different kind of citizen, living citizen. Once this drinking citizen come in, this destroy all the people in Australia.

One centre of drinking and fighting was Albert Namatjira's camp. He was living at Morris Soak on the outskirts of Alice Springs after trying unsuccessfully to secure a block of land in town. He was one of the few fullblood Aborigines in the Northern Territory to have been granted Australian citizenship after a vigorous public campaign had been waged on his behalf, especially in the southern cities. Namatjira himself had not applied for citizenship, and Albrecht personally had the impression that he had not wanted it.

Albrecht was increasingly perturbed at the conditions in the artist's camp. In just one court session which he attended on a Monday morning, twenty Aborigines from Namatjira's group were arraigned for drunkenness and disorderly behaviour over the weekend. Several of the women had hair matted with blood, and bloodstains on their clothing. Namatjira himself had ceased attending church regularly, and Albrecht found communication with him more and more difficult. His painting too had deteriorated noticeably though, in Albrecht's view, a drive for perfection had always been a feature of his work. The implications for others were even more disturbing. Many of those whom Albrecht considered the best men at Hermannsburg had come into town and were living at Namatjira's camp for months at a time, claiming financial support through tribal relationship. In many cases, their wives and families remained at Hermannsburg supported by the mission. Several men had had serious vehicle accidents while drunk, and one had been killed. Another woman in the camp had one arm permanently paralysed after being stabbed in the throat by a man called Police Paddy who, ironically, was the Aboriginal tracker who accompanied the Coniston punitive expedition.

Early in August, a young Aboriginal woman was murdered at Morris Soak, and the evidence of heavy drinking on the night of the murder led to a court warning to the artist that he would face a gaol sentence if he was caught supplying liquor to wards, and that he was not to take liquor to his camp. Namatjira and some of his family returned to Hermannsburg to live. But the flamboyant lifestyle continued. Hired taxis—at £12 a trip—were the normal mode of transport for the artists for the eighty-mile drive to town, and taxis came and went, sometimes three or four a day. In the meantime, many of the artists were contributing little or nothing to the maintenance of their families, and the mission seemed power-less to prevent it. Even in his time as superintendent, Albrecht had fretted and fumed about 'loafers' in the camp who did not work and then claimed rations from relatives. But the problem had grown to massive proportions with the earnings coming into the community with the art movement. There was plenty of money, but no respon-sibility in using it. Men who lived with Namatjira were fully supplied with free food and drink, taxi rides and film shows. It was in keeping with Aboriginal tradition, but Albrecht feared that many of the younger generation were being ruined for life. 'The only work worthwhile in the opinion of many of them is to be like Albert', he wrote.

Later that month, Manasse found Henoch Raberaba on the road at Hermannsburg, too drunk to stand. He had come out in a taxi with Namatjira and obviously had been given liquor. The next day three young men at the mission openly admitted they had been drinking, using Namatjira's supplies. Acting Manager Ralph Ker-nich reported both incidents to the police, but for some weeks, no action was taken. Albrecht felt strongly that something had to be done. 'If Albert is allowed to go on supplying, Hermannsburg will soon be another Morris' Soak, with all the fighting included.' It was obvious that through Namatjira and the other exempted Aborigi-nes, drink would come more and more into the community unless the law on supplying to wards was enforced, and he was relieved when four summonses were finally served on Namatjira.

Albrecht attended the whole of the court hearing, though Minna was far from well. The summer heat was setting in, and she was nervy and depressed. Albrecht was glad that Marianna could be there during the day, though he came home for the midday meal. Namatjira was found guilty of supplying liquor to Henoch, but not guilty on the charge of supplying to the other three men. Albrecht had the impression that the magistrate had bent over backwards not to make the additional charge. On the first charge, the artist was given the minimum sentence of six months' imprisonment with hard labour. A nationwide protest broke out.

'This agitation, and to an extent, the public reaction, is only understandable because people are not sufficiently informed, therefore come to a wrong conclusion', wrote Albrecht in a circular on the subject. He traced out some of the background to the present crisis: Namatjira's lavish spending; the various attempts by mission staff, then government Department of Welfare officers, to stabilize his finances and safeguard the prices and sales of his paintings; recent problems over the authenticity of a large number of paintings he had signed and sent to his Sydney agent, John Brackenreg. Even Namatjira's own family life was being wrecked. Rubina, his wife, had been to Minna and others for clothes, saying her husband had bought her nothing for a year. But after an incident in which he had threatened to shoot her, she left him and returned to Hermannsburg to live, telling Pastor Gross that Namatjira had said he was a free citizen and could kill her if he liked. 'If nothing else, this incident clearly shows the confusion that has come upon this fine man as he was in the past.'

Albrecht thought one of the most regrettable aspects of Namatjira's case had been the influence of some Europeans who had encouraged him along the road to drinking and citizenship rights without any understanding of the difficulties they created for a tribal Aboriginal. Now, with voices everywhere clamouring that the famous artist be released from gaol, the pastor who had known him for over thirty years drew another conclusion:

> In our opinion, a term in gaol where he is kept away from alcohol, will do Albert a lot of good: he will greatly improve physically, and it may help him get back into a normal life, which he has lost. One of the worst aspects of the agitation by people who don't know the position, is now to try and let Albert get free of the consequences of his way of life . . . if he is to be trained into full citizenship, this can never be done by treating him like a ward one day, or like a minor, and then again tell him he has full citizens rights. Albert deserves our deep sympathy, but he will never be helped by being treated like some pet, instead of as a responsible person.

At first, artist mob were drinking in Alice Springs. Albert didn't know till they took him to Sydney, Melbourne. At Sydney, he had a friend, and they share little bit wine, those people taught him to drink, his friends. Then he came back to Alice Springs, and he was number one artist, and he start to drink, because he had learned in those places. Then he gave drink to his relatives.

In the Aboriginal congregation at Maryvale station, the evangelist Paulus had been teaching a baptism class for some years. Towards the end of 1958, Albrecht examined them individually and decided that ten adults and three children were ready. Baptisms were a highlight of congregational life, and Albrecht noticed when he arrived on the day that the whole camp had been raked and swept, including a place under a big ironwood tree for his tent. About seventy came, too many for the little bush church, but the overflow outside was as quiet as those inside, as each person was baptized in the name of the triune God.

Although Maryvale was originally Aranda territory, none of those baptized were Aranda-speaking people. Most had migrated there from considerable distances, some from as far away as the other side of Ayers Rock. Ngarabaia, now called Magdalena, was well over seventy, and her face deeply furrowed with the hardship of years. Albrecht had never really expected her to advance sufficiently for baptism. Not only was she old—and he had found many of the older people unable to absorb the new teaching—but the language question seemed almost insurmountable. But she had managed to learn the Apostles Creed in Aranda, and the answers to some of the baptism questions. Asked why she believed in Jesus, she said, 'because He died for us'. As she spoke, Albrecht felt a radiance in her face despite its furrows.

In his Christmas trip to the southern stations, Albrecht met a man called Junkuman who came originally from the Petermann Ranges, and had been one of the tribal people to befriend the prospector Lasseter in the last weeks of his life in 1931. Junkuman had helped to carry the ill man eastward to Winter's Glen where he died. Apparently Lasseter could still walk when they had found him, though very slowly. He had tried to collect bush food and to catch little animals for meat. But his eyes became infected and dysentery sapped his strength. 'I was young man', Junkuman told Albrecht, 'I could carry him just like nothing'.

The national furore over the case of Albert Namatjira continued in the last months of 1958. In December, an appeal to the Northern Territory Supreme Court against his conviction and sentence failed, though Justice Kriewaldt reduced the sentence to three months. The case was becoming increasingly entwined with the issue of citizenship rights for all Aborigines. Public figures argued vociferously on both sides. Some wanted the immediate granting of full citizenship to Aborigines; others did not oppose this in principle, but said it was premature. It seemed quite possible that the agitation would propel the Commonwealth government into early legislation on the matter.

Like many in the Northern Territory community at the time, Albrecht felt this would be disastrous. Early in January, he and twelve other Alice Springs citizens sent a signed statement of their views to national newspapers throughout Australia. They included four clergy, three Legislative Assembly members, Rex Battarbee, a stipendiary magistrate, a miner, an engineer and Eddy Connellan, pastoralist and founder of Connellan Airways. All had extensive experience of Aborigines and part-Aborigines in welfare, education and employment. The statement concluded that the granting of citizenship to Aborigines without proper preparation was tanta-mount to writing their death sentence. Citizenship could not be given simply by legislative enactment, but only after a period of proper preparation in vocational, social and religious fields, and when the candidate had a sense of its responsibilities as well as its privileges. Most Aborigines, it said, still required a period of protection—not now so much from the Europeans as from them-selves—and in this time a realistic training for citizenship. Present government policy was not providing sufficient employment oppor-tunities, or training for employment. It concluded:

> The Government settlements are indispensable as a first step in keeping the natives away from disastrous contact with the white man's towns with their associated vices, but if nothing more is done than to provide food, clothing and medical facilities, they turn a race of people formerly proud and industrious in their tribal life, with strong moral sanctions, into a parasite race hanging on to the fringes of white society, without proper moral sanctions to guide them.

The statement evoked a great flurry of response, the most vocal from the Victorian Aboriginal Advancement League, led by part-Aboriginal Church of Christ minister, Pastor Doug Nicholls. Dr Charles Duguid, now president of the Aboriginal Advancement League in South Australia, also drew exception to the statement, saying that the suggestion that Aborigines should be candidates for citizenship in their own land was a gross insult. His conclusion, however, that 'all aborigines who have been educated in State schools, who work in our civilization as trained personnel, and pay income tax, should be citizens in their own right ... [and] that citizenship must be recognized as a principle for aborigines every-where to operate for tribal and semi-tribal people as soon as they can use it' would hardly have drawn disagreement from Albrecht.

The debate continued for some time, exacerbated by the release of figures showing that the number of Aboriginal wards brought before the Alice Springs court had increased almost 500 per cent in the last three years, the steep rise coinciding with the lifting of drinking restrictions on part-Aboriginal people. Responding to a member of the Victorian Aboriginal Advancement League who had contacted him personally, Albrecht replied:

> In my opinion, it is wrong to pin too much hope on the granting of citizens rights, better food and housing, education as we know it, and equal pay with other Australians. I don't want to be misunderstood: I have prayed and worked for these ideals as much as I could, and I would feel a happy man if I could see these ideals materialised before my working days are over. However I am convinced that if we tackle this problem mainly from the angle proposed by so many, i.e. the granting of citizenship, then I am sure we shall miss the mark once more, much to the detriment of the Aborigines.

He simply could not see how legislation in itself could instil overnight the values inherent in European-style communities—the motivation to work, the feeling for a home and for maintaining it, a pride in ownership which only created problems within an Aboriginal group. As he put it: 'The sense for values is lacking because as nomads nobody could accumulate anything'. And elsewhere:

> ... as long as the old tribal cohesion continues—and it will for some long time yet—then the individual who takes a pride in his possessions is immediately ostracised: he is sticking his head above the level of the tribe and this is not appreciated. Rather, he had to share, and not in accordance with the need of his fellow tribesmen, but according to the degree of relationship and the amount at his disposal.

Albert Namatjira's conviction and prison sentence was never far from the newspapers in early 1959. Paul Hasluck, Minister for Territories, decided to let Namatjira serve an 'open' sentence at Papunya, now the official government settlement at Popanji Bore, some twenty miles north of Haasts Bluff. He was placed under the custodianship of the superintendent, Ern Fietz. He was the husband of former Hermannsburg school teacher, Hilda Wurst, who had also served on one of the mission art councils set up in the earlier days of the art movement, and was an old associate of the Aranda man whose success had brought him such mixed blessings.

Albrecht himself was as busy as ever. The area of influence of the mission in Alice Springs was steadily increasing, and he and

Paul, who was now living in town, were in contact with almost
1050 Aborigines. Between the two of them, they were regularly
visiting twenty-one stations, Paul travelling to the north of Alice
Springs, and he to the south. Art Latz had become the mainstay
of much of the town work. The business of the store had doubled,
trebled, and doubled again in the last eighteen months. Art also
worked in a way that allowed time to talk to people. Part-Aboriginal
children living close to the mission block regularly found their way
into the store, ostensibly to help him, but more to spend time with
the quietly spoken man behind the counter. For church, he faithfully attended to the arranging of the amplifier and speakers. And
on Tuesday nights, he had begun to show documentary films,
preceded by religious film strips.

After a bout of ill health, Albrecht was advised by his doctor in
Alice Springs to have an operation for gallstones. He brought his
will up to date, and asked Ossie Heinrich to be his executor in case
of death. He also decided to give up smoking. He had smoked for
years—anything he 'could lay hands on'—though a box of cigars
was a special treat. 'Him all pinished now', as he wrote to Lou
Borgelt who sent him Manila cigars after an overseas trip. He no
longer drank alcohol either. 'Although not a teetotaller by principle, [the drinking] would make me a real Cain with my people
here, and that could never be.'

The gallstone operation went well, and Albrecht had many
visitors as he recuperated. Several of the part-Aboriginal children
from his instruction classes came in the afternoons after school,
sitting on every corner of his bed, and inspecting the gallstones he
had kept in a bottle to show them. Some of them were very close to
'Papa' as they called him, popping in and out of the little house on
the mission block, showing him their school books, offering to
help pull weeds in the garden or carry things for him. Even if he
were busy, he tried to give them time, knowing that it was important to them, and that he reaped the benefit in the better attention in
classes. Some, he knew, had little stability in their home lives, and
drew affection and security from their contacts with the Latzes and
themselves. At school holidays, he always took children on the
trips to the stations, or organized a special outing for them like a
picnic at the swimming hole at Standley Chasm. Minna went if she
was well enough, sitting in a chair under a tree. Usually he swam
too, the children laughing at his white legs. He had always worn
long trousers.

Late in the afternoon of Saturday 8 August, he was called

urgently to the Alice Springs hospital. Albert Namatjira had been brought in from Papunya with heart trouble two days before. He had collapsed suddenly and severe pneumonia developed. Rubina came in from Hermannsburg, and she and Albrecht prayed by his bed. The man was obviously in considerable pain and breathing with difficulty, but they felt he was aware of everything. During the Lord's prayer, he tried to join in though every word seemed an immense effort. He died two hours later, a few weeks after his fifty-seventh birthday. The phone in the Albrecht house on Gap Road hardly stopped ringing on Sunday, but arrangements proceeded for the funeral that afternoon at four. At the grave, Aranda hymns were sung, but Albrecht gave the address in English. As often, he grasped the uniqueness of the moment:

> Never before in the history of this country has an Australian Aborigine been borne to his last resting place under conditions as we witness today. His passing, within hours, was flashed as news from one corner of our vast continent to the other . . .
>
> Through his art he had interpreted the beauty of this country to a vast multitude of people. He had made them see our ranges, trees and landscapes in that glorious sunshine, and under those changing colours as perhaps no other corner of our globe knows of . . .

Taking as his text a verse from Corinthians, 'By the grace of God, I am what I am', he spoke of Namatjira's life and his development as an artist. Simply, yet profoundly, he recalled the day in 1932 when Rex Battarbee and John Gardner exhibited their paintings in the old schoolroom at Hermannsburg, and Namatjira had said, 'I can do that, too'.

It was characteristic of Albrecht to try to trace the fundamentals of the man's life and identity. Namatjira was, and had remained, a member of the Aranda tribe in Central Australia, and in this basic alignment he had received every encouragement from the mission. Albrecht paid tribute to the man's great power of concentration and his determination to keep going despite initial failures and discouragements, especially in the total absence of analogous Aboriginal experience on which to draw:

> His greatest difficulty came when he reached the top . . . He would not have been human if the praise he received had not affected him, even if outwardly he showed very little of it. People would come to greet him, expressing themselves in such words: 'Albert, to shake hands with you, is the greatest moment of my life' . . . Many of his newly won friends encouraged him to lay special emphasis on his tribal life . . . for a considerable time he became a stranger in the

church ... it almost looked as if he was going to cast aside his Christian faith and revert back to his heathen ancestral beliefs ... By doing it, he would have given up the very ground on which he had developed and on which he stood ...

In spite of many honest attempts at making them happy and valuable members of our society, we have fundamentally failed ... If we have not found a formula as yet according to which we may transform the life of a nomad and make a producer out of a food collector, we may be sure of succeeding eventually if we rely on God for guidance, rather than follow our own ways of thinking ... God in His grace will not fail us.

Given his unceasing drive for the Aboriginal race as a whole, it would have been impossible for Albrecht not to draw wider reference from the occasion. To him, the predicaments of Namatjira's life typified the enormous complexity of the task of Aboriginal rehabilitation.

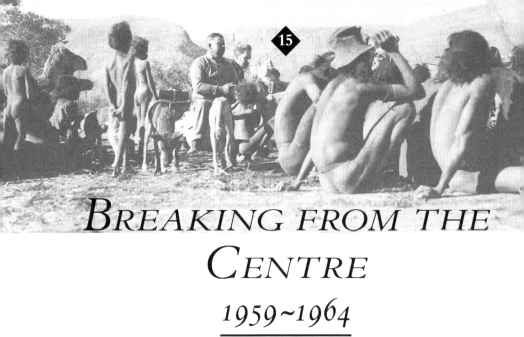

BREAKING FROM THE CENTRE
1959~1964

He always looked after people, worried about them, preached the gospel and taught them about Jesus. Really cared for them, kata mea nunaka *[like a mother and father]. Still today, everybody [especially older people] think that way.*

The day after Albert Namatjira's funeral, his Sydney agent, John Brackenreg, wrote to Albrecht. Rubina had often expressed the wish for a house of her own. Though it had never become a reality in Albert's lifetime, Brackenreg was keen that Rubina should be provided for without delay. The costs could be covered by royalties, and if necessary he would contribute personally. Albrecht replied promptly and in practical terms. Quotes were secured, a contract signed, and the keys of the completed house at Hermannsburg handed over to Rubina by November. However he did not want permanent responsibility for Albert's financial affairs. He and Vic Carrington had been named in Albert's will as trustees, but he resigned this role as early as possible and put the will in the hands of an Alice Springs solicitor.

He had recently attended an official opening ceremony at the new government settlement at Papunya and, after the formalities, an Aboriginal woman approached him. He recognized her immediately, though he had not seen her for many years. Ngalunta was a young woman when she had been brought to him, desperately ill with yaws, in a bush camp on one of the camel treks in the 1930s. Her mother was caring for her, as her husband had rejected her. Albrecht gave her an injection immediately, but knew she would never survive without a course of treatment. His proposal that she return to Hermannsburg on the camels with them was met with a flat refusal from the old men. She might die, they said, and then she could not be buried in her own country. Their opposition put him in a dilemma. Obviously, she would die if she remained there. Yet if she died on the trip—as well she might—they would hold him responsible and all the standing he had built up with these people over years would be destroyed. It was irrelevant that he had told them that she would get well only with God's help and if she was brought to the station. He knew their minds did not work like that. Yet he felt he had to try to convince them. Lying in his tent, he heard them arguing far into the night. In the morning, one of his camel men came to him to say they would let her go. The first afternoon they made camp early to let her rest, but she could not sleep and groaned incessantly. Fearing she would die of exhaustion, Albrecht offered her warm brandy mixed with sugar. She refused, wrinkling up her face at the smell. He took a sip himself and urged her again. This time, she drank it and fell asleep. Taking the journey in easy stages, they made it back to Hermannsburg.

The girl recovered and was returned to her tribe. Some months later, Albrecht heard a knock one night at the window of his study. It was Ngalunta with a young man. She had refused to return to her first husband, and she and the young man had run away together. When they wanted to return to their people six months later, he sent several strong messages asking that they be treated with clemency. He knew that by tribal law they were liable to severe punishment for taking matters into their own hands, and he knew of another man who had been killed under such circumstances. Now, twenty years later, Ngalunta stood before him, perfectly well, asking if he would like to see her family. The sight of her and her nine healthy children gave him immense pleasure.

It was a graphic illustration of how the whole work with Aborigines in Central Australia had changed. In 1930 when he had begun his camel treks into the Haasts Bluff area, they had estimated that about 200 people were living there. Last November there were well over 700 at Papunya, and over the year there had been 42 births and 5 deaths. Approximately 300 lived at Areyonga now, and over

520 at Hermannsburg. Clearly, the mission's work and the efforts of the government in providing better food and medical services had produced results that even twenty-five years before would have seemed unbelievable. Australian Aborigines were no longer the 'dying race' they had been in the 1920s and 1930s.

If their physical survival was now secure, Albrecht could not feel the same confidence that they were starting to function in the economic system. Three of the pastoralist families were making some attempt to continue, but the scheme had failed to draw any larger number of people. Even the cattle industry—the traditional avenue of employment for Territory Aborigines—was being mechanized. Jobs like droving were becoming obsolete as the Landrover replaced the boundary rider and musterer, and more and more cattle stations were run without a single Aborigine living and working there. If Aboriginal men were losing even this kind of employment, Albrecht could see no economic future for them at all unless young boys were trained for specialized work. But that clearly had to be done on an individual and intensive basis, which on the large settlements and missions was impossible. More and more he was convinced that such institutional centres were negative in their effects in the long term. Yet if Aboriginal people were not obtaining ordinary employment, what alternative was there?

The disparity between the old and the new in Aboriginal life occupied him constantly. Polygamy was an area of traditional Aboriginal life which was currently challenging the mission to rethink church rules and practices. In his work on the northern cattle stations, Paul had encountered several men with more than one wife who were seeking baptism, and the issue was discussed at length at a field conference at Hermannsburg at the end of 1959. For Albrecht, it revived a painful episode from his early days at Hermannsburg when a man and his two wives from Tempe Downs station had come faithfully to instruction classes and asked for baptism. At the time, Albrecht felt he had no choice but to make the surrender of one of the wives the condition of the man's baptism, and the man and his wives had left the mission in considerable bitterness.

The conference came to provisional agreement on a new guideline. In the Aboriginal situation which seemed somewhat analogous to the Old Testament, polygamy should not debar any person who had come to a saving faith in Christ from being received into full church membership through baptism. But no-one once received into church membership could take additional wives, and polygamists could not hold church office. The issue was referred to a larger Lutheran Church council to seek the experience of Lutheran churches in indigenous societies in other parts of the world. A second conference resolution sought the liberalization of present government regulations on the marriage of Aboriginal 'wards' to 'non-wards'.

Another important issue was further responsibilities for the experienced Aranda evangelists. Conrad Raberaba at Hermannsburg had been preaching in the church for many years, taking the Aranda service in the morning, and teaching religious instruction in the school. In November, he and Paulus Wiljuka of Maryvale had attended and addressed the Australia-wide Lutheran synod held in Nuriootpa. It was evident to Albrecht that the time was approaching for Aboriginal evangelists to be fully ordained Lutheran ministers. 'Our main effort must be to train their own leaders; we shall never be able to do what such men can do', and, a decade later, 'a missionary who sees his task only in preaching and teaching, will inevitably arrive at a dead end'.

But he was strongly opposed to any idea of formal seminary training in the south, maintaining that for Aborigines, that form of education was an artificial culture. Back in their own situation, it did not survive. A far better way was to find the existing leaders from among the people, and try to equip them further for the task of leadership. It was eventually decided that additional classes would be held at Hermannsburg—Albrecht would be responsible for one next winter. 'Pray for me', he wrote to Lou Borgelt; 'It is important work, and I feel so inadequate for it. It would be ever so much simpler to face a group of white people than prepare for these men'.

Minna was not especially well in the early months of 1960. Yet, as Albrecht wrote to Duguid, 'even from her bed, she runs the house and controls all activities in the garden'. Towards April, the weather became cooler and some of her old energy returned. She spent time in the garden, digging and weeding—always a sure sign of improvement in her health. Sometimes Albrecht joined her, sitting awkwardly on the ground on his lame leg. In May, she and Martin left to go south for five weeks.

Albrecht had shed much of his administrative harassment in leaving Hermannsburg. But his correspondence was as voluminous as ever, and occupied part of most days. Perhaps, too, going into his study and shutting the door had become, in his busy life, a way of being alone. Physically, too, he needed rest. His lame leg had always been a hindrance, and now that he was in his late sixties, both legs were getting weaker.

The correspondence was larger and more varied than it had ever been—hundreds of letters each year from a miscellany of friends, researchers, journalists and writers. The Territory was commanding an increasing interest both in Australia and abroad. Several queries came from people writing about Albert Namatjira. Frank Hurley, whom Albrecht had met many years before, sought advice and some text for his new book of photography on Central Australia. Mervyn Hartwig, a student at Concordia College in Adelaide, wrote for information on the killings at Coniston in 1929. Albrecht thought it 'indispensable' that Hartwig come north to talk with the Aborigines concerned while that was still possible, and offered practical suggestions as to how that could be done. When it became impossible for Hartwig to come, Albrecht typed several pages of answers to a long list of questions.

For many people and groups, the Lutheran pastor was an essential contact and intermediary. Passing on scores of messages of condolence to the Namatjira family, advising the government chest X-ray scheme on the cattle station centres, distributing gifts of money or used clothing, responding to a request from Ted Strehlow who was recording traditional songs at Erldunda station. Back at the University of Adelaide in December, Strehlow wrote again, as he did each Christmas, enclosing a list of names of old Aboriginal friends and associates and a cheque for Albrecht to distribute gifts on his behalf—ten shillings or a pound to each.

In June, Albrecht was sicker than he had been for a long time, suffering a very severe gastro-enteritis that was sweeping the town. Six babies died in the Alice Springs hospital. Albrecht slowly recovered, though he told a friend that it had nearly flattened him. Perhaps it was this as well as his concern for Minna which prompted Lou Borgelt to raise again the question of their leaving Central Australia:

> Now you *must* come down this summer, in any case Minna told Hertha she doubted if she could see another summer out in Alice Springs. It looks as if you may have a major problem on your hands ... If you *must* leave Alice Springs, be near the Chairman at Nuriootpa and continue the literary work.

It had been discussed between them before, but it was a move which Albrecht had not felt as particularly imminent. There were practical obstacles too. Paul could not possibly do all the Alice Springs work alone, and mission finances might not run to establishing another household for a new man. But at heart he was not yet ready to leave. 'I feel there is still too much left in me, some strength which I can put to good use.' When Minna returned north, Albrecht found her unbelievably well, the best he had seen her in ten years. She was taking full advantage of her recovery, cooking, gardening, even painting the kitchen. Six or eight weeks later, she had a relapse. Along with her physical symptoms, she was again restless and anxious.

By 1959, a number of part-Aboriginal children had gone to foster homes in the south, and five girls went in 1960. All did well at school, and four returned south again at the beginning of 1961. Albrecht had made most of the arrangements personally, knowing that success depended to a great extent on a wise choice of home and foster parents for each particular child. Equally, he saw to it that the children came home on holidays at least once a year, feeling it was a grave mistake to try, like some government agencies and missions, to cut off the children completely from their home background, sometimes even changing their names so that nothing would remind them of their past. Sometimes he had been approached by people wanting to adopt a young Aboriginal child or baby. He had always refused, believing that it was essential for an Aboriginal child to establish their Aboriginal identity within their own setting in childhood. In the 1930s he and Ted Strehlow had vigorously opposed the practice of taking part-Aboriginal children away from their fullblood mothers.

 I was at Henbury when the policeman wanted to take me, he don't like see any halfcaste in the camp. Pretty tough. When I was at Henbury, and see policeman comin' on the camel, I run in the scrub, that happened a lot of times. Ted Strehlow saved me and sent me to Hermannsburg, to school.

But for children of eleven or twelve years, Albrecht felt a wider experience could be very valuable, especially for the part-Aboriginal girls for whom early adolescence often seemed a critical period in their lives. Many became pregnant in teenage years, automatically married, and later found themselves tied to someone they might never otherwise have chosen. Albrecht thought a stay in a suitable Christian home in the south introduced them to another kind of 'ordinary' life. They went on outings, attended church with their foster families, and went to young people's groups. Later on, if they could not find work in Alice Springs, they would have the confidence to go elsewhere.

He consulted carefully about each child with Harry Giese, the Director of the Aboriginal Welfare Branch, though the government had given no financial support to the scheme. He also kept in touch with the foster parents and wrote regularly to the girls themselves, usually in a joint letter which he duplicated and distributed to each. 'Dear girls', he would begin, giving them news of their relatives, or life on the stations, always encouraging them to make the best of the time, though he was aware that the real value of the experience would not emerge until years later.

The sense that much of life ran at a level invisible in day-to-day experience was something that had grown in him over the years. Not only was much of life mysterious. It was the deeper, more important aspect that worked itself out, for the most part, invisibly. 'The best part of our life is, and remains, hidden some-how, yet comes up from time to time', he wrote to Ossie Heinrich in the latter part of 1960. It was a reflective letter, precipitated by a long one from Ossie expressing disappointment at the mission board's lack of response to a church commission report the previous year—he and other church members had been asked to review management and decision-making in the mission organization. Albrecht continued:

> I feel what you must have told them is a little beyond their present 'digestive' powers; one day you may be surprised what it all leads to. Then, the difference of those 1000 miles is and remains a terrific obstacle to understanding . . .
>
> Also, with all their faults, I firmly believe our Boardmembers do their work prayerfully, and if so, then some day some good must come of it. When during the time we were going to buy the [Kaporilja] pipe material for which we had money, but not for the freight, I went to the Board meeting and asked them would they at least provide for the freight. I was bluntly told no . . . When I returned to Point Pass where we were staying, I don't mind telling you, Ossie, I was not far off a real good cry: it was bitter, as to us it was a matter of life and death. Yet, even then it turned out a good thing. The public meeting in the Adelaide Town Hall was organised, the *Advertiser* became interested, and even if I had the 'pleasure' of climbing stairs and walking the streets of Adelaide collecting— which was a condition of the paper to ensure the success—it all turned out to the good. I can still praise God for all that, even if at that time it brought me right up to the very limit of what I thought I could possibly go.

It was one of his greatest strengths that he never knew a time limit. For anything really important, he had an almost infinite capacity to wait. 'I still think there will be repercussions of the right kind in the end.' Undoubtedly, it came from his faith that in the final analysis, 'we are not working for a Board, nor for any human organisation or institution'.

In June 1961, Minna had another heart attack and went south by air. For the second time, her Adelaide doctor told her there was no question of returning to a hot climate to live. Their house in Alice Springs was sold to the mission, and for an almost equivalent sum of money they purchased a house in Burnell Street, Linden Park, two blocks from Helene. On his way back to Alice Springs in mid-September to finalize arrangements there, Albrecht attended an inter-mission conference at Ernabella.

Albrecht's relations with the Ernabella staff had always been most cordial, even if he had reservations about some of their policies, especially their support of traditional Aboriginal religion. But he was open, reflective rather than opinionated, about the differences. Perhaps this time, too, there was a deeper nostalgia stemming from the uncertainty about his own future. Reverend William Edwards, superintendent at Ernabella for the previous three years, was surprised by the humility of the man—thirty years his senior both in age and in mission experience. He told Edwards he had taken too strict a stand against traditional culture in the early days, and he regretted that Hermannsburg had not instituted a total ban on alcohol from the beginning for staff and Aborigines alike. For his part, Bill Edwards was conscious that the Lutherans were further ahead with the training of Aboriginal men for leadership in the church. They seemed to have less difficulty with church structures, though he reflected that Albrecht's personality and experience must have carried many issues through. Watching the older man, he was struck by Albrecht's empathy with the people, as he sat cross-legged in the dust with the old men, talking and swapping stories.

A baptism service at Maryvale was planned for the last Sunday in September. Albrecht had always had an especially affectionate relationship with the Maryvale people, and the last service there moved him deeply. Seventeen people were baptized, some of them quite old, and there was a memorial service for Gamaliel who had died in 1959. Several men spoke, including Rufus, who said that though Gamaliel had never learned to read or write, he had in his heart a shining light, and this was so bright that he made it shine into the hearts of others who in turn saw the light of God and turned to Him. The people had collected money for a marble gravestone for Gamaliel and, at the end of the service, the old camp sheet covering it was pulled away to reveal a text from Revelation in Aranda inscripted in gold letters: '*Kaiaka etna nama . . .*' (Blessed are they that have cleansed their robes in the blood of the Lamb).

There was pleasing progress in literacy. For over a year, a woman, two young girls and the young evangelist Paul Ungkwanaka—the son of the former gardener, William Ungkwanaka, at Hermannsburg—had been teaching the older people to read and write. The practice had been to buy an Aranda New Testament from offerings, and to give it to each person who learned to read, even if poorly. Reading classes were conducted daily in front of the evangelist's 'manse'—a rough construction of desert oak, some old timber from the Bungalow, and galvanized iron. Each person read in turn, and Albrecht noticed the pride with which each finished their part and turned to the next person. He felt the reading was opening up a new world to them.

Two Sundays before, he had been at Henbury, where the once flourishing congregation of a hundred people had dwindled to thirty. Albrecht thought the process had been accelerated by the manager who wanted only workers on the place. Albrecht had noticed the same trend on some other stations, though he knew it was also exacerbated by the drought conditions. Albrecht's last Sunday in Alice Springs was 8 October 1961. Packing had been almost impossible during the previous week, with people stopping by for a last chat. Many spoke their feelings for him in words and gestures not found among Europeans, and he thought what warmth and feeling there was in Aboriginal people—hard to describe and harder still to forget. Many of the children, too, came in little groups to say goodbye.

For all of the immediate imperative to move south created by Minna's health, Albrecht's long-range plans were hardly certain. Despite the farewells, a sense of uncertainty, almost a vacuum, hung over him in the first months at Linden Park. 'After all the rush up there, this life is very tame and quiet', he wrote to one of the Alice Springs Sunday School teachers, two weeks after leaving Central Australia:

> Even the street where we live here, is a quiet corner, not many cars pass us here . . . What I miss a lot is my Native friends coming and going, of which I had a good share in Alice Springs.

Ted Strehlow was one of the few people at the time who saw clearly that it was the end of an epoch. Sending Christmas wishes in December 1961:

With your departure from the Centre, another age in the history of the Hermannsburg Mission has ended—just as the departure of my father from Hermannsburg a few days before his death in 1922 closed the pioneering age of that station.

You can look back upon a period of rich development in mission work; and when you look at the present numbers of the native congregations, you cannot fail, I am sure, to be comforted by the knowledge that it was the mighty hand of God Himself, which brought about this miraculous expansion after debts and drought years and disastrous epidemics had threatened to extinguish Hermannsburg soon after you first came to the Centre . . .

With all good wishes . . . T. G. H. Strehlow

Minna's health in the last months of 1961 was uncertain. She was not in pain, and much of the time could help prepare meals, organize the shopping, and even water the garden. But her heart was weak, and even a small amount of movement quickly tired her. Albrecht did not feel it was safe to leave her alone, yet could not help chafing at being tied to the house day and night.

He wrote a large number of letters north, partly to complete a multitude of small tasks left undone before his hurried departure, undoubtedly also from his own need for some links with the work he had not really relinquished. He wrote to the board expressing his sense of urgency that the building of the children's accommodation in Alice Springs be started without delay. Cottage homes with house mothers had been planned, each caring for a small number of children. A note went to Mervyn Hartwig, asking for a copy of his research on the Coniston killings for the Lutheran President General, Dr Max Lohe. 'I don't think that any such work exists anywhere, and I also think that it may never see the public press as it is such a terrific indictment. Yet, if we are to redeem our past sins in this country, it will be only if people's eyes are opened wide to facts as you have dug up.'

Though not a man to create deliberate controversy in the public domain, Albrecht had an acute sense of the importance of facts and the historical record. Speaking at the Northern Territory centenary celebrations in Alice Springs the previous year, he had referred not only to the hardship inherent in the pioneering days of the Territory, but to the dispossession and injustice suffered by Aboriginal people. He also wrote several pages to the owner of Maryvale station, Con Dracopoulos, after Paul reported Con's concern that one of the Aboriginal evangelists had thrashed a boy for not attending church. To Albrecht, it was essential to see the incident within its cultural context:

To our way of thinking and feeling, it is repulsive to try and force one's religion on someone else, 'forcing it down his throat' as the saying is. Here one has to keep in mind the past from which the Natives come. Under old conditions, if a man is invited to an important corroboree, he has to come; if not, he is killed . . . Even if the men at Maryvale are mostly Christian, this feeling still lives in them, has been taken over from their past.

It was easy, he said, for Europeans to think that it was therefore high time that the old custom was discontinued, that Aborigines be told that 'our way is best in such matters'. But to interfere with this pattern of authority often meant that young men grew up knowing no authority, and were much the worse for it. He explained that he had made similar mistakes in his early days at Hermannsburg when he used to feel deeply sorry for the lads who were being treated and trained by the old men:

For instance, if at Hermannsburg I thought, being in charge, I could step in and say what in my opinion the Natives did wrong—say a father to his son. That assumption on my part was entirely wrong; at this stage of their development, we as white people cannot directly take over such a function without doing a lot of harm, even if unknowingly. In this particular instance, the boy Roy would suffer in his future development more than anyone can predict, if he was not told to do what the men tell him. As a matter of fact, one day such a boy could well develop into some sort of a rogue, as one who owes allegiance to nobody; that definite feeling of belonging is not developed, neither the feeling for responsibility . . .

He had pondered the encounter of Aboriginal and European, Aboriginal and Christian, for decades, and the truth seemed to grow more complex as he grew older. Writing to a fellow missionary in 1962, he cautioned him against speaking of corroborees as an evil. 'To approach them from the angle of forbidding it is to assume the role of Moses, the Law giver, and not the Gospel.' A letter from a Bible translator at Ernabella asking advice on translating culturally sensitive material opened up similar questions. Circumcision was discussed very openly in the New Testament, but for an Aborigine, explicit reference to circumcision was likely to be highly offensive, since it was part of initiation ritual and therefore secret to the men. How should such passages be translated: indirectly so as not to offend in the Aboriginal context; or literally, to preserve the clear meaning of the text and its message for salvation? For Albrecht, both principles were important, and in the final analysis he thought the translator could be guided only by the Holy Spirit. But he readily acknowledged that the Lutheran tradition into which he had stepped when first coming to Hermannsburg had been one-sided and overly negative towards Aboriginal culture:

> I think your way there is better than ours, where from the first the missionaries had nothing but a definite no to everything that the Natives had. The result was that the circumcision was continued underhand, underground so to speak, and has remained so to the present day with the majority of the people there. I would feel that it is better to let them do it openly, but at the same time, make the full truth of the Word known to them, unadulterated and without compromise.

Early in 1962, a niece arrived from Germany to live with them. Erika Gevers had been an appealing twelve-year-old when he and Minna visited Germany in 1952, and she had grown up with a lively interest in the aunt and uncle in Australia. With the extra company for Minna in the house, Albrecht decided to go back to Central Australia for two or three months. It would be some time before his replacement, Ralph Kernich, could come, and Paul was taxed to the limit.

He arrived in Alice Springs and took up many of his old responsibilities including the six-weekly trips to the southern stations, Henbury, Palmer Valley, Erldunda, Maryvale. There were full-time evangelists now at eleven stations, and three part-time men. At each place the numbers of Aboriginal people were decreasing. Much of the country was drought stricken, so the stations needed few workers and extra campers were discouraged or hunted away. He thought the Welfare Ordinance was actually encouraging this trend, since station management was held responsible for Aborigines living there. It was liable, for example, for a woman living there who was not supported by a male relative. The station could claim on the government for support, or otherwise see to it that she was not camped on the property. On many stations, wandering Aborigines were simply kept moving. It meant that the large settlements in the district—Jay Creek, Amoonguna, Areyonga, Papunya, and Hermannsburg—were attracting everyone not actually employed. Again, Albrecht thought that the settlements would have to concentrate more on training the future generation if they were to compete with European labour.

He started again with the children's instruction classes after school. About forty came, in two different classes. Lessons were held on four days of the week, so as to leave the children two days free for play. Most of the children were part-Aboriginal or 'coloured', with a few Europeans and one or two fullblood Aborigines. Several came from Christian families living on the cattle stations, and stayed with relatives in town to attend school. Many lived in what seemed appalling circumstances, like the camp on a vacant block adjoining the mission area from which he frequently heard brawls and fights Many of the children coming to classes could barely look forward to a night's sleep, let alone anything one could think of as a home life. The places were overcrowded, with not even a table or chair, so homework could not even be thought of. Some of the bigger children tried to work on their own, but for the most part he accepted that all memory work, like Catechism, scripture texts or hymns, had to be done in class. That was how the frequent classes had developed. And the children liked it. After class, he gave them a little dried fruit, and they sat with him on a little form outside the church and talked before going off. Albrecht felt the regular contact was valuable in their development.

He was experimenting with his cooking, trying—as always—to lose some weight, and developed quite a satisfactory cottage cheese made with powdered skim milk. But he wasn't having too much success in losing weight, and wryly concluded that the case must be chronic. Several hours each day were spent at the typewriter. Sermon writing took time, two or three days on some, and then the duplicating. He made about sixty copies, and sent them out to the evangelists at the various centres, hoping that eventually there would be a book of sermons in Aranda, one for each Sunday of the year. He thought it was important to get some written material to them, since they had access to no literature apart from the New Testament, the Catechism, and the small amount of Bible history included in the hymn book. Sometimes he added a news sheet with the sermons. One man told him that some had been 'hard food', but there were positive comments too. 'You put new thoughts into our heads, don't know where to get them otherwise', said one. One was an article on alcohol in Aranda, '*Rela ba njuntjamea ekalta*' (Man and strong drink). Often he spoke directly to drinkers about alcohol, trying to explain that it was destroying them and their families. Even if the present response was rejection, it might mean something in the future.

There were times when he did not feel too well himself. If he was too busy, he suffered giddiness and a feeling of pressure in the head. It came mostly when he had taken both services on a Sunday. But basically, 'him alright', as he thought to himself, falling naturally into Aboriginal parlance. When Ralph Kernich arrived in October, Albrecht took him out to the station congregations, introduced him to other parts of the work, and went with him to a field conference at Hermannsburg. When the sessions were over, he made a point of speaking personally with the new superintendent, Garry Stoll, congratulating him on the job he was doing. There is a good atmosphere about the place, he told him, better than I managed to achieve when I was here. The comments were generous, coming from the 68-year old missionary to a man in his twenties who had come to Hermannsburg on relieving work only three years before.

Albrecht's last task in Central Australia was teaching a three-week course in November at the government settlement at Amoonguna, and he was pleased to find that for the first time, two women were in the class. He had selected for study Biblical passages that he thought would be relevant to the situations in which Aborigines currently found themselves: the issue of citizenship, for example, and the difficulties under which many Aboriginal people worked. And an afternoon was spent in instruction on voting rights and procedures, a subject of considerable interest, and two afternoons on the drink problem. None of those present drank alcohol themselves. But in recent years, twelve people from the mission community had died as a direct result of drinking, five in a single incident. The latter included the former mission evangelist, Rolf. In 1930, Rolf had survived walking overland without water or supplies from Ayers Rock to Hermannsburg with the mechanic of the Lasseter expedition. Now, he and four companions had died near Coober Pedy after using up all their water on the leaky radiator of their car. All appeared to have been drinking heavily.

Albrecht's leave-taking that year seemed to have a greater note of finality about it than the hurried departure of a year earlier. He had officially resigned from the mission, and handed the *Freizeit* refresher teaching file to Paul with the feeling that one of his last ties to the work was cut. By far his best Christmas present was Minna's bright spirits. But in the weeks following Christmas, she became fretful and depressed. The fact that physically she was reasonably well only underlined her feelings of inadequacy. Being unable to cope emotionally seemed to her spiritual failure as well. 'If I was sick', she said, 'I could simply withdraw. But as it is, I feel as if I should be able to manage'. It was probably harder for him to cope with her difficulties now that there was no work to turn to for relief or escape. He spent many hours writing a long article on the war years at Hermannsburg for the Lutheran yearly *Almanac*, then a detailed account of their experience with the Lasseter expedition, also for the *Almanac*.

The Lasseter story had become something of a legend in Australia, and Albrecht was conscious of the numerous inaccuracies. He also felt that the heroic overtones were sadly misplaced. To him, Lasseter was a man who had perpetrated a swindle and had unfortunately suffered the worst possible consequences. Yet he also felt deeply sorry for him. When he sent a copy of the article to Harry Giese in Darwin, Giese replied appreciatively, 'I feel that unless people like you are prepared to write down some of your experiences and views, a tremendous amount of valuable information will be lost about the early years in Central Australia'.

Yet the writing, even sermon writing for the evangelists, gave him no real feeling of connection with the work in Central Australia. 'Our life here in the south is so different to what it used to be, like a train shunted to a dead end', he wrote to a friend. Yet the very ground of his Christian conviction would not allow him to rest in dissatisfaction, and he constantly tried to content himself with his lot:

> Yet, it would be quite wrong to look at it from that angle only, there is another side to it, and a happy one. If 37 years ago, we were looking ahead, very often with great anxiety, we are now able to look back, and at every turn thank God for His goodness and the power of His Grace.

Aborigines in the Territory gained voting rights in 1962, and D. D. Smith, former government engineer in Alice Springs, solicited their votes in his successful candidature for the seat of Stuart. Albrecht's feelings for the man were mixed. They'd had their differences in the past, particularly over the building of the Kaporilja pipeline. But Smith had won his qualified support by a strong statement of his intention to try to get better conditions for Aborigines, and to work towards gaining Aboriginal representation in the Legislative Council. Albrecht knew no other Member had worked for that before. After the election, he wrote to Smith suggesting specific areas for change. Many Aborigines on stations still had the most inadequate of housing, which seemed to Albrecht needless hardship. At his instigation, twenty simple prefabricated houses had been built on Maryvale station and some other stations were following the lead. Elderly people could pay some rent from their pensions. He was also concerned about the way maternity benefits were administered. Aboriginal mothers had been entitled to the benefit for some years but, in practice, many never received it. With his natural sensitivity to injustice, he had always felt it shameful that the European station-owner's wife was able to collect her benefit promptly, yet the stockman's wife, working at the same station, might not have enough money to buy a nappy.

He and Minna were both able to go to Central Australia in April, he to conduct the five-week evangelists class at Hermannsburg. Teaching was one of his greatest joys in these years, and he conducted courses at Hermannsburg in 1964 and 1965, each of several weeks duration.

Early in 1963, Albrecht received a letter from the superintendent of Hope Vale Mission in North Queensland. Kevin Kotzur had been one of a group of students who had come through Alice Springs and Hermannsburg some years before. Now he found himself, a young man, in charge of a community of almost four hundred people, attempting to fulfil the responsibilities of missionary, manager and magistrate simultaneously. He wrote to Albrecht for advice on discipline, and about the role of evangelists in a largely Christianized mission. Albrecht sympathized with the difficulty of being both law-keeper and missionary. 'That is something that in the end just weighs you down. It is an unusual combination, and one that would be entirely intolerable in our society.' Carl Strehlow, in an earlier era, had run the mission with total authority. Albrecht had, from the first, tried to develop a wider community discipline and leadership through the elders and later the Aboriginal representatives on the field conference, but he was all too aware of the difficulties. The training of evangelists was closer to his heart than anything else in mission work. 'The Lord told his disciples: ye will be my witnesses. There was no mention made of training or education, no, witnesses . . . here are a few stepping stones.' He encouraged Kotzur to spend time daily to discuss Bible stories 'in the light of everyday life', and the lives of church fathers like Augustine, and made some practical suggestions:

> A little later, let him conduct a burial service, after discussing the formal procedure, and especially let him speak to the people. The Natives are born speakers, and you will probably be surprised to see what he can do . . .
>
> If such talents are in a congregation, and not utilised, it ever so often happens that this is turned to bad use. Old Brother Schwarz, like Strehlow at Hermannsburg, was a domineering character, and as such he could do much, once his authority had been fully

established. However, there are not many who can step into such boots and continue; it is not normal either . . . We are certainly going ahead in trying to make more and more use of our Native Evangelists and even try to lead them into a full pastorate.

Increasingly, he was emphasizing the face-to-face, personal aspect. Training might involve teaching, but at its heart was a nurturing of individuals and their spiritual growth and understanding. It differed little from what he had always done at Hermannsburg—personal contact had always been his *modus operandi*. But there had always been so many other battles as well—issues of physical survival, reserves, employment, officialdom.

In the following year, he and Minna travelled to North Queensland following a request by the Queensland church to report on the missions at Hope Vale and Bloomfield. All the years in the Centre—in a setting both similar and different—sharpened his questions and observations. He observed peanut growing on a share-farming basis—which he could not but compare to the Aboriginal pastoralists scheme—the cattle industry in both places; station management; the running of the store. He advised on techniques and equipment for the beginning efforts at tanning. But, for Albrecht, one question was fundamental: what stage had the people reached in being able to live and work alongside other Australians?

At Hope Vale, he found the issues of freedom and protection very much alive, with people expressing a variety of feelings in a public meeting—the desire for greater freedom, fear about surviving in the outside community, memories of the suffering during the war when the community was moved to Woorabinda, concern whether people would lose their spiritual life if they left the congregation. Albrecht's comments in an article soon afterwards indicated his acceptance that the age of protection was ending. As he sometimes thought to himself, a person will learn to swim only in the water, not as an onlooker.

Leaving Queensland via Mount Isa, they spent several weeks in Central Australia where he taught another course at Hermannsburg. By the end of August, Central Australia was already warming up and, after several years of drought conditions, there was plenty of dust. Among the people in his class were two evangelists preparing for formal ordination, Conrad Raberaba and Peter Bullah. They would be examined separately by President Lohe and others from the south. He and Minna were back in Linden Park when the two men were ordained at Hermannsburg in November 1964—the first ordained Aboriginal pastors in the Australian Lutheran Church. For Albrecht, it brought a profound sense of completion and gratitude. Corresponding with Kevin Kotzur in Hope Vale, he wrote:

> It was a great day, sure, when the first two were ordained at Hermannsburg. Now, the last stone has gone into the arch, and I can withdraw, have to decrease, praise God for everything. May He graciously forgive me all what I have done wrong and missed, and may His grace let even mistakes turn into blessing. Sending you a picture of our last Course, with crosses indicating the two ordained . . .

I was preaching sermon in church when I was young fellow. Old Moses taught me, too, and my uncle [Abel]. Then after that, I was learning every time after Christmas, for a course. Moses tell me, you're becoming a minister, you'll be taking my place later on. When he was pass away, I was teaching in the school first, took over from my uncle, preach on Sunday too. We learn every night at my uncle's place.

I told Pastor Albrecht when I was young, eh, Pastor Albrecht, I like to push out to learn, to learn and 'come minister. He never said no. He say, we'll see first. And church work, he showed me then. Later, he asked me, eh, you want to 'come minister? I was thinking, I never been in the college yet, and later on, I told Pastor Albrecht, YOU MY COLLEGE, you teaching me all my word.

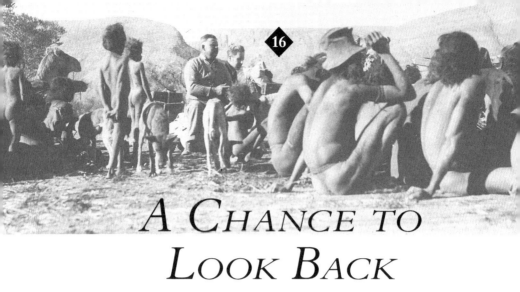

A CHANCE TO
LOOK BACK
1965~1976

*I regret many things in my life, but one thing I do not regret is that
I tried at all times and all places to be of service to anyone, and if I
sometimes failed, God only knows why.*

(F. W. Albrecht, late years)

The first half of 1965 was good. Minna was her old self, digging
in the garden, convincing Papa that some of the lawn would
be better turned into a vegetable area, preserving summer fruit for
the first time in years. Albrecht was busy too. He went up and
down to the shack at Sellicks Beach, doing repairs, painting, and
improving the place. He loved it as much as ever, and frequently
offered it to friends. He had never forgotten the lifesaver it was for
him in the stress-filled years of the war. Few weeks went by
without invitations to talk to one group or another—guilds, mission festivals, Rotary meetings, welfare clubs. In June, he had high
blood pressure. The doctor put him under 'house arrest', telling
him to cut down on his speaking engagements and to go back to a
stricter diet—'largely going hungry', as he told a friend.

By August, he was well enough to go north by train for a six-
week teaching course. Also travelling north was a lecturer from
a teacher training college in Melbourne with a party of female

students. The girls responded warmly to the 71-year-old missionary, plying him with questions about pioneering days in Central
Australia, doubtless responding instinctively to his unassuming
friendliness and the sense of a rich personal experience. He was a
man rich in stories, always 'people' stories, and most often out of
his Aboriginal experience—funny, odd, sad. He showed them the
copy of the latest *Almanac* with the article on Lasseter, and sold a
dozen subscriptions on the spot.

There were thirty-three Aboriginal men in the course at
Hermannsburg. He had the feeling that the fact that he was there
for the third time although no longer in the service of the mission
made an impression. One man lifted his hand to his chin, saying
'You are filling us right up', and there was hardly a devotion in
which the chairman for that day did not pray for the *kngaribata* (old
man) who had come to teach them. Again, he wondered at the
depth of their prayers and the short addresses during morning
devotions. European Australians so often assumed that Aborigines
could not comprehend the finer and deeper things of life. Yet he felt
these prayers bespoke a deeper spiritual experience than some of the
prayers he heard at church conventions, even from learned men.

That year he included twenty lectures on Communism. His
family had been harassed by the Russian régime, and he was well
aware of the record of some Communist governments—persecu-
tion of Lutherans in Latvia and Estonia, millions of deaths under
Stalin. Duguid had expressed concern more than once at Communist sway in the Victorian Aboriginal Advancement League, and
Albrecht had heard that the Darwin branch of the Aborigines Uplift
Society was strongly influenced. Now that all Aborigines in the
Territory had voting rights, he felt they were wide open to political
propaganda which they would not understand without some preparation. As he wrote to a colleague:

> Unfortunately, many of the cattle station owners have behaved in a
> most miserable way with them . . . and this is deeply ingrained in
> their attitude. I shall make no attempt in glossing this over, sin is sin.
> However they must also see the other side, with an . . . infinitely
> heavier debit balance.

To explain Communism in the modern world—something
different from the 'everything in common' concept of the early
Christian church and also inherent in traditional Aboriginal life—he
tried to explain an alternative economic system such as existed in
Australia. He used examples they would understand, referring to

the cattle stations and their need for workers, or the flour mill at Laura. He was unpleasantly surprised to discover that hardly one of the men had any idea of the system they lived in, where most goods were produced in large factories, and obtained by people in exchange for labour, and so on. They didn't have exactly the 'cargo cult' idea of many New Guinea peoples, but seemed to have the impression that there was an unlimited supply of goods available. The only question was one of obtaining them.

Again and again he asked himself how it had happened that they could have grown up under such an impression. How had the mission failed to communicate something so fundamental? He could only conclude that it was a result of their old life: since it was dictated by necessity, they had not had the opportunity to exercise responsibility towards more material things. But he could see that they were growing in their understanding, and many said so appreciatively. He had always emphasized the importance of adult education for Aborigines, on social issues as well as religious teaching.

He was starting to feel like an old man, noticing that he tired more easily. He was rarely to bed before eleven at night, and was up again by six in the mornings. Yet the fatigue aside, the work was deeply satisfying. He had a room to himself, with a table for his typewriter. His midday meal he had with the current missionary, Pastor Radke, and his wife, on six days a week. One day a week, he preferred to go without, feeling it was good for his health. Mornings and evenings he ate alone, mostly fresh fruit and rye bread. Looking around the mission, he was conscious of the time he had been gone. A new church was being built, using stone from the nearby hills. It would be quite a large building, at least eighty feet long, but necessary for the population explosion that was going on. Looking at all the young people in church, he could not help thinking of the drought years when so many babies died. Now there were so many young people he wondered where they would go. Yet let us praise God for the challenge, he thought.

By 1966, Erika was gone from Linden Park to be married. The house seemed empty, too big for two people. Mail still came from other parts of the world concerning the Aboriginal work. Sometimes it was an enquiry about Albert Namatjira, sometimes questions about Aboriginal culture and religion. Responding to one, he wrote:

> There are very many [Christians] to whom it was gospel truth that cleanliness comes next to godliness. Now in the Centre the people hardly had enough water to drink and cook a meal now and then,

but seldom enough to wash themselves. To enforce our way of life on such people at the same time as they are taught the Bible, and insist on them keeping clean and tidy, in order, very often, to show others what we had achieved with them, is just plain nonsense . . .

Has Christianity failed? asked the same person. One might equally ask, replied Albrecht, has Christianity failed in our society and among the Europeans generally, especially as one looked back on the last war? The better question was to ask where we had failed to bring Christianity to the Aborigines.

Another letter, from someone in the British and Foreign Bible Society, asked him about the results in individual people of having the New Testament translated into Aranda. His response could only have been written by someone who was multi-lingual and whose own religious experience had worked deeply in his life:

> Religion is closely bound up in our feelings, and if people are to be approached with the Gospel truth, this is best done through the language where they have their deepest feelings, their mother tongue. It is from here where their whole life is permeated, every aspect of it . . .

As an example, he cited a man in Alice Springs, Joker Doolan:

> He had a job in town, but at night he often came to learn to read his Aranda New Testament. He was camping, at that time, on the mission block . . . One night I watched him closely bent over a small fire in order to read . . . there was a drizzle, yet, with a blanket over his head so as to protect the book he still read his New Testament. When we met again . . . I asked him about it, and he just smiled: 'Yes, I like it'. He had been reading, even with great difficulty, parts of the Sermon on the Mount—God's truth in his mother tongue had set his heart on fire. I find it hard to imagine whether this would have touched him that deeply if it had come to him in any other language.

Having been again invited to teach at Hope Vale, he could not take the courses in Hermannsburg the following year. But their time in Central Australia on the way home from Queensland was a happy one. The new church at Hermannsburg was dedicated, he travelled to Angas Downs station to dedicate the little bush church there for which Minna had collected much of the money, and he dedicated the foundation stone for a new church in Alice Springs.

He had been asked by Pastor Radke to put together some of the early mission history, and he re-read some of the letters and reports sent south by the first missionaries eighty years before. The resulting sketch characteristically blended homespun, practical details of the early years with his never-ceasing ponderings on the basic issues, the methods and assumptions with which the early missionaries had begun work among the Aborigines. Could it have been done differently?

> One of the first things such men would have encountered would have been the sight of old or other helpless people, whom they could not have ignored without denying their Christian witness ... They had no choice but to undertake bodily support of the people, act as a welfare agency, and delve into the multifarious aspects of mission work to the Aborigines as we know it.

Yet he well knew the difficulty in balancing the physical welfare of the Aborigines with the spiritual work proper. Many people either refused to engage in the physical, believing it was outside their appropriate work, or became absorbed in welfare work to the exclusion of the spiritual. 'At bottom of either attitude was misunderstanding and lack of preparedness to meet the peculiar situation of our Aborigines.' He still believed strongly that the nomadic Aborigines presented a challenge different from any other people in the world both for missionary work and for their integration into the larger society.

He was more conscious than ever that European missionaries had come to the Aborigines with mistaken assumptions. They had thought the Aborigines lacked any religious sense. Translating one of Hermannsburg's founding missionaries, Hermann Kempe, 'We have found no trace even of idolatry, or sanctification to idols, so that even the most primitive heathen in Africa may be looked upon as of a much higher standing than these here.' He himself had only come gradually to an appreciation of the depth of their spirituality. For years he had struggled to cope with Aboriginal behaviour that he found difficult or even repugnant. Yet even in those early days, he had also encountered new depths of experience, like the time he heard Abel pray ('as I never heard before') after the death of his son. He had also come to a deep appreciation of the efficacy of their traditional background in their daily lives:

> These Aborigines who had to face the nothing every day [the struggle of bush life], if they had not had a strong spiritual background, they could never have survived. The fact is that their whole life, from early infancy to the last day in this world, was surrounded and entirely lived within their religion; there is nothing else that could have carried them through.

As he had said elsewhere, 'When we first came here we thought we had found the only people in the world without a religion. Now we have learnt that they are among the most religious people in the world'.

He and Minna returned to Central Australia a few months later, in April 1967. On the Sunday following their arrival, Albrecht preached in the old church in Alice Springs. The pulpit was badly eaten with white ants, and he was apprehensive it might collapse at any moment. There must have been 250 people present, some inside and the others outside listening through the loudspeaker system. Two weeks after, he preached the last sermon in the old church, and the congregation walked in procession to the new building. He was vividly reminded of the day in 1938 when a smaller procession, mostly Aborigines, had walked in similar style from the gum tree in the Todd to the little church of mud bricks funded by old Mr Materne of Greenock. The day was perfect, still and warm, the sky intensely blue against the red rocks of the surrounding ranges. He thought the new building the most beautiful church of that size he had seen, though he worried slightly whether the Aborigines would feel at home in it. 'I would have been happier if the whole would have been so as to attract them more and make *them* feel at home.'

Marianna was in hospital with a bad ulcer on her leg. It was almost healed when she died suddenly, evidently due to heart complications. Paul officiated at her funeral, though Albrecht had thought he would like to say a few words. But when the time came, he was overcome with tears and could not speak. He was well aware that he could not have done his own work without Marianna so completely behind Minna in the household. Anything she did, he reflected, she had done as a service to God. That was the secret of her outstanding life. As he wrote to her daughter, Laura:

> Whenever she was . . . left with the children it was as if one of us was with them; we could never have done more than she did. She always knew how to handle them, without making much fuss about it. And whenever we had sickness in the house and at times did not know whether the one or the other would not recover . . . her tears told us where she stood with her feelings.

Minna stayed well for most of the year, and they were often out of the little house in Linden Park for lectures and talks. Schools too were paying more attention to the Aborigines and their traditional way of life, and Albrecht sometimes spoke to classes, especially in the Lutheran day schools in the Barossa Valley. He was at his best talking to children. He always enjoyed them, yet never talked down to them, but rather took them and their education seriously. He read their Aboriginal projects with as much care as he gave to any researcher. For a class at Angaston, he wrote three pages of detailed comments on different kinds of corroborees, the importance of the marriage systems, and the differences between hunting and killing boomerangs. He encouraged the children not to measure Aborigines by European standards, but in their own context.

Some of Albrecht's mail continued to come from an earlier circle of young friends. Several of the girls who had gone south to foster homes wrote from time to time, and he took a close and affectionate interest in their progress. Three had gone to the Lutheran College at Walla Walla in New South Wales, and from there had found employment. He was delighted to hear they were saving money, and making their own travel arrangements. 'In future Australia will be open for them.'

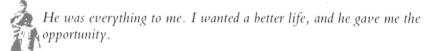 *He was everything to me. I wanted a better life, and he gave me the opportunity.*

A letter came from one of the girls while she was home on holidays on Maryvale station, and Albrecht was pleased to sense in the news about mustering that she still felt at home there. They need their own background, he often thought, 'the soil' in which they must remain rooted if their life was to grow and mature normally. He sometimes thought of others he had known—Aboriginal or part-Aboriginal children completely removed from their Aboriginal background in childhood—in whom feelings of insecurity and uncertainty had built up and finally erupted in adulthood.

By the end of the 1960s, he was almost a decade away from the former life in Central Australia, though he had made one more trip to Hope Vale for four weeks of teaching, which included the ordination of two Aboriginal men, George Rosendale and Alec Cameron. His correspondence was as intensive, but it was becoming more personal, individual. A reference for a former mission employee; letters in Aranda; letters to and from Henbury, Maryvale, Erldunda; news of births, sicknesses, deaths. He regularly visited Aborigines in Adelaide hospitals, especially those sent down from Central Australia. Often they were frightened and disoriented in their strange surroundings, confused by endless corridors, sometimes unable to see where the sun rose and set, and cut off from ordinary communication by the language barrier. He also visited the gaol. Convicted murderer Rupert Stuart was one of many whom he saw regularly.

Visiting grandchildren periodically galvanized the Burnell Street household into life. The extra commotion was sometimes difficult for Minna, but the house felt empty when they left. 'It feels as if our feathers have been pulled out,' she said once. She loved to see the families, conscious that she had missed this experience with her own parents. Minna rarely argued with her children. Nor did she nag them to come more often, as he sometimes did. Without the busy life which the mission work had always meant, he tended to assume that his children and their families would fill the gap. Occasionally Minna reminded him that he had not really spent the time with them when they were younger. He was starting to realize that it was only too true, and the realization wasn't pleasant.

Minna was well enough in the winter of 1967 for them to take a car trip through Victoria to Sydney to see Martin, and they renewed contacts with others like John Brackenreg. The next year they drove via the Murray River to Broken Hill, where Ted and his family were living. Minna had never seen the Murray towns, and they were happy. Sometimes he had a deep sense of completion, yet a feeling of the essential mystery of things. 'I always think that the best a man has to give and leave behind is something he knows little about.' Often he thought about his life, and the inexplicable weaving of events. If it were not for his leg—which had caused him such anguish as a child—he would never have had the interest in reading, and would never have become a missionary. There were other themes, too. He spoke often of their ageing, the shadows lengthening, as if they couldn't expect too much now. Perhaps it was an attempt to account for that feeling which still recurred, of being out of the stream of life. He accepted preaching and speaking invitations whenever possible, but sometimes they felt like a poor substitute for the real thing. The nearest to that was probably the occasional visits of Aboriginal people from Central Australia to the little household at Linden Park.

While we were down there, old Ephraim and me went round to see old Albrecht. He was happy to see us, old Pastor Albrechta, he asked lot of questions about people here, people he taught, because he saw old Ephraim, and that reminded him. Others were passed away, only few are left now, that sort of thing, old Ephraim told him, and then he showed us photos, where he went before, the places—Haasts Bluff, west of Haasts Bluff, all places.

The older people at Hermannsburg often talked about Albrecht, especially the men that had worked most closely with him. They told stories about him, remembering his toughness, his eccentricities. With their unerring sense for individual idiosyncrasy, they delighted in stories about his thriftiness, how he never wasted anything. The stories were all the better for their long familiarity, and the Aboriginal gift of mimicry. They loved to take off his expressions, the way he spoke Aranda.

In the eight or so years of his retirement, Albrecht had spoken on radio a number of times. In 1969, he and Minna were interviewed at length in their Linden Park home and four programmes were televised in several Australian states. After seeing a preview of 'The Call to Hermannsburg', he wrote to the producers suggesting they include two items to convey the real meaning more adequately. Concerning the struggle to secure the 8000 square mile Haasts Bluff block for the Aborigines, 'I should have added at the end the following, 'This is the only known occasion in Australian history where the Aborigines have been preferred before the bullocks'. He also wanted to clarify that while the Aboriginal pastoralists scheme had been a financial success—the men having repaid their loans and finishing with substantial bank balances—the scheme had essentially failed. 'It is obvious, therefore, that the present policy which expects the solution of the problem from making bigger and bigger payments to the Aborigines, is doomed to failure, much of which could be avoided if our experiment would be studied carefully'.

He had always tried to learn from experience. And he had learned so often that white man's schemes and policies for Aborigines frequently did not work. Repeatedly he had reached a point where something did not go forward: it might have seemed logical, even desirable, for the Aborigines, yet somehow it had failed to reach their deeper feelings. It was an impasse that came up against some of his own deepest premises—a European notion of work and economic independence, and an idea of work being integral to personal responsibility. Yet at another level, the impasse was transcended by his personal relationships with Aboriginal people which continued as they always had done.

Paulus Wiljuka of Maryvale wrote the most frequently:

Ingkata tjina nukai [Pastor, my friend] ... Another matter, dear pastor, would you be able to ask Dora why she does not write at all? ... Her mother and father are waiting, too ... perhaps you could wake her up in case she has gone to sleep.

By his late seventies, there was still a range of correspondence: Charles Duguid (ten years his senior) working on a second book, asked about his address at John Flynn's burial in 1952. Albrecht was unable to lay his hands on it, but could give Duguid the gist of what he said, as he well remembered his mixed feelings at the time. It had been no easy matter to give a fair and honest statement on Flynn's life and work. At a personal level, he had always been deeply appreciative of the services of the Australian Inland Mission. At the same time, Flynn himself had little time for Aborigines. He had often told Albrecht that their outlook in life was hopeless, and Duguid had clashed with Flynn on the same issue. Yet to Albrecht, Flynn clearly had been 'a tool in God's hands'. Flynn may have intended the aerial medical service in the first place for the European settlers, yet God had had his own plans for the Aborigines—in fact, many more Aborigines than Europeans had benefited from the service. Albrecht was also acutely aware of the constraints within which the man had been forced to work. Flynn's hostel and medical service would never have gained acceptance among Europeans had he admitted Aboriginal patients in the early days. 'Had he tried, at that time, to combine the two he would probably have lost both.' He also felt that Flynn's disparaging view of Aborigines came from his ignorance of the Aboriginal context and values.

There were also queries about Albert Namatjira and, for Albrecht, they raised wider issues. So much had been said and written about the conflict between his tribal law and the law of white Australian society. Albrecht thought the case had been overstated. That there was a conflict was undeniable, but he also felt strongly that the way of life Namatjira had eventually developed went strongly against his Christian conscience. This, he wrote, would have been as important to him as the tribal constraints:

> It has been said that he died of a broken heart, after he had been sentenced to a term in gaol . . . What irked him was that journalists in Alice Springs had told him times and again; they will never touch you, leave alone putting you in; you are far too big a man for them . . . However, apart from his hurt feelings, I do not think that this brush with the white man's law meant much to him at all. At the same time, the many incidents when he had acted against his conscience and offended against the law of God, he more and more felt as a tremendous burden on his mind. Repeatedly he stated: only the Lord Jesus can help me now.
>
> There is a trend in our days to blame the white man, the Government, for everything detrimental among our Aborigines. I, too, know something of this burden of guilt resting on our white society,

concerning the Aborigines. However, I am sure that the Aborigines must accept their share of the blame, too. The Aborigines, if not adversely influenced, readily accept this. Like in Albert's case, the final decision rests with them. This is a point which is mostly overlooked in our days when speaking and writing about Aborigines.

The question of a book about his own life was frequently put to him. To Albrecht, it was a project fraught with difficulty. 'If I wrote a true book', he often said, 'I would spend the rest of my life in court on libel charges. And if it wasn't an honest book, what would be the use of it?' Uppermost in his mind seemed to be the countless incidents, especially in earlier days, of the widespread indifference and heartlessness towards Aboriginal people, often by government officials. To bring it all out would also create difficulties for those still in the work. As Art Latz had commented in a note, 'Read your Luth. *Almanac* last night, sure some write up, and very good, but thought to myself what you didn't write too'. The question of a book continued to be broached, but the necessary energy never seemed to be there.

More of his mail these days seemed to be in German, as if the decline in the mass of contacts generated from his years in Central Australia was yielding space to an earlier part of his life. He was to receive singular acknowledgment from his country of ancestry. In a ceremony at Luther Seminary in Adelaide in September 1983, he was presented with the *Bundes Verdienst Kreuz (erster Klasse)*—a Special Order of Merit (first class)—a rarely bestowed award from the West German government for humanitarian work by Germans in any part of the world. It was a fitting tribute to a man who, while he had thoroughly committed his life to Australia, had always understood and valued his European roots. That part of him came out in a hundred ways: politely refusing the suggestion from a military officer in Alice Springs during the war that he change his name; his enthusiasm for foods like sauerkraut or rollmops; building the little smokehouse at Hermannsburg.

In 1971, two more Aboriginal men were ordained in Central Australia. Colin Malbanka had been especially close to their household in the early days at Hermannsburg. Paulus Wiljuka had been influenced firstly by Gamaliel at Henbury, then spent a year learning with Albrecht in Alice Springs. In the old cemetery, Manasse had erected a tombstone for Moses, with a plaque commemorating the man who had been an outstanding teacher, leader, evangelist, storyteller and historian to his people. Albrecht heard it all with deep thankfulness. There were so many problems with drink at

Hermannsburg. Yet there was still a vital contact with the people, and a spiritual life still evident. He felt deeply that the pathway by which the Aboriginal men were finding their way into the ministry was the right one. Writing to John Pfitzner, the current missionary at Hermannsburg:

> So many attempts, and very honest attempts, have been made to get ministers from among the Aborigines by training them in accordance with the white youngsters—primary school, college, seminary. But this has failed every time it was started. On the other hand, men who have a thorough understanding of the way of salvation as we find it in the New Testament and who have proved themselves, like Colin and Paulus, in the field, can and will accept responsibility for this work . . . In our home we have not been so well, my wife . . . has to take it very, very quietly . . . Still, we have no complaints, the Lord has been so good to us for so many years.

All his life, he had practised gratitude.

In Australia generally, the climate of public opinion surrounding Aboriginal issues was evolving rapidly. In 1967, Australians voted to give the Commonwealth government power to legislate on behalf of Aborigines in all Australian states and, under the new Labor government in 1972, Aboriginal land rights were becoming an important issue. Early in the year, the Australian Council of Churches made a submission on the matter and Albrecht was asked for comment. Characteristically, he was cautious, making practical suggestions rather than endorsing wide-ranging principles. But he was unequivocal about the need for land for Aborigines living on or near cattle stations:

> These people are deserving of special consideration. In most cases, their fathers and grandfathers have already worked at the place and have essentially helped to build it up. Yet, even on a large cattle station, there is not an inch of ground they may call their own . . . In view of the tremendous benefit the Aborigines would derive from such a step, and not only the present generation, I would regard this aspect of Land Rights of far greater importance even than anything else . . .

Hermannsburg in the early 1970s was going through a difficult period. An old order was breaking up under the various impacts of increased drinking, greater financial independence through basic wage payments and social services, and a changing ethos in which Aborigines, government and public alike looked for Aboriginal participation in the management of missions and settlements. An Aboriginal council was elected at Hermannsburg, but the breakdown in order only grew worse. Albrecht, at Linden Park, felt out of touch. What news he did hear confused and depressed him.

Pas' Albrecht was the pastor here. Teach all the people. It was a good life, that time. Everybody was here, Pas' Albrecht was more stronger, talk to people. Today, can't see. People go anyways here today in Hermannsburg. Drunken people singing out, fighting, they never do this way, before. He was strong for rules. Oh yes, tough to make people understand properly. Keep away from bad things, drinking, fighting. He and Pastor Gross.

Consulted about the increasing disorder in the Aboriginal community at Hermannsburg, a University of Queensland anthropologist advised the mission staff to try to locate the traditional authority structures in the community, most likely via the kinship systems. Staff members spent much time and effort—with immense support from the Aboriginal community—drawing up family genealogies and establishing kinship networks. They felt they were coming to a new understanding of how the community worked, its hierarchies of authority and responsibilities, its communication systems. 'Understanding the culture' became a crucial focus in a situation which seemed to be slipping completely out of control, though there were also mission workers who felt the senior staff were going to the other extreme, and applying cultural criteria more rigidly than the Aborigines.

We bin trying to tell these things to you for years. But we just worked out that white people must be stupid because they couldn't understand it.

Albrecht was not unsympathetic to these efforts, though he probably felt they were receiving undue time and attention. There were other aspects which he viewed with increasing perturbation. Early in 1974, two Aboriginal families moved away from the main Hermannsburg community to more isolated parts of the mission lease, partly because of the prevalent drinking and fighting. By the middle of 1976, seventeen outstations had been established beyond the precincts of the Hermannsburg township.

Main reason I left was drink. It started in Hermannsburg from the artists, and from the halfcastes who were free citizens. Afterwards, everybody become citizen. Drink still a really big problem. Hermannsburg is supposed to be dry, people still bring grog in. Not in my place.

I don't know about other outstations. Today, I only know myself and my family. Children today in Hermannsburg, I don't know them, they stranger to me . . . It's changed a lot.

Albrecht had long felt the need for some dispersion of the large population in the town itself. His pastoralists scheme in the 1940s had aimed partly at this, and his writings in the 1950s had often commented on the desirability of smaller communities. But he felt that decentralization had to be balanced with encouraging the unity and mutual support inherent in his notion of a Christian community. Hermannsburg seemed to be undergoing a progressive splintering. He also questioned the implications for education. Mission teachers were travelling out to teach children several days a week at the outstations, and the formerly wide curriculum of a decade before had shrunk to English and mathematics. Western-style pottery introduced by a former craft teacher was now deemed culturally inappropriate. Albrecht, with his fundamental belief in education as an equipping and training for life within a wider Australian society, felt there were sadly regressive aspects.

The fact that his son, Paul, was now field superintendent only exacerbated his unease. For his part, Paul made many attempts to explain the new climate, the pressures, the reasons behind mission policies. His father would appear to see the point. Later, the old arguments would emerge all over again. At heart, Paul felt his father had never really retired, never truly relinquished the work and his own understanding of it.

 Yes, he had a strong feeling about the congregation. He was thinkin', what's going to happen with my congregation.

Doubtless it was virtually impossible for Albrecht—given his age and the theological, pietistic emphasis of his original missionary orientation—to alter his basic perception of 'mission work' and everything it implied. With almost nothing in the way of a sociological approach to culture provided in his early training, he would have lacked the conceptual tools by which he might have been able to approach Aboriginal culture in a mode that was more open, less theologically committed, indeed to be also more aware of the 'cultural factors' in his own outlook and Christian understanding.

His conflict in the matter came to a head in July 1976 with a series of articles in *The Lutheran* on recent developments at Hermannsburg. Aboriginal ceremonies had increased and were being performed openly and discussed with senior staff and, on invitation, staff were attending them. Such ceremonies, it was said, had never really ceased but had been forced underground by the disapproval of former mission policy. Acceptance of the ceremonies was opening up a new and more open communication with the people, an opportunity to work together at what it meant to be both Aboriginal and Christian. According to Paul, who had spent a year in India in 1969–70 studying sociology and social change:

> Sociologically, it indicates that people are taking strong initiatives to try and correct the imbalances and social malfunctionings of their social system. A factor we are now beginning to realise is that the training and teaching of the young, for example, can take place only within the traditional framework. If the framework is interfered with, so is the teaching process. This applies to most other educative and social control functions in Aboriginal society. In the past, by taking a negative attitude to certain Aboriginal ceremonies, we did not simply interfere with the ceremonies, but with the vital social processes of the people; and then we wondered why, for example, the people were not bringing up their children properly.

Albrecht, now eighty-two, was appalled. He felt the new emergence of ceremonies was a symptom of the general decline in Christian life in the community which he felt had begun in the years when Albert Namatjira was spending vast sums of money freely among the young Aborigines. He had gradually accepted a considerable amount of traditional culture and, in fact some of what Paul had written was little different in principle to what his father had written to Con Dracopoulos fifteen years before. But for Albrecht, the ceremonies were symbolic of the very heart of former Aboriginal religious life. That Christian staff should be attending them, and thereby in his view affirming their meaning, struck at the very centre of his whole concept of mission work and his own life's task. Since it also constituted, in his eyes, a complete reversal in the working policy of the mission, he felt he would have to make a public statement.

New mission policy stressed the need to give 'positive recognition to the culture'. In his statement Albrecht said that the mission had always respected the language and the marriage laws, and maintained tribal organization as far as possible. But where 'culture' approached explicit religious belief, he was simply unable to see it apart from superstitions and untruths which had to be abandoned. This clear stand against former religious beliefs had, he said, been maintained equally strongly by an earlier generation of Aboriginal

Christians. His various attempts to reintroduce the non-religious or 'play-about' corroborees had failed, since the older men told him that there was little if anything that was not connected to their old beliefs. He recalled the incident in 1928 when the community had reprimanded him for allowing the University of Adelaide party to record corroboree music at the station; and the incident at Maryvale where the people had burned ceremonial objects—on that occasion there had not even been a European man present.

Albrecht, he say Aboriginal religion wrong. But that was right. Everything wouldn't have come, wouldn't have happened if he wouldn't have said that. The [old] religion would have been still strong. [It was good that he took a hard line, so that people had to choose, sort out what was important.] People now understand, they realise what's been happening in the past, we still believe those, still today. I believe too, some of my religions. But I see there's no life in it . . . because God is stronger than everything . . .

It's still separated today, God's way and our way, our culture. That still on [Aboriginal culture]. People still using it . . . but we can't bring it into God's way, we can't join it.

Albrecht's personal experience of traditional Aboriginal culture dating back fifty years had included things that were simply impossible to take into the life of a Christian congregation. He recalled a time in the 1940s when he had arrived in a large camp in the Haasts Bluff area. The people had been unduly subdued, and he discovered that an old man had driven his spear through his wife's womb, apparently because she had been nagging him over a young girl he had taken as an additional wife. She had died on the spot. As an old man, it was an act that he was entitled to. Yet Albrecht, as a Christian, felt he had to say it was murder, and he also felt that the people had expected him to take that stand. If their culture was their final authority, how far was it to be taken?

Old people's laws have gone into the background, because a lot of it too hard. [Christian teaching did change things. Over a period of time people changed their lives including not having more than one wife, and not murdering people.] Those things gone now. But if any fighting, they still use the same [kinship] system to settle own fight. Every family had own representative, one in each family to control the family. Still like that today.

Much of Albrecht's formative experience had derived from a earlier era. Both his age and his lack of contact in later years would have made it difficult to appreciate the gradual evolution of Aboriginal traditions and belief. And theologically, he was conservative even in the Christian context. He saw within modern Christianity itself, and especially in some denominations, trends he thought were giving away the essential foundations of the faith—decreasing emphasis on the centrality of the Bible, and symbolic rather than literal interpretations of cardinal events like the Virgin birth and Christ's resurrection. 'All this watered down religion is worth nothing', he often said. 'When it comes to the test, the real crunch, the whole thing collapses. It's absolutely no use at all.' In many aspects of his life, Albrecht had showed great capacity for risk and change. What was not open to change was his understanding of Christian truth. For him God's truth was clear. The only thing in question was one's response. He wrote:

> I readily admit that in a developing community as at Hermannsburg changes from time to time are necessary and are wholesome. However, if it is a matter of changing the attitude towards the eternal word of God, then it is only one step towards removing the very ground on which we stand.

This concern was also rooted in the tradition of his own church. Albrecht was deeply Lutheran in his belief in the importance of right doctrine—words were crucially important in the transmitting of truth, even if religious experience might finally transcend the words. It was hardly surprising that he could not interpret an entirely different tradition—the Aboriginal myths and stories—as anything else but 'untruths' beside the Christian revelation.

Albrecht thought if God's word was true, nothing else is true. But we think both are true. Christian Aboriginals like Moses, Martin, they thought Aboriginal part important too. Some things in Aboriginal culture they thought were not true, same like teaching in the Old Testament. A lot of things was dropped, like fighting all the time, that's not law, that's bin dropped. Some good things bring along from old time, from right back there, can keep them, like story, teach your kids. And add Bible stories, bring 'em in, add the old stories to the Bible. Together.

Yes, still tell children some of the old stories. Tell them story, but put it in the light, from darkness to light. That changes the story a little bit. Now, we bin see with the light, you understand more, can see further.

Albrecht sent a copy of his statement to the mission board and to *The Lutheran*. Not that he expected it to influence the board or present policies at Hermannsburg—he felt he was regarded as being thoroughly out of step with current thinking. But his longing for the simple human contact with Aboriginal people that had been such a fundamental part of his life sounded in a letter to evangelist Obed Raggatt at Papunya. 'I thank you for your love which you show again and again ... I am now a wobbly old man. Many who in the past were close to me, now stand far away. But not you ... At times I have a great homesickness to see you and others again, but I don't know if this will be possible or not.'

Minna had recently written an article on experiences in her life of answered prayer. Simply and economically written, the four or five pages which Albrecht typed up and duplicated for distribution to a few close friends revealed a person of great inner strength and steadfastness. Seeking God and His will had been one of the shaping forces of her life. Albrecht's awareness of her essential strength, even through the years of illness, had only increased in the years of their retirement. 'She was a rock', he often said, 'she was far stronger than I'. The theme of sacrifice was one he often pondered. 'You see, without some sacrifice, you can't do anything in this world. That's what I shall never forget with my wife. She was prepared to go through thick and thin.'

He was starting to write again himself. A book was being prepared for the centenary of Hermannsburg's founding the following year, and he had been asked to write a section on his period at the mission. It was a large task, and he prayed for strength and wisdom to complete it.

LEAVE-TAKINGS

1977~1984

Came down to Adelaide just the right time. Never forget this one, always talk about this one. We want to see them two old people, we might see last time, Mrs Latz too.

The first months of 1977 saw a flare-up of the running controversy surrounding Professor Ted Strehlow and the custodianship of his extensive collection of Aboriginal recordings and artefacts. There were assertions that he had no right to them, that artefacts had been given to him only on loan, that they should be returned to Central Australia. Court action was threatened. Albrecht could only believe that 'impudent white men' were behind the controversy, and said so in a letter to the Adelaide *News* in May. Tribes were being named as claimants, he said, that he had never heard of in thirty-five years of living and working among Aborigines in the Centre. Strehlow, he said, had had the fullest confidence of the men who brought *tjurungas* to him. They had done so because they thought he would be their best guardian—this excluded any thought of a loan. The assertion that the tribe wanted them back he dismissed as sheer nonsense: *tjurungas* were always owned by individuals, not by a tribe. He stated in strong terms that the charges made were completely out of character with Strehlow's record in his work and dealings with Aborigines. Assertions that Strehlow paid for artefacts with 'bully beef and tea' did not tally with his own experience in the 1950s when Strehlow had annually sent him a cheque of £100 to distribute to old Aboriginal friends and associates. Despite summer heat, dust and flies, Strehlow had chosen to live for years in tents at Jay Creek in order to work more effectively with the people, and he had been instrumental in the establishing of the Haasts Bluff-Papunya reserve. He warned:

> If the *tjurungas* would be taken from the professor and handed back to the people who allegedly demand their return, they would not know their meaning, as this was always confined to their owners who have died long ago. This means these *tjurungas* would become dead relics which would be quickly forgotten, or left rotting in some cave in the Centre, instead of being preserved for posterity. To interrupt what the professor is doing at the present time in evaluating these objects is criminal folly because it breaks up a development which is entirely unique in this country. There is no other man in Australia who grew up with the Aborigines as Strehlow did, who speaks their language and shares his innermost feelings with them.

Albrecht disclaimed any personal interest in the matter. He was seeing little of Ted Strehlow, and had been enormously saddened by the break-up of his first marriage. But his respect for the man's work and a general sense of his integrity was undiminished, and he could not be indifferent to what he saw as contemptible and untruthful attacks on his character and reputation.

But in his emphasis that *tjurungas* were always owned by individuals, not by a tribe, Albrecht perhaps undervalued the extent to which the gift and the guardianship of *tjurungas* included the notion that they would eventually be passed on. The purpose of guardianship had always been the preserving of the tradition, and perhaps some of these processes were re-emerging in Central Australia more than he realized. Yet in his sense of the irrevocable decline of traditional Aboriginal culture, he was not alone. The notion of himself as a 'last custodian' pervaded much of Strehlow's thinking. Both men had been significantly shaped by their experiences in the 1930s and earlier, an era which had seen enormous destruction of Aboriginal life and tribal organization, and a time in which Aboriginal elders themselves could hardly have known if or how their traditions could be preserved.

Much of Albrecht's time in the first six months of 1977 was taken up with writing his section of the Hermannsburg history, the years between 1926 and 1962. The fifty pages was Albrecht's writing at its best, thoughtful in its tracing of developments yet at the same time totally personal, filled with simple yet memorable descriptions: a Pintubi woman, for instance, grinding seeds to feed her children at Ilbilla, or the unforgettable words of men like Moses as they spoke at gravesides in the drought:

> Since my knowledge of the language was still inadequate, one of the Aboriginal elders usually preached a sermon at the graveside. Some such occasions were highlights of our congregational life, and I repeatedly felt the desire that, at the end of my days, one such Aboriginal preacher might testify at my graveside in like manner and eloquence.

The centenary itself was a moving experience for him. Superintendent Garry Stoll drove him around the station—so familiar, yet with new developments such as the power house and the huge water storage tanks. It was the water supply which most staggered him. The scarcity of water had always been such an issue, and they had prayed for it so often and earnestly. Now there were bores yielding 1000 and 1500 gallons per hour, and not even used. And this in areas where they had been told that boring would not yield water. He could not have imagined it in his wildest dreams. But there was also the achingly familiar. Driving out to Kaporilja, the hills whose very contours were etched into the mind, Mount Hermannsburg and its purple shadows across the Finke 'which witnessed some of the deepest experiences ... when the children were so desperately ill and we had no way of contacting help. Mum and I looked up to those hills in prayer, and the Lord was not far. To us, that is holy ground.'

The Sunday of the centenary itself, 12 June, was a big day and very tiring. About two thousand people were present. Hymns were sung in Aranda and English; Scripture lessons read in English, Aranda and Pitjantjatjara. Pastor Conrad Raberaba preached the morning sermon in the new Bethlehem church. In the afternoon, the large assembly gathered in front of the old church for the unveiling of a memorial stone to commemorate the centenary. Paul conducted the service, and with him at the memorial stone were senior evangelist Obed Raggatt, and Clara Inkamala, the oldest member of the Hermannsburg community.

Albrecht preached the sermon. It was as much as he could manage, though Garry had taken him in a wheelchair as near to the front as possible. It was fifteen years since he had left the Centre, and twenty-six since his last service in the little church behind him. He felt, as he spoke, that he was breaking a long silence. With all his heart, he encouraged them to move on in the confidence that God had made them his own—to affirm their faith, establish themselves in the wider community, to seek guidance and clarity in their tribal associations. 'May these words coming from one who may have been forgotten with the passing of many years, find an echo in your hearts. God bless you all, Amen.'

It was also a day of greetings and reunions. From the time he had arrived, there had been a stream of the older people coming up to shake his hand. Sometimes the men waited, and the women came up first to hug him. He took away an impression that the Christian women were the real backbone of church life. It was a rich time. Yet unanswered questions remained in his mind, variations on themes that he had been wrestling with for fifty years. The underlying philosophy of mission staff at present seemed to be to wait for initiatives from the Aborigines, then to be ready to help them. But would the people ever take that step? He could see that the situation which had frequently prevailed in his own time— where Aborigines simply worked as a gesture of response or personal loyalty to Europeans—was undesirable. But was there a middle path?

It seemed to him that in areas such as employment 'the Aborigines have moved more and more to the periphery'. On this visit to Hermannsburg, one of the European mission staff had driven him in and out to town. Yet, he reflected, Eli Rubuntja had been his driver for years. And despite his years of effort to employ Aboriginal men in the mission-run stores at Haasts Bluff and the Jay, he had not noticed any Aboriginal assistants working in the Hermannsburg store. He still felt strongly that there was no substitute for the personal work with individuals—challenging them to take up responsibilities, swallowing the disappointments, trying again, and trusting that the efforts would eventually bear fruit. Writing to John Pfitzner, he drew not only on his own experience but on that of others who had pioneered Lutheran mission effort in Australia:

> What Strehlow achieved was largely done through his personal, individual contact, step by step. It was the same in Hope Vale, with old Missionary Schwarz. There would not be an Alec Cameron at the place, who saved the congregation at Woorabinda, if Schwarz had not had a very personal and individual contact with him over the years.

Meeting Manasse had been one of the sadder moments. He had abandoned the house built for him in Hermannsburg after his wife and a son died, and was now living at the Five Mile. He looked dirty and dejected, and Albrecht had the feeling his mind was going. Perhaps seeing his longtime superintendent stirred some of the old reflexes in Manasse. He told Albrecht he had tried to get the tannery going again, but had been unable to get on with his sons, but he would like to start a tannery at the Jay, and at Finns Gap . . . Albrecht felt very sad as he said goodbye to him. He had been such a capable and faithful worker, but had lost his bearings in the new ethos.

It was hard for Albrecht to comprehend that some projects, like the tannery into which he had put so much effort, had lapsed, even though he knew that very different economic factors were now operating for tanning generally in Australia. Similarly with the fancywork that had been an important activity in his time. Since the women had to be paid full wages for it now, it simply did not pay. Yet he still believed that such work was valuable for the individuals concerned and a way to help them achieve a measure of economic independence. The present situation, where the government footed the bill for capital developments like tanks and boring as well as most of the salaries, left him uneasy. At the same time, he complimented Paul and Garry on the good relationship with government that had been achieved.

Life in the household in Burnell Street grew steadily smaller in its scope. Speaking engagements became a thing of the past as physical limitations increased. For the first time in their lives, there was no real garden apart from fruit trees. But their companionship only deepened as their world grew smaller. Visitors from the north who were used to Albrecht being the main talker noticed that he sat back to let Minna recount a recent healing experience after a stroke. It was the most animated they had seen her for a long time.

Even his correspondence was thinning out, and his energy for other efforts was failing. When the editors of the journal *Aboriginal History* wrote from the Australian National University seeking any reminiscence or documentary record of Hermannsburg's history, he reluctantly declined. It had been rare that he had ever turned away such a request. Even in 1977, despite caring for Minna after a third stroke, he had read and commented on an extensive paper on Papunya, as requested by a study team within the Department of Aboriginal Affairs. But he no longer had the capacity. Another part of his life came to a close when Ted Strehlow died suddenly in October 1978. Albrecht had seen him only a few weeks before, apparently well. 'Especially we in the Finke River Mission must ever remain grateful for what he has done for us and the Aborigine people', he wrote to a friend, 'We have never had one like him, and it is doubtful whether we shall ever have one his like again'.

Albrecht was delighted in late 1980 to receive a letter from John Brackenreg of the Legend Press in Sydney about the possible establishment of a scholarship in memory of Albert Namatjira. Characteristically, he tried to think of ways in which European education could be adapted to suit Aboriginal patterns. He thought it essential that education be centred on their local communities:

> I would suggest to widen your scope, so that men of a mature age would be eligible, and not only artists, rather men with ability and outstanding gifts for leadership ... In Aborigine society the individual has to be helped through the community. That has been overlooked with Albert Namatjira, with tragic results.
>
> Another way of assisting the artists and furthering their ability and bringing some needed moral support to them, would be to commission some suitable white artist to go up, live with them like Rex Battarbee and teach them in their surroundings, and the scholarship to meet the costs. In my view, this would be the most promising step in helping them effectively, without bringing harm to them. The person chosen for the job would be of paramount importance, would have to be of highest integrity.

Late in November 1980, he had a bad fall. Since neither he nor Minna could walk alone, they were taken first to a hospital and eventually to a nursing home in the Adelaide suburb of Fullarton. Despite his lack of physical capacity, there was some surge of inner energy, the old imperatives asserted themselves briefly. Surely there was a little more he could do:

> To be faced with the end of the road brings up many thoughts we never had before, and there is so much one would like to finish. I am thinking of writing some articles on our Aborigines, but now I don't know whether I will have the time. Our Aborigines and their future are still largely a closed book, and if I could bring even a little more light into this problem ... If possible, I would like to write something for the family. I regret that my busy working days meant that the family was neglected; Minna had to make up for it. If God gives me time I shall try and repay my debt, even if belated.
>
> Finally, there is our dear Church. If I can I shall write something regarding our work in the Mission. It is over 55 years since we came to South Australia, then proceeded to Central Australia.

There was to be time, but not the capacity.

At Fullarton, weeks went by before there was any feeling of belonging. Albrecht reflected to himself that he had never realized that this would be such a difficult stage of life. One had to adapt to a whole new way of living at the same time leaving behind so much that had been important. They were unable to share a room, though they spent the day together. 'It is like committing a part of one's life to death', he wrote to friends almost a year later. Some of the staff observed their closeness, and the way he devoted himself to Minna's every need—getting her a cup of tea, encouraging her to eat.

In October 1981 they were visited by twenty-four Aboriginal women from the Hermannsburg choir on a visit to Adelaide. There was hugging and kisses and laughter and tears all at once as they crowded around the two old people in their wheelchairs, and fast talking in Aranda, everybody trying to say something. Many they had known since childhood. Afterwards, they were still shaken in a joyful kind of way. It had brought back so much. They remembered the beginnings of their friendship, how others had disapproved of their marriage plans, the silly girl who was told she could never have children. An overwhelming sense of the remarkable providence of God welled up, things brought to fulfilment they could not have dreamed of, confirming all over again an understanding Albrecht had lived by all his life. He spoke of it often, almost like a refrain:

> Leave it in God's hands and you can't do better, you can't do more. You may go through deep waters. We have had times at Hermannsburg where we were up against the wall, no doctors, no medicines, the nearest doctor 400 miles away. It brought us down to bedrock, but it was worthwhile.

On June 2 1982, the Finke River Mission surrendered its Hermannsburg lease, and the Commonwealth government passed the land to five Aboriginal land trusts, representing five tribal leaders who in the eyes of the Hermannsburg community were the traditional owners of the land. After that date, neither the land nor the improvements on it belonged to the Finke River Mission. It was the culmination of five years of intensive work by mission staff in co-operation with Aranda leaders and government officials. Under the Northern Territory Land Rights Act of 1976, the sole trustee for the vesting of land to Northern Territory Aborigines was to have been the Central Land Council. But it had become clear that the Hermannsburg community did not want the legal title of the land given to a group of people who traditionally had no relationship with it. Nor did the Land Rights Act itself reflect their ways of owning land. Under Australian law, Hermannsburg was one tract of land. To the Hermannsburg community, it was five separate pieces of land, the title to which was based on Dreaming stories, with five separate land-holding groups of people. After much work, and a special Act of Parliament, the traditional ownership was formally enacted. Albrecht had gleaned what he could of the process. On the whole he felt there were definite advantages in the Aborigines owning their land though, as always, the more crucial question for him was the Gospel itself and its transforming power. Again and again in his last years, he referred with enormous feeling and gratitude to the Aboriginal ministry and the response of Aboriginal congregations, like the recent request for baptism of a whole group at Ammaroo. Amid the collapse of so many of the things he had worked for, it was his deepest consolation.

All the time, when I bin 'coming pastor, I remember all the time what him preach, this way, that way. What Gospel, Old Testament, New Testament, I know all that, remember all the time.

When I was at Undandita, every weekend, Pas' Albrecht come with the truck, bring the Bible, teach the people. When I grew up, then I understand, that's a pastor. When little, I went running cos we want a lolly, next time he come, sit down and talk to us, teach the Bible ... old people tell me, ingkata. *When I grew up, I thinkin', that's Pastor Albrechta, teaching. Then evangelist course, I was evangelist at Areyonga with Pastor Leo Kalleske, and other evangelists, two at Docker River, three hundred people at Docker River, Pitjantjatjara. They gone back to their country, feel safe there now. People talking now, old people, that is where Pas' Albrecht came with the camel. Everybody know that, old people.*

There were hard times too. For Minna, there were periods of acute distress and mental confusion in which she would beg to be taken out of there, or 'let me go and stay with my father'. Sometimes she longed to return to Germany, as though a sense of it as home had never entirely left her. Unlike her husband, she had never become totally at ease in English, and the English she did speak was hesitant and often incorrect.

Albrecht had no instinct to return to Europe. His profoundest bond there had died with his mother in 1922, and the rest of his family had been scattered by two world wars. For him, it was Central Australia and its Aboriginal people that, apart from Minna herself, still lay deepest in his heart. He suffered no acute distress, and could content himself with his lot. But at a deeper level, there recurred the sense of living a useless life. He was almost ninety now, and as he sometimes thought to himself—'on the way out'. His life had been so full—yet now it all felt stale.

Around 12 November 1983, Minna suffered a deterioration in her health. As each day passed, she became weaker and her breathing more and more erratic. Near the end of the week, twenty Hermannsburg women on a trip to Adelaide came to the Fullarton home, and three or four of the older ones were allowed to see Minna. Later that evening, she slipped into unconsciousness and died the following day, 18 November.

Minna's death was a blow that Albrecht had never really expected, and from which he never recovered. It was a measure of his profound dependence on her, so deep as to be almost invisible. 'The light in my life has gone out', he said to Helene. It was evident to everyone that he had no wish to live.

Friends and family did their best, but his health steadily deteriorated as the weeks went by. Yet the physical distress in no way displaced his deep inner bereftness, a darkness deeper than anything he had known. In all the hundreds of deaths he had attended in his long lifetime, nothing, it seemed, had quite prepared him for this. 'But our Heavenly Father knows best', he said sometimes. Now, it was the slenderest of threads. In February, Nahasson Ungkwanaka came down from Central Australia:

> He was in bed when I came, he couldn't see much, I think he must have been very tired, he couldn't talk much, only few words he said to me, I'm happy to see you, he said, and I said few words to him.
> Well, what I said, I'm happy to see you, God has kept you for long time, gave you long life, you are in very old age, and God has blessed you. And I said thank you, because of all Aborigines, because of what he had done, only few words I said. Because I could know in his face, he didn't look far, just saw half way.

He died early on Friday evening, 16 March. His funeral service was conducted in St Stephen's Lutheran church in Wakefield Street in the city. Afterwards the cortege drove east out of the city to the Lutheran section of the Centennial Park cemetery. Three Aboriginal pastors from Central Australia helped to carry his coffin: Conrad Raberaba, Eli Rubuntja and Traugott Malbanka. Before the coffin was lowered into the grave, Conrad stepped forward to speak. His mother had been one of the Aborigines who had accompanied Carl Strehlow on his last journey. But for him and another generation of Aboriginal people, that bonding had been with Albrecht. He had shed the long white surplice he had worn as

he walked in the long procession of pastors into St Stephen's church
an hour or so before. Now he stood, a 67-year-old Aboriginal man
in long trousers and a brown cardigan, and spoke in Aranda to the
Albrecht family.

> '*Kaiyaka nama errilkngirrperra etnathoa* . . . Happy are those who . . .
> die in the service of the Lord. Yes, indeed, answers the Spirit. They
> will enjoy rest because the fruits of their service go with them.'
> That's the word I have chosen.

It was characteristically Aboriginal that he spoke not of general
facts and events about the European pastor's life, but out of his own
relationship with Albrecht:

> *Ingkata Albrecht Ntariurna pitjika* . . . Pastor Albrecht came to
> Hermannsburg when I was a small boy. At Hermannsburg, when he
> came, there was a very bad drought, seven year drought. I was a boy
> and willing to learn, and Pastor Albrecht taught me all the word of
> life. As I was learning, I became convinced I wanted to become an
> evangelist and follow in his steps. He worked with me, teaching me.
> He confirmed me. I joined the class for evangelists. Later on I went
> out with Pastor Albrecht when he was travelling with the camels.
> I went happily.
>
> I worked with him in this way when Papunya was yet to come,
> Haasts Bluff was yet to come, Areyonga was yet to come, and all the
> other outstations had not even been thought of. He continued to
> work. As I am preaching here I recall how Pastor Albrecht, our
> father, taught and strengthened me over the years and today I am
> standing here, in his place as it were . . .

Sometimes the noise of passing traffic on the highway muffled the
Aboriginal words. Sometimes the wind took them away, blowing
down the long slope of the cemetery to the distant ocean. Almost
all of the hundred or so people standing at the graveside service
were European, but stood silently as the Aboriginal pastor continued intently and deliberately:

> He came to Hermannsburg without any children. There were just
> the two of them, your father and mother. All you children here
> today were born at Ntaria later. You are part of Ntaria . . . Greetings
> were sent today from the Hermannsburg people. Today they are
> remembering how he, the father of us all, taught us over the years.
> He fed us with God's Word and Sacrament . . . All of us at Ntaria are
> his offspring . . .
>
> I wanted to speak in Aranda to you his children who were born at
> Hermannsburg and grew up as Aranda. Pastor Albrecht became an
> Aranda at Hermannsburg . . .

He ceased, and raised his arm high to make the sign of the cross. '*Retnjala Altjira Kataka, Aliraka, Enka Alkngaltaraka tuta*' (In the name of the Father and of the Son and of the Holy Spirit).

Ingkata inurra, *(lame pastor) . . . people still calling him that today. Only that name he had, not just pastor. That name bin given from here, from Hermannsburg . . . Because he was at Henbury, Tempe Downs, Middleton Ponds, all those places. After, when word bin spread about him to other countries, then they knew, then they were expecting him . . .*

Still today, no matter if he was passed away. Because by that name, they make it more clear, people can understand, we know who that old man was. Because he was really kind to them. And because of God's message, he brought God's message, he took it every places, and everybody became Christian through by him, only through by him, that's the main one. Still today, people never forget. In every place, in every outstation, every cattle station, on settlements, people . . . remember his journey, his trip. People still remember his kindness, and he helped a lot of people while they were sick, with the pray, and with little bit medicine, and with God's message. People talking about ingkata inurra, *because they said, old Albrechta went to every places, he had to visit them, he had to put all his life into them, never mind they were running away, still he had to chase them, still he had to brought them back, because he really loved them.*

Notes

All writings are by F. W. Albrecht unless stated otherwise.

ABBREVIATIONS

F.R.M.   Finke River Mission
L.A.   *Lutheran Almanac—Yearbook of the United Evangelical Lutheran Church in Australia*
L.H.   *Lutheran Herald*

PAGE

xvii. 'If he had something to say'. Pastor Nahasson Ungkwanaka, 1986.

 1. 'Pastor Albrecht, he come from somewhere else'. Pastor Eli Rubuntja, 1986.

 1. 'Yet, if it were not for that'. Interviews with author, 1983.

1–8. Details of early life drawn from 'From the Pinnacle of Eighty Years', *The Lutheran*, 27 January 1975; 'Road to Hermannsburg', *L.H.*, 5 January 1976; interviews by David Shrowder and author; information from the Albrecht family.

8–14. Early Lutheran mission effort in Australia. Leske, *Hermannsburg*; Schmiecken, The Hermannsburg Mission Society in Australia; Jones and Sutton, *Art and Land*.

 9. 'The first time my grandfather saw the missionaries'. Joylene Abbott, 1986.

11–12. This account of the first decades of European–Aboriginal contact in Central Australia, including the interaction between the Western Aranda-speaking people and the Lutheran mission, is drawn largely from Hartwig, Progress of White Settlement; Powell, *Far Country*, and Leske, *Hermannsburg*. Alan Powell in *Far Country* refers to the Hermannsburg mission as 'an oasis of peace amid the bitter war between pastoralists and blacks', p. 136.

 13. Baldwin Spencer's work. With F. J. Gillen, Spencer published *The Native Tribes of Central Australia* (1899), *The Northern Tribes of Central Australia* (1904) and *Across Australia* (1912).

 14. 'Yes, I remember Pas' Strehlow'. Pastor Conrad Raberaba, 1984.

 14. 'especially as we have had the Word of God'. Leske, *Hermannsburg*, p. 36.

 15. 'I remember the day that Pastor Albrecht arrived'. Edwin Pareroultja, 1984.

 16. Spencer visited Hermannsburg with the Horn Expedition in 1894 after the first missionaries had left, and in 1910 when the Strehlows were on leave in Europe, and in 1923 after Strehlow's death.

 16. Sexton's report. Revd J. H. Sexton, Report to the Home and Territories Department on the Hermannsburg Mission Station, 1925.

 16. 'If we turn to the problem of financing'; 'Then we feel compelled'. Revd J. J. Stolz to Hon. G. F. Pearce, 11 March 1926.

17–21. Arrival at Hermannsburg. 'First report of our Missionary Albrecht', *L.H.*, 7 June 1926; Leske, *Hermannsburg*, p. 43; interview with David Shrowder.

 22. Moses' life. 'Old Blind Moses', *L.H.*, 24 July 1954; H. Heinrich, 'Mose, a Biographical Sketch', *L.H.*, 16 February 1926; interview with author.

 24. Albrecht's early encounters with Revd John Flynn. 'Flynn of the Inland', *L.H.*, 24 November 1951; Leske, *Hermannsburg*; an undated, untitled recollection of

289

Flynn (typescript); letter to Dr Charles Duguid, 26 March 1971; interview with David Shrowder.

26. 'We have not as yet made much progress'. The Hermannsburg Congregation—a Review, 1926–56 (duplicated paper).

26. Albrecht's sense of Carl Strehlow's era as a 'patriarchy'. *Albert Namatjira: Native Artist* (printed pamphlet), Aborigines' Friends' Association, *c.* 1948; letter to Revd Kevin Kotzur, 4 February 1963.

27. 'dip into our own pockets'. Report of the Sixth Session of the S.A. District Synod of the U.E.L.C.A., 1926.

27. 'letting this work of the Lord perish by sheer indifference'. Report of the Seventh Session of the S.A. District Synod of the U.E.L.C.A., 1927.

28. 'No [government] rations that time'. Edwin Pareroultja, 1984.

28. Cash payments. Leske, *Hermannsburg*, p. 43.

29. Baldwin Spencer's comments on education at Hermannsburg. Spencer, Report on Hermannsburg Mission Station, 1923 (duplicated paper).

29. Cawood's visit. Leske, *Hermannsburg*, p. 48; letter to M. Hartwig, 18 April 1960.

30. 'My mother came from the country south-west of Mount Olga'. Pastor Nahasson Ungkwanaka, 1984.

30. 'Yesterday we dug the ninth grave'. To Riedel, 24 February 1928.

32. 'dreaming and doing sweet nothing'. To Riedel, 15 May 1928.

32. Moses' Christian teaching. 'Mission News', *L.H.*, 10 September 1928.

33. 'I used to go mustering cattle'. William Ungkwanaka, 1984.

33–4. Distribution of blankets. Rowley, *The Destruction of Aboriginal Society*, p. 233. Rowley refers to 1928 as 'the nadir in Commonwealth control of the Territory', not only in relation to Aborigines, but in the ineffectiveness of the administration. See also, Departmental communication about blankets for missions in Central Australia.

33. Letter of Secretary, Home and Territories Department, to Parsons, 25 February 1928; Rowley's discussion of J. Bleakley's 1929 report: '[Bleakley] pointed to the incredible situation in Central Australia, "where no medical help whatever is available": he recommended more blankets and relief' (p. 268).

34. 'Bob Buck from Middleton Ponds station'. To Riedel, 19 April 1928.

34. 'I wonder if the author'. Pray and Work, Pray and Tell the Truth (duplicated articles), 1928.

35. Albrecht's discouragement. To Riedel, 23 March 1928.

35. Issuing guns to Aborigines. To Riedel, 11 April 1929.

36. 'Yes, big mob come in during the drought'. Edwin Pareroultja, 1984.

36–8. This account of the Coniston massacre is drawn from Cribben, *The Killing Times*, and from Albrecht's written answers to questions from Mervyn Hartwig about the events and their context, 18 April 1960. In this letter Albrecht states that according to Aboriginal thinking and values, 'this killing [that of Brookes] was completely justifiable'.

36–7. 'What use is a wounded black feller'. Cribben, *The Killing Times*, p. 114.

37. '. . . From Yimampi [Coniston station]'. Excerpts from an Aboriginal account of the Coniston massacre were taken from Japangardi, *Yurrkuru-kurlu* (Coniston Story).

37. '. . . ten or twelve men had been shot'. Information from Aboriginal respondents to Garry Stoll; information from Joylene Abbott.

38. 'spectacular injustice' and events in Arnhem Land in the early 1930s. Rowley, *The Destruction of Aboriginal Society*, pp. 288–305.

39. 'He was up late at night'. Pastor Conrad Raberaba, 1984.

41. Journey north. 'Mission News', *L.H.*, 13 May 1929.
41. 'We will have to become accustomed'. Letter to mission friends (duplicated), 4 April 1929.
41–2. Aboriginal dependence on mission food. 'Mission News', *L.H.*, 27 May 1929.
42. 'First time to Hermannsburg'. Darby Jampijimba, 1984.
42. 'I've come to the stage'. To Riedel, 18 April 1929.
43. Burials in the drought years. Leske, *Hermannsburg*, pp. 46–7; interview with David Shrowder; information from Helene Burns.
43. 'But I thank God'. Moses quoted in duplicated letter to mission friends, 1 August 1929.
43. 'To be able to give thanks'. *L.H.*, 14 October 1929.
43. 'The Christians all die', and Mortana's opinions. Ibid.
43. The belief that the mission had been 'sung'. Jampijimba thought that the illness and deaths had been caused by someone casting an evil spell on the mission. Information to author from Jampijimba.
44. Howley's prescriptions. To Riedel, 21 April 1929.
44–5. Problems of nursing and winter cold. To mission friends, 1 August 1929; *L.H.*, 14 October 1929.
45. 'Consideration has been given'. Secretary, Department of Home Affairs to Riedel, 15 August 1929.
46. 'In the circumstances'. Secretary, Department of Home Affairs to Riedel, 19 August 1929.
46. Report on mission by Adelaide University Expedition. Statement of Prof. Dr Clealand [*sic*] and Dr Fry, of the Adelaide University Expedition, as regards nutrition and general health of Natives at Hermannsburg, Central Australia (typed copy).
47. Dr Davies's recording. The Hermannsburg Congregation—a Review, 1926–56. Albrecht's feeling that, from a certain viewpoint, the congregation could be regarded as right would probably have been based on St Paul's discussion in the New Testament (1 Corinthians) of whether Christians should eat foods which had been dedicated to idols. Paul advised that while nothing was forbidden for a Christian, not everything was helpful, and it was important to consider the feelings of Christian brethren less established in their faith who could be confused and offended by such an action.
50. 'It was the first time'. Darby Jampijimba, 1984.
50ff. Some station news in this chapter is taken from Annual Report of the Finke River Mission Station for the Year 1930/1931, *L.H.*, 24 August 1931.
51. 'Well there was not much to eat'. Seth Pareroultja, 1984.
52. Pastor Lehmann's comments on Hermannsburg visitors. 'Our Finke River Mission', *L.H.*, 13 October 1930.
53. 'Manangananga cave, he was dangerous place'. Joseph Mantjakura, 1986.
54. 'We had a service there'. Edwin Pareroultja and Pastor Traugott Malbanka.
54. Opening of Manangananga cave. The Hermannsburg Congregation—a Review, 1926–56; information from Pastor Traugott Malbanka and Edwin Pareroultja.
54–62. Albrecht gave a very detailed description of the 1930 camel trek in *L.H.*, 26 January, 9 and 23 February 1931; see also Leske, *Hermannsburg*, pp. 48–50.
56. 'he demonstrated the ceremony'. A characteristic 'creation' ceremony in which the observance of the ritual is believed to assist in the continuation of the seasonal cycle.
57. 'Bush people really trusted Albrecht'. Pastor Conrad Raberaba, 1986.

57–8. Albrecht's encounter with Aborigines at Pikilli is also described in a letter to
Revd T. J. Fleming, 21 January 1968, and in interview with David Shrowder.
58. ' "unoccupied" Crown land'. In the European thinking and legal language of
the day, Crown lands not licensed or leased were 'unoccupied', Aboriginal
populations notwithstanding.
59–65. Albrecht's contact with the Lasseter expedition. 'On Lasseter's Trail',
L.A., 1964; 'Lasseter' (duplicated article), 1982; interview with David
Shrowder.
59. 'First time Albrecht went'. Jimmy Jugadai, 1986.
66. 'When the white man came'. Peter Bullah, reported by Paul Albrecht.
66–71. Albrecht's views at this stage on the depopulation of tribal lands and the
responsibilities of European Australia to provide an alternative livelihood to
the dispossessed Aborigines are expressed in his Annual Report 1930/31
to Government Resident, 15 July 1931, which was also published in *L.H.*,
24 August 1931.
67. 'It would take the whole lifetime'. *L.H.*, 29 June 1931.
67. 'Pas' Albrecht looking for hungry people'. Jimmy Jugadai, 1986.
70. 'If the actual position of the Natives'. To Hon. Secretary, Association for
Protection of Native Races, 4 November 1931.
70. 'It always meant either Natives'. Report to Association for Protection of
Native Races, published in *L.H.*, 18 January 1932.
71–2. Trek west in 1932. Leske, *Hermannsburg*; interview with author.
72–3. Petering's arrival in Central Australia. Interview with David Shrowder.
74–5. Albert Namatjira's introduction to Western painting. Leske, *Hermannsburg*,
pp. 70–1; and other articles on his life and painting including Albrecht's
address at his funeral, 9 August 1959.
75–6. T. G. H. Strehlow described his return to Hermannsburg at the end of 1932
in Dark and White Australians. See also McNally, *Aborigines, Artefacts and
Anguish*.
77. 'My parents' country was Napperby'. Pastor Cyril Motna, 1984.
79–80. Description of trek west and comments on impact on Aborigines of
European civilization. *L.H.*, 10 and 23 October 1933. Asked by M. Hartwig
what more the government of the time should or could have done to avert
disasters like the Coniston expedition, Albrecht replied (18 April 1960),
'Should have acted lawfully; to say, shall teach them a lesson, is in effect an
entirely lawless act, as it gives the individual a free hand'. See also, letter
concerning tribal people in Petermann Ranges to A. Le Soeuf, 30 November
1933.
80. 'In those days, people didn't thought about that [their land]'. Pastor Nahasson Ungkwanaka, 1984.
81. 'about Epafras and Victor'. To Riedel, 4 August 1933. See also letters to
Riedel, 20 November 1932, 1 July and 9 October 1933, 23 February 1937.
82–3. Neglect of the sick, and other problems. *L.H.*, 21 January and 5 August
1935.
82. Comments on Loritja men. *L.H.*, 21 January 1935.
83. Albrecht's worries about Aboriginal health and the disinclination of the
people to grind whole wheat or go out to look for bushtucker. To Riedel,
25 October 1935.
83. 'When we spend so much time'. *L.H.*, 5 August 1935; see also *L.H.*,
21 January 1935.
84. 'What the women have to undergo'. *L.H.*, 5 August 1935.
84. 'it is simply impossible'. To Duguid, 7 August 1940.

84. Minister's visit. To Riedel, 1 July 1933.

85ff. Details of the Kaporilja scheme are found in several articles including Kaporilja Spring Water Pipeline Scheme for the Natives in Hermannsburg, Central Australia: an Appeal by the Finke River Mission Station, early 1932 (duplicated paper); Hermannsburg Mission Water Scheme, June 1935 (duplicated paper); 'Twenty-Five Years Kaporilja Water', *L.A.*, 1960; 'Kaporilja Pipeline', *The Lutheran*, 17 May 1976; and many letters.

86. 'Anyway, we and Mr Kenyon feel'. Una Teague to Riedel, 16 August 1934.

86. 'the drought has got so bad'. To Riedel, 17 August 1934.

86–7. Government medical officer's instructions. To Albrecht, 28 September 1934.

88. 'Old man [Albrecht] take the camel one day'. Pastor Traugott Malbanka, 1984.

89. 'Now . . . have we a right here to dispossess the Native?' To Duguid, 11 May 1935.

90–2. Account of trip west. 'Going West', *L.H.*, 16 September, 25 November and 9 December 1935.

93–4. Lutheran contact with Aborigines in Alice Springs. The History of the Alice Springs Lutheran Church (duplicated paper), *c.* 1960s.

94. '. . . establishing a station directly'. To the Minister for the Interior, 14 August 1935.

95–6. Albrecht's anxiety. I was Afraid (duplicated paper), March 1976.

96. 'Some of us started the garden then'. Pastor Conrad Raberaba, 1984.

96. 'Albrecht said we want to try to get the water here'. Edwin Pareroultja, 1986.

97. 'Old man Albrecht, sometimes he take the big school kids'. Seth Pareroultja, 1984.

98. 'Karma and Serena'. To Riedel, 2 August 1932. Discussions with Hermannsburg community following court case. To Riedel, 21 April 1936.

99. 'As a rule'; 'My opinion about this'. To Duguid, 24 April 1935; see also letter to Riedel, 30 June 1935.

100. 'When I go through the garden now'. To Riedel, 21 April 1936.

101–2. Camel trek west. About our Work with the Natives (duplicated paper), *c.* August 1936; *L.H.*, 4 January and 1 February 1937. Duguid wrote of the camel trip west in *No Dying Race*, pp. 36–50.

101. 'First time he had service here'. Jimmy Jugadai, 1986.

103–4. Differences in approach to mission work. Interview with author.

103. 'From our point of view'. 'Deal thy Bread to the Hungry' (duplicated paper), November 1935; also published in *L.H.*, 25 November 1935.

104. 'This "laziness"'. To Riedel, 20 November 1935.

104. 'They [would] rather beg or starve'. To Riedel, 25 October 1935.

104. 'We carry one bag at a time'. Bert Nananana, 1986.

104–5. Strehlow's activities. To Riedel, 22 October 1936.

105. 'Strehlow has returned'. To Sexton, 24 October 1936.

106. 'Mr Braitling was allowed to go to the Davenport Ranges'. To Sexton, 23 January 1937.

106. 'All my endeavours'; 'This is the most difficult problem'. To Riedel, 17 November 1936.

107. 'In those early days'. Pastor Nahasson Ungkwanaka, 1986.

108–9. Haasts Bluff lease cancellation. Leske, *Hermannsburg*; interviews with David Shrowder and author.

108. 'But above all, being humans as we are'. To Deputy Administrator, 28 January 1937.

109. Duguid's account of ministerial action on Haasts Bluff. Duguid, *No Dying Race*, p. 50; letter to Albrecht, 24 February 1937; interview with author. Also described by Albrecht in Dr Duguid's Intervention in the Haast's Bluff Lease (duplicated paper), June 1972.
111. 'When we started with our work'. To Riedel, 29 September 1937; see also letter to Riedel, 25 July 1937, and *L.H.*, 21 January 1935.
112. 'Vagrants are a big problem here'. To Riedel, 29 September 1937.
112. 'Old Albrecht, he didn't understand lite of families'. Pastor Nahasson Ungkwanaka, 1986.
113. 'There was not too much trouble'. Pastor Traugott Malbanka, 1986.
114. 'Firstly, I point out'. To Riedel, 5 November 1936.
114–15. Peterings' visit to the west. Information from Revd and Mrs Werner Petering.
116. Riedel's views on mission work. To Sexton, 14 June 1937.
117. 'There was spear-throwing'. Pastor Nahasson Ungkwanaka, 1984.
117–18. Albrecht's encouragement of non-secret ceremonies and the elders' disapproval was discussed between Albrecht and Ronald and Catherine Berndt in the 1940s. Information from Ronald Berndt.
118. 'When I was a boy at Hermannsburg'. Pastor Eli Rubuntja, 1986.
119. Description of train journey north and mission life. Information from Elizabeth Pech.
119–20. Bryan Bowman's relationship with Albrecht. Information from Bryan Bowman.
121. 'You wrote that you cannot understand'. To Riedel, 22 July 1938.
123. 'Also with a car'. To Riedel, 10 December 1938.
123. Albrecht's speaking arrangements conflicting with baby's baptism. Information from Minna Albrecht, 1983.
124. 'the whole future of the natives of Central Australia'. Strehlow to Chief Protector, 30 June 1938.
124. 'the policy of isolation is impracticable'. Ibid, 8 August 1938.
126. Albrecht's report. To Hon. J. McEwen, Minister for the Interior, 5 August 1938.
127. 'Petermann people frightened at an aeroplane'. Unidentified Aboriginal respondent, translated by Pastor Traugott Malbanka, Areyonga, 1986.
127–31. Expedition to the Petermanns. F.R.M. Report for July 1939–June 1940, *L.H.*, 2 December 1940; 'Journeying with Missionary F. W. Albrecht in 1939', *L.A.*, 1965, pp. 37–47; information from O. Heinrich. Described in Duguid, *No Dying Race*, pp. 55–71.
130. 'The older people know this is the sign'. Comments by Albrecht written on expedition photographs.
131. 'It is obvious that they cannot be left under present conditions'. To Sexton, 3 November 1939.
132. 'Brother Vogelsang mentioned that you are not well'. Riedel to Albrecht, 12 September 1939.
134. 'Titus became boss for people around there'. Jimmy Jugadai, 1986.
135. 'It is one of their weakest points'. Account of Christmas 1940 (including visit to Pitjantjatjara camp at Undandita) in duplicated letter to mission friends, January 1940.
136. 'He wasn't interested in those stories!!' Pastor Eli Rubuntja, 1986.
137. First months of Sam Gross's time at Hermannsburg. Gross to Riedel, 9 January 1940.
137. 'It is very, very hard to understand'. To Duguid, 29 June 1940.

138–9. Changing marriage customs, Haasts Bluff. To Riedel, 8 August 1940; 'Allocation of Wives', *The Lutheran*, 3 May 1976; interview with David Shrowder.
139. 'Albrecht used to bring all the people together'. Jimmy Jugadai, 1986.
140ff. Search of Hermannsburg, 1940, and other issues between Hermannsburg and the Alice Springs military. To Riedel, 8 August 1940, 24 May 1942; 'Hermannsburg in Central Australia during the War', *L.A.*, 1964.
141–3. Development of Haasts Bluff ration depot. To Riedel, 11 December 1940; to Sexton, 26 December 1940.
142. 'Long way round'. Bert Nananana, 1984.
142. 'It was a nice experience'. To Riedel, 29 June 1941.
143. 'It is my opinion'. To Sexton, 31 December 1941.
143. 'I would like to ask you'. Riedel to Albrecht, 17 March 1941.
144. 'As far as we know'. Riedel to Albrecht, 23 September 1941. Water investigations at Haasts Bluff. To Riedel, 16 November 1941.
146. 'Soldiers used to go down to Palm Valley'. Pastor Conrad Raberaba, 1984.
146. Northern Territory at war. Powell, *The Shadow's Edge*.
146–7. Second search and Bowman's comments. Information from Bryan Bowman and Pastor Traugott Malbanka.
148. 'When schoolchildren heard the planes'. Pastor Traugott Malbanka, 1986.
148–9. 'Rev. Love believes'; 'The exhortation to be good boys'. *L.H.*, 16 January 1943. See also, Revd J. R. B. Love, Ernabella Newsletter, November 1942.
150. Albrecht's return to Hermannsburg. Letters to Riedel and Duguid, 5 September 1942.
150–1. Aboriginal labour gangs. To Riedel, 26 April 1943; Notes for Review of 1942.
151. 'It was nice, everything is one'. Ephraim Wheeler, 1984.
151. 'Army bit rough!' Pastor Eli Rubuntja, 1986.
152. 'From my previous experience with Titus'. To Riedel, 23 September 1942.
152–3. Death of Priscilla. To Riedel, 5 and 25 November 1942.
154. 'Maybe God might be working this way'. Joseph Mantjakura, 1986.
154–5. Minna's journey north. Undated letter by Minna Albrecht.
155–6. Dams, tractor and scoop. To Riedel, 18 December 1942, 26 February 1943.
156–7. Tanning developments. To Riedel, 24 June 1943.
157. New dispensary and Manasse's road. To Riedel, 30 May 1943.
157–8. Difficulties at Haasts Bluff. To Riedel, 18 December 1943.
158. 'enquire from the proper authorities'. Riedel to Albrecht, 26 October 1943.
159. 'You are under the impression'. To Riedel, 18 December 1943.
159. 'Our station or stations'. Riedel to Albrecht, 26 October 1943.
159. 'We must not overlook'. To Riedel, 18 December 1943.
160ff. Early developments for Areyonga. To Riedel, 20 August 1943.
161. 'At first Areyonga thought a dangerous place'. Joseph Mantjakura, 1986.
161. 'One of your co-workers'. Riedel to Albrecht, 14 September 1943.
161. 'Only then would you be able to see'. To Riedel, 2 October 1943.
162. 'They were obviously in a great hurry'. Leske, *Hermannsburg*, pp. 60–1.
162. 'That story, all run to the truck'. Joseph Mantjakura, 1986.
163. 'Hoping our visit has been of some benefit'. Riedel to Albrecht, 28 March 1944.
163. 'Pastor Albrecht start a new thing'. Ephraim Wheeler, 1984.
164. 'Above all ... this whole scheme'; 'The biggest drawback'. To Riedel, 31 August, 16 June 1944. Aboriginal Pastoralists Scheme, see also letters to Riedel, 17 July, 2 and 5 August, 10 September 1944.

165. 'In the Western Macdonnells'; 'Seasons of drought'; 'Yet the fact remains'. 'Natural Food Supply of the Australian Aborigines' (pamphlet), Aborigines' Friends' Association, Adelaide.
166. Reece expedition. Report of the Expedition investigating the Possibilities of Mission Work amongst the Aborigines N. W. of Alice Springs, L. Reece.
166–7. Albrecht's response on Baptist mission proposal. To Sexton, 5 October 1944.
167. Albrecht's concerns for Hermannsburg community. To Riedel, 17 July 1944; notes for his report for 1944.
168. 'Few things he bin gone pretty strong'. Helmut Pareroultja, 1986.
168–9. Revision of Aranda New Testament. See also letters to Riedel, 24 July 1944, 20 January 1945.
169. 'If it were not the Bible'. To Riedel, 31 August 1944.
170. 'One thing seems established'. To Riedel, 10 September 1944.
171. 'they are going to the other extreme'. To Riedel, 15 April 1945.
170–1. Further developments at Haasts Bluff and Areyonga, see letters to Riedel, 8 April, 11 May and 15 June 1945.
171. Baptisms and confirmations. To Riedel, 15 November and 26 December 1944.
173. 'Over a period of time'. Jimmy Jugadai, 1986.
174. Visit to Haasts Bluff. To Riedel, 15 June 1945.
175. Discussions with mission board. Notes for board meeting, April 1946.
175. 'Before . . . we were only tolerated at decisions'. To Riedel, 13 December 1945.
176. 'I got another two small buildings'. To Revd Gordon Rowe, Aborigines' Friends' Association, 6 September 1946.
176. Developments at Haasts Bluff and Areyonga, see also letters to Riedel, 9 July, 1 and 22 August 1946.
177. Consie's death. To Riedel, 22 August 1946.
178. Albrecht's opinions about location of Yuendumu. To Revd T. J. Fleming, 14 April 1968.
178. Simpson Inquiry. To Riedel, 30 October 1946.
179. 'Rex Battarbee take me that exhibition'. Edwin Pareroultja, 1984.
179. Comments on Aranda art movement. *Advertiser*, 22 May 1945.
180. 'After talking . . . Dr Lum allowed me to go'. To Riedel, 22 November 1946.
180. 'Very unfortunately, you are not the only one'. To Riedel, 10 December 1946.
181. 'I couldn't remember before Minnie and Martin'. Helmut Pareroultja, 1986.
181. Children's activities. Information from Min, Paul and Martin Albrecht, and Helmut Pareroultja.
182. 'After I cleared out from school'. Jack Coulthard, 1986.
183. 'I have had several nights'. To Riedel, 30 March 1947.
185. 'I have tried, therefore, to devise some scheme'. To Riedel, 5 February 1948.
186. 'What he has done is truly remarkable'. To Riedel, 5 February 1948.
186. Strehlow's revision of Aranda New Testament, see also letter to Riedel, 21 March 1948.
186–7. Spearing at Haasts Bluff. To Riedel, 11 April 1948.
187–8. Pressures on Albrecht. To Riedel, 11 January and 5 May 1948.
188. 'ideas and well prepared plans'. Address to St Stephen's Auxiliary Meeting, 14 December 1948.
188. 'The fact remains'. Address at Murray Bridge, 5 October 1947. Aboriginal–European cultural gap. See many other writings including The Future of our

Aborigines, Address to Church Synod (undated); Attempts at Economic Rehabilitation of Nomadic Natives in Central Australia (duplicated paper), c. 1948.

189. 'I might as well give him thanks'. Helmut Pareroultja, 1986.
190. 'I was working with Sister'. Joyce Malbanka, 1986.
191. 'What a change in the attitude of officialdom'. To Riedel, 13 June 1948. See also letter to Riedel, 2 July 1948.
191. Government–mission conference in Darwin. To Riedel, 13 September 1948.
193. 'How little we can see through God's ways'. To Riedel, 1 December 1949.
193. 'November 25, Titus passed away'. F.R.M. Report for 1949, 5 January 1950.
193. 'Old Titus, Rengkareka'. Edwin Pareroultja, 1984.
193–4. Further developments at Haasts Bluff. To Riedel, 16 December 1949.
194. 'Now these men have paid their debts'. To Riedel, 28 April 1950.
194. 'I was at Undandita'. Ephraim Wheeler, 1984.
195. 'I am writing about his case fully'. To Riedel, 28 April 1950.
195. 'Had I said much'. To Riedel, 18 May 1950.
196. Government policy on Aboriginal education. To Riedel, 3 August 1950.
196. 'Wherever the people have to be fed'. To Duguid, 20 September 1950.
197. 'In spite of his achievements'. 'Albert Namatjira: Native Artist', Aborigines' Friends' Association, Adelaide, c. 1948.
197. 'If this continues'. To Riedel, 2 July 1948. Art developments, see also letter to Riedel, 15 August 1951.
198. Namatjira's application for pastoral block. To Aborigines' Friends' Association, 2 December 1949; F.R.M. Report for 1949.
198. 'One would say nothing against it'. To Riedel, 23 December 1950.
198. 'The average Native'. To Rowe, 21 February 1951.
199. 'There is always money in the camp'. To Riedel, 9 August 1951.
199. '. . . it is practically impossible to segregate them'. To Riedel, 9 August 1951.
199. 'I got idea about work'. Helmut Pareroultja, 1986.
200. 'Native Christians have occasionally told us'. The Gospel and the Nomadic Aranda in Central Australia (duplicated article), November 1950.
200. 'The dominant factor was simple faith in God'. Into the Heart of a Continent (duplicated article), October 1950.
201. 'One was in connection with the water scheme'. To Riedel, 8 November 1950.
202. 'She is always willing'. To Reuther, 23 December 1950.
202. Role of elders. To Reuther, 30 January and 31 March 1951.
203. 'Yes, seven years drought'. Pastor Conrad Raberaba, 1984.
203. Death of Klementine. To Reuther, 23 February 1951; to Duguid, 4 December 1950.
203. 'One does regret the time'. To Reuther, 2 June 1951.
204. 'The Native Elders'. To Reuther, 12 April 1951. See also, letters to Reuther, 30 January and 31 March 1951.
205. 'recognised, with Bishop Gsell'. Lockwood, The Mail, 25 March 1950.
205. 'Perhaps it is true that my past'. To Reuther, 10 September 1951.
206. Albrechts' farewell. 'Pastor Albrecht leaves Hermannsburg', L.H., 22 December 1951.
206. 'We are getting ready to leave here tomorrow'. To Reuther, 17 November 1951.
206. 'In that time earlier'. Helmut Pareroultja, 1986.
207. 'Went to Tempe Downs'. Joylene Abbott, 1986.
208. Burning of ceremonial items at Maryvale. F.R.M. Newsletter, 30 December

1953; also described in 'What God Made of an Aboriginal', *L.H.*, 25 July 1959.

209. 'It is a strange thought'. Strehlow, *Songs of Central Australia*, p. xlvi.
209. 'Old men still alive today'. Pastor Nahasson Ungkwanaka, May 1986.
210. 'Over the past 70 years'. Paul Hasluck, quoted in report on conference, *L.H.*, 26 December 1953.
211. 'The Pareroultja brothers are brothers to Namatjira'. Helmut Pareroultja, 1986.
211. 'The Question of Economic Rehabilitation of Aborigines', paper presented to missions–administration conference, Darwin, December 1953.
211. 'Henbury was my home'. Joylene Abbott, 1984.
212–13. Sending part-Aboriginal children south for high school education. F.R.M. Newsletter, April 1954, and elsewhere.
214. 'Instead of helping them to see some responsibility'. F.R.M. Newsletter, April 1954.
214–15. Moses' death and Albrecht's reflections. F.R.M. Newsletter, December 1954; 'Old Blind Moses', *L.H.*, 24 July 1954; interview with author.
215. 'If somebody took you to that old cemetery'. Pastor Nahasson Ungkwanaka, 1986.
215. Hermannsburg school anniversary. 'Seventy-five Years of School Work at Hermannsburg', *L.H.*, 11 December 1954.
216. 'I used to work mostly Tempe'. Jack Coulthard, 1984.
217. 'It is about time'. To his children, 2 November 1955.
217. Strehlow's comments to field conference. Ibid.
218. 'It must be borne in mind'. F.R.M. Newsletter, May 1957. Tribal killings, see also F.R.M. Newsletter, March 1955. Albrecht reiterated his sense of the highly developed feeling for justice among traditional Aborigines in letter to M. Hartwig, 18 April 1960.
219. Philipp Scherer's visit to northern stations. Haasts Bluff Newsletter, 9 August 1955.
219–20. Murray Downs killings and subsequent events. To his children, 26 September 1955; The Gospel versus Sorcery in Central Australia (duplicated paper), *c.* 1964; interview with David Shrowder, and elsewhere.
221. Jonathan Namatjira's death. 'Jonathan Namatjira', *L.H.*, 24 March 1956.
222. 'In my thoughts I am often in Australia'. F. Strehlow to M. Albrecht, 10 March 1957.
223. 'Old Albrecht look after all Aboriginal people'. Joylene Abbott, May 1986.
223. 'I was small when they came to Hermannsburg'. Pastor Eli Rubuntja, 1986.
224. 'If he had something to say'. Pastor Nahasson Ungkwanaka, 1986.
225. 'Church then in the morning'. Pastor Eli Rubuntja, 1986.
224–5. Albrecht's visits to the cattle stations are described in many of the F.R.M. newsletters in the 1950s; see also, Aspects of Mission Work among Aborigines Living at Cattle Stations, paper presented at joint conference between representatives of Yuendumu Baptist mission, Ernabella Presbyterian mission, Lutheran Finke River Mission, Alice Springs, October 1956.
227. 'Assimilation means'. Hon. Paul Hasluck, Commonwealth–State conference on native welfare, quoted in Powell, *Far Country*, p. 232.
228–9. Conversations with Fleming. Information from Revd T. Fleming.
228. 'There have been times'. Stages of Transition (duplicated paper), 1961.
229. 'they find it almost impossible'. To A. Tauscher, 6 May 1976.
230. 'Not that they lack brains or intelligence'. Apprenticeship Paper for Aborigines, paper presented at missions–administration conference, Darwin, 1955.

230. 'Until about twenty or more years of age'. Albrecht here is drawing both on Ted Strehlow's knowledge, and his own reading of Revd Carl Strehlow's anthropological volumes, which he had managed to purchase.
230. 'The pressure is to give them freedom'. A. P. Elkin, Comments on Pastor Albrecht's Apprenticeship Paper (Aborigines), 6 August, 1958.
231. 'These Aboriginal men'. Pastor Eli Rubuntja, 1986.
231. 'When sent here by our United Evangelical Lutheran church'. Duplicated letter to mission friends, 30 June 1958.
232. 'Ladies and gentlemen, it is nearly thirty years'. Notes on address to naturalized citizens, Alice Springs, undated.
233. 'After Albert was citizen'. Pastor Nahasson Ungkwanaka, 1986.
234. 'If Albert is allowed'; 'This agitation'. Albert Namatjira Sentenced to 6 Months Gaol (duplicated pamphlet), 10 October 1958. For accounts of Albert Namatjira and increasing Aboriginal drinking, see also duplicated letter to mission friends, 1 October 1959.
235. 'At first, artist mob were drinking in Alice Springs'. Pastor Nahasson Ungkwanaka, 1986.
236. Junkuman. Smoke Signals, March 1959, duplicated magazine of Welfare Branch, Northern Territory Administration.
237. 'The Government settlements are indispensable as a first step'. Albrecht and others, open letter to newspapers, 5 January 1959.
238. 'In my opinion, it is wrong'. To T. V. Weir, 12 February 1957.
238. 'The sense for values is lacking'. Accepting the Aborigines into our Society (duplicated paper), December 1971.
238. 'as long as the old tribal cohesion continues'. Some Notes on the Question of Full Citizenship for Aborigines (duplicated paper), c. January 1959.
240. 'Never before in the history of this country'. Address at Funeral of Albert Namatjira (duplicated paper), 9 August 1959.
242. 'He always looked after people, worried about them'. Pastor Nahasson Ungkwanaka, 1984.
243. Ngalunta. 'The Story of Ngaluntu', *The Lutheran*, 31 May 1976; interview with author.
244. Aboriginal employment. F.R.M. Report for 1959 (duplicated).
244–5. Aboriginal polygamy. Minutes of Third Missionaries' Conference of Finke River Mission, 17/18 November 1959.
245. 'Our main effort must be'. L.H., 22 December 1962.
245. 'a missionary who sees his task only in preaching and teaching'. To Revd J. C. Pfitzner, 23 July 1970.
245. 'Pray for me'. To L. Borgelt, 2 September 1960.
246. Coniston research. To M. Hartwig, 18 April 1960.
246. 'Now you *must* come down this summer'. L. Borgelt to Albrecht, 15 June 1960.
247. 'I feel there is still too much left in me'. To L. Borgelt, 9 November 1959.
247–8. Albrecht's belief that it was vital for Aboriginal children to retain their links with their families. Many statements including letter to K. Schulz, 22 April 1967.
247. 'I was at Henbury'. Joylene Abbott, 1984.
247. Value of wider experience. F.R.M. Report for 1959 (duplicated).
248. 'The best part of our life'. To O. Heinrich, 12 October 1960.
249. 'we are not working for a Board'. To Revd Philipp Scherer, 3 December 1967.
249. Visit to Ernabella. Information from Revd W. Edwards.

249–50. Maryvale baptism service. *L.H.*, 25 November 1981.
250. 'Even the street where we live'. To J. Burger, 28 October 1961.
251. 'With your departure from the Centre'. Strehlow to Albrecht, 15 December 1961.
251. 'I don't think that any such work exists anywhere'. To M. Hartwig, 2 December 1961.
252. 'To our way of thinking and feeling'. To C. Dracopoulos, 26 November 1961.
252. 'To approach them from the angle of forbidding it'. To Revd L. Kalleske, 21 February 1962.
253. 'I think your way there is better than ours'. To Mrs Elliot, 14 May 1962.
253–5. Temporary period in Centre. Report for Field Conference (Alice Springs–South) October 1962, *L.H.*, 22 December 1962.
255. Amoonguna course. Brief report on the Refresher Course held at Amoonguna October 29–November 9.
256. 'I feel that unless people like you'. H. Giese to Albrecht, 30 May 1963.
256. 'Our life here in the south is so different'. To V. Schwedes, 3 March 1963.
257. 'That is something that . . . just weighs you down'. To K. Kotzur, 4 February 1963. Albrecht referred to Carl Strehlow's era as a 'patriarchy' in 'Albert Namatjira: Native Artist' (printed pamphlet), Aborigines' Friends' Association, *c.* 1948.
258. Visits to Hope Vale and Bloomfield. Visiting Hope Vale and Bloomfield Missions (typescript), 1964; Some Observations on Mission Work in North Queensland (duplicated paper), 1964.
259. 'It was a great day'. To K. Kotzur, 20 December 1964.
259. 'I was preaching sermon in church'. Pastor Conrad Raberaba, 1984.
260–1. Aboriginal spiritual experience. To Revd L. H. Leske, 6 November 1965; to Mr and Mrs W. R. Edwards, 6 January 1966; to Mr and Mrs L. A. Borgelt, 9 October 1965; interviews with David Shrowder and with author.
261. 'Unfortunately, many of the cattle station owners'. To W. Fritsch, 5 September 1965.
261–2. Lectures on Communism. Communism: an English translation of lectures held in Aranda before a group of 33 Aborigines, including two pastors and evangelists, Hermannsburg, September/October 1965.
262. Albrecht's reflections. To P. Albrecht, 15 September 1965; to Revd D. J. Radke, 2 August 1965.
262. 'There are very many [Christians]'. To B. Teasdale, 4 September 1963.
263. 'Religion is closely bound up in our feelings'. To G. Kilham, 10 April 1966.
264. 'One of the first things'; 'These Aborigines who had to face the nothing'. Notes for address at dedication service of Hermannsburg church, 1966.
264. Death of Abel's son. The Gospel versus Sorcery in Central Australia (duplicated paper), *c.* 1964.
264. 'When we first came here'. Quoted in Broome, *Aboriginal Australians*, p. 119.
265. 'I would have been happier'. To Mr and Mrs L. A. Borgelt, 24 April 1967.
265. 'Whenever she was . . . left with the children'. To Laura Mulkatana, 1 July 1967.
266. Response to Angaston children. To Miss Jacob, 20 April 1967.
266. 'He was everything to me'. Mary Wolski, 1987.
266. Albrecht's reflections. To Mrs Schwedes, 5 October 1968.
267. 'While we were down there'. Pastor Nahasson Ungkwanaka, 1984.
268. 'I should have added'. To H. Cowgill, 8 October 1970.

268. *'Ingkata tjina nukai'*. Paulus Wiljuka to Albrecht, undated.
269. Letter about Revd J. Flynn. To Duguid, 26 March 1971.
269. 'Had he tried, at that time, to combine the two'. Duplicated article about Revd J. Flynn, undated.
269. 'It has been said that he died of a broken heart'. To Ure Smith Publishers, 16 March 1971.
270. Writing a book about his life. Comments from several informants.
271. 'So many attempts, and very honest attempts'. To J. Pfitzner, 13 November 1971.
271. 'These people are deserving of special consideration'. Comments on Australian Council of Churches Submission on Aboriginal Land Rights (duplicated article), 29 February 1972.
271–2. Hermannsburg in the early 1970s. Information from Paul Albrecht, Garry Stoll, Robert Arnold, Pastor Eli Rubuntja, Pastor Nahasson Ungkwanaka, Doris Kubisch.
272. 'Pas' Albrecht was the pastor here'. Pastor Cyril Motna, 1986.
272. 'We bin trying to tell these things'. Pastor Eli Rubuntja, recounted by Garry Stoll.
272. 'Main reason I left was drink'. Pastor Nahasson Ungkwanaka, 1986.
273. 'Yes, he had a strong feeling'. Pastor Nahasson Ungkwanaka, 1986.
274. 'Sociologically, it indicates people are taking strong initiatives'. P. Albrecht, 'Winds of Change', *The Lutheran*, 12 July 1976.
274. Albrecht's statement on new mission policy. Changes in the Missionary Policy in the Finke River Mission (duplicated paper), September 1976. See also, letter to Revd J. Pfitzner, 29 July 1976.
275. 'Albrecht, he say Aboriginal religion wrong'. Pastor Nahasson Ungkwanaka, 1986.
275. 'Old people's laws have gone into the background'. Jimmy Jugadai, 1986.
276. 'All this watered down religion'. Interview with author.
276. 'I readily admit'. Undated notes, *c.* 1970s.
276. 'Albrecht thought if God's word was true'. Pastor Eli Rubuntja, 1986.
276. 'Yes, still tell children some of the old stories'. Pastor Traugott Malbanka, 1986.
277. 'I thank you for your love'. To O. Raggat, 16 November 1976.
277. Minna's article. Experiences in my Life of Answered Prayer (duplicated paper), *c.* 1976.
277. 'You see, without some sacrifice'. Interviews with David Shrowder and with author.
278. 'Came down to Adelaide just the right time'. Joylene Abbott, 1986.
279. 'If the *tjurungas*'. News, 5 May 1977.
280. 'Since my knowledge of the language'. Leske, *Hermannsburg*, pp. 46–7.
280–2. Hermannsburg centenary celebrations and later reflections. 'The Day the Lord Made: Hermannsburg, June 12, 1977', and 'Hermannsburg Centenary Sermon', *The Lutheran*, 4 July 1977; letter to Mr and Mrs G. Stoll, 28 June 1977; information from Revd T. J. Fleming.
280. 'which witnessed some of the deepest experiences'. Duplicated letter to friends, 17 June 1977.
281. 'the Aborigines have moved'; 'What Strehlow achieved'. To Revd J. Pfitzner, 30 June 1977.
283. 'I would suggest to widen your scope'. To J. Brackenreg, undated [1980].
283. 'To be faced with the end of the road'. Duplicated letter to friends, 20 December 1980.

284. 'It is like committing a part of one's life to death'. Duplicated letter to friends, 19 December 1981.
284. Reunion with Hermannsburg women. Interview with David Shrowder.
284. 'Leave it in God's hands'. Interviews with David Shrowder and with author.
284. Surrender of mission lease. *Advertiser*, 29 May 1982. Information from Garry Stoll and David Shrowder.
285. 'All the time, when I bin 'coming pastor'. Pastor Eli Rubuntja, 1984.
285. 'When I was at Undandita'. Joseph Mantjakura, 1986.
285. Sense of living a useless life. Communication with author.
286. 'He was in bed when I came'. Pastor Nahasson Ungkwanaka, 1986.
287. 'Happy are those who . . . die in the service of the Lord'. Pastor C. Raberaba, address at graveside, funeral of F. W. Albrecht, 19 March 1984.
288. *Ingkata inurra* (lame pastor)'. Pastor Nahasson Ungkwanaka, 1986.

A NOTE ON SOURCES

Pastor F. W. Albrecht's correspondence was voluminous from his first years in Australia until the last decade of his life. From his early years at the mission he wrote regular and detailed reports to the mission board in South Australia about many aspects of mission life. A considerable amount of this correspondence has survived and was made available to me (though I was not able to have translated all of the letters which Albrecht wrote in German). This material has enabled me to provide at times a level of detail in description that some readers of the manuscript have assumed to be fictionalized. This is not the case. It is impossible to give source references for all information, but I have attempted to do so for the more significant events and issues.

Pastor Albrecht was a natural communicator, and believed strongly that other people—church supporters, the general public, politicians etc.—needed to understand Aboriginal and mission issues if they were to support the mission financially, make policy decisions, and generally work toward the integration of Aborigines into the wider Australian community. To this end, he wrote circulars and letters for special distribution to 'mission friends', articles for Lutheran newspapers, and sometimes letters to the general press. Albrecht's writings, therefore, form the primary source material for this biography. Occasionally his letters contain minor errors of spelling or punctuation and I have tended to correct these. David Shrowder generously made available the transcripts of a considerable number of interviews he conducted around 1981 with Pastor and Mrs Albrecht and others connected with the Albrechts' time at Hermannsburg, and I was able to interview both Pastor and Mrs Albrecht in November 1983. Interviews with Aborigines and Europeans with first-hand experience of the mission and of Pastor and Mrs Albrecht are the other main primary source.

SELECT BIBLIOGRAPHY

Australia, Department of Territories. *Progress Towards Assimilation*. Canberra, Department of Territories, 1958.

Batty, Joyce. *Namatjira: Wanderer between Two Worlds* Melbourne, Hodder & Stoughton, 1963.

Bell, Diane. *Daughters of the Dreaming*. Melbourne, McPhee Gribble/George Allen & Unwin, 1983.

Blackwell, Doris and Lockwood, Douglas. *Alice on the Line*. Adelaide, Rigby, 1965.

Blainey, Geoffrey. *Triumph of the Nomads: a History of Ancient Australia*. Melbourne, Macmillan, 1982.

Broome, Richard. *Aboriginal Australians: Black Response to White Dominance*. Sydney, George Allen & Unwin, 1982.

Cribben, John. *The Killing Times*. Sydney, Fontana, 1984.

Duguid, Charles. *No Dying Race*. Adelaide, Rigby, 1963.

Duguid, Charles. *Doctor Goes Walkabout*. Adelaide, Rigby, 1972.

Elkin, A. P. *Aboriginal Men of High Degree*. Brisbane, University of Queensland Press, 1977.

Gibbs, R. M. *A History of South Australia*. Adelaide, Balara Books, 1969.

Gill, Walter. *Petermann Journey*. Adelaide, Rigby, 1968.

Hartwig, M. Progress of White Settlement in the Alice Springs District. B.A. thesis, University of Adelaide, 1960.

Japangardi, Tim. *Yurrkuru-kurlu* (Coniston Story), ngarrurnu (told by) Tim Japangardirli, yirrarnu (written down by) George Jampijinparlu, kuruwarri kujurnu (illustrated by) George Jampijinparlu. Yuendumu School, 1978. Text in Warlpiri with English translation.

Jones, P. and Sutton, P. *Art and Land*. Adelaide, South Australian Museum/ Wakefield Press, 1986.

Leske, E. (ed.). *Hermannsburg: a Vision and a Mission*. Adelaide, Lutheran Publishing House, 1977.

McNally, Ward. *Aborigines, Artefacts and Anguish*. Adelaide, Lutheran Publishing House, 1981.

Powell, Alan. *Far Country*. Melbourne, Melbourne University Press, 1982.

Powell, Alan. *The Shadow's Edge: Australia's Northern War*. Melbourne, Melbourne University Press, 1988.

Reynolds, Henry. *The Other Side of the Frontier*. Melbourne, Penguin, 1982.

Reynolds, Henry. *Frontier*. Allen & Unwin, Sydney, 1987.

Rowley, C. D. *The Destruction of Aboriginal Society*. Melbourne, Penguin, 1979.

Schmiecken, H. J. The Hermannsburg Mission Society in Australia. B.A. thesis, University of Adelaide, 1971.

Stanner, W. E. H. *After the Dreaming*. Boyer Lectures, 1968, Sydney, Australian Broadcasting Commission, 1972.

Strehlow, T. G. H. *Aranda Traditions*. Melbourne, Melbourne University Press, 1947.

Strehlow, T. G. H. Dark and White Australians. Paper given originally to South Australian Peace Committee, North Adelaide, 6 April 1957.

Strehlow, T. G. H. Nomads in No-Man's-Land. Address to Ninth Summer School organized by Adult Education Department, University of Adelaide, 1960.

Strehlow, T. G. H. *Journey to Horseshoe Bend*. Adelaide, Rigby, 1969.

Strehlow, T. G. H. *Songs of Central Australia*. Sydney, Angus & Robertson, 1971.

Thomson, Donald. *Donald Thomson in Arnhem Land*. Melbourne, Currey O'Neil Ross, 1983.

Wise, Tigger. *The Self-Made Anthropologist: a Life of A. P. Elkin*. Sydney, Allen & Unwin, 1985.

INDEX